Johann Sebastian Bach, Concertmeister and Court Organist in Weimar.

JOHANN SEBASTIAN BACH

Johann Sebastian Bach

THE CULMINATION OF AN ERA

KARL GEIRINGER
IN COLLABORATION WITH
IRENE GEIRINGER

NEW YORK

OXFORD UNIVERSITY PRESS

1966

Library of Congress Catalogue Card Number: 66-22262

Copyright © 1966 by Oxford University Press, Inc.

20 19 18 17 16 15 14 13 12

PRINTED IN THE UNITED STATES OF AMERICA

PREFACE

BACH research has made spectacular progress in recent years. Every aspect of this vast and highly complex area has been re-examined. New discoveries were made and a multitude of significant details has come to light.

Under these conditions it seems appropriate to take stock of the present state of our knowledge and to weave the new strands into a larger fabric. This applies in particular to the English-speaking countries.

It may well be argued that to publish such a study now is still premature, Bach research being in a constant flux, with many problems remaining unsolved. However, even a confirmed optimist cannot assume that definite solutions will be achieved in the near future; indeed it seems more likely that certain answers will never be forthcoming. Such considerations encouraged the author to offer the present general account of Bach's life and work, though he is well aware that future new evidence may necessitate a revision of specific points. In view of the complexity of the subject, corrections and suggestions will be gratefully accepted.

For practical reasons, the biographical material was separated from the analysis of the music. In the latter, the different categories of Bach's compositions were, as far as possible, presented in chronological order. It was the author's aim to outline Bach's artistic development within each group of works. Characteristic examples were analyzed, but no attempt was made to treat every work within the composer's vast output. An introductory chapter deals with the history of the musical forms inherited by Bach. Bibliographical information regarding specific problems is to be found in footnotes, while a selected bibliography of a more general nature is presented at the end of the book.

The chapter on J. S. Bach in the author's book *The Bach Family* served as a starting point. In that work the over-all plan imposed restrictions and necessitated a somewhat cursory treatment. The author attempted to rectify this in the present book, which aims to be more thorough as well as more up-to-date. The new chronology of Bach's output established in recent years gives us a different view of the master's creative process. Periods of violently erupting productivity alternate with phases of relative inactivity. Bach, as we see him now, is more human, though certainly no less the supreme genius.

The author feels deeply indebted to the scholars who revolutionized Bach research in our time. Their names and works appear again and again in the pages of this book. Some of them extended valuable direct assistance in this study. Professor Friedrich Smend, Berlin, made noteworthy material accessible. Professor Werner Neumann, Director of the Leipzig Bach-Archiv, and his assistant, Mr. Hans-Joachim Schulze, kindly read large sections of the manuscript and made significant comments. Unfailing assistance was given by the Music Division of the Library of Congress, Washington, D.C., in particular by Messrs. Harold Spivacke, Edward Waters, and William Lichtenwanger. Generous help was also extended by Mr. Frank Campbell of the Music Division, New York Public Library; the Music Library of Yale University; Dr. William H. Scheide, Princeton, N.J.; the Morgan Library, New York; Dr. Karl-Heinz Köhler, Director of the Music Division, Deutsche Staatsbibliothek, Berlin; the Bach-Archiv, Leipzig; Dr. Wilhelm Virneisel, Stiftung preussischer Kulturbesitz, Tübingen; the Anger Museum, Erfurt; the Schlossmuseum, Weimar. Valuable last-minute suggestions were made by Professor Gerald Abraham, London.

Mr. Sheldon Meyer of Oxford University Press and his staff proved most helpful and patient in the ultimate revision of the book.

Dr. Irene Geiringer (Mrs. Karl Geiringer), who has assisted the author in his previous literary efforts, extensively collaborated in the writing of the present book, particularly with regard to the biographical section.

Karl Geiringer

University of California, Santa Barbara
April 1966.

TABLE OF CONTENTS

vii

ILLUSTRATIONS

following page 84

PLATE V:

View of the Thomas School after two stories were added to the building in 1732. Engraving by Krügner. Stadtgeschichtliches Museum, Leipzig.

At the solemn inauguration of the enlarged building a new Bach Cantata (BWV Anh.18) was performed.

Interior of the Ducal chapel, Weimar, called 'Castle of Heaven.' Painting by C. I. Richter, around 1660. Schlossmuseum, Weimar.

In this chapel Bach's cantatas were performed.

PLATE VI:

Receipt of a payment made to Bach for the loan of a clavier. Autograph, Library of Congress, Washington, D.C.

The practical-minded composer was not averse to such extra income.

Explanation of different ornaments entered by Bach in the *Clavier-Büchlein* for his son W. Friedemann. Autograph, Yale University, New Haven, Conn.

PLATE VII:

J. S. Bach. Pastel by Gottlieb Friedrich Bach, a son of the composer J. Ludwig Bach. Property of Paul Bach, Munich.

The most intimate picture of the Thomas Cantor.

J. S. Bach. Painting by Elias Gottlob Haussmann, 1748. Property of W. H. Scheide, Princeton, N.J.

This second copy of the famous Haussmann painting is superior to the original portrait of 1746 which was restored and overpainted in the nineteenth century.

PLATE VIII:

Sonata in G minor for unaccompanied violin, first page. Autograph, Stiftung preussischer Kulturbesitz, Tübingen Depot.

This shows a typical fair copy that demonstrates the beautiful Baroque curves Bach liked to display in the music he wrote; compare this autograph with the 'working score' shown in Plate II.

ABBREVIATIONS

BG   J. S. Bach's Collected Works published by the Bach Gesellschaft in 46 volumes, Leipzig, 1851-99; supplement, 1932.

BJ   *Bach Jahrbuch*, Leipzig and Berlin, 1904 —.

BWV   Thematic catalogue of the works of J. S. Bach in W. Schmieder, *Thematisch-systematisches Verzeichnis der musikalischen Werke J. S. Bachs*. Leipzig, 1950.

J.S.B.   Johann Sebastian Bach.

KB   Kritischer Bericht zu J. S. Bach, *Neue Ausgabe sämtlicher Werke* (the critical commentary accompanying each volume of the new Collected Edition of J. S. Bach's works), Kassel, 1955 —.

MGG   *Die Musik in Geschichte und Gegenwart* (Musical Encyclopedia), edited by F. Blume, Kassel, 1949 —.

MQ   *Musical Quarterly*, New York, 1915 —.

NBA   J. S. Bach, *Neue Ausgabe sämtlicher Werke,* edited by the J. S. Bach Institute, Göttingen, and the Bach Archiv, Leipzig (the new Collected Edition of J. S. Bach's works), Kassel, 1954 —.

P   J. S. Bach's organ works as published by C. F. Peters in nine volumes.

fl., gr., pf.   The German Gulden (florin) was usually subdivided into 20 Groschen (gr.), each Groschen comprising 12 Pfennige (pf.).

Part I

THE LIFE OF BACH

GENEALOGICAL TABLE OF THE BACH FAMILY

Veit
d. 1619

Johannes
d. 1626

Lips
d. 1620

Wendel
1619–82

Jakob
1655–1718

J. Ludwig
1677–1731

Johann
1604–73

Heinrich
1615–92

Christoph
1613–61

J. Egidius
1645–1717

J. Christoph
1642–1703

J. Michael
1648–94

J. Ambrosius
1645–95

J. Bernhard
1676–1749

J. Nikolaus
1669–1753

Maria Barbara
1684–1720

J. Christoph
1671–1721

J. Jakob
1682–1722

J. Sebastian
1685–1750

Anna Magdalena
Wilcken 1701–60

J. Ernst
1722–77

W. Friedemann
1710–84

C. P. Emanuel
1714–88

J. G. Bernhard
1715–39

Elisabeth Juliane
F. (Altnikol) 1726–81

J. C. Friedrich
1732–95

J. Christian
1735–82

Wilhelm Fr. E.
1759–1845

INTRODUCTION: THE ANCESTORS

THE history of Johann Sebastian Bach's paternal ancestors can be traced back through five generations, thanks to a unique chronicle[1] in which the composer himself took a hand. It is obvious why Sebastian felt the urge to leave to posterity a history of the Bach clan: from his great-grandfather onward the family had produced a multitude of professional musicians serving as organists, town pipers, or members of a court band in Thuringia, a small state in eastern Germany with a predominantly Protestant population. From this account we know that a number of them had considerable creative talent. Sebastian gathered compositions of these forebears and thus established a highly significant collection, which was faithfully preserved by his son Carl Philipp Emanuel and has come down to us.[2]

Johann (1604-73) and Heinrich (1615-92), brothers of Sebastian's grandfather, were prolific composers.[3] Of particular significance was Heinrich's son, Johann Christoph (1642-1703). He wrote outstanding works which Sebastian praised as profound, while Philipp Emanuel

1. It is entitled *Ursprung der musicalisch-Bachischen Familie*. Cf. *Bach-Urkunden* edited by M. Schneider in *Veröffentlichungen der Neuen Bach-Gesellschaft*, XVII, 3, 1916, and C. S. Terry, *The Origin of the Family of Bach Musicians*, London, 1929. When C. P. E. Bach sent the chronicle in 1774 or 1775 to J. N. Forkel, he remarked that his father had 'written the first section . . . many years ago'. Whether this means that Sebastian only contributed the beginning of the chronicle or that he had started on it many years ago, cannot be ascertained today. The latter seems more likely, however. Anyway the *Ursprung* supplied by Emanuel to Forkel, which is preserved today in the Staatsbibliothek, Berlin, seems to be a copy of a former document. According to recent research it was penned by Emanuel's daughter, Anna Carolina Philippina Bach. Cf. Hans-Joachim Schulze, 'Marginalien zu einigen Bach-Dokumenten' in *BJ* 1961, p. 79 ff.

2. Cf. M. Schneider, 'Thematisches Verzeichnis der musikalischen Werke der Familie Bach' in *BJ* 1907, and publications of these works in *Das Erbe deutscher Musik*, vols. 1 and 2, Leipzig, 1935.

3. For a detailed report on the lives and works of the various Bach musicians, see Karl Geiringer, *The Bach Family. Seven Generations of Creative Genius*, New York, 1954.

3

Bach extolled their expressive power. It is noteworthy that the eight-part motet *Ich lasse dich nicht* by this greatest of the earlier Bach musicians was for a long time ascribed to Johann Sebastian.

In contrast to this branch of the family, Sebastian's grandfather, the Arnstadt town piper Christoph Bach (1613-61), and his father, the Eisenach town musician Johann Ambrosius Bach (1645-95), seem to have been merely fine and versatile performers, and their descendant was—for all his family loyalty—not able to lay his hand on any composition written by either of them. Sebastian's grandfather somewhat diverged from family tradition in another respect, too. While his two brothers, like various other relatives, married daughters of Thuringian musicians, he chose a descendant of Saxon farmers. The highly imaginative Thuringians differ from the more realistic Saxons. Through the union of Christoph Bach with a farmer's daughter from Saxony new and important strains were added to the Bach patrimony. They were balanced in a most auspicious way through Sebastian's maternal heritage. Johann Ambrosius married Elisabeth Lämmerhirt, descendant of a family that had lived in the state of Silesia, eastern Germany, until in 1620 persecution of the Protestant religion forced these deeply religious people to move to Thuringia. In this respect their action significantly matched that of Sebastian's great-great-grandfather, Veit Bach, who, as the chronicler remarks, 'was compelled to escape from Hungary because of his Lutheran faith.' The Lämmerhirts settled down in the town of Erfurt, where they were prosperous furriers. At the same time they became ardent followers of a mystic named Esaias Stiefel, who preached according to the tenets of the Anabaptists. The Lämmerhirt family faithfully attended his services, and even when Stiefel was sentenced to jail because of his heretic leanings, they courageously proclaimed their allegiance to him. A streak of mysticism and a passionate striving for the individual vision of God, Sebastian may have inherited from his maternal forebears. His father supplied a tremendous musical potential and a vital concern for Lutheran Protestantism, the spiritual force dominating the Bach musicians of the time.

I. APPRENTICESHIP

(1685-1703)

IN the northern side-aisle of the *Georgenkirche* in Eisenach there stands a baptismal font erected in the year 1503. This venerable relic, which is still intact today,[1] has witnessed many significant events through the centuries, but none more so than the ceremony on March 23, 1685, to which the pastor still refers today whenever a baby is christened there. On that day the town musician Johann Ambrosius Bach had a son baptized under the name of Johann Sebastian. Of the two godfathers, one, the town musician Sebastian Nagel, came all the way from the city of Gotha; the other, Johann Georg Koch, was a ducal forester in Eisenach.[2] It seems deeply symbolic that Sebastian Bach was made a member of the Christian community in a church steeped in German tradition and legend. At St. George's the saintly Elisabeth was wedded to the Landgrave Louis IV of Thuringia, originator of the Tournament of Song in the Wartburg. From St. George's pulpit Luther, on May 3, 1521, thundered his sermon of defiance after returning from the fateful *Reichstag* at Worms. But even apart from such historical considerations, the church meant much to the Eisenach Bachs as the center of their musical activities. Now, in the building in which Johann Christoph, the most eminent among the older Bach musicians, had been serving as organist for the past twenty years, the

1. It remained intact in spite of the fact that the church itself suffered various injuries both outside and inside from air pressure during bombing raids. According to information kindly supplied by Eisenach residents, the repairs needed to make the beautiful building fit for use again were completed by 1951. However, except for the late Baroque incasement, the organ is no longer in existence.

2. C. Freyse, in *Eisenacher Dokumente um S. Bach,* thinks it probable that Ambrosius Bach, who also lodged for several years with a forester, was a member of the *Schützengilde* (shooting association), founded in the 13th century, which had St. Sebastian as their patron saint. If the assumption is correct, it would imply that Ambrosius enjoyed a certain social standing in the community.

member of the family who was to excel him by far was being baptized.

Few definite facts are known about Sebastian's early youth, but it seems safe to assume that he was taught to play stringed instruments by his father, an outstanding violinist, while his second cousin, Johann Christoph, may have started him on the organ. When he was eight years old, he entered the Eisenach Latin school,[1] attending it at the same time as his brother, Johann Jakob (1682-1722), and two of his cousins. The pupils usually started at the age of seven, and remained in each class for two or three years, until ready for promotion. Sebastian advanced very quickly, holding a slightly higher place than his brother Jakob, who was three years older. He excelled in other than scholastic subjects too. Naturally he was among those pupils for whom the school choirs were of paramount importance and he was rapidly promoted from the *Kurrende* choir, which sang one-part hymns, to the *Chorus Symphoniacus* performing motets and cantatas. The congregation of St. George's was fortunate indeed to enjoy the Sunday music provided by the Bachs, with Johann Christoph producing magnificent sounds on the organ, Ambrosius performing in a masterly manner on a stringed instrument, and little Sebastian singing in a pure soprano voice,[2] joined by other relatives, who were all intensely musical. And fortunate were the Bach children who grew up in this atmosphere of deep-rooted and natural musicianship.

It was only for a brief space of time that Sebastian was granted the happiness of so sheltered an existence. The boy's frequent absences from school—95 hours in the first school year and 103 in the one following—testify to the upheaval in his domestic situation. He lost his mother when he was nine years old, and his father less than a year later. Now the family was called on to help. Both Sebastian and his brother Jakob were admitted to the home of their eldest brother,

1. From 1544 the school was housed in a former Dominican monastery built in 1232. In 1707 the institute was raised to the rank of a *Gymnasium*.

2. Sebastian's fine, penetrating soprano voice of great range and flexibility is mentioned by J. N. Forkel, the composer's first biographer, who derived his information from Philipp Emanuel Bach. Forkel's biography, *Über J. S. Bachs Leben, Kunst und Kunstwerke*, 1802, is available in a modern reprint edited by J. Müller-Blattau, Kassel, 1950. An English translation of 1808 can be found in H. T. David and A. Mendel, *The Bach Reader*, New York, 1945, p. 293 ff. Our quotations are in part based on this version. C. S. Terry offered a profusely annotated translation of Forkel's book (London, 1920).

Johann Christoph (b. 1671), organist at the little Thuringian town of Ohrdruf. In accepting them, Johann Christoph followed the family tradition of mutual assistance which had greatly contributed to the success of the Bach musicians. We can imagine, however, that the offer of such hospitality was not easy for him. The ties of blood had never been strengthened by a home life enjoyed in common, for shortly after the birth of Sebastian, Johann Christoph had left his parents in order to study in Erfurt with the great organist Johann Pachelbel; so his young brothers were really strangers to him. Besides, he had married only a few months previously, a child was on the way, and the stipend paid by the Ohrdruf Council was extremely meager.[1] It is understandable that the elder of Johann Christoph's two charges, Jakob, after attending Ohrdruf's Latin school for a year, left his brother in order to be apprenticed to the Eisenach town musician who had succeeded Ambrosius Bach.

Sebastian, however, stayed on in Ohrdruf for five years. During this time he contributed to the household expenses by earning a not inconsiderable amount as a singer;[2] but such work did not prevent the precocious youth from a brilliant career at Ohrdruf's renowned Latin school. His promotions followed one another very rapidly, and Sebastian was usually not only the youngest in his class but also one of the top-ranking pupils. He became a senior at fourteen, while the average age of his classmates was 17.7 years. In this school, which he attended at the same time as his cousin, Johann Ernst (1683-1739), he received a thorough training in Latin and, what was important for his subsequent religious attitude, in Lutheran orthodoxy. His keen mind must have enjoyed the intellectual gymnastics of theological dialectics. He later was to develop a hobby probably unique among composers, that of collecting theological books and pamphlets and reading them as a form of relaxation.

Nevertheless, school work could take up no more than the outer fringes of his wide-awake mind. What really mattered to Sebastian was the thrilling voyage of exploration into the immense domain of

1. He received 45 fl. a year plus allowances in rye and wood. In 1696 he was granted an increase of 10 fl. after he had refused an offer from Gotha.

2. The prefect of the chorus was Johann Avenarius, whose cousin, J. G. Schübler, became Sebastian's pupil and publisher. Cf. G. Kraft in *J. S. B. in Thüringen*, edited by H. Besseler and G. Kraft, Weimar, 1950, p. 187.

music. He had the opportunity to store away a great deal of practical knowledge by observing the construction of a new organ at his brother's church. In this as in all musical matters Johann Christoph was his mentor, a guide of high quality, trained by his father, Ambrosius Bach, and by the great organist and composer Johann Pachelbel. It may be assumed that he was artistically on the same high level as so many other Bachs, a conjecture borne out by two entries made by his superior, Superintendent Kromeyer. When Johann Christoph married, Kromeyer noted in the church register: 'young, but artistic,' and when the organist died in 1721 he described him in the death register as 'an artist of the first rank.'[1] According to Forkel, Johann Christoph taught Sebastian the clavier; but we can safely assume that he also instructed him in other instruments, as well as in the elements of composition.

Young Sebastian absorbed all instruction as readily as a sponge does water. His thirst for new information was unquenchable, and continued so throughout his life. There is the touching story, first reported in Mizler's Obituary,[2] of how Sebastian took a volume of music by leading clavier composers that his brother had denied him as being too advanced; how, lacking candles, he copied it painstakingly by the light of the moon, thus seriously injuring his sight; and how he suffered the worst possible blow when, after months of toil, he was found out and deprived of the copy he had made. If the story in this form is true, it would make Sebastian's eldest brother appear a singularly unpleasant person. But it may be that he normally treated his brother quite decently, and that it was only exasperation with the young genius's unceasing battery of questions and a sudden jealous awareness of Sebastian's superior gifts that provoked this spiteful outburst. That Sebastian was, on the whole, not treated too harshly in Ohrdruf is apparent from his subsequent attitude toward his relatives there. He dedicated one of his early clavier works to Johann Christoph (cf. p. 261), and repaid his elder brother by giving two of the latter's sons musical training in his own house. Yet it seemed impossible for him to remain

1. Cf. F. Reinhold, 'Die Musik-Bache in Ohrdruf,' *Ohrdruf Festschrift,* 1950.
2. The article, which appeared in 1754 in Mizler's *Musikalische Bibliothek,* was written by Philipp Emanuel Bach and Sebastian's pupil, Johann Friedrich Agricola, and is one of our main sources for the details of Sebastian's life. It is reprinted in *BJ* 1920.

much longer at Ohrdruf. Johann Christoph's home was becoming more
and more crowded, owing to additions to his family; while the school
on the other hand, unlike other institutions of its kind, did not place
impecunious students in houses of rich citizens. Nor could Sebastian
have recourse to the expedient of joining any other member of the
family for further training, as had been the practice in previous generations, since the number of Bach musicians had been sadly reduced
during the preceding decades. Thus young Sebastian began to search
eagerly for an opportunity to study in another part of the country.

Luck, or fate, would have it that a new Cantor by the name of Elias
Herda had recently joined the Ohrdruf school faculty. Although a
Thuringian himself, Herda had as a student held a scholarship at St.
Michael's in the city of Lüneburg in northern Germany. He knew
that good singers were in great demand for the church's exquisite
Mettenchor, which consisted of 12 to 15 musicians who took over the
solos or led the choir of the *Ritterakademie*, a school for young noblemen whose schedule did not include musical training. The choir members, according to the statutes, had to be the 'offspring of poor people,
with nothing to live on, but possessing good voices'; in addition to free
board and tuition they were entitled to a small monthly income.

As Herda taught music at the Ohrdruf school, Sebastian could not
fail to hear of his teacher's experiences in Lüneburg. The boy, once he
learned of such a fine opportunity, was most eager to grasp it. The
great difficulties involved in traveling 200 miles without adequate
funds did not scare him in the least. He felt quite ready to exert himself to the utmost, and to limit his appetite to the scantiest rations, if
this could bring him to an institution which for long had been a re-
vered center of choral singing. Fortunately, a schoolmate of his, Georg
Erdmann, was interested in the same project; being a friend, maybe
even a relative, of Herda's, from whose native village he came, he succeeded in obtaining the Cantor's full assistance for himself and Sebastian. Herda contacted Lüneburg, and his report on Sebastian must
have been enthusiastic indeed; for the answer was positive, despite the
fact that as a rule St. Michael's only accepted younger boys able to
serve for a longer period, or pupils of seventeen or eighteen, whose
voices were full-grown. Thus, early in March 1700, two eager youths,
Bach, not quite fifteen, and Erdmann, aged eighteen, set out on the

arduous trek to Lüneburg. They left Ohrdruf just in time, for we see from the church registers that soon afterward a terrible epidemic struck the little town.[1]

In April the list of the Lüneburg *Mettenchor* mentions Bach among the sopranos receiving a monthly payment of 12 groschen. This seems very little, but fortunately it did not constitute his whole income; for he was entitled to a share in all the monies earned for singing in the streets, performances at weddings, funerals, etc. As, moreover, his domicile and board as well as a supply of firewood and candles were provided, his financial position was certainly not worse than it had been in Ohrdruf. As to the educational opportunities, they were ideal for a youth with so ravenous a musical appetite. Lüneburg differed in many ways from Ohrdruf. The church of St. Michael itself was of breathtaking loftiness, and the famous high altar with its centerpiece of pure gold interspersed with lovely enamels, near which the choir had its position, must have impressed young Sebastian as deeply as it did many of his contemporaries. The music offered was worthy of so exquisite a setting, and in its great variety most helpful in providing a young musician with a thorough knowledge of contemporary and older choral literature. Ever since the first Protestant Cantor had established an imposing music library at St. Michael's in 1555, the tradition had been faithfully continued by his successors. The Thuringian Cantor, Friedrich Emanuel Praetorius (1623-95), in particular, had done a great deal in this respect, with the result that the collection included, besides a huge amount of printed music, some 1100 manuscript compositions by 175 composers, among them even two members of Sebastian's family, Heinrich Bach and the great Johann Christoph. Thus the church had huge resources on which to draw, and the programs accordingly included a wealth of fine music unknown to Sebastian, with which he became familiar through performing it.[2]

Not long after his arrival he lost his fine soprano voice. This did not

1. Cf. Günther Kraft, p. 29.

2. G. Fock in his valuable study *Der junge Bach in Lüneburg*, Hamburg, 1950, considers the former assumption that Sebastian copied many of the works in this collection to be erroneous. He contends that the music was partly the private property of the Cantor, who had bought it from the estate of Praetorius, and that it was probably housed in its entirety in the Cantor's rooms, to which a pupil of the school would hardly have had admission.

mean dismissal, however, as young Joseph Haydn was to experience
in a similar position at St. Stephen's in Vienna. In Lüneburg it was
the custom to let the scholarship boys continue as best they could as
tenors and basses. In Sebastian's case, moreover, his various excellent
qualifications made him extremely valuable in other respects. It is
significant that just in the year 1700 the church employed only three
instrumentalists (against six in 1660, and ten in 1710), and fifteen-
year-old Sebastian was probably from the outset admitted because of
his usefulness as a violinist or viola player in the orchestra and as an
organist.

Added to a very heavy schedule of musical duties was the curriculum imposed by the *Michaelisschule,* a Latin school for non-aristo-
cratic youths, where Sebastian studied religion, rhetoric, logic, Latin,
and Greek, mainly under Rector Johann Büsche. Since the teacher was
an orthodox Lutheran, the religious foundations initiated in Ohrdruf
were greatly strengthened and were to remain of vital importance to
Sebastian throughout his life.

While the scholarship boys had to attend the *Michaelisschule,* they
roomed and boarded in the old convent, where the *Ritterakademie* was
housed. In some ways this was not too pleasant an arrangement; for
young noblemen were apt to treat poor singers scornfully, and to require many a menial service from them. Sebastian, however, who had
not been exactly spoiled in his brother's home, cannot have minded
this overmuch; and he was, on the other hand, fully aware of the tremendous advantages he derived from living close to these aristocrats.
The Academy was a center of French culture. French conversation,
indispensable at that time to any high-born German, was obligatory
between the students; and Sebastian with his quick mind may have
become familiar with a language which he had no chance to study in
his own schools. There were French plays he could attend and, what
was more important, French music he could hear, as a pupil of Lully,
Thomas de la Selle, taught dancing at the Academy to French tunes.
Most likely it was de la Selle, noticing the youth's enthusiastic response, who decided to take Bach to the city of Celle, where he served
as court musician.[1]

1. Fock, p. 47, has succeeded in establishing in the person of de la Selle, employed both in the *Ritterakademie* and at Celle, the person most likely to have been

Celle, residence of the dukes of Brunswick-Lüneburg, was at that time ruled by Duke Georg Wilhelm, who, like so many German sovereigns with small domains and large ambitions, did everything conceivable to create a miniature Versailles at his court. His French wife fully shared his enthusiasm, and between them they created a veritable center of Gallic culture in Celle. French Huguenots who had fled from their country were sure of hospitality there and enjoyed the French musicians and singers, who produced an unending series of performances. The Duke could certainly expect a high artistic standard, as he spent huge sums (for instance, some 14,000 thalers in 1690) on his music and theater. It is significant that one of the greatest oboists of the time, Johann Ernst Galliard,[1] was trained at the Celle court; the Duke paid Galliard's teacher 100 thalers a year for instructing the promising youth.

We can well imagine what the visits to Celle must have meant to an artist with a mind so wide open to new experience. There Sebastian may have become familiar with the idiom and style of Couperin and other keyboard masters; he heard French instrumental music and listened to French organ compositions in the castle's exquisite Renaissance chapel with its jewel of a small organ. Various copies made by him[2] testify to the eagerness with which he applied himself to these studies.

It was a stroke of luck that Sebastian happened to go to Celle at that particular time; a few years later the artistic Duke Georg Wilhelm

responsible for Sebastian's admission to the court of Celle, about which the Obituary reports. None of the previous theories sounded very convincing. A. Pirro (L'Esthétique de J. S. B., Paris, 1907, p. 423) assumed that Bach was introduced by the court physician, Scott, son-in-law of Lüneburg's mayor; W. Wolffheim (Festschrift für Rochus v. Liliencron, Leipzig, 1910, p. 430) pointed to the trumpeter Jan Pack in the Duke's service, who might have been a kinsman. It was also conjectured that the Celle town organist Brunckhorst, with whom Bach had contact after 1703, was the link. (Cf. P. Spitta, J. S. Bach, Leipzig, 1921³, I, p. 198; an English translation of this basic biography was offered by C. Bell and J. A. Fuller-Maitland, London, 1884-85, reprinted, New York, 1951. In the present book, quotations are based on the German original of Spitta's work.)

1. Galliard was subsequently court conductor in London, and Handel's predecessor.

2. For example, the suites by Nicolas de Grigny and Charles Dieupart, and the former's Livre d'orgue.

died, the orchestra was dismissed, and the little court ceased to be a center of French music.

In Lüneburg there were also other interesting persons living in the convent which housed the Academy. In 1701 the excellent organ builder Johann Balthasar Held stayed there while he was repairing St. Michael's organ. With what interest must Sebastian have watched him, and listened to the reports about the outstanding instruments in Lübeck and Hamburg, on which Held had worked! Young Bach was thus able to acquire more knowledge about the construction of organs —a field in which he was to become the greatest authority.

He seems also to have established a very important contact with Georg Böhm,[1] organist of Lüneburg's *Johanneskirche*. Born in 1661 in a village near Ohrdruf, this musician naturally had various links with the Bachs. It is probable that he studied at the school in Ohrdruf that Sebastian had just left; later he attended the Gotha Latin school with a kinsman of Sebastian, and he studied at the University of Jena together with three men who subsequently became Bach's teachers at Ohrdruf. Thus it may not have been difficult for Sebastian to gain access to the great organist and composer. Though not proved by any documentary evidence, it appears very likely that a youth driven by so insatiable a craving for musical knowledge should have approached the eminent Thuringian musician. Anyway, Sebastian's early organ works clearly reveal the influence of the Lüneburg organist, and C. P. Emanuel Bach testifies to his father's admiration for Böhm.[2]

Bach also underwent a highly significant experience on his visits to Hamburg, where he heard the outstanding organist J. A. Reinken, then seventy-eight years old. The thirty miles' distance and lack of

1. The connection with another Lüneburg organist, Johann Jakob Löw(e), conjectured by Spitta and Terry (*Bach, A Biography,* London, 1928), seems of minor importance. Löw was not really a Thuringian, but a Viennese who called himself 'von Eisenach' because this was his father's native town. When Sebastian came to Lüneburg, Löw was 72 and probably not interested in a young musician.

2. Cf. his letter of 1775 to Forkel, edited by Max Schneider in *Veröffentlichungen der Neuen Bach-Gesellschaft,* XVII, 3, 1916. Almost all organ and clavier works by Böhm which have been preserved may be traced back to copies owned by Sebastian's kinsman J. G. Walther (cf. p. 36); Fock, p. 86, believes it not unlikely that Walther received them from Bach. Erich Valentin maintains a different viewpoint in *MGG* (II, p. 12) and assumes that Bach got to know Böhm's works through Walther at Weimar.

funds were negligible matters once Sebastian's artistic curiosity was aroused. He walked to Hamburg, and so great were the impressions he received from the aged artist and his magnificent organ at St. Catherine's (renovated in 1670),[1] so fascinating was Hamburg's bustling musical life, with the great Reinhard Keiser at the opera house, that Sebastian seems to have repeated the visit more than once. How he managed in Hamburg without starving, we do not know. Perhaps he received shelter and a little help from cousin Johann Ernst, his former classmate at Ohrdruf, who had also gone to Hamburg to improve his musical knowledge.

Thus the young genius had an abundance of musical experiences. With passionate eagerness he absorbed them all—Reinken's virtuosity; the Hamburg opera; the elegant French *manières*, Böhm's individual language; the old choral music—until they became an integral part of his own personality. Lüneburg, with its peculiar location near two important, and so very different, musical centers, was indeed an ideal place for Sebastian's musical training. At the same time nobody could have displayed a fiercer determination to get hold of, and to exhaust to the uttermost limit, all the golden opportunities within his grasp.

1. This is the only organ about which Sebastian Bach's praise has been recorded. Cf. Agricola in J. Adlung, *Musica Mechanica Organoedi,* Berlin, 1768 (facs. ed., Kassel, 1931). The organ was destroyed during World War II.

II. YEARS OF GROWTH

(1703-1708)

BY Easter 1702[1] Sebastian had finished his studies at the *Michaelis-schule* and was ready for a university. Attending any such institution without funds would have presented a big but not insoluble problem to so energetic and resourceful a youth. Apparently Sebastian did not seriously consider studying at a university; he was most eager to start musical work in earnest and felt ready for any position that might come his way. In later years he may have regretted this decision, for in 18th-century Germany attendance at a university made a tremendous difference to a musician's standing, both socially and economically. For this reason, when it came to his own sons, he was eager to give them a university education, although there was no doubt in his mind that they would eventually choose musical professions. But as a youth of seventeen Sebastian was not far-sighted enough to adopt such a policy. Where to look for suitable employment was the question that now arose. Significantly enough, he did not consider staying in northern Germany, where he had established numerous contacts which might have led to an appointment. For purposes of study and artistic improvement this part of Germany had been excellent. But when it came to settling down, he decided to travel the 200 miles back to Thuringia, where his forebears had tilled the musical soil for almost two centuries. This he did out of a deeply rooted allegiance to the family tradition, and out of longing for contacts with his kinsfolk, a longing particularly strong in one who, since the age of ten, had missed normal family

---

1. The assumption of former biographers that Sebastian stayed at the Latin school in Lüneburg for three years seems unfounded (cf. Fock). Sebastian had already started work on the last class of the Latin school in Ohrdruf, and in view of his former scholastic progress it cannot be assumed that it took him more than three years altogether to master the curriculum of the senior year. What he did until he found a position in 1703, and where he lived, is not known.

ties. Apart from this consideration, there were also practical reasons in favor of Thuringia. There the very name of Bach was honored and would be enough to secure the beginner a position. The family was also sure to lend all the help it could, just as Sebastian was to do again and again for other musicians of the clan, and its members were often in possession of the necessary inside information regarding a vacancy which sometimes spelled the difference between success and failure.

In 1703 three different organist posts were due to be filled in Thuringia. One was at the *Jakobikirche* at Sangerhausen, the organist of which had died in July 1702. That Sebastian applied is revealed in a letter he himself wrote some thirty years later to a Sangerhausen Council member. From it we learn that after all the votes had been cast in his favor, and the post promised to him, the lord of the town, a Duke of Saxe-Weissenfels, had interceded, as he wanted the position to be filled by a more mature musician, Joh. Augustin Kobelius. Naturally the Duke's protégé was appointed, and Sebastian had to content himself with a promise of subsequent favors (a promise he was to redeem successfully for one of his sons).

At Eisenach, also, the town organist's position became vacant through the death of Johann Christoph Bach on March 31, 1703. Sebastian may have been greatly attracted by this opening in the city of his birth. Whether he applied for the position or not, we do not know. At all events the post was given to an older and more renowned member of the family, Johann Bernhard Bach (1676-1749). A more promising opportunity, however, seemed to be materializing in another Bach center, Arnstadt. There the old church of St. Boniface, which in 1581 had been devastated by fire, had been rebuilt some hundred years later and was now once more in use under the name *Neue Kirche*.[1] At first it had no organ at all, but eventually enough money was collected to start building an instrument, for which an organist would be needed before long. Early in 1703 the work was nearly completed, and Sebastian's relatives began to exert themselves on his behalf. Naturally such endeavors could not be rushed, and in the meantime Sebastian had to earn his daily bread. He therefore took the first position that presented itself, entering as a 'lackey and violinist' the small chamber orchestra[2]

1. In 1935 its name was changed to *Bach Kirche*.
2. Sebastian possibly received the position through the intervention of a member of this orchestra, his distant kinsman David Hoffmann.

of Johann Ernst, a younger and very artistic brother of the reigning Duke of Weimar. It looked as though Sebastian was following the tradition established by his father and grandfather (the latter had also begun his career at Weimar in the double capacity of servant and instrumentalist), but he was really only marking time until an organist's post, on which he had set his heart, was offered to him. Meanwhile he tried to play the organ as much as possible, acting as deputy for the aged court organist Johann Effler. This was not only a valuable experience for young Sebastian, it was also helpful for the negotiations in Arnstadt. Martin Feldhaus, mayor of the town and kinsman to the Bachs, did not fail to make good use of this fact. Indeed, when he succeeded in having the eighteen-year-old Sebastian Bach invited to test the new organ, the receipt he drew up on payment of Sebastian's expenses gives the youth the exaggerated title of 'Princely Saxonian Court Organist at Weimar,' which seems not to be in accordance with the facts.

Testing and playing the new organ, young Sebastian had a chance of revealing his stupendous mastery to the Arnstadt citizens, and there is no doubt that he swept them off their feet. The usual procedure of inviting several candidates for trial performances was dispensed with, and hardly a month after his appearance, Sebastian received a contract granting him a yearly salary of 50 fl., plus 34 fl. for board and lodging.[1] This income for an organist in those days was excellent. Sebastian's great-uncle, the eminent Heinrich Bach, had never received so much during his fifty years' service at Arnstadt, nor was Sebastian's eldest brother in Ohrdruf ever to earn what his pupil was granted from the outset. It is significant that Sebastian, although eager to work in the same capacity and in the same town as his kinsmen, was, even as a youth of eighteen, determined to build up his life on more favorable material conditions.

On August 14, 1703, the new organist entered upon his duties. These were not extensive; he was to play every Sunday from 8 to 10 a.m., every Monday at an intercessory service, and every Thursday

---

1. Sebastian was paid 25 fl. out of the beer taxes, 25 fl. out of the church treasury, while the additional 34 fl. were granted by the hospital 'on command of the Princely Consistory.' This did, however, not necessitate Bach's performing in the hospital where services were held but rarely as the pensioners were expected to attend the 'New Church.' Cf. K. Müller, *Der junge Bach*, in *J. S. Bach und seine Verwandten in Arnstadt*, ed. by F. Wiegand, Arnstadt, 1950.

from 7 to 9 a.m. Since his church had not engaged a Cantor, he was supposed, although his contract did not specifically mention it, to train a small choir formed of pupils from the Latin school for performances during the Sunday service. It seemed to be an ideal position for a young musician who needed plenty of time for his own improvement and creative work. Arnstadt, a city of 3800 inhabitants, was also a pleasant place to live. Its many linden trees had earned it the name of the 'Linden-town'; the gardens surrounding its castle, with their flower-beds arranged in patterns of beautiful tapestries, their grottoes and fountains, were considered outstanding in Germany, while the Medie-val *Liebfrauenkirche* and the Renaissance Town Hall were among the gems of Thuringian architecture. In the reign of Anton Günther II,[1] various prominent men were assembled at the small court; among them, in charge of the numismatic collection, was the learned Andreas Morelli, who had formerly been attached to the Paris court.[2] The court orchestra was directed by Paul Gleitsmann, and as it did not con-sist only of court employees, the conductor would certainly have se-cured the services of so gifted and versatile a musician as Sebastian.

In addition to the advantages of a good position, there was the pleas-ure of renewing contact with members of his own family. There were three cousins, among them Johann Ernst, with whom he had shared unforgettable artistic experiences in Hamburg. Most important, how-ever, was Maria Barbara (1684-1720), youngest daughter of the late organist and composer Johann Michael Bach, a cousin of Sebastian's father. Both the girl's parents were dead by 1704, and she lived with her uncle, Mayor Martin Feldhaus, and an aunt, Regina Wedemann, in the house named 'The Golden Crown,' where, according to docu-ments preserved, Sebastian also boarded for some time. Sebastian and Barbara were of approximately the same age; both had been reared in homes where music was considered of paramount importance; and both were orphans drifting along without strong personal ties. Each could lighten the other's solitude and provide the anchorage both needed. No wonder the two young people were drawn toward each other, and 'The Golden Crown' witnessed the growth of an idyllic love affair.

1. He was elevated to the rank of prince in 1697, but only used the title as late as 1707.

2. From 1689 to 1697 the poet, Salomo Franck, was active there as 'government-secretary.' Sebastian was to meet him subsequently in Weimar and set various cantatas of Franck's to music.

The blood relationship was considered too remote to present an obstacle, since they were second cousins. However, several years were to pass before they could get married, years which were not too easy for either of them.

There were certain difficulties involved in Sebastian's work, which in course of time assumed larger and larger proportions. The choir he was supposed to train was small and of very poor quality. As the 'New Church' was the least important in Arnstadt, it was inevitably allotted the worst material, while the good singers were employed in the other two churches of the town. Not only were Sebastian's charges mediocre musicians, they were also an unruly lot, behaving (as the City Council complained to the Consistory) in 'a scandalous manner.' To achieve good results with such an unco-operative group, a mature man of high authority was needed; a musician like Sebastian, who was younger than some of the singers, had a difficult position indeed. These complications were further aggravated by the young genius's lack of patience with incompetent musicians, and by his temper, which, when provoked, could assume violent proportions. Thus his relations with the recalcitrant group was by no means characterized by the dignified behavior to be expected of a servant of the church. After two years of unpleasantness, things came to a head in a street brawl between the organist and a particularly offensive rowdy by the name of Geyersbach. The latter, by three years Sebastian's senior, happened to meet Bach on a dark night and attacked him with a stick, calling him a 'dirty dog' because the organist had made fun of him as a 'nanny-goat bassoonist.' Sebastian drew his sword, a fight began, and blood would have been shed had not the spectators intervened after sundry holes had been pierced in Geyersbach's camisole. The incident made Sebastian even more disgusted with the choir, and gradually he stopped working with it. Various unpleasant cross-examinations by the Consistory followed (of which the files have been preserved). Again and again his superiors urged him to accept the 'imperfect conditions,' which they readily admitted, and work with the choir, but he stubbornly persisted in his point of view that the contract did not provide for this work, and that it should be entrusted to a choir master.[1]

---

1. It seems that when Sebastian refused to co-operate, the training of the choir was entrusted to a distant kinsman, Andreas Börner, husband of the late Heinrich Bach's granddaughter.

Maria Barbara must have worried a good deal over this conflict between her dear cousin and the authorities, but she could not learn too early the hard lesson that there was no pliability in Sebastian's nature. When he considered his claim justified, he would fight for it to the bitter end, even at the risk of endangering his own position. Indeed, the choir was not the only point of difference between the youthful organist and his superiors. Soon after the Geyersbach affair, Sebastian, eager to forget his personal problems in a great musical experience, asked for four weeks' leave to visit the famous organist Dietrich Buxtehude, in Lübeck, and suggested that his cousin Johann Ernst should act as his substitute at the 'New Church.' The Consistory well understood their gifted young organist's desire to improve his art and gave him permission to make the trip. So Sebastian turned again toward the north, this time traveling a distance of 230 miles.[1] His plan was to attend the famous *Abendmusiken* (evening concerts) which Buxtehude conducted at St. Mary's on the last two Sundays after Trinity and the second, third, and fourth Sundays of Advent. As a contemporary document states, 'in this way best thanks could be musically rendered to the Almighty at the end of the year for all favors granted.'[2] Bach arrived in Lübeck just in time for these events and found that the reality exceeded his high expectations. Buxtehude had forty musicians at his disposal who were placed on four platforms especially erected for the performances. The orchestra of twelve to fourteen players was of a high calibre, and the seven town musicians co-operating were said to be 'not mere pipers but excellent artists and fine composers famous at princely courts.' But it was naturally Buxtehude himself who both as a composer and organist made an overwhelming impression on young Sebastian. He had a chance of also attending the stirring performance of Buxtehude's *castrum doloris*, written in memory of the deceased Emperor Leopold I, as well as the celebration of the new emperor's accession, for which the composer provided his *templum honoris*. Sebastian was held spellbound in Lübeck, and the idea of returning to his post at the end of the four weeks' leave did not enter his mind. The only thing that mattered was to absorb all the intrica-

1. The Obituary states that he made the trip on foot, but this seems unlikely because of the short time available.
2. Cf. Wilhelm Stahl, *Dietrich Buxtehude*, Kassel, 1952.

cies of Buxtehude's art. These were indeed glorious days for Bach, who was forever making new and exciting discoveries, which were to be most fruitful in his own creative work. For Barbara, far away at Arnstadt, worrying over the reaction of Sebastian's superiors, it must have been a difficult time. However, Sebastian while profoundly stirred by what he heard and learned, did remain faithful to her. When it was hinted to him that he might become Buxtehude's successor, provided he married, according to custom, the master's daughter Anna Margreta, then thirty years old, he declined, although the position at St. Mary's must have seemed most alluring to the organist of the smallest church in Arnstadt.[1]

It was after an absence of four months instead of four weeks that Sebastian reappeared in Arnstadt. Soon the congregation noticed a change in their organist's playing. Encouraged by what he had heard in Lübeck and overflowing with new ideas, Sebastian became rather unconventional in his accompaniments of the hymns, and his improvisations between the verses seemed never to come to an end. The congregation was amazed, bewildered, outraged, and at times unable to stumble through the chorales. Finally the organist was again called before Superintendent Olearius, who, after reproaching him for his overlong absence, took him to task for the 'many curious variations . . . confusing to the congregation' he was inserting into the accompaniment. Strict orders were given him 'if he used a *tonum peregrinum* (a strange melody or tonality) to hold it out and not quickly to pass on to something else or even, as he liked to do, to use *a tonum contrarium* (a tune or key conflicting with the former one).'

Sebastian could do nothing but obey these instructions, and the joy went out of his work. If the good burghers wanted a dull organist, no doubt he could satisfy them, he thought. Hence, where he had previously done too much, he now did too little; and this time he was criticized because his preludes were too short. So went the year 1706: complaints, cross-examinations, ultimata issued to the organist, who promised to answer in writing and never did. Barbara seems to have been the cause of another disagreement with the Consistory when she sang

1. Buxtehude had also tried unsuccessfully to win first Mattheson, and later Handel, as successor and son-in-law; he eventually achieved his aim with J. Christian Schiefferdecker, who was Bach's age, and ten years younger than the bride.

to his accompaniment at a time the church was empty. Their music-making must have delighted them both and further strengthened the bond between them, but the aftermath was not so pleasant. In Arnstadt nothing remained a secret for long. Someone had heard Barbara singing, tongues were set wagging, and Sebastian was again summoned by the Consistory to explain the presence of a 'strange maiden' in the organ gallery.

The organist was now aware that he would have to look for another position. Fortunately a good opportunity presented itself before long. In the Free Imperial City of Mühlhausen the highly renowned composer and organist of St. Blasius', Johann Georg Ahle, had died in December 1706. Once more the family got busy to secure the position for Sebastian. Maria Barbara was related on her mother's side to the Mühlhausen Councillor, Johann Hermann Bellstedt,[1] and it was he who carried on the negotiations with young Bach. His recommendation was probably supported by the Mühlhausen organ builder J. F. Wender, who had built Arnstadt's new instrument, which Sebastian had tested and approved in 1703. Thus it came about that young Bach was invited to give his trial performance at Easter 1707. Again he overwhelmed the congregation with his superb playing, and the pattern established at Arnstade repeated itself.

The authorities were truly eager to secure his services and even prepared for financial sacrifices. Asked to state his terms, Sebastian requested the salary he got at Arnstadt; and although Ahle, in spite of the esteem he had enjoyed, had received only 66 fl. 14 gr. yearly, the new organist was granted a yearly income of 85 fl. plus the amounts of grain, wood, and fish allowed to Ahle. The Council also undertook to send a wagon to Arnstadt to transport his belongings.

In June Bach again appeared before the Arnstadt Consistory, but with very different emotions! No recriminations this time, no evasive answers on his part; he merely notified the authorities of his appointment at Mühlhausen and asked for permission to hand back the keys of the organ. Everything went smoothly, and young Sebastian in voicing his thanks displayed for once all the courtesy that was demanded.

1. Susanna Barbara Wedemann, aunt and godmother of Maria Barbara Bach, had married in 1680 Johann Gottfried Bellstedt, a kinsman of the Mühlhausen Councillor.

This was most necessary, for the Consistory had, in effect, the power to annul his appointment by not accepting his resignation; and he knew that it was for such reasons that both his father, Ambrosius, and the latter's cousin, Johann Christoph Bach, had been compelled to refuse outside offers and stay on in Eisenach. However, nothing of this kind happened, and the Consistory felt friendly enough toward the Bach clan to appoint as Sebastian's successor his cousin Johann Ernst, though with one significant stipulation: Johann Ernst's salary was to be 40 fl., less than half Sebastian's stipend.

Sebastian was now twenty-two years old and eager to end his bachelor existence. Having exchanged a good position for another equally good, he felt able to take care of a wife and children. If he had any fears about the extra expenses he would incur over the wedding and the furnishing of a modest home (responsibilities which he might have to shoulder alone, as his fiancée was an orphan without means), such fears were dispelled by a small legacy that came his way just at that time through the death of his uncle Tobias Lämmerhirt.[1] At first Sebastian went to Mühlhausen alone, to start his work and to find suitable accommodation; but it was not long before he returned to Arnstadt for his bride. On October 17, 1707, the little church of Dornheim, a village near Arnstadt, witnessed the simple wedding ceremony of Sebastian and Barbara Bach. The choice of this church was due to the family's friendship with its pastor, Lorenz Stauber, who himself was to marry Barbara's aunt, Regina Wedemann, a few months later.[2]

So Sebastian Bach assumed the responsibilities of a married man at a very young age. This was entirely in keeping with the family tradition, although it seems early to us who are inclined to consider freedom from personal ties and responsibilities as one of the requirements for the development of a young genius. But such freedom was not what

1. By a curious coincidence another legacy reached him fourteen years later, when he was about to conclude a second marriage. This time it came from the widow of Tobias Lämmerhirt.

2. Stauber's first wife was a Hoffmann, probably a kinswoman of the Bachs. The wedding of Stauber and Regina Wedemann occurred on June 5, 1708, and was attended by the young Bach couple. It is possible that Sebastian's wedding cantata, *Der Herr denket an uns* (BWV 196), was written for this occasion. The friendship between the Staubers and Bach was maintained even after the latter's removal to Leipzig. When Regina died in 1731, her last will provided a legacy for the Thomas Cantor and his second wife.

Sebastian needed. To him, who at the age of ten had been deprived of his parents, nothing seemed so desirable as a peaceful home where he really belonged. If ever a genius was suited to the state of matrimony, it was Sebastian Bach. He chose his partner with deep wisdom (such as neither Haydn nor Mozart displayed in the same situation), and made of each of his two marriages a full success. Home meant for him not only material comforts, but the sharing of his most profound interests. His spouse had to be more than a good housekeeper; she had to be a musician, able to appreciate her husband's work. Sebastian's second wife was a professional singer. Although no evidence has come down to us about Maria Barbara's musicianship, we can reasonably assume that someone who was descended from a line of outstanding musicians, and who became the mother of two of Sebastian's most talented sons, was also a real helpmate to her husband in artistic matters.

The newly-wed pair spent a few days with their kinsfolk in Erfurt, and then traveled to Mühlhausen, where Sebastian threw himself vigorously into his new duties.

The position at St. Blasius' conferred greater distinction than that at Arnstadt's least important church. The city of Mühlhausen had harbored a number of eminent musicians, and during the past fifty years St. Blasius' in particular had possessed quite outstanding organists in Johann Rudolph Ahle and his son Johann Georg. Sebastian could not fail to be stimulated by the standard set by such renowned predecessors. All his aspirations for the improvement of church music, which had lain dormant in the uncongenial Arnstadt atmosphere, now manifested themselves with elemental force. The way he shouldered his new responsibilities would have amazed his former employers. Once more the contract merely stipulated that he should play the organ at all the services held at St. Blasius'. This time, however, such work was by no means sufficient for Sebastian. He felt responsible for all the music offered in his church, and, furthermore, he even took a lively interest in the musical progress of the neighboring villages. At St. Blasius' he found the repertory somewhat old-fashioned, as the Ahles had mainly favored the simple sacred aria with instrumental ritornelli, neglecting the type of cantata developed by Buxtehude and other north German masters. This had of course to be changed, and so Sebastian, together with his pupil Johann Martin Schubart, diligently set about copying suitable works for the church library. For the solemn inauguration in February 1708 of the new burgomasters and members of the Council, he wrote the 'congratulatory motet' *Gott ist mein König* (BWV 71) making splendid use of what he had learned from Buxtehude. The congregation could not help being thrilled by this solemn music, and his employers were so pleased that they had the music printed. (This was by no means the rule. In the years 1710-13, for instance, the Mühlhausen authorities published the text only of such congratulatory motets, not the music.)

The Councillors' appreciation of their new organist was further heightened when he handed them soon afterwards a careful survey of the deficiencies of his organ with advice on how to repair the instrument. So convincing was the craftsmanship and intrinsic knowledge revealed in his suggestions that his basic ideas were accepted without demur, and an organ builder was entrusted with their execution. Sebastian's specifications have been preserved, and from them we may reconstruct the young organist's conception of a good instrument. He liked the Baroque arrangement of the organ registers in groups, the members of which are closely interrelated in construction and tone quality, while each group is sharply contrasted from the remainder in sonority and timbre. As he wished to increase the possibilities of such contrasts in dynamic power and tone color, he wanted the addition of a third manual to the two manuals and pedal of the Mühlhausen organ, as well as an increase in the number of bellows. It is interesting to note that the organ suggested for Mühlhausen had much in common with the remodeled instrument of the Eisenach *Georgenkirche*, which his great kinsman Johann Christoph Bach had planned. Although the reconstruction work at Eisenach was not begun until a year after Sebastian left, he doubtless had heard all the details of it from his relatives, and had perhaps even examined the instrument itself after its completion in 1707. That he let Johann Christoph's plan influence him strongly in rebuilding his own organ shows how firm were the artistic ties that bound him to his forebears.

Although his advice regarding the organ was fully heeded in Mühlhausen, troubles arose for the young organist in other areas. The Superintendent at *Divi Blasii*, J. A. Frohne, had decided leanings toward

Pietism, a new trend developed within the Lutheran church and emphasizing a more subjective faith. It had been born out of a reaction against the increasing petrification of the Lutheran doctrine as preached in the orthodox churches. In their striving for a religious revival the Pietists shunned much that played an important role in the Protestant service. Some of them felt that music could become dangerous if it had too strong an effect on the senses, and fought against the inclusion of elaborate music in the service,[1] decrying it as 'siren songs disturbing meditation, mixing the world's vanity with the sacred, and corrupting the gold of divine truth.'[2] It was an anti-artistic attitude very much like that of the Puritans.

Possibly Pastor Frohne was responsible to some extent for the musical austerity prevalent at St. Blasius' before Sebastian arrived, and when he found his organist bent on remedying such shortcomings, he may have hesitated to support him. Nor can we assume that the congregation eagerly followed the newcomer's lead. Reforms are always reluctantly accepted by the majority, and Mühlhausen certainly was no exception to the rule. What they had been accustomed to hear in the thirty-three years' service of Johann Georg Ahle (who, after all, was a native of Mühlhausen, and not just an outsider like this young Bach) was good enough for them, they felt. So quite a few would have rejected the organist's innovations as 'too worldly' and 'carnal.' Nevertheless, such difficulties might eventually have been smoothed out and a compromise agreed upon with Pastor Frohne, who was not a fanatic and was likely to have appreciated his organist's true faith. But, unfortunately, Sebastian seems to have taken sides in a feud between Frohne and the pastor of St. Mary's, Georg Christian Eilmar, on matters of dogma. The latter, a passionate upholder of orthodoxy, had started violent attacks against Frohne's Pietism as early as 1699. At that time the Council intervened and interdicted any further dispute of the kind. Now, however, the old conflict was again brought into

1. This was not true of all the Pietists. Some sects, for example, the *Herrenhuter*, were in favor of elaborate church music; on the other hand, there were also orthodox pastors who condemned too brilliant an organ style. Cf. H. Besch, *J. S. Bach, Frömmigkeit und Glaube*, Kassel, 1950.[2]

2. These remarks are quoted by Bach's predecessor, J. G. Ahle, in a new edition of his father's *Kurze und deutliche Anleitung zu der lieblich und löblichen Singekunst*, Mühlhausen, 1704.

the open and the fight conducted in anything but a Christian spirit. Eilmar was the more aggressive, and his rigid insistence on the letter of the dogma does not put him in too pleasant a light. But to Bach he had one point in his favor: he allowed music an important part in the service. One may assume that he wrote libretti for Sebastian's cantatas,[1] and apparently he thought much of the organist's talent. To receive encouragement both in his general aims and in his creative efforts from so important a man must have meant a good deal to the young composer, and it naturally drew him toward the pastor. He closed his eyes to Eilmar's reactionary formalism and became sufficiently friendly with him to suggest his being godfather to the first child which Bach's young wife was expecting. Eilmar accepted, and when the girl was born in December 1708 he went to Weimar, where the Bachs had moved, to attend the christening ceremony. The friendly connection continued, and for Sebastian's first son, Friedemann, Eilmar's daughter, Anna Dorothea Hagedorn, was godmother.

Sebastian's attitude in the unpleasant feud between the two pastors was a typically youthful one. He saw the picture in black and white and let his actions be determined by his artistic interests, his upbringing, and the family tradition (though not that of his mother!). To him the Pietists who rejected an elaborate church music were enemies to be defeated; the orthodox Lutherans who saw in music an important means of glorifying the Lord were his friends. Beyond that he did not venture. This does not mean, however, that he maintained so intransigent an attitude throughout his life. There is no definite proof that he remained intolerant in his adherence to orthodoxy;[2] certainly the texts he used for some of his cantatas show him to be rather attracted by the spirit of Pietism.

But whatever his subsequent attitude may have been, young Sebastian realized that the prospect of carrying on at Mühlhausen did not

---

1. This is likely for *Gott ist mein König* and also for *Aus der Tiefe rufe ich* (BWV 131), which bears at the end the note 'at the request of Mr. Georg Chr. Eilmar set to music by J. S. Bach, organist at Mühlhausen.' Eilmar may also have provided libretti for other cantatas of this period.

2. As a proof of Bach's orthodoxy his library is usually referred to, which contained some eighty theological works, most of which were by leaders of Lutheran orthodoxy. This certainly reveals the composer's strong interest in these problems, but we cannot deduce from it that he completely shared the several authors' views.

appeal to him. He was eager to assume duties of a different kind, and a position at a princely court seemed to offer far greater attraction than service in the Imperial City. Thus, less than a year after starting work at Mühlhausen, he began to look around for something more desirable. Luck was with him. In Weimar a court organist was needed to replace the aged and infirm Johann Effler, and Sebastian presented himself in June 1708, gave his trial performance, and was accepted. Thereupon he wrote the following letter to the Mühlhausen Council:

Magnificence, High and very Noble, High and
          Learned Sirs, High and Wise Sirs,

   Most Gracious Patrons and Gentlemen,
   This is to express to ycur Magnificence, and to my highly esteemed Patrons who of your grace bestowed on me, your humble servant, the office, vacant a year ago, of Organist to the church of St. Blasius, and granted me the enjoyment of a better subsistence, that at all times I desire to recognize your favors with obedient gratitude. I have always kept one end in view, namely, with all good will to conduct a well regulated church music to the honor of God, in agreement with your desires, and besides to assist, so far as possible to my humble ability, the church music that has grown up in almost all the neighboring villages, which is often better than the harmony produced here. To that end I have obtained from far and wide, and not without expense, a good collection of the choicest pieces of church music. Furthermore I have laid before you the report of the defects in the organ needing repair, and at all times and places have with pleasure fulfilled the duties of my office. Yet this has not been done without opposition, and at present there is not the slightest appearance that things will be altered, though in time our congregation might be brought to approve for their own spiritual benefit. Moreover I have humbly to represent that, modest as is my way of life, with the payment of house-rent and the purchase of indispensable articles of consumption, I can only with difficulty carry on a fitting establishment.
   Now God has so ordered it that a change has unexpectedly been presented to me, in which I foresee the attainment of a more sufficient subsistence and the more effective pursuit of my aims in the due ordering of church music without interference from others, since His Ducal and Serene Highness of Saxe-Weimar has graciously offered me the *entrée* to His Court Capelle and Chamber Music.
   In consequence of this privilege I hereby, with obedience and respect,

represent it to my Most Gracious Patrons, and at the same time would ask them to take my small services to the church up to this time into favourable consideration, and to grant me the benefit of providing me with a gracious dismissal. If I can in any way further contribute to the service of your church I will prove myself better in deed than in word, as long as life shall endure.

I am, Most Honorable Gentlemen, Most Gracious Patrons,

Your Most Humble Servant,

Joh. Seb. Bach.

Mühlhausen, June 25, anno 1708.

The concluding remark evidently refers to the organ repairs started at his instigation. The authorities, while regretfully consenting to the organist's departure, asked him to continue to supervise the work; he promised gladly. Indeed, his relations remained so friendly with the Mühlhausen Councillors that he was again commissioned, in 1709, to write the 'congratulatory motet' for the inauguration of the new Council.[1]

On Reformation Day 1709 he also tested the renovated organ and performed on it. It seems likely that he wrote for the festive occasion his magnificent chorale fantasia *Ein feste Burg* (BWV 720).[2]

Before leaving, Sebastian was able once more to suggest a cousin as his successor. The Council agreed, but insisted (again in the pattern of Arnstadt) that the new organist should receive a much lower salary. Thus Sebastian was replaced by Johann Friedrich (son of the great Johann Christoph of Eisenach), who, in the good old family tradition, retained the position to his death in 1730. But such stability was as yet impossible for Sebastian, and so we see him in July 1708 zestfully starting a new life at Weimar.

1. Although this cantata was printed too, no copy has been traced so far, and we do not even know its title. Yet the Mühlhausen files prove irrefutably that Bach wrote such a work. Cf. *Mühlhäuser Geschichtsblätter*, 1932, p. 294.

2. Cf. Werner David, *Johann Sebastian Bachs Orgeln*, Berlin, 1951, p. 35.

III. THE GREAT ORGANIST

(1708-1717)

THE distance between Mühlhausen and Weimar is not more than forty miles. Socially and economically, however, Sebastian traveled a long way when he exchanged his position in the Free Imperial City for one at the ducal court. From the outset his new salary was almost twice what he received in Mühlhausen, and it was destined to grow throughout his stay at Weimar. And although succeeding the Ahles, father and son, at St. Blasius' had been a privilege indeed, yet, in the eyes of the world, a good position at a ducal court bestowed still more prestige. Added to the material advantages there were other considerations which meant much to the organist. His new patron was a fervent and deeply religious Lutheran, who valued music as an important means of glorifying the Lord. Here Sebastian found encouragement for carrying out his schemes for 'a well-regulated church music,' and no opposition was to be anticipated from other religious sects, as the Duke, who ruled his land with an iron hand, would not tolerate anything but orthodox Lutheranism.

Later in the century, the small court of Weimar was to become the Athens of Germany, witnessing the golden age of literature dominated by the gigantic figures of Goethe and Schiller. Like a magnet, Weimar was to attract men eminent in all the realms of culture, men who were to find in the small residence of the enlightened Duke Carl August a most congenial atmosphere. In Bach's time there was as yet hardly a breath of that invigorating cultural climate, but even then Weimar was clearly different from the average small German court. Here religion was the axis around which everything revolved. The serious-minded Duke Wilhelm Ernst, in the forty-five years of his rule, struck this note, and the court followed his lead. All ducal servants had to attend daily devotions and take turns in reading the Bible aloud. To let the attention wander during a sermon was highly dangerous, for the Duke had the unpleasant habit of questioning his servants personally on every detail of the chaplain's discourse. It was also the Serenissimus himself who worked out the order in which his employees were to appear at the altar for communion. Not only was the Duke engrossed in matters of religious dogma, he also attempted to lead a truly Christian life. Hence there arose at Weimar an atmosphere of austerity which was in strong contrast to the frivolity and extravagance prevalent at other German courts. Not a glimmer of light was visible about the castle after 8 p.m. in the winter and 9 p.m. in the summer. Festivities were rare, and even the troupe of actors[1] which the Duke had employed for some years was dismissed before Sebastian's arrival. Wilhelm Ernst's tastes were frugal, but he insisted on a supply of fresh flowers every day; to meet his needs he had the castle's bearpit, where his predecessors had kept wild beasts, transformed into a beautiful garden. While allowing only a small budget for entertainment, the Duke spent considerable sums on welfare and cultural institutions, showing himself in all such enterprises an important precursor of that type of enlightened ruler which Germany and Austria were to produce some fifty years later. Yet, on the other hand, he was convinced of his absolute power, and accepted as a matter of course the idea, characteristic of the epoch, that an unbridgable gulf existed between his august self and his subjects. He was, in short, a despot, though a well-meaning one.

Fortunately in the field of music, Bach's ideas seemed to move along the same lines as those of the patron. The Duke came to value his organist's gifts, and to trust his judgment in musical matters. Although the organ of the *Schlosskirche* had been reconstructed as recently as 1708 by the organ builder Weishaupt, Bach succeeded in inducing his patron to spend further substantial sums on it. First he had a set of chimes installed, and before long he suggested a complete reconstruction, which organ builder Heinrich Trebs executed between 1712 and 1714.[2] The Duke's co-operative attitude was all the young musician needed to unfold his genius. It was at Weimar that Bach the organist climbed to the loftiest heights. As his patron allowed him frequent

1. In 1696 the theater was inaugurated with a work bearing the characteristic title 'Of virtuous Love as opposed to sinful Desire.'
2. Cf. R. Jauernig in *J.S.B. in Thüringen*, p. 77 ff.

absences, during which his competent pupil J. M. Schubart deputized, Sebastian often played at other courts and cities too, and his fame as an organ virtuoso spread all over Germany. Legends began to circulate: how all unknown he had visited a village church and coaxed such magnificent sounds out of a wretched instrument that the village organist whispered: 'This can only be the devil or Bach himself!' But the awe and admiration of his contemporaries for Sebastian's stupendous virtuosity are also laid down in authentic reports. Constantin Bellermann, a rector of Minden, describes Bach's performance at the court of Cassel thus: 'His feet flew over the pedals as though they had wings, and powerful sounds roared like thunder through the church. This filled Frederick, the crown prince, with such astonishment and admiration that he drew from his finger a ring set with precious stones and gave it to Bach as soon as the sound had died away. If the skill of his feet alone earned him such a gift, what might the Prince have given him had he used his hands as well?' To which we may add: and what would have been the just reward to the composer of the works that the performer interpreted so miraculously? For simultaneously with the organ virtuoso the organ composer Bach climbed to the peak of his creative mastery, and the majority of his important organ works were written or at least started in Weimar. Kindled by the prevailing religious atmosphere they achieved a 'disembodied spirituality' (Forkel) which has perhaps been best characterized by the Weimar genius who heard them a century later. Goethe, listening to Bach's organ works, wrote: 'It is as though eternal harmony were conversing with itself, as it may have happened in God's bosom shortly before He created the world. Thus profoundly was my soul stirred and I felt as if I had neither ears nor eyes nor any other senses, and had no need of them.'

Such insight was not given to Sebastian's contemporaries. Though learned musicians could not fail to be impressed by Bach's profound knowledge and superb craftsmanship, to most listeners his dazzling exploits as a performer necessarily obscured his creative achievements. Sebastian's own attitude in this matter will never be known. His was not an age of self-expression and introspection. What he is reported to have said about his own work is therefore quite unrevealing. Complimented on his great organ playing, he answered deprecatingly: 'There is nothing to it. You only have to hit the right notes at the right time and the instrument plays itself.' And Forkel reports: 'When he was asked how he had contrived to master the art to such a high degree, he generally answered: "I was obliged to work hard; whoever is equally industrious, will succeed just as well." ' Utterances of this kind reflect to some extent the rationalistic attitude of the time. Mostly they were dictated, however, by innate reserve and a natural contempt for people who asked questions that defied a real answer.

There is yet a third aspect of Sebastian's activities in connection with the organ. He gradually attained the position of a highly skilled expert on the construction of the instrument, and in this capacity he constantly received invitations to test newly completed or repaired organs. 'He was,' as Forkel reports, on the basis of information from Philipp Emanuel Bach, 'very severe, but always just, in his trials of organs. As he was perfectly acquainted with the construction of the instrument, he could not be in any case deceived. The first thing he did in trying out an organ was to draw out all the stops and play with the full organ. He used to say in jest that he must know whether the instrument had good lungs. After the examination was over, he generally amused himself and those present by showing his skill as a performer. . . . He would choose some subject and execute it in all the various forms of organ composition, never changing his theme, even though he might play, without intermission, for two hours or more. First he used it for a prelude and a fugue, with the full organ. Then he showed his art of using the stops for a trio, a quartet, etc. Afterwards there followed a chorale, the melody of which was playfully surrounded in the most diversified manner by the original subject, in three or four parts. Finally, the conclusion was made by a fugue, with full organ, in which either another treatment of the first subject predominated, or one or two other subjects were mixed with it.'

Success won outside Weimar naturally had some bearing on his standing there; this was particularly true in the case of Halle. Five years after his arrival in Weimar, Sebastian visited this town and was greatly impressed by the plans for a rebuilding of the huge *Liebfrauenkirche* organ. To work on such an outstanding instrument (with 63 stops!) was tempting indeed; and as the organist's position, held up to 1712 by Handel's teacher Friedrich Wilhelm Zachau, was still vacant, Sebastian applied for it. The Halle authorities showed themselves very interested, and at their request Sebastian not only gave the customary performance on the organ but also produced a cantata of his own composition. The electors were naturally much struck by his mastery, and hardly had Sebastian returned to Weimar when he received a contract from Halle for signature.[1] The conditions, however, were not too attractive. The yearly salary paid in Halle was 196 fl. (to which some *accidentien* for weddings, etc. could be added) whereas in Weimar he received 229 fl. He therefore wrote back noncommittally and tried to obtain better conditions. Halle remained firm, however, and while Sebastian was weighing its artistic attractions against the financial loss involved, his Duke considerably improved the Weimar contract, with the result that Sebastian now definitely declined the Halle position. The electors were mortified and hinted that the organist had used them simply as a means of securing better conditions at Weimar. Such insinuations he contested in an energetic letter, and his arguments must have been persuasive enough to calm the Halle authorities; for, two years later, when the great organ was completed, it was Sebastian who, together with organ experts Johann Kuhnau and Christian Friedrich Rolle, was invited to test it. Bach, delighted with the Halle electors' change of mind, accepted with alacrity and had a very good time indeed. Not only was it fascinating to try out the new organ, but he also enjoyed co-operating with the Leipzig Thomas Cantor, Kuhnau. Halle, on the other hand, outdid itself in courtesies to the three organists. Servants, coaches, and refreshments were more than plentiful. The menu of the concluding banquet is certainly impressive and deserves to be quoted in full:

> Boeuf à la mode.
> Pike with Anchovy Butter Sauce.
> Smoked Ham.
> Sausages and Spinach.
> Roast Mutton.

1. Paragraph 4 of this contract stipulated that the organist should accompany the hymns 'quietly on 4 or 5 stops with the Principal, so as not to distract the congregation . . . eschewing the use of Quintatons, reeds, syncopations, and suspensions, allowing the organ to support and harmonize with the congregation's singing.' This shows that Arnstadt's earlier complaints against young Sebastian's too elaborate accompaniment were quite in keeping with the prevailing opinion.

Roast Veal.

Peas. Potatoes. Boiled Pumpkin. Asparagus. Lettuce. Radishes.
Fritters.

Candied Lemon Peel. Preserved Cherries.

Fresh Butter.

The wine is not mentioned especially, but there is every reason to believe that the guests of honor sampled no small amount of it.[1]

From now on work in Weimar was even more absorbing. At the
beginning of his employment, Sebastian had been engaged as court
organist and chamber musician, the latter title meaning that he also
played the violin in the ducal band. A contemporary chronicler reports:
'The Duke's ears frequently enjoyed the playing of sixteen well-disci-
plined musicians clad in Hungarian haiduk uniforms,' and on these
occasions Sebastian probably had to appear in this fanciful attire. Nom-
inally the conductor of the band was Johann Samuel Drese, but in-
firmity and old age made him unable to officiate. For a considerable
time his place had been filled by deputies, the last being Drese's own
son, Johann Wilhelm, who had been trained at the Duke's expense in
Italy and now held the rank of vice-conductor. The Duke, although
supporting the Dreses out of loyalty to an old servant, could not help
realizing that it would be a wise move to entrust part of the conductor's
duties to his fine organist. So, when Sebastian received the invitation
from Halle, the new post of concertmaster was created with a salary of
268 fl., and the obligation of composing and performing a new cantata
every month; leaving to the younger Drese the duty of supplying the
court with new secular music.[2]

The result was that Sebastian now had an opportunity of working
with both singers and instrumentalists, and was able to lay the foundations of his mastery as a conductor. The rehearsals, like the performances, took place in the court chapel, a Baroque monstrosity in the
worst taste,[3] which, however, bore a name most appropriate to the

1. In Sebastian's expense bills the item for wine was quite a considerable one. For
instance, when he went to Gera in 1724 to examine a new organ, he received 30 fl.
as a fee, 10 fl. for transportation, 17 fl. 8 gr. 8 pf. for food, and 7 fl. 8 gr. for wine.

2. Cf. Jauernig, p. 57.

3. The chapel was destroyed by fire in 1774 together with the castle, and new
buildings were erected according to Goethe's plans.

music resounding in it, being called the 'Castle of Heaven.'[1] This time the conductor, who led the group with his violin, had no trouble with the singers. There were twelve to fourteen well-trained vocalists at his disposal, among them the excellent altist (countertenor), Christian Gerhard Bernhardi, himself a composer, for whom Bach wrote some very intricate parts.[2] The widening of his musical duties brought much joy to the new concertmaster, and great cantatas (some of which used texts by the eminent Salomo Franck, secretary of the Consistory) first saw the light in Weimar.

In other respects, too, life was satisfactory at the small Court. Sebastian's home was a happy one. Children arrived regularly, among them three sons—Wilhelm Friedemann, Carl Philipp Emanuel, and Johann Gottfried Bernhard—destined to display outstanding musical talent.

Godparents for the Bachs' offspring were not chosen locally, and it is interesting to note that among fifteen persons who acted in this capacity, thirteen came from other places. It would seem that Bach, deeply absorbed in creative work, had not too much time for establishing new contacts in Weimar. Yet there was one fellow musician with whom he struck up an important friendship: the town organist Johann Gottfried Walther (1684-1748), a pupil of Sebastian's relative, Johann Bernhard Bach, and, moreover, a distant kinsman on the Lämmerhirt side, who had spent his childhood in the house 'The Three Roses,' where Sebastian's mother was born. The two Weimar organists were both newly married, and when Walther's first son was born, Bach was godfather. In Walther, an eminent organist and a composer of outstanding organ music, Sebastian found a congenial spirit; in his zeal for self-improvement he discovered that much could be learned from his colleague. In particular, their common interest in Italian music formed a strong bond, and there was a friendly competition between them in the arrangement of Italian concertos for keyboard instruments. According to Walther, Bach presented him with no less than 200 compositions, partly his own and partly Böhm's and Buxtehude's. Friendly relations were also established with Johann Mathias Gesner, vice-prin-

1. It was originally called 'Path to the Castle of Heaven' on account of a small pyramid which rose from the altar to the ceiling carrying little cherubs toward Heaven.
2. Cf. Cantatas 132, 161, 185.

cipal of the Weimar *Gymnasium,* who became one of Sebastian's staunch admirers. Of course there was also frequent intercourse with kinsmen and with musicians in nearby places. In Eisenach there was his second cousin, the organist Johann Bernhard Bach, and from 1708 to 1712 the celebrated and prolific Georg Philipp Telemann (1681-1767), who, after moving to Frankfurt, acted as godfather to Sebastian's second son, Carl Philipp Emanuel (1714-88). The city of Jena, which formed part of the Duke of Weimar's territory, was within reach and visits to the senior member of the clan, the organist Johann Nicolaus Bach (1669-1753), could be arranged easily.

Gifted pupils provided a further enrichment. Among them were two excellent organists, Johann Martin Schubart and Johann Caspar Vogler, and also Johann Tobias Krebs, a cantor who for seven years walked regularly from the village of Buttelstädt to Weimar in order to receive instruction from Walther and Bach. Continuing an old family tradition, Sebastian undertook the training of two young kinsmen, one of them a son of Sebastian's own teacher and eldest brother, Johann Christoph of Ohrdruf. With four children, various pupils, and one of his wife's sisters living with them, Sebastian's home at Weimar displayed the features his son Emanuel was later to summarize to Forkel: 'it was like a beehive, and just as full of life.'

He also had pupils of a more exalted rank. The princely patron whom he had served when first working in Weimar for a few months in 1703 (cf. p. 17) died in 1707, but he left two sons in whom Sebastian was greatly interested. The younger, Johann Ernst, had a really outstanding musical talent, and some of his violin concertos were transcribed by Bach for keyboard instruments; these works written in the Italian style were even granted the honor of being mistaken for compositions by Vivaldi. Johann Ernst's real teacher was Walther; but there was undoubtedly much artistic intercourse between the court organist and the young prince, and Sebastian must have grieved indeed when a tragic fate carried off the talented youth in 1715 at the age of nineteen.

But there was an elder brother, Prince Ernst August, who was also interested in music, and he studied the clavier with Bach. Ernst August was not what one would call a lovable character; contemporary reports make him appear a highly eccentric man, whose actions sometimes bordered on insanity. His ideas about government were decidedly old-fashioned; for when he succeeded his uncle Wilhelm Ernst as a ruler of Weimar, he issued an edict threatening any subject proved to have 'reasoned,' i.e. criticized conditions in his land, with six months' imprisonment. At the time of Sebastian's work at Weimar, the Prince's views had not yet assumed so excessive a character. Bach spent a good deal of time in Ernst August's 'red castle,' taking part in its very active musical life,[1] and the Prince, according to a statement from Emanuel Bach to Forkel, 'particularly loved him and rewarded him appropriately.'[2] This was destined to be fatal to Sebastian's position in Weimar. The relations between Wilhelm Ernst, the reigning sovereign, and his nephew and heir, Ernst August, were very strained indeed. According to the charter of the duchy of Saxe-Weimar, all executive power was centered in the eldest duke, his younger relatives having a purely consultative role in the government. So vague a provision naturally opened the door to family quarrels of all kinds, and during Sebastian's stay at Weimar these assumed inordinate proportions. Duke Wilhelm Ernst definitely had a mind of his own and did not relish any advice from his nephew. Ernst August, on the other hand, insisted on voicing his opinions, and there was constant friction and antagonism. These were difficult times for the court employees, who needed a good deal of tact not to become involved in the feud between the two princes. The court musicians in particular found themselves in a sad predicament when Duke Wilhelm Ernst, on pain of a 10 thalers fine, forbade them to play in his nephew's castle. This was most unfair, as the musicians counted among the 'joint servants' and were paid from the joint treasury. Bach's sense of justice and his independent spirit made him pay no heed to so unreasonable an order. Indeed, on Duke Ernst August's birthday he performed a cantata with musicians from the nearby court

1. Jauernig points to items in the *Particulier Cammerrechnungen der Fürstl. Sächs. Jüngeren Linie* revealing considerable expenses for copying music and buying instruments. One of these was a *Lautenwerk*, a harpsichord with gut strings and a lute-like tone, acquired for the price of 41 fl. 3 gr. from the Jena Bach, Johann Nicolaus, who was famous for his construction of such instruments. Around 1740 Sebastian himself had a similar instrument constructed in Leipzig. It was a *Lautenclavicymbel*, equipped with both gut and brass strings. The notes it produced sounded like those of a theorbo or lute (cf. J. Adlung, *Musica mechanica.* Berlin, 1768, II, p. 139).

2. Cf. letter to Forkel of January 13, 1775 (see footnote 2, p. 13).

of Weissenfels, and handed the Duke a birthday poem bound in green taffeta, for which he was handsomely rewarded. Naturally the elder Duke's ire was roused and he soon found a way to punish his concert-master.

In December 1716 old Drese, the Kapellmeister, died, and by all rights the position should have been conferred on Sebastian Bach, who in the past two years had assumed most of its duties. This was what Sebastian himself expected as a matter of course. The Duke, however, first tried to secure Telemann, and when this proved impossible he conferred the position on the former vice-conductor, Johann Wilhelm Drese. Sebastian's disappointment and humiliation at having been passed over for a nonentity like young Drese were intense, and the work at Weimar lost its attraction for him. It is significant that after old Drese's death no trace of any cantatas written by the concertmaster is to be found. Even at the Bicentenary of the Reformation, celebrated in grand style, the fervent admirer of Luther remained silent. It is possible that the Duke, when conferring the conductorship on young Drese, expected him henceforth to supply all the new cantatas required. In view of Sebastian's behavior in Arnstadt, however, it seems not un-likely that the headstrong concertmaster simply stopped composing for his patron in order to express his grievance.

The sequence of events bears an interesting resemblance to that in Mühlhausen. Again Sebastian was drawn into a conflict that did not really concern him; just as he had supported Eilmar against his own superior in Mühlhausen, so in Weimar he revealed his attachment to the younger Duke, and infuriated his actual patron. In each case a less straightforward nature could have avoided entanglement in such feuds. Sebastian, however, was anything but a diplomat. Indeed, there was a definitely pugnacious streak in his disposition; far from trying to avoid difficulties, he acted rather to provoke them, and then used all his energy and resourcefulness to overcome the resulting trouble.

Accordingly, after nine years of service at Weimar, Sebastian began to consider moving again. The friendly relations with the younger Duke that had spoiled his promotion now helped him to reach his goal. Duke Ernst August had married in 1716 a sister of Prince Leopold of Anhalt-Cöthen, the young ruler of a tiny principality that had come into existence through the partition of the little duchy of Anhalt. Bach was on excellent terms with the Princess, and it did not take long for her brother to discover what a prize he could acquire for his own court. His interest was still strengthened when he heard the exquisite 'hunt' cantata presented by Bach for the birthday of Duke Christian of Saxe-Weissenfels (BWV 208). He therefore decided to reorganize his music staff; his conductor was to retire in August 1717, and the Prince offered the position to Sebastian on highly favorable terms. The character of the work was the diametrical opposite of that in Weimar. No organ playing and no composition of church music was expected from the conductor; for the Cöthen court had adopted as early as 1596 the Reformed (Calvinistic) Church, which meant that except for certain feast days only the simplest kind of unadorned psalmody was permitted in the service. On the other hand, the Prince was deeply interested in instrumental music, and in this field the conductor was expected to be constantly at work. Acceptance of the Cöthen position therefore meant breaking with almost everything that Sebastian had hitherto aimed at and accomplished. As a musician with a consuming zest for experimenting he could not fail to be fascinated by the very novelty of his prospective artistic duties. So, although Sebastian did not uphold the religious doctrine of the Cöthen court, he accepted the offer; and from August 1, 1717, he was on the princely payroll, despite the fact that he had not yet received his leave from Weimar. At the same time the generous Prince Leopold paid him an additional amount of 50 thalers to defray the expenses of moving, and it appears that Sebastian settled his large family in Cöthen before matters were straightened out in Weimar.

In September he traveled to Dresden, where at that moment a French organist and clavier player, Louis Marchand, was making a tremendous impression. Sebastian, who had known and admired Marchand's compositions for some time, naturally did not want to miss so good an opportunity to hear the great man perform and possibly to meet him. Little did he suspect that instead of his honoring the French master, the honors would be bestowed on him. For as soon as his presence became known in Dresden, an influential courtier (possibly Count Flemming) suggested holding a competition on the clavier between the French and German masters. The challenge was accepted on both sides, but when Sebastian presented himself before the exalted audience which was to witness the contest, his opponent was not there. After a prolonged wait, a messenger sent to Marchand brought word that the Frenchman had secretly left Dresden that very morning, thus admitting the superiority of his German rival. Any disappointment the guests may have felt at missing so thrilling a spectacle was quickly dispersed by the inimitable art of Bach, who now entertained them on the clavier.

With the enthusiastic acclaim of the Dresden nobility still ringing in his ears, Sebastian returned to Weimar to settle the little formality of getting official release from his duties. In his former appointments this had never presented any difficulty, and apparently Sebastian did not anticipate any trouble in Weimar. His pupil Johann Martin Schubart, who had deputized for him on the organ, would be well qualified to succeed him. The post of Kapellmeister, with all pertaining duties, was held by the younger Drese, and a concertmaster was no longer needed. With Duke Wilhelm Ernst, however, such reasonable arguments counted as little as the fact that Bach was offered a substantially higher stipend at Cöthen. Changes in his personnel were always annoying to him; he even retained old servants who were of no use. Moreover, although he was angry with Bach, his renowned organist was an asset to the court which he did not like to surrender. Finally, it would be most vexing to let Bach go to the Prince of Cöthen, who, as the brother-in-law of Prince Ernst August, naturally belonged to the enemy's camp. He therefore refused to release Bach, and thought that the organist, though upset at first, would eventually calm down. In this assumption he was mistaken, however, for Bach did not submit to the decision of his patron. Indeed, so outspoken was his insistence that (according to the court secretary's report) 'he was put under arrest for too obstinately requesting his dismissal.' From November 6 to December 2 Sebastian remained in jail, possibly making the best use of his enforced leisure by working on his *Orgel-Büchlein*; but as he showed no inclination whatever to give in, and as the Duke on the other hand did not care for an open wrangle with the Cöthen court, the recalcitrant organist was at last released 'with notice of his unfavorable discharge.' As was to be expected, Schubart was appointed his successor and retained this position until his early death, at the age of thirty-one, in 1721, when he was replaced by one of Bach's best pupils,

Johann Caspar Vogler; thus the Bach tradition of organ playing was kept alive in Weimar until Vogler's passing in 1763.

This does not mean, however, that Sebastian Bach was kindly remembered in Weimar's official circles. Two facts clearly illuminate this unrelenting attitude. Walther treated Bach in his *Musiklexikon* in a strangely superficial manner; he did not even list those works which he himself had received from Sebastian. This was not due to an estrangement, for we know from other sources[1] that Walther continued to feel the greatest esteem for this 'cousin and godfather,' whose 'Well-tempered Clavier' he copied and whose chorale arrangements he diligently collected. Yet, as an employee of the city of Weimar, he apparently had to heed the dictates of the local censor. The same official exercised his veto when, five years later, Wette published a history of Weimar; in it, among the names of the Weimar court organists, the one who had conferred lasting glory on the town was simply left out.[2]

Sebastian Bach's determined defiance of his patron's wishes constitutes an important, though as yet isolated, landmark in the artists' fight for social freedom. At this point of his career he certainly broke with the family tradition. His father Ambrosius Bach and his eminent kinsman Johann Christoph had both been forced to stay on in Eisenach against their will; Sebastian refused to be cowed by similar restrictions. How gleefully would his forebears have applauded had they been privileged to hear his 'stiff-necked protestations,' which finally opened the jail doors for him!

1. Cf. Schünemann, in *BJ* 1933, p. 86 ff.
2. Significant is the remark on the title page of Wette's book: 'Unter hoher Censur und Bewilligung des Hochfürstl. Ober-Consistorii ans Licht gestellet' (Issued under exalted censorship and with the approval of the Princely High Consistory).

IV. COURT CONDUCTOR AND PRINCELY FRIEND

(1717-1723)

W HEN Barbara's seventh child was born, an august group of godparents assembled at Cöthen for the christening; three members of the princely family joined with a Court Councillor and the wife of a Court Minister, both members of the aristocracy.[1] This fact clearly shows what a prominent position Sebastian held at Cöthen. At Weimar such exalted godparents had not been available for any of the six Bach children born there. The Cöthen Court Conductor, however, was a person of high standing. His salary of 400 thalers equalled that of the Court Marshal, the second highest official, and his princely patron treated him as a respected friend. Prince Leopold, 23 years old, and thus nine years his conductor's junior, was a true lover of the Muses. He brought back home valuable objects of art from a trip to Italy, and he greatly enlarged the court library. In music, he was much more than a mere enthusiast. He played the violin, viola da gamba, and clavier with professional skill; moreover he was a competent singer with a pleasant baritone voice. Sebastian bestowed on him the highest praise in claiming that the Prince 'not only loved but *knew* music.' The profundity of Leopold's understanding is indeed revealed by the works which the new conductor wrote for his master. Compositions such as the sonatas for violin solo and the suites for violoncello solo can be only truly appreciated by someone with the deepest musical insight.

Under the rule of Prince Leopold's widowed mother the small court of Cöthen had been run on strictly economical lines; music had hardly any place in it, and only three musicians had been employed in the princely service. As soon as Leopold came of age, decisive changes were made. An orchestra of seventeen players was established, and the Prince was fortunate in securing some eminent players in Berlin,

---

1. The child received with such pomp died after ten months.

43

where the anti-musical King Friedrich Wilhelm I had dissolved his own band in 1713. When Bach took over, he found a well-trained instrumental body.[1] Gradually fine instruments were purchased too, such as a harpsichord, which Bach was sent to Berlin to acquire, and two Stainer violins. Inspired by the new possibilities thus opening to him, and by his patron's passionate interest and delighted approval, Bach now created a profusion of works. The accounts of the bookbinders who bound the parts copied from Bach's scores show the new conductor's frenzied productivity;[2] on the other hand, the sums spent on the acquisition of music from outside were negligible. A great part of Bach's output in these years is lost; but what has been preserved—works like the six Brandenburg Concertos—reflect the exuberance of an artist discovering new means of expression, and the peace of mind of the composer who had found real understanding and appreciation in his new patron.[3] These first years at Cöthen were peaceful indeed, and this, significantly enough, in spite of the fact that the tiny principality itself was by no means free from the religious dissensions prevalent in Bach's time. The Prince's parents had belonged to different denominations. His father had fallen in love and married Gisela Agnes von Rath, although this was socially and religiously a *mésalliance;* for his bride came from the ranks of the lesser nobility and was a Lutheran, while he himself, like the majority of the Duchy's population, belonged to the Reformed Calvinistic Church. Neither of the two part-

1. The accounts mention one solo trumpeter and eight soloists designated as 'chamber musicians'; these received higher salaries than the ripienists (players of reinforcing and accompanying instruments). The chamber musicians took care of the following instruments: two violins, one cello, one viola da gamba, one oboe, one bassoon, two flutes. The lack of a chamber musician for the viola is explained by Bach's predilection for the instrument, a predilection which Emanuel Bach reported to Forkel. Among the soloists, Christian Ferdinand Abel (1682-1761) should be mentioned, a virtuoso on both the viola da gamba and the violoncello. Sebastian's suites for unaccompanied cello, were probably written for him. Cf. also Ernst König, 'Die Hofkapelle des Fürsten Leopold,' *BJ* 1959, p. 160 ff.

2. F. Smend, who carefully went through the accounts in the *Landesarchiv* Sachsen-Anhalt at Oranienbaum, estimates that in 1719-20 at least fifty works of ensemble music must have been bound. Cf. his *Bach in Köthen,* Berlin, 1951, p. 151.

3. Smend has proved that Bach also composed a number of cantatas in Cöthen, some for the Prince's birthday, some for New Year's Day and similar occasions. In some cases this music was later used for church cantatas of the Leipzig period (cf. Nos. 32, 66, 120, 134, 173, 184), while the music of others is lost.

ners changed his or her religious persuasion, and Gisela Agnes did her best to obtain privileges for her fellow Lutherans. Yielding to her persuasion, the happy husband allowed a Lutheran church and school to be built in Cöthen, thus provoking the wrath of his own Consistory. Heated feuds raged over the allotment of church taxes, the use of the Calvinistic church bells, etc., and finally appeals to revoke the Prince's decisions were made even to the Emperor. When the young Prince Leopold assumed the government, he confirmed his father's policy, claiming that the 'greatest happiness of his subjects depended on their freedom of conscience being safeguarded.' A very enlightened point of view, to be sure, but unfortunately one that was not shared by the majority of the citizens. Thus at the time when Bach came to Cöthen religious quarrels and disputes had by no means abated. The Sebastian of Mühlhausen would have felt duty bound to take up the cudgels and fight for his own denomination. Not so the Cöthen court conductor. For the time being, he was much more interested in musical than in religious problems. From the onset he had been aware that he would find a religiously uncongenial atmosphere at the Cöthen court, and apparently decided to take this in his stride. Naturally he never conceived the idea of adopting his patron's religion. On the other hand, he did not intercede in favor of his fellow Lutherans. He contented himself with attending the Lutheran church and sending his children to the Lutheran school. Beyond that he let things alone, and was very happy indeed in his artistic work and in the economic and social prestige he had achieved.

A new source of satisfaction was opening to him in his children. By now it had become clear that the eldest son, Wilhelm Friedemann (1710-84) possessed great talent, and the father decided to train him in earnest. On January 22, 1720, when Friedemann was nine and a half, Sebastian started a 'clavier book' for him. It is a most interesting document on Sebastian Bach the teacher, revealing his pedagogical bent, his methodical mind and the peculiar fingering technique he employed (cf. p. 269). This *Clavier-Büchlein* belonged to the series of books of instructive keyboard music already started in Weimar, a series which comprised such masterworks as the Orgel-Büchlein, the Inventions, and the 'Well-tempered Clavier.' Bach apparently enjoyed creative work which served educational purposes; in this respect he certainly occupied a unique position among the great composers. The planning of a systematic course of instruction satisfied his keen and logical mind. His creative fire was always kindled by self-imposed restrictions, and the challenge afforded him by the solution of certain problems of teaching inspired him to real works of art. Forkel, relying on the testimony of Philipp Emanuel Bach, described Sebastian's method as clavier instructor as follows:

The first thing he did was to teach his pupils his peculiar mode of touching the keyboard. . . . For this purpose he made them practise for months nothing but isolated exercises for all the fingers of both hands, with constant regard to the production of a clean, clear tone. For some months no pupil was excused from these exercises, and, according to his firm opinion, they should be continued for six to twelve months at least. But if he found that anyone, after some months of practice, began to lose patience, he was so considerate as to write little connected pieces, in which these exercises were linked together. To this type belong the six little Preludes for beginners, and still more the fifteen two-part Inventions. He wrote down both during the hours of teaching, and, in so doing, attended to the immediate requirement of the pupil; afterwards he transformed these pieces into beautiful and expressive little works of art. With the finger training . . . was combined the practice of all the ornaments in both hands. After this he set his pupils to the task of studying his own greater compositions, which, as he well knew, would give them the best means of exercising their powers. In order to lessen the difficulties, he made use of an excellent method; this was first to play to them the whole piece which they were to study, saying: "This is how it must sound."

Forkel goes on to describe at length the way this excellent method worked, and one cannot but agree with him. Listening to the masterly performance of a Bach composition, before starting to work on it, the pupil was able to set himself a definite goal; to reach it he was prepared to undertake the practice required.

This system, besides being eminently practical, must also have been most congenial to the teacher. J. N. Gerber, Bach's pupil in Leipzig, reports that 'he had his most blissful experiences when Bach, feeling no inclination toward instructing, sat down at one of his exquisite instruments and transformed hours into minutes.' One can well understand the composer's attitude and only wonders why he persevered in different teaching tasks and was even willing painstakingly to train beginners struggling with their first exercises. Apparently he regarded music as a craft he was obliged to hand on to his 'apprentices' just as his father and kinsmen had done. What mattered was the pupil's talent. Bach was the perfect teacher for gifted youths, but he was unable to put up with mediocrity.

There was, to be sure, no musical mediocrity in Sebastian's children; they were, as he proudly wrote to his former schoolmate, Georg Erdmann, 'all born musicians,' and the father found delight in teaching them. Going carefully through Friedemann's clavier book, one has the impression of the boy's fast progress. On the other hand there are touching instances of the father's understanding for his son's immature taste. After setting him a tough task with one of his own compositions, Sebastian relented and attempted to amuse the boy with a dance by a fashionable composer like G. H. Stölzel (1690-1749).

In July 1720, when Friedemann had reached his tenth year, an event occurred that tragically broke up the Bachs' idyllic existence in Cöthen. While Sebastian was at the Bohemian spa of Carlsbad, accompanying his patron, who did not want to forgo the enjoyment of chamber music while taking the waters, Barbara was suddenly prostrated by illness. There was not even enough time to summon her husband; when he returned, a scene of desolation greeted him, and he had to be told that his beloved wife had died and been buried. The children, aged twelve, ten, six, and five, had lost their mother, and Sebastian was without the devoted companion who had shared courageously the vicissitudes of his early struggles. This was indeed a cruel fall from security and gaiety to loneliness and grief, and to bear it he needed all the spiritual resources his faith provided. To Sebastian Bach death had always seemed as a release fervently to be longed for, which in destroying the body would simultaneously relieve the soul of its sins. Death was for him not the end, but the culmination of spiritual life. Possibly during the first joyful years spent at Cöthen he had to some extent put aside such thoughts. Now, however, he turned to them again, and religious experiences assumed their old significance for him. He began to realize that for all the satisfaction he derived from the association with his patron, there was something lacking in his existence at Cöthen, and he was again filled with a longing to express his innermost faith through church music.

Just at that time the organist of Hamburg's *Jakobikirche* died,[1] and eight musicians, among them Sebastian Bach, were invited to compete for the position. To Sebastian, Hamburg was still hallowed by the youthful impressions he had received there, and eagerly he traveled to the northern city to find out more about the vacancy. He learned that the trial performances were to take place on November 28, and that three Hamburg organists, among them venerable Reinken, had been named adjudicators. The date did not suit Bach, who had to return to Cöthen in order to prepare for the celebration of his patron's birthday, but he arranged to play before that day on Reinken's organ in the *Catharinenkirche*. The very same chorale, *An Wasserflüssen Babylon,* which in Reinken's dazzling treatment had held young Sebastian spellbound some twenty years previously, was chosen as subject for the improvisations out of courtesy for the veteran master. For a long time he played, piling one gigantic structure on the other and revealing his stupendous mastery. Finally Reinken, who as a rule did not indulge in praise of other musicians, exclaimed: 'I thought this art was dead, but I see it still lives in you.' Whether the Obituary is right in reporting that Bach played 'before the Magistrate and many other distinguished persons of the town, to their general astonishment,' or whether the master performed only to the three musical experts, is not known. Anyway there is no doubt that the Hamburg Council favored his appointment.

But there was one serious drawback. Sebastian was informed during his visit that it was customary at Hamburg to sell certain offices to the highest bidder; even in the churches a newly appointed employee was expected to make a handsome payment. A passage in the minutes of the meeting determining the policy regarding the election of the new organist for the *Jakobikirche* reads thus: 'The capacity of the candidate should be considered more than the payment, but if the chosen candidate of his own free will desires to make a contribution as a token of his gratitude, it will be accepted for the benefit of the church.' In spite of such cautious language it was clear to everybody concerned that such 'voluntary' payment could not be dispensed with. This must

1. This was Heinrich Friese, who died on September 12, 1720.

have displeased Sebastian greatly. He probably did not have the money available, but even if he had, it would have been a matter of pride for him not to pay for a position in which he would make an outstanding contribution to the religious life of Hamburg. He left the town promising to write to the Council; and the decisive board meeting was postponed for a whole week until the arrival of Bach's letter. The contents cannot have been encouraging, for after reading the letter (which is not preserved) the committee decided to appoint a certain Johann Joachim Heitmann, who acknowledged his gratitude by paying the tidy little sum of 4000 Marks. The pastor of the church, Erdmann Neumeister (famous for his cantata texts, several of which Bach had set to music), was disgusted indeed with the affair. As this happened shortly before Christmas, he found a chance of airing his grievance in the festival sermon. Speaking eloquently of the angelic music at the birth of Christ, he remarked acidly that if one of those angels came down from Heaven wishing to become an organist at his church and played divinely, but had no cash, he might just as well fly away again, for they would not accept him in Hamburg.

On his return to Cöthen, Bach set to work on a meticulous copy[1] of six orchestral concertos which he sent in March 1721, with a courteous French dedication, to Christian Ludwig, Margrave of Brandenburg, an uncle of King Friedrich Wilhelm I of Prussia. He may have met the Margrave in 1718, when he went to Berlin to purchase a new harpsichord for the Cöthen court. At this occasion he seems to have been invited to submit a new composition to the august music friend. In order to comply with this request Bach selected for his dedicatory copy works written for, and performed by, the excellent Cöthen orchestra, as is proved by details of the orchestration. Margrave Christian Ludwig, however, had no musical resources of this kind available, and it is not surprising that Bach's score was never used at his court.[2]

1. Despite the beauty of the handwriting, the autograph is by no means free of errors. Evidently the composer started with some reluctance to produce the fair copy (cf. P. Wackernagel, 'Beobachtungen am Autograph von B.s Brandenburgischen Konzerten,' in *Max Schneider-Festschrift*, Leipzig, 1955, p. 129).

2. H. Besseler remarks in *BJ* 1956, p. 18 ff., that, contrary to prevailing assumption, the score was not auctioned off after the Margrave's death, but included in the estate inherited by different members of the royal family (cf. also his KB to NBA, Series VII/2, Kassel, 1956, p. 14 ff).

At this time the composer was also deeply engrossed in his work on the first set of the 'Well-tempered Clavier.' Such creative activities helped to heal the wound inflicted by Barbara's death and made Bach ready to face the necessity for establishing a new home. Remarrying after a very short lapse of time was the general custom in his family (and indeed in his time), and it proves Bach's deep attachment to Barbara that he waited from June 1720 to December 1721 before being joined in holy matrimony again. His bride, twenty-year-old Anna Magdalena Wilcken, the daughter of a court trumpeter, was descended from musicians on both sides of her family; and in her own right she was an excellent soprano singer, who since the autumn of 1721 had been employed by the Cöthen court, which she seems to have visited as early as 1716. The young singer retained her position after she married the court conductor, and earned half as much as her husband. The disparity in age between the girl of twenty and the man of thirty-six was balanced by their common interests. Magdalena may well have been more concerned with operatic music than was her husband (it was her youngest son who was the only one of Sebastian's children to become a successful opera composer), but she was certainly able to appreciate Sebastian's greatness, and young enough to adopt his own artistic creed. When she started her married life, Magdalena may have been afraid of her new responsibilities, which included looking after four stepchildren, the eldest of whom was a girl only seven years her junior. We don't know how her young charges acted toward her. In the case of the eldest boy, Friedemann, then eleven years old, the possibility cannot be excluded that he resented seeing his mother supplanted by a stranger, and that this experience contributed to the shaping of his difficult personality. But while we are in the dark as to her stepchildren's attitude, we have reasons to assume that for her husband Magdalena succeeded in creating a cheerful, comfortable home. Visiting musicians and an endless stream of kinsfolk were received cordially, and felt happy with the Sebastian Bachs. Magdalena knew the secret of enjoying the simplest pleasures with all her heart. Once when she was given a present of six yellow carnation plants, she 'treasured them more highly than children do their Christmas presents and tended them with the care usually bestowed on babies.'[1]

1. Cf. the letters of Johann Elias Bach reproduced by Pottgiesser in *Die Musik*, 1912-13.

This disposition helped her a great deal in a life that was filled to the brim with the duties of running a large household most thriftily, a life in which she had to go through the ordeal of child-bearing thirteen times, and seven times saw a child of hers carried to the grave. How Sebastian on such occasions tried to instil courage into her suffering heart is revealed in Magdalena's music book, which he presented to her in 1725 to be filled with music of various kinds. Twice he wrote into it a different version of his aria (BWV 511, 512) based on Paul Gerhardt's hymn, *Gib dich zufrieden und sei stille* (Fret not my soul, on God rely) meant to lift her out of the day's turmoil with simple and deeply felt music.

We know nothing of Magdalena's appearance. Her husband had her painted by Cristofori—at that time quite an unusual distinction for a woman of her social standing—but the portrait, which was listed in Emanuel's collection, has been lost. So we must content ourselves with the mental picture of a hard-working, warm-hearted, and highly musical woman; a true helpmate to her husband, one who gloried in his artistic achievements, undertook to copy some of his music despite her many other duties, eased the strain of the many professional crises created by Sebastian's fighting spirit, and shared with fortitude the burdens that life imposed on them.

Shortly after they were married, the outward conditions of Bach's existence underwent a decisive change. Up to that time, as he later stated in a letter to his old friend, Erdmann (cf. p. 9), he had intended to spend the rest of his life in the service of Prince Leopold. Now, however, the Prince gave up his bachelor existence and married a princess of Anhalt-Bernburg. Even before the ceremony, the happy bridegroom had been so occupied with redecorating his quarters, creating a new 'princely guard,' whose exercises and parades he attended, and preparing for the festivities which were to last through five weeks, that he was unable to give much thought to music. And when things finally calmed down at Cöthen, life assumed a different aspect. The young princess was, according to Bach's verdict, an 'amusa,' a person without love for music or art. It seems possible that she was somewhat jealous of the court conductor's influence on the Prince, and set on breaking up this close relationship. Gradually music was removed from the center of the Prince's activities and Bach felt neglected and more or less superfluous. As months went by and Leopold maintained his 'somewhat lukewarm' attitude, his conductor began to ask himself whether under such conditions it was worth while to stay at the little court. Would not a position with wider responsibilities, in particular one where he could again serve the Lord in a church, and through the power of his music lead a large congregation toward Christ, give him deeper satisfaction? He had also to consider his sons, who, he felt, should enjoy the benefits of a university education, of which he himself had been deprived. Thus he gradually began to recognize that the secluded and secure existence in Cöthen had only been a happy interlude ultimately to be exchanged for the weightier duties and inevitable struggles of a position in a more important musical center.

V. THOMAS CANTOR AND DIRECTOR MUSICES

(1723-1730)

THE manner in which Sebastian Bach received his appointment in Leipzig supplies a *leitmotiv* for the twenty-seven years he was destined to spend there. He offered his services reluctantly, and was accepted reluctantly, a decisive factor for the appointment being the candidate's willingness to assume various teaching duties.

When the great Johann Kuhnau died on June 5, 1722, the question of his successor in the post of the Leipzig Thomas Cantor occupied the minds of musicians all over the country. In Protestant Germany the position, combined as it was with the musical directorship of Leipzig's churches, enjoyed a very high prestige; for Leipzig at that time was a bastion of Protestantism, a city where religion was a living, driving force.[1] Ever since its foundation in 1212 the Alumnate (choirschool) of St. Thomas' had supplied singers for the church services, and the venerable institution could look back with pride on a line of great Cantors (among them the illustrious Johann Hermann Schein), whose creative work had greatly contributed to the growth of German church music. The opening in Leipzig seemed to offer all that Bach had been missing in Cöthen. Nevertheless it took Sebastian six months to make up his mind about the desirability of the position, and he was

1. An abundance of services was offered in Leipzig. On Sunday, worship at St. Thomas' and St. Nicholas' occupied the greater part of the day. It started with early Matins, followed by the main service lasting from 7 to 11 a.m. Half an hour later the noon service took place, and at 1.30 p.m. vespers followed, which took up about 2 hours. On every weekday there was a service at 6.45 a.m. in one of the main churches and an hour of prayer in the afternoon. On Saturday at 2 p.m. a very important service was held in preparation for the communicants of the following Sunday. To discharge these extensive duties, no less than five ministers were officiating at St. Thomas' as well as at St. Nicholas.' The other churches, too, engaged a comparatively large amount of clergy to satisfy the spiritual needs of this city of 30,000 people.

first mentioned as an applicant in December 1722. The reasons for his long pondering were manifold.

From a previous visit to Leipzig in 1717, and from his conversations with Kuhnau, Bach was aware that the Thomas Cantor's position was altogether different from his present one. While the Cöthen *Kapellmeister* had to comply with the wishes of a single patron, the Thomas Cantor had something like two dozen superiors. In his educational work he had to conform to the ruling of the rector of the school. But the running of the institute was in the hands of the City Council, consisting of three burgomasters, two deputy burgomasters, and ten assessors; and it was this body of fifteen which engaged the Thomas Cantor and kept a check on all his activities. Finally, there was the ecclesiastical authority of the Consistory, which was responsible for the services in the churches, and became therefore the chief arbiter in all matters concerning the music to be offered by the Thomas Cantor in his capacity as church music director. To be dependent on these different governing bodies, which, as might be imagined, would not always live in perfect harmony, did not seem too pleasant a prospect for any man, least of all for one who had so little of the touch of the diplomat. There was also the matter of social rank, to which Sebastian was by no means insensitive. According to the general view, a court conductor was on a higher social level than a cantor, and Sebastian found it somewhat strange (as he admitted to his old friend, Erdmann) to climb down the ladder. As to financial considerations, he did hope to earn more in Leipzig than in Cöthen, but the former pleasant feeling of security would be lacking. The basic salary in Leipzig was low, not more than 100 fl. a year, less than one-fourth of what Prince Leopold paid his conductor. To it were added the *Accidentien,* a certain percentage of the statutory fee for funerals, weddings, etc., and one-fourth of the weekly tuition fee of six pennies which the boarders had to pay, and which, when lacking funds, they collected every week from charitable families. The cantor's income might grow out of pennies and farthings to the sum of 700 thalers (more than 1000 florins), but there was no certainty about it; and when 'a healthy wind was blowing'[1] and the death-rate went down, the receipts showed a sad decline.

1. Cf. Bach's letter to Erdmann of 1730 (p. 72), in which he complained about this, for him, unfavorable wind.

Anna Magdalena Bach may have felt even more reluctant than her husband to go to Leipzig. At Cöthen she held a good position as court singer, which brought her a yearly salary of 200 thalers. In Leipzig she would be deprived of an artistic career and an income of her own. The wife of the Thomas Cantor would have to lead a very secluded and unobtrusive existence. She might enjoy singing Sebastian's music in the privacy of their own home, but it would be utterly out of the question for her to undertake a solo in a church, in which women were not allowed to perform. Thus to the young singer the removal to Leipzig would mean the renunciation of any professional activity of her own.

And yet, in spite of such various misgivings, Sebastian was drawn toward the new position. At the Thomas School, and subsequently at the renowned University of Leipzig, his gifted sons would be given the right kind of education, which provincial Cöthen was unable to offer. He himself would be in entire charge of the church music of an important city, and would thus be able to make his ideas for its improvement a reality. Tremendous forces within him urgently sought release in the composition of sacred music and after months of wavering, the voices of caution were silenced. Driven by his daemon, Bach decided on the Leipzig position in order to fulfil his artistic destiny.

In the six months since Kuhnau's passing, the Leipzig Council had been singularly unsuccessful in their attempts to secure a suitable Thomas Cantor. At first matters had seemed to shape just perfectly. Among the six applicants was Georg Philipp Telemann, newly appointed Music Director and Cantor of Hamburg; from his former activities as organist of Leipzig's New Church, as a composer of, and singer in, popular operas, and as an extremely successful conductor of a Collegium Musicum, he was highly regarded by the Leipzig citizens. The Council was delighted to acquire so spectacular a musician and, the day after he had conducted a cantata of his own composition in Leipzig,[1] the members voted unanimously for his appointment. Telemann, noticing Leipzig's eagerness, managed to obtain important concessions. He caused the city fathers to waive one part of the Thomas Cantor's statutory duties, viz. the teaching of Latin in certain classes, and he secured the musical directorship of the University church. Armed thus with all the requirements necessary for a satisfactory posi-

1. The Council even printed the libretto of this cantata for the use of the congregation.

tion in Leipzig, he returned to Hamburg to press for a higher salary. His policy proved successful, and the badly disappointed Leipzig Council had to continue their search. Yet when Sebastian Bach made his application in December 1722 he was not considered the most desirable of the candidates. There was Christoph Graupner, who, as a former pupil of St. Thomas' and the highly renowned conductor of the Prince of Hesse's orchestra in Darmstadt, seemed much better qualified. Graupner was invited to direct the Christmas music (including a *Magnificat* of his own), and some weeks later to conduct a cantata, all of which he did with so much success that the position was offered him. But Leipzig had bad luck again. The Prince of Hesse firmly refused to let his conductor go, and as he added very strong arguments in the form of a raise of salary and a munificent gift, Graupner was not too reluctant to stay in Darmstadt. He explained the situation to the Leipzig Council and warmly recommended Bach as a musician as competent on the organ as he was in directing church and orchestra music. However, at the time the letter arrived, it was outdated by the recent events. Bach was no longer a stranger to the Leipzig community. He had performed the required 'trial cantata' of his own, probably singing the bass solo himself.[1] The Council was now determined to engage Bach in the event of Graupner's refusal.

Their initial lack of enthusiasm for the Cöthen candidate is not hard to understand. Bach's tremendous fame as an organist did not count for much, as the Thomas Cantor was not supposed to play this instrument. Of Bach's creative work the Council could know nothing, for no composition of his except the two Mühlhausen cantatas had ever been printed. In the eyes of the Leipzig authorities, a candidate's present position was of paramount importance, and it cannot be denied that the conductor of the tiny court of Cöthen enjoyed less prestige than the Hamburg or Darmstadt music directors. Finally, Bach seemed inferior to the majority of former Thomas Cantors because he lacked a university education. Kuhnau, for instance, had been a successful jurist before being appointed to St. Thomas', and had published mas-

1. It was the Cantata No. 22, *Jesus nahm zu sich die Zwölfe*, in which the bass solos are unusually high, in accordance with the composer's own voice. Cf. Arnold Schering, *J. S. Bach und das Musikleben Leipzigs im 18. Jahrhundert*, Leipzig, 1941, p. 30 ff.

terly translations from the Greek and Hebrew. Compared with him, Sebastian Bach could hardly be called erudite. On the other hand, the Council was thoroughly tired of the unsettled conditions that had prevailed since Kuhnau's death, and so was willing to engage Bach. This time, however, they wanted to take precautions against another failure, and Bach was requested to supply a letter of dismissal from his patron before the final election took place. Prince Leopold, though grieved at his conductor's decision, was certainly not going to put any obstacles in his way, and wrote a very gracious testimonial for the 'respectable and learned J. S. Bach.' Another point of contention between the various candidates and the Council was removed by Sebastian's pledge either to instruct the pupils in Latin or to remunerate another teacher undertaking the work in his stead. When all difficulties were thus overcome, the formal election took place on April 22, 1723. The minutes of the meeting are significant. Burgomaster Dr. Lange, who had conducted the negotiations, did his best to make the appointment palatable, mentioning Bach's excellence on the clavier, and even venturing to declare that 'If Bach were chosen, Telemann, in view of his conduct, might be forgotten.' The other Councillors followed his lead, but they stressed, as the main point in the candidate's favor, his willingness to teach Latin and the Latin catechism. It was characteristic that although the city fathers had naturally all attended Bach's trial performance, only one referred to him as a composer, and this with the sole object of emphasizing that his church music should not be 'too theatrical,' a stipulation which was promptly included in the contract.

Bach, determined now to get the position, signed whatever was requested of him; he also promised meekly not to leave town without the permission of the Burgomaster (with the mental reservation that he would break such a pledge whenever necessary). He then passed the requisite theological examination, and was declared fit for the office of Thomas Cantor.

Before these irrevocable steps were taken, fate seemed to give Bach a last chance of staying on in idyllic Cöthen. The Princess, whose lack of love for music Bach had so deplored, died on April 3, and the conductor could have expected to see the old state of affairs revived. But his was a nature not easily turned off a path once chosen. It had been a long and arduous struggle to make up his mind; now, however, he was ready for a new adventure, and ten days after the Princess's death, on April 13, 1723, the bereaved husband signed the letter of dismissal for his conductor. Nevertheless, their friendship persisted, and in spite of his many new duties, Bach found time to visit Cöthen regularly for some fine music-making, especially in celebration of Leopold's birthday on December 10. He had the joy of seeing his Prince united two years later to a music-loving wife; for her birthday he wrote the cantata *Steigt freudig in die Luft* (BWV 36a), which he performed with his Leipzig singers, while Prince Leopold took over the important bass solo in the tradition of their former delightful days. When the Prince's son was born in 1726, Bach dedicated to the infant his first clavier partita, adding a congratulatory poem (possibly written by himself). These pleasant ties were tragically severed by Leopold's sudden death in November 1728. Bach came to Cöthen for the last time to perform an imposing funeral music on the night of March 23, 1729, when the body was interred, and another cantata (BWV 244a) on the following day, when the funeral sermon was preached.[1] Under Leopold's successor the orchestra declined steadily, until even its last five members were dismissed. Clearly Bach had done the right thing when he decided not to tie his fate to the little principality.

On May 31, 1723, the new Cantor was formally installed. Various addresses were given, music was sung by the pupils, and the new official responded in a dignified speech promising to serve a 'Noble and Most Wise Council' to the best of his abilities. There was, however, a slightly discordant note in the ceremonies, typical of the state of affairs in Leipzig. The Consistory had requested the pastor of St. Thomas' to welcome the new Cantor in the name of the church authorities. This act of courtesy did not please the town officials, who considered the installation of the Cantor their prerogative and claimed that never before had a church official taken part in such a ceremony. A discussion ensued that was subsequently continued in a lengthy correspondence. The new Cantor may have been somewhat perplexed by this incident; however, he could not learn too quickly that henceforth he would have

1. Cf. Smend, *Bach in Köthen*. The connection with the Cöthen court was not severed even after Sebastian's death. When Friedemann Bach's daughter, Friederica Sophia, was christened on February 15, 1757, two members of the princely house of Anhalt-Cöthen were among the godparents.

to deal with a host of officials, all of whom, minor as well as major, insisted on the full recognition of their vested rights. To find a path through the maze of prerogatives and conventions determining the work of the various city and church employees, and to learn how to observe the countless unwritten rules, seemed almost a full-time occupation, and there was so much else for the new Cantor to do! He found the school in a shocking state of disorganization. Rector Johann Heinrich Ernesti, a weak and tired man of seventy-one, had for years been unable to exercise control, and the standard of the institute had steadily declined. The students consisted of a number of paying day scholars and some fifty-four foundation scholars, mostly sons of poor parents who on account of their musical talent were admitted as boarders for a nominal payment. Some of these boys had not received a good upbringing at home, and a firm hand was needed to keep them in decent discipline. This unfortunately the rector did not possess. Furthermore, it was almost impossible to obtain good order in a building that had hardly been altered since its erection in 1554, and was now completely outdated and overcrowded. There was not even a separate bed available for each boarder, and one classroom had to accommodate three classes at the same time, besides serving as a dining-room. The pupils' schedule was bound to fill Bach with even greater concern. The few capable musicians were sadly overworked and unable to keep their voices in good condition. The pupils had to accompany every funeral (except those of the very poor), singing hymns —rain, storm, or snow making no difference; and who could suggest a change in these conditions, when the fee for funerals meant so much to pupils and teachers? From New Year's Day to the middle of January most Thomasians sang daily in the streets, naturally often in bad weather, in order to attract charitable contributions; and again nobody dared raise his voice against this lucrative old custom. Fatigued, poorly fed, and badly housed, these pupils easily succumbed to illness, and contagious diseases were bound to spread rapidly in the unsanitary, overcrowded school building.

Between the teachers relations were not too harmonious. Indeed it was a turbulent and rather frightening world for which Sebastian Bach had surrendered the idyllic seclusion of the Cöthen court.

He had to live in the very midst of it. His quarters, occupying the

left wing of the school building,[1] had a separate entrance; yet his
sanctum, the *Componierstube,* traditionally reserved for the Cantor's
creative work, was separated from the classroom of the sixth form by
only a plaster wall. How much concentration must it have required not
to hear the loud voices of his young neighbors! Yet even such little
privacy as this was not granted him continuously. Every fourth week,
for the seven full days, the Cantor had to serve as inspector, maintaining discipline from 4 or 5 a.m., according to the season, when the
boarders rose, through prayers, meals, and lessons, up to 8 p.m., when
it was his duty to extinguish all the lights after the boys had retired.
These thirteen weeks a year (sometimes even more if one of the other
high-ranking teachers was not available) meant work of the most uncongenial kind. They must have unsettled Sebastian's creative activity
and called for a special expenditure of nervous energy, inasmuch as the
maintenance of discipline did not come easily to a man of his quick
temper. Fortunately the other extramusical work was negligible. As
Bach's Latin classes were taken over by a colleague, for a sum of 50
thalers paid by the Cantor, he had only to teach Luther's Latin catechism once a week, which could not have been a burden to one so
fully conversant with and interested in the Protestant dogma.

The bulk of his duties were of an artistic nature and were covered
by the title 'Director musices,' which Bach always used with his signature, thus stressing that it was the one he held to be important. He was
responsible for the musical program in all the municipal churches, two
of which, St. Thomas' and St. Nicholas', had very elaborate music on
Sundays, especially during the main service, which lasted for four
hours.[2] The main musical work was the cantata, performed alternately

1. It was inevitable that Sebastian should bring disease germs from the school into
his own quarters, and this was probably the main cause of the death of so many of
Anna Magdalena's babies.

2. Bach noted the order of Divine Service in the score of his Cantata No. 61. His
aide-mémoire reads as follows:

'1. [Organ] prelude; 2. Motet; 3. Prelude on the Kyrie, which is [afterwards] performed. . . . 4. Intoning before the altar; 5. Reading of the Epistle; 6. Singing of
the Litany; 7. Prelude on the chorale [and singing of it]; 8. Reading of the Gospel;
9. Prelude on [and performance of] the main music work; 10. Singing of the Creed;
11. The Sermon; 12. After the Sermon, as customary, singing of several verses of a
hymn; 13. Words of Institution [of the Sacrament]; 14. Prelude on [and performance of] the composition [2nd part of the cantata]. Afterwards alternate preluding

at St. Thomas' and St. Nicholas' by the best singers of the school (the so-called 'first *Cantorei*') and conducted by the Cantor himself, while the performance of the preceding motet and the direction of music in the other three churches was largely entrusted to senior students appointed as assistant conductors. Of the two churches, Bach preferred St. Thomas'. The organ had recently been repaired, and the building itself remodeled, and the church was considered, according to a chronicler of the time, 'one of the most elaborate and beautiful places of worship in existence . . . adorned with an exquisite and costly altar.' The music director was particularly pleased with the very convenient wooden galleries placed on the left and right of the organ. While the choir stood in front of the instrument, the galleries accommodated the instrumentalists and were admirably suited for double choirs, inspiring Bach to use them, for instance, in the St. Matthew Passion. In addition to the large organ, there was a small instrument placed high up on the altar wall[1] which Bach liked to use for special effects, such as the playing of the cantus firmus in the first chorus of the St. Matthew Passion. The church of St. Nicholas had no such advantages and the choir loft was smaller. Bach therefore avoided it for more elaborate works. When his St. John Passion had to be produced there in 1724, he insisted on some repairs being carried out so as to have more space available in the choir loft for his performers. On the other hand, the organ at St. Nicholas' was more powerful, and Bach preferred to use it for works employing the organ as a solo instrument. Either at St. Thomas' or at St. Nicholas' a new cantata adapted to the special liturgical requirements of the day had to be offered on every Sunday and all the feast days of the ecclesiastical year. The only exceptions were the last three Sundays of Advent and the five Sundays of Lent; but these provided no real rest-period for conductor and performers, since particularly ambitious and extensive programs had to be prepared for Christmas and Easter (two performances each on December 25, 26, 27, as well as on Good Friday, Easter Sunday and Monday). As to the works performed, the majority were composed by the music director himself. Bach threw himself into this part of his duties with breath-taking vigor. Of cantatas

---

and singing of chorales to the end of the Communion, and so on' (see the fascimile in NBA vol. I/1).

1. It was removed in 1740/41.

alone he supplied, according to Forkel's statement, five complete sets for the entire ecclesiastical year, nearly 300 works in all. Even if we grant that a number of these were older compositions or rearrangements of secular music, we may still accept as a fact that at the outset Bach presented approximately one new cantata per week. And besides cantatas he had to provide Passions for Good Friday, motets for important funerals,[1] music for weddings, festive compositions for the yearly inauguration of the new City Council, for visits from royalty, etc. The first Christmas at Leipzig gives a good idea of the creative fury that possessed Bach. On each of the three feast-days he offered a new cantata, while in the vesper service his new *Magnificat* was performed; in spite of this he had another composition ready for New Year's Day. And thus it went on, with hardly any let-up, the extent of his creative work being miraculously matched by its superb quality.

The other civic churches,[2] using the inferior singers of the school, called for little work by the music director, except in the allotment of the performers to the different groups, which were continually fluctuating in numbers or competence owing to illnesses or other causes.

In addition to the directorship in the four civic churches, it was important for Bach to have charge of the music at St. Paul's as well. This was the University church, which in former times had offered services only on the high feast days and the quarterly solemn orations, on which occasions the Thomas Cantor had been responsible for the music. But from 1710 onward the University, in addition to this 'Old Service,' inaugurated a 'New Service' for every Sunday, and Kuhnau had had great difficulties in securing the musical directorship of this, as the University wanted to be as independent as possible of town officials. After his death, J. G. Görner, a former organist of St. Paul's, filled the position temporarily, and was far-sighted enough to refrain from asking for a remuneration. This impressed the University officials so favorably

1. For instance, shortly after his arrival in Leipzig, he was called on to compose music for the commemoration service held for the wife of a high official. It is likely that the motet *Jesu, meine Freude* (BWV 227) was written for this occasion.

2. They were the church of St. Peter and the 'New Church.' In the latter more elaborate music was performed on holy days and during the Leipzig Fair. For this the church organist was responsible (on Bach's arrival, G. B. Schott, and after 1729, J. G. Gerlach) and he had the help of University students and professional musicians.

that they graciously acceded to his subsequent application and, a few weeks before Bach's appointment, they conferred on him the directorship of the 'New Service,' while reserving the 'Old Service' for the Thomas Cantor. Bach was anything but pleased about this turn of events. The University appointment seemed important for more than financial considerations; it was useful for establishing contacts with University students performing at St. Paul's, who might be willing to help the music director on other occasions. Bach, convinced that the position ought to be his by precedent, valiantly strove to regain it. On his settlement in Leipzig he immediately started work at St. Paul's by providing beautiful music for Whitsunday, May 16, 1723, which happened to occur even before he was formally installed in his new office. He continued in this way through the following three years, offering his services for as many as eleven festive occasions. The University was not displeased with this state of affairs, but when it came to payment, Bach was unable to obtain the statutory stipend of 12 thlr. per annum. After many discussions he was given half of what constituted the former salary due to the Cantor from the University, while the rest went to Görner. This seemed important enough to Bach to justify direct appeals to the highest authority, Augustus 'the Strong,' Elector of Saxony. If it appears rather surprising to us that the composer should have bothered his monarch regarding a comparatively insignificant payment, we must not forget that the Cantor's income was made up of small items, careful attention to which provided the difference between an adequate and an insufficient sustenance. Most of all, it was not in Bach's nature to put up with what he felt to be unjust. So he dispatched in the last months of 1725 no less than three petitions to the Elector; the third, a masterwork of logical presentation and clarity of diction, amounted to some 3000 words. He asked for the restitution of the lawful emoluments and for the directorship of both the 'Old' and the 'New Service.' The University submitted a detailed, strongly worded reply[1] which in various ways contradicted Bach's assertions and caused the Elector to decide against him. The Cantor, he ruled, was to receive the statutory salary for the 'Old Service' traditionally forming

1. It is reproduced for the first time in *Bach Dokumente,* ed. by W. Neumann and H. J. Schulze. Leipzig and Kassel, 1963, p. 42 ff.

part of his office, but the University was free to settle the question of the 'New Service' in whatever way it wanted. As a result Bach lost interest in St. Paul's and had the music for the 'Old Service' conducted by his prefects. On the other hand, his energetic action had not exactly endeared him to the academic authorities; from the outset they had looked down on the new Cantor's lack of academic training (a shocking state of matters that had not occurred in Leipzig during the past century!), and they now did their best to bypass Bach whenever a special composition was required for a festive occasion, thus depriving him of not insignificant fees.

Their hostile attitude is best illustrated by an incident that happened two years later. In September 1727 there occurred the death of Christiane Eberhardine, wife of the Elector of Saxony, who was dearly beloved in Lutheran Leipzig because she had remained faithful to the Protestant religion when her husband adopted Catholicism in order to gain the Polish throne. To express the prevailing emotion, an aristocratic University student, Hans Carl von Kirchbach, volunteered to hold a commemorative service in the University church at his own expense, in which he was to deliver the funeral oration. When he was given permission for this act of loyalty, he commissioned the poet, Johann Christoph Gottsched, to write a funeral ode, and Bach to compose it. He could certainly not have made a wiser choice—although this was by no means the opinion of the learned professors. Their colleague, Gottsched, a great reformer of the German language, was eminently suitable, but his ode, they contended, should be set to music by Görner. When Kirchbach refused this suggestion, claiming that Bach had already done the work (BWV 198), he was informed that the composer would not be allowed to perform the music, as this was Görner's duty. In high irritation, the young nobleman threatened to give up the whole project, whereupon a compromise was reached. Görner was to receive a present of twelve thalers from the student, and Bach was to sign a statement that the actual commission was a 'mere favor not to be considered as precedent for the future.' The first part of this arrangement worked out satisfactorily; Görner received his money and was content. But as to the statement, the University official dispatched to Bach's lodgings to obtain the signature of the document had no success; the Cantor refused in no uncertain words to sign it. What the eminent Gottsched thought about the controversy, we do not know.

Maybe Bach's composition did not meet with the poet's full approval, as the Cantor had dared to change the ode's structure by loosening the nine uniform stanzas and creating ten musical sections out of them.

There was one brighter aspect to this unpleasant episode: young Kirchbach's insistence on Bach's composition. While to the erudite professors the work of a third-rate musician like Görner (who, as Bach once shouted in a fit of fury, 'would have done better as a cobbler'[1]) seemed in no way inferior to that of Bach, the young people fell under the spell of the great man at the Thomas School. They were eager to secure his co-operation when they prepared musical entertainment for some special occasion, and several of Bach's secular cantatas owe their existence to such commissions.[2] What was even more important, gifted University students were attracted by his genius and took part in the church music directed by him. We know, for instance, from a testimonial Bach wrote for C. G. Wecker, subsequently Cantor at Schweidnitz, that this student of law gave him 'creditable assistance' both as a singer and instrumentalist. Young J. G. Gerlach, who had graduated from the Thomas School in 1723, was also a valuable helper, whom Bach rewarded by recommending him successfully for the position of organist and music director at Leipzig's 'New Church.'[3] Likewise Bach's future son-in-law, J. C. Altnikol, when entering Leipzig University, served for four years in the Thomas Cantor's performances as a bass singer and instrumentalist.

Thanks to talented and enthusiastic aides, not forgetting Bach's own three sons, who were gradually developing into first-class musicians in their own right, the master was able to carry out one of the most ambitious projects of his whole career. On Good Friday, 1729, his St. Matthew Passion had its performance at St. Thomas'.[4] The

1. Cf. C. L. Hilgenfeldt, *J. S. Bach's Leben, Wirken und Werke*, 1850. Bach had plenty of opportunity of seeing Görner at work. The latter was his subordinate as organist of St. Nicholas', a position which Görner gave up in 1729 for a similar one at St. Thomas'.

2. Cf. Friedrich Smend in *Archiv für Musikforschung*, 1942.

3. Bach took Gerlach as soloist to Weissenfels in 1729, to take part in the celebration of Duke Christian's birthday, which certainly brought the young singer a handsome fee.

4. It has also been suggested that the first performance took place as early as 1727 (cf. *Beiträge zur Musikwissenschaft*, 1960, p. 84), but no proof has so far been established. The libretto preserved by C. F. Zelter, but lost today, showed the date of April 15, 1729.

body of executants must have seemed quite enormous compared with those usually employed in Leipzig churches. The parts used in a subsequent performance under Bach's direction have been preserved, and they show that seventeen players were employed for each orchestra, twelve singers for either of the two choruses, and a third group of 3 to 6 vocalists for the chorale in the first piece. In 1729 the number of singers was somewhat smaller, as the cantus firmus was not sung, but played on the little organ over the altar; nevertheless the group of executants far exceeded the customary body of performers. In spite of its considerable length (well over three hours), the Passion was performed within the framework of the traditional Good Friday services, for which the following schedule was laid down: (1) 1.15 p.m. ringing of all bells; (2) the hymn *Da Jesu an dem Kreuze stund* sung by the choir; (3) Passion music, first part; (4) versicle, *Herr Jesu Christ, dich zu uns wend;* (5) sermon; (6) Passion music, second part; (7) motet, *Ecce quomodo moritur* (Jacobus Gallus); intonation of Passion versicle; collection; hymn, *Nun danket alle Gott.*

It is hard for us today to estimate Leipzig's response to the sublime work. Bearing in mind the reactionary attitude prevailing in Leipzig and the pledge Bach had signed not to write operatic church music, it is to be feared that a good many listeners may have been confused, if not actually shocked, by the poignancy of this music.[1] On the same Good Friday another Passion was performed too. At the New Church, Gottlob Fröber offered his composition of Brockes' *Der für die Sünde der Welt gemarterte und sterbende Jesus* and as he was a candidate for the directorship, the Leipzig burghers may have been more interested in this work than in their Thomas Cantor's contribution.

But whatever the response of the congregation may have been, it must be reported that neither the work itself, nor the tremendous achievement in presenting it, helped to impress Bach's superiors favorably. Their attitude is clearly reflected in an incident that happened in the very same year. Every spring new pupils were admitted to the Thomas School to replace those graduating. In May 1729, a few

---

1. It is usually assumed that the St. Matthew Passion is referred to in Gerber's story about the elderly lady who on hearing the Passion threw up her hands in horror, exclaiming: 'God help us. 'Tis surely an opera-comedy.' Smend in *Bach in Köthen* gives the entire quotation from Christian (not Heinrich Nikolaus) Gerber's *Geschichte der Kirchen-Ceremonien in Sachsen,* 1732. Apparently the passage read in its entirety points to Dresden rather than Leipzig.

weeks after the performance of the St. Matthew Passion, Bach handed the Council a detailed list of the candidates he had examined, naming those he found suitable and unsuitable respectively, and the Rector seconded his recommendations. The city fathers, however, had their own opinions: they admitted four candidates the Cantor had warned against, one he had not even tested, and only five he had recommended. Apparently they were not really interested in obtaining good musicians for their church music and selected the candidates on the strength of other qualifications. Their attitude may to some extent have been dictated by a feeling of animosity toward Bach. The report on a Council meeting taking place a year later is typical. At this occasion the shortcomings of a certain Magister Petzoldt, Bach's deputy for the Latin classes, were under discussion, and this led to complaints about the Cantor himself. 'He has not conducted himself as he should,' criticized one of the members; 'he is doing nothing,' complained another; while a third described him as 'incorrigible.' Not a single voice was raised in Bach's defense; nobody even mentioned the St. Matthew Passion or Bach's other outstanding contributions to Leipzig's church music. Finally, it was decided to punish the Cantor for his many deficiencies by reducing his income. A change in the contractual salary and the statutory allotment of *Accidentien* was impossible, but the Council could, and did, restrict the offender's share in unexpected revenues.[1]

The city fathers' animosity toward Bach was heartily reciprocated by the Cantor, who felt that his superiors' lack of co-operation prevented him from carrying out his artistic plans. In August 1730, Sebastian, maybe still unaware of the punitive action planned against him, submitted a memorandum in which he pointed out that the admittance of unsuitable pupils and the lack of adequate funds were jeopardizing his efforts to maintain the church music at a high level. The very title of the document, and the condescending manner with which all the details of an organization well known to the officials were explained in it, must have been irritating to the recipients:

1. The following instance reveals their policy. After the death of the old Rector in October 1729, and until a new official was installed, Bach had to conduct the school inspection every third, instead of every fourth, week. Later, when it came to allotting the Rector's very considerable share of *Accidentien*, the two other teachers who had taken over extra duties received sizable shares of this money, while Bach was left out and got nothing at all.

'A short, but indispensable sketch of what constitutes a well-appointed church music, with a few impartial reflections on its present state of decline

'For a well-appointed church music, vocalists and instrumentalists are necessary. In this town the vocalists are provided by the foundation pupils of St. Thomas', and these are of four classes: trebles, altos, tenors, and basses.

'If the choirs are to perform church music properly . . . the vocalists must again be divided into two classes: concertists [for the solos] and ripienists [for the chorus]. There are usually four concertists, but sometimes up to eight if it is desired to perform music for two choirs. There must be at least eight ripienists, two to each part. The instrumentalists are also divided into different groups, namely, violinists, oboists, flutists, trumpeters, drummers. *N.B.* The violinists comprise also players of viola, violoncello and double bass.

'The number of the resident pupils of the Thomas school is fifty-five; these are divided into four choirs, for the four churches in which they partly perform concerted music, partly sing motets, and partly chorales. In three of the churches, i.e. St. Thomas', St. Nicholas', and the New Church, all the pupils must be musically trained . . . those who do not know music and can only sing a chorale at need go to St. Peter's.

'To each choir there must belong, at least, three trebles, three alti, three tenors, and as many basses, so that if one person is unable to sing (which often happens, and particularly at this time of year, as can be proved by the prescriptions of the school *medicus* sent to the dispensary), a motet prescribing double chorus can at least be performed. (*N.B.* How much better would it be, if it were so arranged as to have four singers available for each part, each choir thus consisting of sixteen persons!). Consequently, the number of those who must understand music is thirty-six persons.

'The instrumental music consists of the following performers:

two or even three	violino I
two or three	violino II
two each	viola I, Viola II, violoncello
one	double bass
two or three, according to need	oboes
one or two	bassoons
three	trumpets
one	kettledrums

In all, eighteen persons at least, for the instruments.

N.B. Since church music is often composed with flutes (be it recorder or transverse flute), at least two persons are needed for them; altogether, then, twenty instrumentalists. The number of players engaged [by the city] for church music is eight, viz. four town pipers, three professional violinists, and one apprentice. Discretion forbids my speaking at all truthfully of their competence and musical knowledge; however, it ought to be considered that they are partly *emeriti* and partly not in such good practice as they should be. . . . The following important instrumentalists needed for reinforcement or for the performance of indispensable parts are lacking: two players each of first and second violin, viola, violoncello, and flute, one player of double bass.

'The deficiency here shown has hitherto had to be made good partly by the University students, but chiefly by the Thomas pupils. The University students used to be very willing to do this, in the hope that one or the other might be rewarded by some kind of stipendium or honorarium (as formerly happened). But since this does not occur [now] and the few small beneficia have even successively been withdrawn, the readiness of the students has likewise disappeared, for who will give his service for nothing? In the absence of more efficient performers, the second violin has been at most times, and the viola, violoncello, and double bass have been at all times played by the Thomas pupils, and it is easy to judge what has thus been lost to the vocal choir. So far only the Sunday music has been mentioned [which takes place alternately in St. Thomas' and St. Nicholas']. But if I come to speak of the holy days, when music must be provided for both the principal churches at the same time, the lack of the necessary players is even more serious, since then I have to give up such pupils as can play one instrument or another, and thus am obliged to do without their assistance [as singers] altogether.

'Furthermore, I cannot omit mentioning that through the admissions hitherto granted to so many boys unskilled and ignorant of music, the performances have necessarily fallen into decline. It is evident that a boy who knows nothing about music, who cannot even sing the interval of a second, has no natural musical talent and can never be of any use in music. And even those who bring with them some elementary knowledge, do not become useful as quickly as desirable. Years are required to train them. However, as soon as they are admitted, they are placed in the choirs where they must at least be sure of measure and pitch to be serviceable. As each year some of those who have done something in music leave the school and are replaced by new pupils who are either not yet ready for the task or else show no ability whatever, it is clear that the *chorus musicus* must suffer. It is well known that my predecessors, Schelle and Kuhnau, were obliged to have recourse to the assistance of the [University] students when they desired to perform complete and well-sounding music, which they were able to do, because several vocalists, a bass, a tenor and even an alto, as well as instrumentalists, in particular two violinists, were favored with individual salaries by a Most Noble and Wise Council, and thereby were induced to strengthen the church music. Now, however, when the present state of music has greatly changed—the art being much advanced and the taste surprisingly altered, so that the old-fashioned kind of music no longer sounds well in our ears—when, therefore, performers ought to be selected who are able to satisfy the present musical taste and undertake the new kinds of music, and at the same time are qualified to give satisfaction to the composer by their rendering of his work, now the few perquisites have been altogether withheld from the choir, though they ought to be increased rather than diminished. It is, anyhow, astonishing that German musicians should be expected to perform *ex tempore* any kind of music, whether Italian or French, English or Polish, like some of these *virtuosi* for whom the music is written and who have studied it long beforehand, even know it almost by heart, and who besides have such high salaries that their pains and diligence are well rewarded. This is not duly taken into consideration, and our German musicians are left to take care of themselves, so that under the necessity of working for their bread many can never think of attaining proficiency, much less of distinguishing themselves. To give one instance of this statement, we need only go to Dresden and see how the musicians there are paid by his Majesty; since all care as to maintenance is taken from them, they are relieved of anxiety, and as, moreover, each has to play but one instrument, it is evident that something admirable and delightful can be heard. The conclusion is easy to arrive at: that in ceasing to receive the perquisites I am deprived of the power of getting the music into a better shape.

'Finally, I feel obliged to list the present foundation pupils, stating in each case the extent of his musical skill, and leave it to further consideration whether concerted music can be properly performed under such conditions or whether a further decline is to be feared . . . [There follows a list of names under the headings 'those who are efficient,' 'those needing further training before they can take part in concerted music,' and 'those who are not musical at all']. Summa: 17 serviceable, 20 not yet serviceable, 17 useless.

Joh. Seb. Bach,
Director Musices.'

Leipzig, August 23, 1730.

This is, indeed, a highly significant document.[1] Not only does it offer valuable glimpses into the performing practice of the time; it allows, too, some insight into Bach's artistic thinking and personality. His emphasis on the 'surprising alteration in the present musical taste' shows that the Thomas Cantor felt to be completely in accord with the trends of his time (a feeling, he was not to entertain for long, however). Yet, had he been more endowed with the graces of diplomacy, he would not have stressed the progressive nature of his music to the tradition-bound Leipzig authorities who were hardly inclined to make allowances for new-fangled methods. Even worse was his praise of conditions in Dresden at the expense of Leipzig. Such a comparison was not quite fair, since Dresden, as the Elector's residence, naturally enjoyed privileges denied to other towns. The wording of the report also reveals the inflexible nature of its author. Bach was angry with his superiors, and when he penned the petition he did not attempt to hide his feelings under the flowery phrases of respect and submission which the exalted officials deemed their rightful due. All this could not but increase the animosity of Bach's superiors.

The burgomaster to whom he handed the report was apparently not at all impressed by it. He did not even mention it at the following meeting, and merely remarked that the Cantor 'showed little inclination to work.' No vote was taken regarding the payment to University students, for which Bach had pleaded so strongly. This must have angered him all the more, as he was well aware that the Council was not as tight-fisted in dealing with another music director. Young Gerlach, who, at Bach's recommendation, had been appointed to the New Church, was granted in this same year a 100 per cent increase in his salary, and allowed 30 thalers for the purchase of new instruments. It really looked as though the Council were eager to develop the musical service in this less significant church at the expense of venerable St. Thomas' and St. Nicholas', which were under Bach's direction.

All this caused the Thomas Cantor to write on October 28, 1730, the following letter[2] to his old schoolmate, Georg Erdmann (cf. p. 9), now settled as Imperial Russian 'resident' (ambassador) in Danzig:

1. A facsimile edition of this document, preserved in the Bach Archives, Leipzig, was presented by Werner Neumann, Leipzig, 1955.
2. English version partly using the translation by C. S. Terry.

Most Honored Sir:

Pray excuse an old and faithful servant for taking the liberty of troubling you with this letter. It is nearly four years since you delighted me with an answer to the last letter I wrote you, when, as far as I remember, you were good enough to desire news of me and my welfare. I will do my best to comply with your wish. You know my *fata* up to the *mutation* which took me to Cöthen as Capellmeister. Its gracious Prince loved and understood music, so that I expected to end my days there. But my Serenissimus married a Berenburg princess, and in consequence, so it seemed, his musical inclination abated, while his new wife appeared to be an *amusa*. So it pleased God that I should be called hither to be *Director Musices* and Cantor of the Thomas school. At first I found it not altogether proper to become a simple Cantor after having been a Capellmeister, and for that reason I forbore from coming to a resolution for three months. However, I received such favorable reports of the situation, that, having particularly in mind my sons' inclination for studies, I at last, in the name of the Lord, made up my mind, came to Leipzig, offered my trial performance, and received the post. And here, God willing, I have remained till now. But unfortunately I have discovered that (1) this situation is not as remunerative as it was represented to be, (2) various accidentia relative to my station have been withdrawn, (3) living is expensive, and (4) my masters are a strange folk with very little care for music in them. Consequently, I am subjected to constant annoyance, jealousy, and persecution. It is therefore in my mind, with God's assistance, to seek my fortune elsewhere. If Your Honor knows of or should hear of a *convenable station* in your town, I beg you to let me have your valuable recommendation. Nothing will be wanting on my part to give satisfaction, show diligence, and justify your much esteemed support. My present station is worth about 700 thaler a year, and if the death-rate is higher than *ordinairement,* my accidentia increase in proportion; but if a healthy wind is blowing, they decrease and for the past year, as it happens, I have received about 100 thaler less than usual in funeral accidentia. The cost of living, too, is so excessive that I could manage better in Thuringia on 400 thaler than here with twice the amount.

And now I must tell you something of my domestic circumstances. My first wife died at Cöthen and I have married again. Of my first marriage are living three sons and a daughter, whom your Honor saw at Weimar and may graciously remember. Of my second marriage one son and two daughters are living. My eldest son is a *studiosus juris,* the other two are at school here in the *prima* and *secunda classis;* my eldest daughter as yet is unmarried. My children by my second wife are still young; the eldest boy is six. All my children are born *musici;* from my own family, I assure you, I can arrange a concert *vocaliter* and *instrumentaliter:* my wife, in particular, has quite a pleasing soprano, and my eldest daughter can give a good account of herself too. I should trespass too far on your forbearance were I to *incommode* your Honor further. I conclude therefore with my most devoted and life-long respect, declaring myself

Your Honor's most obedient servant,
Joh. Sebast. Bach.

Reading the complaints in this letter, and bearing in mind the annoyance and tribulations to which Bach was subjected from his superiors, one cannot help feeling outraged by the city fathers' narrow-mindedness. But it must not be forgotten that one of the main sources of Sebastian's feud with the authorities lay in the twofold nature of his position. He was engaged as teacher (cantor) and music director. To Bach only the music directorship mattered, while to the Council the duties of the cantor seemed of paramount importance. The city fathers may have heard of lack of discipline at the school, of outburts of fury on the part of the irascible cantor, and of lengthy visits to various courts, for which he did not ask permission, and they knew that his prefects often took over the singing classes which he was supposed to hold. Other cantors before him had taken similar liberties, but these had known how to ingratiate themselves by submissive and deferential behavior, whereas this 'incorrigible' Bach acted with maddening presumptuousness. Altogether, it was one of these human relationships which defy a satisfactory solution; for the engagement of a composer at the peak of his creative productivity as school official and disciplinarian in a badly organized institution is a contradiction in itself. Bach would have been better off at the court of an important sovereign, who would have expected nothing from him but musical compositions and performances. As no such opening presented itself, he was forced to remain in Leipzig.[1]

The two sections of Bach's letter to Erdmann illuminate two different aspects of his life in Leipzig. As a matter of fact they afford a

---

1. We do not know whether Erdmann, in answer to Bach's appeal, did anything to find a congenial position for his old schoolmate. Any plans he may have entertained for bringing Sebastian to Danzig were cut short by the ambassador's death in 1736.

glimpse at two different sides of his personality, a glimpse which is still clarified by two portraits painted during the composer's service in Leipzig. One was produced by Elias Gottlieb Haussmann toward the end of Bach's life (cf. p. 94), the other in the 1730's by a young kinsman, Gottlob Friedrich Bach (1714-85), eldest son of the Meiningen court conductor, Johann Ludwig Bach, with whom Sebastian had established a close artistic contact (cf. p. 169 f.). Haussmann's portrait shows a man of tremendous power and stubborn energy, whose face reveals the suffering, the disappointments, and the bitter fights which formed so decisive a part of his life as Thomas Cantor. This is the Bach with whom the Leipzig authorities had to deal: clearly a formidable man who made the good burghers feel uncomfortable and only too often definitely hostile. In the kinsman's beautiful pastel,[1] Sebastian's characteristic features—the lofty brow, fleshy face, prominent nose, stubborn mouth—are the same, but the expression is a very different one. Gottlieb Friedrich painted his relative as he saw him when visiting Sebastian's hospitable home. Here, at the center of his own private world, Sebastian was by no means the man whom the Leipzig Council resented and feared. He was generous and helpful; he rejoiced in his children and kinsmen, training them in his art and assisting them in every conceivable way. The man whom the Meiningen painter portrayed was not harassed by 'jealousy and persecution.' There is strength and determination combined with joy and pride in his face, pride in his position as the father and mentor of the gifted young people who sat at his feet and drew inspiration from his supreme mastery and powerful personality.

The picture we have given so far of Sebastian's life in Leipzig would therefore be incomplete were we not to follow him into the privacy of his home and watch the destinies of the younger generation take shape under his guidance.

When Bach moved to Leipzig in 1723, four children accompanied him and his young wife.[2] The eldest, Catharina Dorothea, was fifteen

1. The pastel belongs to Mr. Paul Bach, a great-grandson of the painter. For more than 200 years it had been kept in the family collection, but it was made available to the present writer and published first in his study The Lost Portrait of J. S. Bach, New York, 1950.

2. It is characteristic of Sebastian's loyalty to the family that shortly after his appointment he had a nephew from Ohrdruf join the school. This was Johann Heinrich

and thus capable of giving valuable help in the household. The three boys, Wilhelm Friedemann, Philipp Emanuel, and Gottfried Bernhard, aged thirteen, nine, and eight respectively, were enrolled in the Thomas School and did well there. Some of Friedemann's exercise books have been discovered, and they reveal him as a very bright boy, well versed in Latin and Greek, and one who, on the other hand, knew how to enliven boring lessons by drawing caricatures and scribbling jokes in his books. Sebastian, who was determined that his sons should enjoy the academic training denied to himself, was pleased to note their scholastic aptitude. It is significant that in the very first year of their arrival in Leipzig, he had Friedemann's name entered at the University for ultimate matriculation, and at Christmas he presented the boy with the certificate of registration. Hand in hand with school work went a most thorough musical education, which must have kept the three Bach boys very busy indeed. They were naturally important members of Sebastian's choir; they studied organ and clavier with him, and they were gradually introduced into musical theory and the science of composition. But Sebastian was still not satisfied as far as his beloved 'Friede' (the nickname of the eldest boy) was concerned. Studying with an eminent violinist seemed to him an essential part of musical training, and therefore, in 1726, he sent Friede to Merseburg, to work for almost a year with the excellent Johann Gottlieb Graun, a pupil of Tartini, and subsequently a colleague of Emanuel Bach in Berlin. The result of the Merseburg studies was probably quite satisfactory; nevertheless Friede's interest remained centered in the keyboard instruments which his father had taught him. As regards the younger sons, musical instruction outside the home did not seem so important to Sebastian. In any case, since Emanuel was left-handed he was not well qualified for playing stringed instruments. The father therefore trained him to become an outstanding clavier player, and he had the satisfaction of seeing Emanuel, at the age of seventeen, engrave a clavier minuet of his own, which was published almost simultaneously with Sebastian's opus I, the *Clavier-Übung* (Part I). Yet it

---

(b.1707), fourth son of Sebastian's eldest brother and teacher, Johann Christoph, who had died not long before. This youth stayed at the Thomas School for four years, receiving ample instruction from his uncle; he subsequently became cantor in Oehringen.

was Friede in whom Sebastian was most interested. He loved doing things in company with his eldest boy, and their trips to Dresden, to attend opera performances and visit the local musicians, were great treats for both of them. The father's sympathy and care, so unstintingly given at all times, at first made life easier for Friedemann, but proved ultimately a fatal gift. Sebastian's genius could not but overwhelm one who was so close to him. Friedemann naturally adopted his father's artistic tastes and opinions, and was unable fully to follow the trends of his own generation. Keenly conscious of the great expectations the father cherished for him, he may have felt alternately inspired and heavily burdened. Emanuel, on the other hand, never achieved Friede's intimacy with his father; he admired Sebastian tremendously, but did not try to imitate him, and thus his own individual style was to develop more freely.

On his return from Merseburg, Friedemann continued at the Thomas School and in 1729 he graduated, acting as valedictorian of his class. He then began his studies at Leipzig University, where he remained for four years, taking courses in law, philosophy, and mathematics. Emanuel closely followed his brother's example; he entered the University two years later, at the age of seventeen, and remained there as a student until 1735.

While the sons from Sebastian's first marriage were growing up, the cradle was never empty at the Thomas Cantorate. In the first decade of their Leipzig stay ten children were born to the couple. But for Anna Magdalena the joy of motherhood was inextricably mixed with tragedy, for seven of these children did not survive infancy and of the other three the eldest, Gottfried Heinrich, caused the parents much grief and heartache. In the Genealogy the note referring to this son reads: 'Gottfried Heinrich, likewise inclined toward music, especially clavier playing. His was a great talent, which, however, remained undeveloped.' These words veil the tragic fact that this son was feebleminded.[1] However, brave Anna Magdalena was granted the joy of highly gifted sons too. In 1732 she bore Johann Christoph Friedrich and three years later Johann Christian, both destined to be eminent musicians.

1. A case of this kind had occurred in an earlier Bach generation, a sister of Sebastian's father having been half-witted.

VI. FRIENDS AND ADVERSARIES

(1730-1740)

AT the time Bach was penning his angry letter to Erdmann, a new situation was developing at the Thomas School which was bound somewhat to ease Sebastian's problems. Johann Mathias Gesner, a good friend from Sebastian's Weimar days, became Rector of the school on September 8, 1730. Gesner is recognized today as one of the pioneers in the field of classical philology. Before him German scholars had been pedantically investigating trifles of antiquarian or grammatical interest; Gesner grasped the very spirit of antique culture and in his lectures and commentaries opened up new vistas to the German mind. This outstanding philologist was at the same time a born teacher, genuinely interested in young people, whose devotion he won by the power of his own humanity and enthusiasm. Thus he was perfectly suited for carrying out the long-needed reforms at the Thomas School. As soon as he started on his duties, he prevailed on the Council to make definite plans for a building program. Before long two new stories were added to the school, and though this entailed a good deal of inconvenience—all the teachers, including Bach, having to find temporary quarters outside the school—the result was well worth the trouble. The Rector also issued new regulations in which music was allotted an important place. He explained to the pupils that their praising the Lord through music linked them with the heavenly choirs and that he expected them to be proud of this privilege and even to sacrifice leisure hours for the sake of good performances. More effectively than by such general advice and the listing of fines to be imposed on those neglecting their musical work, the Rector succeeded in improving the pupils' attitude by changing the general at-

77

mosphere of the school. It was a much happier group that now worked there, and naturally in all fields better results were obtained.

As for the Cantor, Gesner endeavored to smooth out his differences with the Council. At the Rector's suggestion Bach was freed from any teaching assignments outside music and instead was put in charge of the daily attendance to the morning service, at which eight choristers alternately provided the music at either St. Thomas' or St. Nicholas'. Gesner also induced the authorities to let the Cantor henceforth have his full share of all accruing monies. Bach, on the other hand, could not but enjoy working with this outstanding Rector who really valued his musical work. This attitude of Gesner's is proved by a delightful description he offered of Bach's art both as a virtuoso and conductor, sufficient in itself to endear the scholar to every music friend. Some years after leaving Leipzig he wrote a Latin commentary to an edition of Marcus Fabius Quintilianus' *Institutiones Oratoriae*. Using the mention of a cithara-player's versatility who had simultaneously to utter words and sounds and mark the rhythm with his foot, he plunged into this panegyric:

All these [outstanding achievements], my Fabius, you would deem very trivial, could you but rise from the dead and see our Bach . . . how he with both hands and using all his fingers, plays on a clavier which seems to consist of many citharas in one, or runs over the keys of the instrument of instruments, whose innumerable pipes are made to sound by means of bellows; and how he, going one way with his hands, and another way, at the utmost speed, with his feet, conjures by his unaided skill . . . hosts of harmonious sounds; I say, could you but see him, how he achieves what a number of your cithara players and 600 performers on reed instruments[1] could never achieve, not merely . . . singing and playing at the same time his own parts, but presiding over thirty or forty musicians all at once, controlling this one with a nod, another by a stamp of the foot, a third with a warning finger, keeping time and tune, giving a high note to one, a low to another, and notes in between to some. This one man, standing alone in the midst of the loud sounds, having the hardest task of all, can discern at every moment if anyone goes astray, and can keep all the musicians in order, restore any waverer to certainty and prevent him from

1. The Latin expression Gesner uses is *tibia,* signifying a Roman instrument somewhat related to the oboe.

going wrong. Rhythm is in his every limb, he takes in all the harmonies by his subtle ear and utters all the different parts through the medium of his own mouth. Great admirer as I am of antiquity in other respects, I yet deem this Bach of mine to comprise in himself many Orpheuses and twenty Arions.

Such genuine admiration from a man of Gesner's intellectual stature must have warmed Bach's heart. Their association may also have stimulated the composer in other ways. In 1731 Gesner's outstanding *Chrestomathia Graeca* appeared, and we can well imagine Bach discussing certain pieces with his learned friend and receiving much food for thought from the Rector's vision of antique glory. Gesner, incidentally, was not the only one in Leipzig who was responsible for new trends in the conception of the past. There was, for instance, Johann Friedrich Christ, professor at the University, who opened the students' eyes to the all but forgotten beauties of ancient sculpture and painting. Bach may have heard about these lectures from his young University friends, and on his visits to Dresden he had a chance to test the truth of Professor Christ's assertions by visiting the exquisite collection of art treasures, which had begun being assembled in 1728.

By a fortunate coincidence the years of pleasant co-operation with Gesner also brought other improvements in Bach's position. He now had some excellent vocalists in his chorus, among them his favorite pupil, Johann Ludwig Krebs,[1] and his first sopranist, young Christoph Nichelmann. Even more important, in 1729 he succeeded G. B. Schott as head of a Collegium Musicum. This institution had been founded by Telemann for regular weekly performances and later met in Zimmermann's coffee-house. Leipzig had two associations of this kind, comprising a substantial number of members, and as they were independent of the University authorities, there was nobody to prevent Bach from assuming the directorship of one of them. These Collegia Musica served a dual purpose: they kept the musicians among the students in good training, and they helped them to obtain recognition and eventually a position. Visitors from outside, especially during the

1. He was the son of Johann Tobias Krebs, Bach's student in Weimar. The older Krebs admired Bach so greatly that altogether he sent three of his offspring to the Thomas School.

Leipzig fair, thronged the two coffee-houses to hear the young musicians display their virtuosity, and valuable contacts were established in this way. The direct financial returns for the players must have been insignificant, if we are to believe the remarks of the poetess Mariane von Ziegler:[1] 'Most of the listeners seem to think that these sons of the Muses just extemporize the music, the reward they get is very poor indeed, and often they have to be content with a bare bone to pick for all the hours of preparation they have put in.' This may have been true for the students, but certainly not for Bach, who would not have directed his group for several years[2] without receiving adequate financial compensation. Zimmermann, the owner of the establishment in which Bach played, probably paid him a fair honorarium, which the astute businessman amply recovered from the customers who enjoyed the artistic treat. In winter the performances took place every Friday from 8 to 10 p.m. In summer the Collegium played in Zimmermann's open-air restaurant outside the city ('vor dem Grimmischen Thor'), every Wednesday from 4 to 6 p.m. The work with the Collegium Musicum inspired Bach to compose a number of delightful secular cantatas, but he did not by any means limit himself to the performance of vocal music. The Brandenburg Concertos, many other chamber music works, and new compositions for keyboard instruments must have resounded at Zimmermann's, together with compositions by other masters. And here ample opportunities were provided for the appearance of Bach's gifted sons.

Some of the performances of the Collegium Musicum took place as an act of homage to the ruling monarch. In particular, the year 1733, when the Elector Friedrich August II succeeded his father, was distinguished by a series of such festive acts. Bach exerted himself by producing no less than three different cantatas during the period from August to December of that year in order to celebrate the name-day of the new ruler as well as the birthdays of the Crown Prince and the Electress; and he continued with equal efforts in 1734. This year wit-

---

1. This outstanding woman supplied numerous texts for Bach's cantatas (cf. p. 161).

2. According to W. Neumann in *BJ* 1960, p. 5 ff., Bach directed the group from spring 1729 to summer 1737 and again from October 1739 to 1741 or possibly even 1744.

nessed a performance of the cantata *Blast Lärmen, ihr Feinde* (BWV 205a)[1] presented by the Collegium Musicum on February 29, 1734, in honor of the Elector's coronation as Polish king in Cracow. When the ruler paid a surprise visit to the Leipzig Michaelis fair in October, Bach succeeded in producing within three days the cantata No. 215 *Preise dein Glücke, gesegnetes Sachsen* commissioned for an evening music by the University students and performed with the greatest splendor on October 5, while 600 torch-bearing students paid their respects to their Majesties.

Yet all these contributions sink into insignificance when compared to the one monumental work he submitted to the monarch. It was a *Missa* consisting of Kyrie and Gloria, those towering products of his genius which in the last years of Bach's life were extended to encompass the whole ordinary of Mass, a sublime work known today as the Mass in B minor. It seems likely that the *Missa* was destined for the solemn service held in Leipzig to celebrate the new ruler's first visit on April 21, 1733, to accept the town's oath of allegiance. In a service of this kind the Kyrie would have expressed the mourning for the deceased Elector, Friedrich August ('the Strong'), while the triumphant strains of the Gloria following the sermon were to convey the joy over the heir's ascension to the throne. This assumption first propounded by Schering and accepted by Smend[2] has not been proved, but various facts seem to speak in its favor. During the official period of mourning after the Elector's death, no polyphonic music was performed in any Leipzig church, and Bach, freed from his routine duties, had the opportunity wholly to concentrate on the work meant to honor the deceased ruler as well as his august successor. The result was a composition outstanding even in his magnificent output. Not only could he achieve a work, every little detail of which bespeaks supreme artistry; he could for the solemn occasion rely on a body of executants widely exceeding the modest contingent usually at his disposal. As a Catholic the Elector, was, significantly, deprived of the joy of hearing the glorious music in his honor. But he may have received favorable ac-

---

1. It is an adaptation of the earlier cantata *Der zufriedengestellte Aeolus* (BWV 205).

2. Cf. Schering, *J.S.B. und das Musikleben Leipzigs*, p. 217, as well as KB to NBA, Series II/1.

counts from those in his entourage attending the ceremony. Anyway Bach felt encouraged to send the parts of the *Missa* to the Elector on July 27, 1733, writing on the cover the following words clearly referring to the Leipzig celebration: "With the enclosed Missa the author J. S. Bach exhibited his most submissive devotion toward His Royal and Electoral Highness." The music was accompanied by the following letter:[1]

Most gracious and illustrious Elector:

With profoundest *devotion* I offer your Royal Majesty the accompanying insignificant example of my skill in *Musique,* with the most submissive demand that your Royal Highness may receive it not as its merits as a *composition* deserve, but with your Majesty's well-known clemency, and condescend to take me under your Majesty's most powerful *protection.* For some years past I have exercised the *directorium* of the music in the two principal churches in Leipzig, a situation in which I have been exposed to one or the other undeserved affront, and even the diminution of the *accidentia* due to me, annoyances not likely to recur should your Majesty deign to admit me to your Court Capelle and direct a *Praedicat* to be issued to that effect by the proper authority. Your Majesty's gracious response to my most humble petition will place me under an enduring obligation, and, with the most dutiful obedience and unflagging diligence, I shall show myself ready to fulfill your Majesty's commands to compose *Musique* for church or *orchestre,* devoting all my powers to your Majesty's service.

> With constant loyalty I subscribe myself
> Your Majesty's most devoted and obedient servant,
> Johann Sebastian Bach

Bach had good reasons for making continual efforts to prove his loyalty to the new ruler. He felt increasingly in need of the Elector's support as the situation in Leipzig was changing again. Rector Gesner had always cherished the wish to lecture at a university, and as this apparently proved impossible in Leipzig, he accepted, after four years spent at the Thomas School, a call to the newly founded University of Göttingen, where he was to serve with the greatest distinction. He was succeeded in November 1734 by the former vice-principal of the

1. English version based on Terry, p. 216.

school, Johann August Ernesti, a man only twenty-seven years of age, who deservedly enjoyed a fine reputation as a classical scholar. In some respects he continued his predecessor's policy by raising the scholastic standard; but in his ambition to create an outstanding institute of learning, the young Rector saw in the students' musical duties nothing but an obstacle to the fulfillment of his plans.

His attitude was not wholly unjustified. The type of school meant to serve both scholastic and musical purposes had become definitely outdated. The range of subjects to be studied was greatly widened in the 18th century, and gradually it became impossible for the young people to cope with all these different tasks. The young Rector wanted to modernize his institute and hated to see his charges waste so much time by singing in the streets, attending funerals or weddings, and rehearsing for performances. His problem was further aggravated by the kind of music the Cantor expected the choir to sing; it often necessitated serious studying and additional rehearsals. All this displeased the Rector exceedingly. He did not, like Gesner, compare the Thomasians to the angelic choirs. Instead, when he came across a boy practising his music, he would remark sneeringly: 'So it's a pothouse fiddler you want to become,' and thus make the performance of music seem an inferior kind of occupation.

To work in harmony with so intolerant and ambitious a superior would have been hard for any musician; it was utterly impossible for Bach. Thus there was tension, more and more of it, until it burst out in a controversy which assumed terrific proportions and lasted more than two years (during which time the two enemies had to live next door to each other!). The incident provoking it was petty, and the details need not concern us today. It had to do with the appointment of musical prefects, those senior pupils who took over much of the Cantor's duties and whose satisfactory work was of vital importance to a smoothly running musical organization. Bach's top prefect provoked the Rector by punishing a recalcitrant young pupil too severely, whereupon Ernesti, against Bach's wish, forced him to leave the school. The Rector then promoted another prefect to the first place, a youth whom the Cantor declared unfit for so responsible a position. Clearly the right was on Bach's side, as no one but he was in a position to judge a pupil's qualifications for the musical prefectship. Unfortunately, however, the hot-blooded Cantor let his temper run away with him. Shocking scenes occurred during the church services when Bach, seeing the hated prefect at work, chased him away with 'great shouting and noise,' whereupon Ernesti sent the youth back, threatening the whole choir with dire penalties if they sang under anybody else.

Thus utter confusion reigned at the Thomas School, and the discipline built up with so much difficulty was carried off as in a whirlwind. Bach, however, insisted on the restitution of his rights, 'cost it what it might.' A stream of reports and appeals began to flow from both adversaries to the authorities. Bach's were models of clarity addressed specifically to the problem in question. Ernesti, on the other hand, not only blamed the Cantor for shirking his duties in various ways, but even contended that Bach was venal and accepted unsuitable candidates whose fathers were prepared to make him a payment. Such a remark about Sebastian Bach, whose unshakable fairness and justice in the examination of organs had become a byword all over the country, shows best with what type of chief the Cantor had to deal.

The Council and the Consistory, receiving various petitions from the two adversaries, found themselves in a most unpleasant situation; they may have felt Bach's complaints to be justified, but they certainly wanted to avoid offending Ernesti, of whom they thought highly. In this quandary the best method seemed to delay answering the complaints and hope that with the graduation of the offensive prefect the storm would pass over. Though the controversy had come into the open in August 1736, they waited until February of the next year, and when they ultimately issued a statement, they pointed to the new school regulation according to which the Cantor was to chose his prefects with the Rector's consent.[1] Bach replied that he did not consider these new rules valid. When they were issued in 1723, the former rector had submitted them to the Consistory for approval and as this had never been given one had to rely on the old rules.

Aware that there was little chance of support for him from the Leipzig authorities, Bach tried to strengthen his position by other means. On September 27, 1736, he submitted a second petition to the Elector to be awarded the title of Royal Polish and Electoral Saxon Court composer, and this time he was successful. Apparently one of

1. The document is reproduced in *Bach-Dokumente*, p. 99.

PLATE I

The Bach House in Eisenach. Painting by Paul Bach.

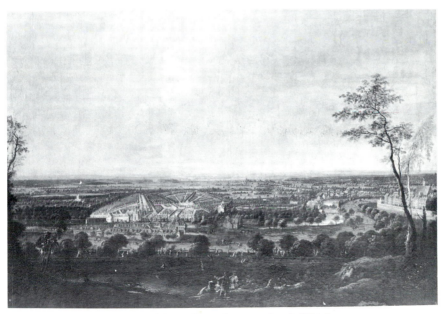

View from Bach's study in Leipzig, by A. Thiele, 1740.

PLATE II

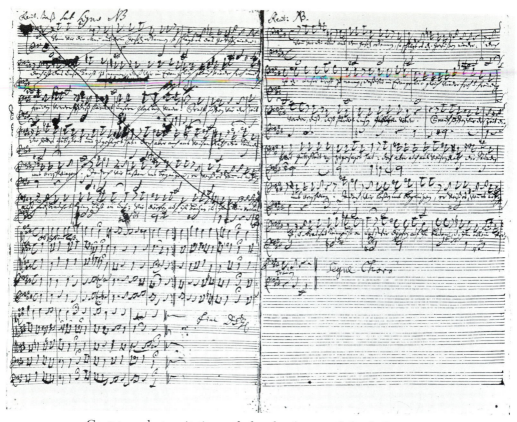

Cantata 9, last recitative and chorale. Autograph by J. S. Bach.

PLATE III

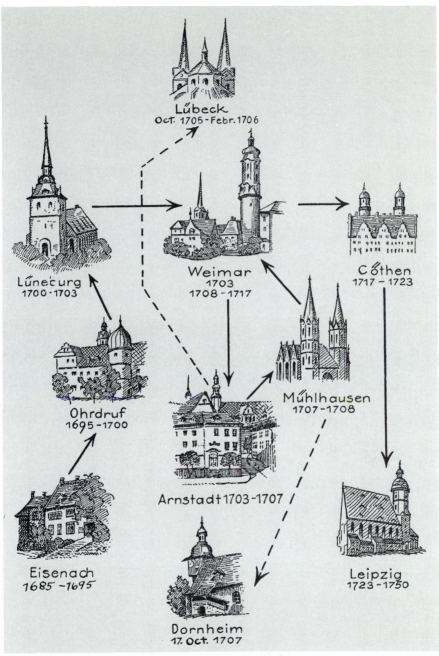

Lübeck
Oct. 1705 - Febr. 1706

Lüneburg
1700 - 1703

Weimar
1703
1708 - 1717

Cöthen
1717 - 1723

Ohrdruf
1695 - 1700

Mühlhausen
1707 - 1708

Arnstadt 1703 - 1707

Eisenach
1685 - 1695

Leipzig
1723 - 1750

Dornheim
17. Oct. 1707

Places significant in Bach's life.

PLATE IV

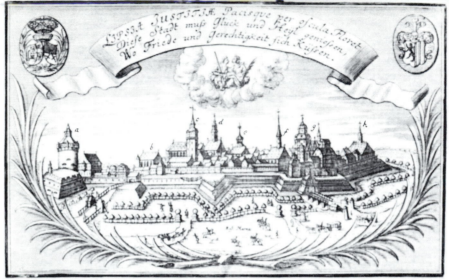

Die Königl. und Churfürstl. Sächs.
Florirende Kauff = und Handels = Stadt
Leipzig im Prospect.

a Vestung Pleissenburg.   c St. Thomas Kirche.   e Rath=Hauß.   g St. Nicolai Kirche.
b St. Peters Kirche.   d Neue Kirche.   f Pauliner Kirche.   h Zucht= und Wäysen=Hauß.

View of Leipzig by C. F. Rumpf, 1713.

Celebration on the market square in Leipzig. Engraving by Sysang, 1733.

PLATE V

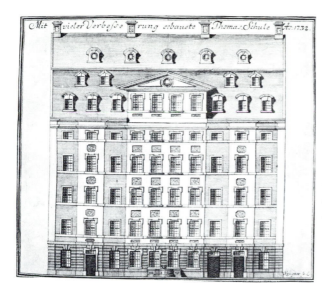

View of the enlarged
Thomas School,
by Krügner, 1732.

Interior of the Ducal chapel,
Weimar.
Painting by C. I. Richter.

PLATE VI

Bach's receipt for a payment received October 5, 1747.

Bach's explanation of ornaments, from *Clavier-Büchlein* for W. Friedemann.

PLATE VII

J. S. Bach. Pastel by G. F. Bach.

J. S. Bach.
Painting by E. G. Haussmann, 1748.

PLATE VIII .

First page of Bach's Sonata for unaccompanied violin. Autograph.

his great admirers at Dresden, Count Hermann von Keyserlingk, serving as Russian ambassador at the Saxon court, interceded on Bach's behalf. Moreover an obstacle to the awarding of the title had been removed when Duke Christian of Weissenfels died on June 28, 1736. The Weissenfels Capelle was thereupon disbanded and Bach lost the title of court composer to this small principality. The Elector was therefore not obliged to be associated with a lower ranking ruler in the titles he awarded. On November 19, 1736, the certificate of Bach's appointment as Royal Polish and Electoral Saxon Court Composer was made out in Dresden,[1] and even before that an order had been issued by the Dresden court to the Leipzig Consistory to re-examine the case and give Bach 'such satisfaction as he might be entitled to.' A few months later, during the royal family's visit to Leipzig, Bach presented (on April 28, 1738) an *Abendmusik* (evening concert) commissioned by the University students in celebration of the nuptials of Princess Amalia to Charles IV of Sicily. The cantata *Willkommen ihr herrschenden Götter der Erde* (BWV Anh. 13, lost today) on a text by Gottsched was performed with the greatest pomp and received with general applause. It seems that at this visit the monarch personally intervened in favor of his composer, for thenceforth the feud at the Thomas School is not mentioned in any official document. This does not mean, however, that either of the two parties forgot or forgave.

The years overshadowed by the feud with Ernesti also witnessed a sad event in Sebastian's family which could not fail profoundly to affect his peace of mind. In 1736 a vacancy occurred at the organ of St. Mary's in Mühlhausen, and Sebastian was eager to secure the position for one of his children. The two eldest sons did not enter into consideration. Friedemann had been appointed organist to Dresden's Sophienkirche in 1733. Independent-minded Emanuel had gone farther away, settling down in Frankfurt-on-the-Oder to continue his university studies while supporting himself as a clavier teacher. Sebastian therefore decided to apply in Mühlhausen for his third son, twenty-year-old Johann Gottfried Bernhard. There was some opposi-

---

2. It is possible that the sumptuous velvet coat seen in Gottlieb Friedrich Bach's pastel portrait of Sebastian (cf. p. 74) was acquired for the visit to Dresden, where the newly appointed court composer had to express his thanks for the conferment of the title.

tion from members of the Council who favored a local organist, but the weight of Sebastian Bach's name, coupled with Bernhard's excellent trial performance, was too strong, and young Bach was appointed. Sebastian had apparently forgotten how difficult he himself had found conditions in Mühlhausen. His life at this moment was dominated by the vicious dispute raging between him and Rector Ernesti, and any other place may have seemed to him preferable to the stormy atmosphere in Leipzig. Besides, he could not yet be sure of the outcome of this feud, and it therefore seemed advisable to make young Bernhard financially independent. This was to prove a fatal decision. Bernhard was no more mature than his brothers had been at twenty, and Sebastian's wise policy of allowing his children to develop slowly would have been beneficial for him. But instead of receiving a full university education he was sent away to Mühlhausen, where difficulties arose at once. The minutes of the Council meetings have been preserved,[1] and they clearly reveal animosity of some members toward the new organist. Their remarks sound like echoes of the complaints raised against twenty-year-old Sebastian in Arnstadt (cf. p. 21). One Councillor argued: 'Bach has preluded far too much and too long, and thus unduly shortened the time meant for the service and devotion. Besides, he often only confuses the congregation with his playing.' Another one exclaimed: 'If Bach continues to play in this way, the organ will be ruined in two years or most of the congregation will be deaf.' The mayor did his best to stem the tide of complaints by stressing Bernhard's artistic qualities, but did not quite succeed. Young Bach could not help noticing the inimical attitude of some councillors; his self-confidence was shaken, and he besought his father to find him another position. Sebastian thereupon managed to have his son appointed to the *Jakobikirche* in Sangerhausen, a position for which he himself had applied in 1703 (cf. p. 16). Bernhard gave notice at Mühlhausen, and the local organist favored by some of the councillors got the position. When in March 1737 Bernhard left Mühlhausen, he might have rejoiced had he not at the very end been treated with wounding suspicion. Those Council members who had objected to his vigorous playing insisted that before his departure another organist should check

1. Cf. Georg Thiele, 'Die Familie Bach in Mühlhausen,' *Mühlhäuser Geschichtsblätter*, 1921.

whether Bernhard had left the organ in good condition. It was a humiliating and, as it proved, quite unnecessary action to take against a son of *the* organ expert, who infused into his pupils a profound knowledge of, and veneration for, the king of instruments. We can imagine Sebastian's anger at this affront. Nor were Bernhard's personal affairs less unpleasant. For the young man, shaken by his problems, had not adhered to the strict standards of frugality instilled into him at home, and had incurred debts. What happened subsequently in Sangerhausen can only be guessed. Apparently Bernhard could not settle down there or rid himself of the habit of spending more than he earned. After less than a year he suddenly disappeared from the little town, leaving various debts behind him. The father, informed thereof, wrote as follows[1] to a certain Mr. Klemm, who had been helpful in securing the appointment for Bernhard:

Most Honored Sir:

You will not take it amiss that I have not till now answered your esteemed letter, for I only returned from Dresden two days ago. So loving and tender a father as yourself will understand the grief and sorrow with which I write this letter. I have not seen my, alas, undutiful boy since last year, when I enjoyed so many kindnesses at your hands. Your Honor will remember that I then paid what he owed for his board, discharged the Mühlhausen bond (which seems to have been the cause of his leaving that place) and left some ducats to meet his other debts, hoping that for the future he would reform his *genus vitae*. You will therefore understand how pained and upset I am to learn that he has again been borrowing money on all sides, by no means changed his way of life, and has even absconded without giving me, so far, the slightest indication of his whereabouts. What can I do or say more, my warnings having failed, and my loving care and help having proved unavailing? I can only bear my cross in patience and commend my undutiful boy to God's mercy, never doubting that He will hear my sorrow-stricken prayer and in His good time bring my son to understand that the path of conversion leads to Him.

I have opened my heart to your Honor, and beg you not to associate me with my son's misconduct, but to accept my assurance that I have done all that a true father, whose children lie very close to his heart, is bound to do to advance their welfare. I recommended him to Sangerhausen when

1. English text based on C. S. Terry.

the vacancy occurred, trusting that its more cultured society and distinguished patrons would incite him to better behavior. As the author of his promotion, I must once again thank your Honor, confident that you will not allow the position to be filled until we have discovered his whereabouts (God, who sees all things, is my witness that since last year I have not set eyes upon him) and learn his future intentions, whether he resolves to change his course, or intends to seek his fortune elsewhere. I shrink from troubling your Council on this matter, and only beg for *patience* until he returns or discloses his retreat. Already several creditors have written to me, whom I am not disposed to pay until, as I am entitled by law, I have come to an understanding with my son about his affairs, face to face or by letter. Meanwhile, I respectfully ask your Honor to discover his whereabouts and let me know, in order that, under God's providence, I may make a last effort to soften his hardened heart and bring him to his right senses. As he was so fortunate as to lodge in your house, may I ask your Honor whether he removed his few pieces of furniture, or if any of them remain behind? Awaiting your speedy reply and wishing you a happier holiday[1] than I shall have, I remain, with humblest respects to your wife,

Your Honor's most devoted servant,
Joh. Seb. Bach

Leipzig, May 24, 1738.

In the meantime Bernhard had gone to the University of Jena to study law. Perhaps he felt that the scholastic training previously denied to him (while his two elder brothers had enjoyed this privilege) might help him to discover the right way of life. The choice of Jena was a wise one. Here his aged kinsman Johann Nicolaus Bach (1669–1753) had been active since 1695 as organist and builder of instruments. Nicolaus Bach's only son had died a few months earlier, and the septuagenarian may have gladly welcomed a gifted relative who could relieve him of part of his duties and eventually become his successor. But whatever Bernhard's plans were, they came to nothing; for only four months after his matriculation, this ill-fated son of Sebastian suddenly succumbed to a "fever" on May 27, 1739 at the age of twenty-four.

The half a dozen years following Gesner's departure from Leipzig

---

1. Reference to the imminent feast of Pentecost.

were certainly a period when various circumstances conspired to upset the composer. In addition to the bitter feud with the head of the Thomas School, and to the grief over an unfortunate son, Sebastian had to experience a vehement attack on his art.

There appeared in Hamburg a new periodical entitled *Critischer Musicus,* which set out to analyze and criticize contemporary music from the viewpoint of the artistic tenets held by the young generation. Its author, who at first preferred to remain anonymous, was Johann Adolph Scheibe from Leipzig, a gifted journalist and a fairly good self-taught musician.[1] As the son of an eminent organ builder who had taken care of the instruments at St. Thomas' and St. Nicholas', young Scheibe was naturally acquainted with the Thomas Cantor, though, significantly enough, he did not care to study with Leipzig's foremost music teacher. Bach had even written in 1731 a friendly testimonial on his behalf, when Scheibe applied for the organist's post in Freiberg, Saxony (an attempt that was unsuccessful). Two years earlier the youth had tried for a similar position at St. Nicholas' in Leipzig, which was, however, awarded to Bach's pupil, Johann Schneider. These two failures apparently greatly upset the young man, and when Scheibe settled down in Hamburg and started work on his critical journal, the pent-up emotions erupted forcefully. In the sixth issue dated May 14, 1737, he obviously attacked Bach, though not really mentioning his name. After praising his brilliant technique as a performer he remarked:[2]

This great man would be the wonder of the universe if his compositions displayed more agreeable qualities, were less turgid and sophisticated, more simple and natural in character. His music is exceedingly difficult to play, because the efficiency of his own limbs sets his standards; he expects singers and players to be as agile with voice and instrument as he is with his fingers, which is impossible. Grace-notes and embellishments, such as a player instinctively supplies, he puts down in actual symbols, a habit, which not only sacrifices the harmonic beauty of his music but also blurs

1. Scheibe was born 1708 in Leipzig. In 1736 he moved to Hamburg; four years later he was appointed conductor of the Margrave of Brandenburg-Kulmbach; in 1744 he became court conductor to King Christian VI of Denmark. Scheibe died 1776 in Copenhagen.
2. Translation by C. S. Terry.

its melodic line. All his parts, too, are equally melodic, so that one cannot distinguish the principal tune among them. In short, he is as a musician what Herr von Lohenstein used to be as a poet[1]: pomposity diverts them both from a natural to an artificial style, changing what might have been sublime into the obscure. In regard to both of them, we wonder at an effort so labored and, since nothing comes of it, so futile.

This criticism was bound to affect Bach, for the writer expressed an attitude widely adopted by the young generation which, in a revolt against the tenets of the musical Baroque, stressed pleasure to the senses and simplicity of expression as the primary goals of a musical composition. Such aesthetic theories had been vigorously attacked by Bach and Picander as early as 1729 in the satiric cantata *Phoebus and Pan* (cf. p. 186), and with increasing age Bach had still stiffened in his reaction against these ideas. It was thus with indignation that he read the attack from Hamburg, which seemed particularly offensive through Scheibe's use, when referring to the Royal Polish and Electoral Saxon court composer, of the German word *Musicant,* a term generally applied at that time to musicians belonging to the lowest strata of society. Considering it beneath his dignity to answer Scheibe in a pamphlet, Bach entrusted a friend, J. A. Birnbaum, instructor in rhetoric at Leipzig University, with his defense. The latter's reply,[2] lengthy though not too effective, appeared in January 1738, and the controversy was carried on for some time, with nobody emerging as a clear victor. Though profoundly vexed by young Scheibe's attack, Bach was objective enough not to let his annoyance influence him when judging a few years later the Johannis organ in Leipzig built by the critic's father. He declared it to be 'faultless,' an admirable act of fairness which was particularly stressed in the Obituary written after Sebastian's death.

The vicissitudes that befell Bach during the late 1730's, were somewhat alleviated through the friendly ministrations of a young kinsman

1. In the 18th century the gaudy and excessively florid diction of the German poet D. K. von Lohenstein (1635-83) was considered definitely outdated, and Scheibe's comparison was meant to be offensive.

2. It is entitled 'Unpartheyische Anmerkungen über eine bedenkliche Stelle in dem 6. Stück des critischen Musicus.' The article was published separately and subsequently appeared in Mizler's *Musicalische Bibliothek* (cf. p. 93).

who joined his household at that time. Thirty-three-year-old Johann
Elias Bach (whose grandfather was a brother of Sebastian's father)
arrived in 1737[1] from the town of Schweinfurt to study theology at
Leipzig University. Sebastian, who had trained Elias's brother many
years ago in Weimar, naturally received the kinsman very hospitably.
Being deprived of his elder sons' assistance, he suggested that Elias
should stay at his home, and in return for board and lodging, do some
secretarial work and teach the three young sons. A contract was concluded, and before long most cordial relations developed between him
and the Thomas Cantor's family. Various drafts of Elias's letters have
been preserved,[2] and they reveal the writer as a lovable person who
participated with faithful devotion in all that happened in the Bach
household. He took his teaching duties very seriously, especially the
preparation of his charges for communion. When in 1741 another position was offered him, he refused it stating that the relatives under his
care, in particular the [feeble-minded] eldest, were 'in the greatest need
of a solid and faithful instruction.' Elias wrote about his eminent cousin's new works to other musicians; he tried to brighten Magdalena's
hard life by obtaining carnation plants and a singing bird for her; and
he urged his sister to send Sebastian a supply of her excellent home-
made cider. Once, when the composer was in Berlin, Elias, knowing
his cousin's tendency unduly to extend absences from Leipzig, reminded Sebastian of the imminent Council election, for which a new
composition by the *director musices* was expected. So Elias was a great
help in many respects and always eager to serve his relatives. On the
other hand, he would not have exerted himself so much had he not, as
he wrote, 'received so much kindness' from Sebastian and the family.
We learn, for instance, that the Thomas Cantor lent Elias his fur-lined
boots and raincoat, both particularly dear to him as the indispensable
paraphernalia of those trips out-of-town which he enjoyed so much.
Sebastian also took his secretary with him on visits to Dresden and
introduced Elias to as high-ranking a music lover as Count Keyserlingk
(cf. p. 85). Most of all, the concerts at the Thomas Cantor's home,
frequently attended by outstanding visiting musicians, must have been

1. Sebastian's petition to the Elector dated Oct. 18, 1737, was written by Elias.
2. A volume of some 250 drafts to letters from the years 1738-42 is known. Several of these were reproduced by K. Pottgiesser in *Die Musik*, XII, 2 (1912).

experiences never to be forgotten by the kinsman from Schweinfurt ('something extra good in the way of music' as Elias described one such event to a stepbrother of his, when Friedemann Bach performed with the two famous Dresden lutenists Sylvanus Weiss and Johann Kropfgans). So greatly indebted to his Leipzig cousin did Elias feel that years after his departure he presented Sebastian with a token of his affection. Unfortunately the desired effect did not quite materialize, as will be presently shown.

VII. NEARING THE END

(1740-1750)

THE rankling experiences of the past decade made Bach grow more and more aloof. As a pleasant relationship with Rector Ernesti seemed out of the question, the Thomas Cantor became less concerned with the duties of his office and neglected them to some extent. In 1740 it became therefore necessary for the Thomas School to appoint a new master for musical theory. In his creative activity the aging composer preferred to devote himself to instrumental composition and to harvest the fruits of his immense output by revising former works and preparing some for publication. The attacks of the young generation merely strengthened his desire to achieve the utmost in the employment of the ancient intricate forms ridiculed by the adherents of the new 'style galant.' The works of his last years provide a superlative expression of his determined adherence to formal Baroque conceptions. Performance was hardly in his mind when he penned some of these compositions. They constitute a kind of abstract music, written for his own satisfaction, as a testament of his artistic faith.

While taking less interest in the affairs at the Thomas School, Bach did by no means withdraw from contact with other musicians. He followed with interest the activities of the scholarly *Societät der musikalischen Wissenschaften* (Society for the Promotion of Musical Sciences) established in 1738 by young Lorenz C. Mizler, a former member of Bach's Collegium Musicum. This society presented every four weeks an issue of its *Neu eröffnete musikalische Bibliothek* dealing with theoretical problems. The society's membership consisted of distinguished musicians who were well versed in all aspects of musical theory. While Bach was at first reluctant to join the society, his attitude changed after Handel had accepted such an invitation in 1745 and become the eleventh member. Even then Bach waited for two more years, and only in June 1747 was he prevailed upon to join. In accordance with the society's rules he contributed as proof of his learning an intricate triple canon in six parts as well as his portrait[1] painted by E. G. Haussmann, which shows the composer with the canon in his hand.

Bach's delay in joining after Handel had become a member might be attributed to a rather strange reason. Most likely it was due to the pleasure he took in the so-called *lusus ingenii* (intellectual games), a predilection he shared with the founder of the society and, as a matter of fact, with many scholars and artists of the era. It was a common practice at that time to substitute numbers for the letters of the alphabet and express a name by a figure. The word Bach corresponds to 14, since *b* is the second letter of the alphabet, *a* the first, *c*, the third, *h* the eighth, the sum of which is 14, which played a very important part in the composer's thinking. Consequently Bach waited until he could join Mizler's society as 14th member. In addition to the canon and the portrait, Bach presented to the society a composition for organ, the canonic variations on the Christmas song *Vom Himmel hoch* ('From Heaven above'; BWV 769), a work displaying the most profound erudition, and admirably fulfilling the aims of the founder.

Outside of Leipzig he was still in great demand for the testing of organs. Bach gladly accepted such invitations, for he loved to travel. He also spent a good deal of time at Dresden, appearing at court, giv-

1. In the 19th century the portrait became the property of the Thomas School and finally it was lent in 1913 to the Leipzig Historic Museum. At this occasion the picture, which meanwhile had suffered considerable damage, was thoroughly restored; parts were painted over and thus some not insignificant alterations occurred. A better preserved version of the Haussmann portrait dated 1748 was made accessible in the Bach year 1950 (cf. Hans Raupach, *Das wahre Bildnis J. S. Bachs*, Wolfenbüttel, 1950). This fine portrait, which may have been produced for C. P. E. Bach, is now owned by William H. Scheide of Princeton, N. J. The so-called Bach portrait by Haussmann of 1723 (cf. Herz, A 'New' Bach Portrait, *MQ*, 1943) does probably not represent the composer. On the other hand Heinrich Besseler (cf. *Fünf echte Bildnisse Johann Sebastian Bachs*, Kassel, 1956) has put in a strong claim for the authenticity of the following five paintings: the miniature by Gottlieb Friedrich Bach; the youthful portrait owned by the Erfurt Museum; that by J. J. Ihle in the Bach House, Eisenach; the portrait by an unknown master belonging to Walter R. Volbach, Fort Worth; and finally a portrait known only through photographic reproduction. (It was discovered in 1941 but destroyed four years later in the war.) Cf. also H. O. R. Baron van Tuyll van Serroskerken, *Probleme des Bachporträts*, Utrecht, 1956, and Besseler in *BJ* 1956, p. 66 ff. See also C. Freyse, *B.s Antlitz*, Eisenach, 1964.

ing organ recitals, and making music with the prominent court musicians, who also came to Leipzig to play at his home.

A unique experience was granted him in a meeting with King Frederick 'the Great' of Prussia. Since his second son, Emanuel, had been appointed in 1740 court accompanist to the enlightened and music-loving ruler, Bach was greatly interested in Prussia's capital, Berlin. It is probably his own opinion that is reflected in the remark of his secretary, Johann Elias Bach (cf. p. 91), that 'at Berlin the golden age of music seemed to be inaugurated.' Sebastian may even have entertained hopes of finding in Berlin the kind of position he was longing for. It is noteworthy, anyway, that as early as 1741 he visited his son there. The time was not well chosen, for the king was involved in the first 'Silesian war' against Austria; besides, Sebastian's sojourn had to be broken off because of a serious illness of Anna Magdalena; as a result, no appearance at court took place. In the following years the monarch was still engaged in the war, which even interfered with Bach's own life. In 1745 the Prussian armies laid siege to Leipzig, ruthlessly burning and ransacking the lovely countryside around it. But as a true son of the period Sebastian was not really concerned with the quarrels of the rulers, and once the danger was over and peace restored, he again planned an appearance at the Prussian court. This time conditions were much more propitious, since a distinguished friend and patron of Bach's art had come to Berlin in 1746 as Russian ambassador. This was the *Reichsgraf* Hermann von Keyserlingk, who had been stationed in Dresden from 1734 to 1745. Keyserlingk was a genuine admirer of the composer's music, and when he received the "Aria with sundry Variations" Bach had written for him (cf. p. 295), he sent the Thomas Cantor a golden goblet filled with a hundred louis d'or. The ambassador's enthusiastic praise of the Leipzig composer naturally excited the Prussian king's curiosity, and so an invitation was extended through Emanuel Bach.

In the spring of 1747 Sebastian complied and came to Berlin, where he also had the joy of seeing his first grandson, Johann August,[1] born

1. It is likely that the 'Capellmeister Bach' mentioned as one of the child's godfathers was Sebastian, but this does not necessarily mean that he attended the christening ceremony. The same applies to Anna Magdalena Bach, who is mentioned as godmother of Emanuel's second child, Anna Carolina Philippina, christened on September 12, 1747 (cf. H. Miesner, *BJ* 1932, p. 157 ff.).

on November 30, 1745. 'Old Bach,' as the king referred to him, was received most graciously. He had to perform on the various organs in Potsdam and try out the pianofortes built by Silbermann that were in the palace; on each he displayed his incredible mastery of improvisation. The king, a composer in his own right, was deeply impressed and was glad, at Bach's suggestion, to offer him a subject for a fugue. The Thomas Cantor was so intrigued by the possibilities of the royal theme that, after improvising a three-part fugue on it for the king, he wrote on his return to Leipzig a truly royal set of polyphonic compositions in the strictest style based on this subject. He had them engraved under the title *Musicalisches Opfer* (Musical Offering) with a dedication to the king, and on July 7, 1747, he forwarded it to Berlin.

The work submitted to the monarch was of the greatest artistic significance. It may be well doubted, however, that the recipient was aware of this. The printing carried out in great haste by Bach's pupil, J. G. Schübler, was done in a rather haphazard way with different numbers squeezed together. Anyone not aware of the composer's intentions would have found it extremely difficult to ascertain the order in which the different pieces were to be heard and thus would have no idea of the underlying structural plan. Moreover the solution of the ten canons included presented formidable problems, as Bach left important points unexplained and occasionally even neglected to indicate at what place the different parts were to come in. The set he presented was bound to be fascinating for an expert in musical theory who was willing to devote ample time to its study, but hardly fit for enjoyment by a king who, despite his love for music, was too concerned with other matters to afford the leisure and patience required for the solution of these intricate canonic puzzles. This may explain why no financial benefits were derived by Bach from the dedication. The king's account books at least make no mention of any payment to the composer, nor is there any record of a performance of the 'Musical Offering' at the Prussian court.[1]

The whole episode throws light on Bach's personality. It is typical of his didactic approach to leave the solution of the canons to the recipients of his work; their laborious efforts to solve the problems must also have appealed to his sense of humor. On the other hand it was

1. Cf. Friedrich Ernst, Bach und das Pianoforte, *BJ* 1961, p. 71.

alien to his nature to anticipate the reaction of other people. Apparently it did not occur to him that a properly ordered sequence of numbers with adequate explanation of each piece would have given the king much more pleasure than the copy that was actually presented. Thus it came about that the 'Musical Offering' shared the unhappy fate of the concertos Bach had sent in 1721 to the king's relative, Margrave Christian Ludwig of Brandenburg. During the composer's visit, however, the monarch seems to have behaved most cordially. Indeed he was so impressed by 'old Bach' that many years later he spoke quite enthusiastically to van Swieten[1] about this meeting.

Though the 'Musical Offering' apparently brought no financial returns from Berlin, it seems to have been well received by Bach's own small circle. When Elias Bach, by that time established as cantor in his native town, asked for a copy of the work, Sebastian had to answer:[2]

Leipzig, October 6, 1748.

Worthy and respected cousin,

Time presses on and I must endeavor to say much in a few words, if only to acknowledge God's grace and bounty, both in the abundant vintage and in regard to the prospective happy event.[3] You ask for the copy of the Prussian fugue; I cannot send you one, for *justement* to-day the edition was used up. Only 100 copies were engraved, and most of them I gave away *gratis* to friends. However, between now and the New Year's Fair more will be published, and if my cousin still desires one, he should at his convenience acquaint me hereof and mail me a thaler, and it will be forwarded. I conclude with greetings from us all,

Your Honor's devoted
J. S. Bach

PS. My Berlin son now has two male heirs. The first was born about the time we, alas, suffered the Prussian invasion. The other[4] is about a fortnight old.

1. Cf. A. Einstein in *Musical Times,* 1936, p. 209.
2. English version based on translation by C. S. Terry.
3. Elias had apparently informed his kinsman that his wife was expecting a child, which was born on December 26, 1748.
4. Emanuel's second son, Johann Sebastian Bach II, was to develop into a gifted painter, but died at the age of thirty. He preferred to call himself Johann Samuel.

Sebastian's reference to the abundant vintage seems to have been caused by Elias's promise to send his Leipzig relatives some home-made wine. The receipt of this gift is confirmed in Sebastian's follow-ing letter dated November 2, 1748:[1]

Worthy and respected cousin,

Your letter, received yesterday, brings me the good news that you and your dear wife are still well. For the delectable cask of wine that came with it accept my best thanks. It is much to be regretted that the cask suffered a jar, or some other accident, on the journey, for on examination here it was found to be almost two thirds empty and containing, the *visi-tator* declares, only six quarts. What a pity that so noble a gift of God should be wasted. Nonetheless I am heartily obliged to my worthy cousin for his kind present and I sincerely congratulate him on the rich vintage he has gathered. *Pro nunc* I am *reellement* not in a position to reciprocate; still *quod differtur non auffertur,* and I hope to find an opportunity some-what to discharge my obligation.

It is unfortunate that we live so far apart, for else I should give myself the pleasure of inviting our cousin to my daughter Liesgen's wedding, which takes place in January 1749 to the new organist Herr Altnikol. However, though for that reason, and because of the inconvenient season, he can presumably not be present, I will ask him to assist them with a Christian wish, and with the same I commend myself to my cousin's re-membrance. With warmest greetings from all here, I remain,

Your Honor's devoted and faithful cousin and servant to command,
Joh. Seb. Bach

P.S. Magister Birnbaum[2] was buried six weeks ago.
P.M. Though my good cousin offers to send me more of the same *liqueur,* I must decline on account of the heavy charges at this end. The carriage was 16 gr., delivery 2 gr., *visitator* 2 gr., provincial excise 5 gr. 5 pfg., general excise 3 gr. So my cousin may calculate that the wine cost me nearly 5 gr. a quart, which is too expensive for a present.

The wedding referred to was the ceremony uniting Sebastian's daughter Elisabeth Juliane Friederica (b.1726) to Johann Christoph Altnikol (b.1719), a former pupil, of whom Bach thought highly, now installed as organist in Naumburg. In a testimonial dated Jan-

1. English version based on C. S. Terry's translation.
2. Cf. p. 90.

uary 1, 1748, he praised Altnikol as a vocalist, performer on various instruments and composer, whereupon he concluded: 'Enfin, he is an ecolier of whom I need not be ashamed.' The ceremony took place on January 20, 1749, an occasion for much rejoicing, as it was the only wedding celebrated in the Bach home, Liesgen being, incidentally, the only daughter married among Sebastian's ten surviving children. On October 4, 1749, a son was born to the couple and christened, as Emanuel's second son had been, Johann Sebastian.

After Liesgen had left home, a very small family-group remained in the Thomas Cantorate. It was further depleted when early in 1750 Sebastian's eighteen-year-old son, Johann Christoph Friedrich, was appointed Kammermusikus to Count Wilhelm of Schaumburg-Lippe in Bückeburg. There remained with Sebastian his eldest daughter, a spinster in her forties; feeble-minded Gottfried Heinrich; two young girls, aged thirteen and eight, and the youngest son, Johann Christian aged fourteen. Sebastian took particular delight in Johann Christian's brilliant musical talent and expressed this by presenting him with three of his claviers. Above all there was Anna Magdalena, ready as ever faithfully to share with her husband whatever life was bringing them, and by her very presence lightening his burden.

He certainly needed all the support and encouragement she could give him during the tribulations that were assailing him at this time. Sebastian's eyesight had been poor for many years, and the constant strain of writing small notes by candlelight finally exacted its toll—as it did with two of his kinsmen, the organist and lexicographer Johann Gottfried Walther and the Arnstadt organist Johann Ernst Bach. In 1749 Sebastian was nearly blind, and rumor had it that his health was badly impaired as well. Whether this was correct and he had had a stroke, as some historians conjecture, can no longer be verified. It is significant that he was unable to attend the christening of his grandson in Naumburg on October 6, 1749, and that a letter of recommendation for his son J. C. Friedrich, penned on December 27, 1749, was written by his wife, who also undertook to simulate his signature.[1] On the other hand the Obituary contributed by Philipp Emanuel and Sebastian's pupil, Johann F. Agricola, stressed that, apart from his eye trouble, Bach had been physically quite fit.

Anyway, the reports about Bach's bad health caused the writing of

1. Cf. H.-J. Schulze, 'Marginalien zu einigen Bach-Dokumenten,' BJ 1961, p. 94.

a letter to Leipzig's burgomaster, in which the Dresden conductor Johann Gottlob Harrer was recommended for the vacancy expected to occur through Bach's death; and it was suggested that Harrer should prove his skill by giving a trial performance immediately. As the author of the letter was the all-powerful Saxonian minister Count Brühl, his suggestion amounted to an order. The good city fathers complied—whether or not with a feeling of guilt at this flagrant lack of respect we do not know—and so it came about that in the inn of the 'Three Swans,' where secular concerts used to take place, Harrer on June 8, 1749, gave a public performance of a church cantata he had brought with him, as a test piece for the 'future position of Thomas Cantor, if the *director musices,* Sebastian Bach, should pass away.' Thus a chronicler[1] records nonchalantly.

Bach could not help hearing of the shameful incident. His fighting spirit was roused; he would prove to them that he was still in the possession of his strength. Tenaciously he continued the struggle for more than a year, and Harrer, dismayed and disappointed, had to go back to Dresden. At that time reports on a visiting English oculist, who had performed amazing operations, spread through Germany. This Chevalier John Taylor happened to pass through Leipzig, and Bach resolved to entrust himself to the surgeon (who was subsequently to treat Handel too). Taylor performed two operations[2] on him, but both were failures; moreover the various drugs administered shattered Sebastian's whole system, and he grew steadily weaker. On July 18, 1750, sight was suddenly restored to him, but a few hours later a stroke occurred, followed by a raging fever, to which he succumbed on July 28, 1750. Musicians and music lovers in Leipzig deeply mourned the loss. The City Council, however, in its next meeting, did not waste much time in eulogies on the departed composer. Some remarks were uttered such as 'the school needs a Cantor, not a conductor' or 'Bach was certainly a great musician, but no school teacher,' and Harrer's appointment was formally decided on. Furthermore, when Bach's widow applied for the customary payment of the Can-

1. Johann Salomon Riemer, *Chronik Leipzigs, 1714-71.* Stadtarchiv, Leipzig.
2. Helmut Zeraschi points out in *BJ* 1956, p. 63, that the first took place between March 28 and 31, 1750, the second between April 1 and 7. Afterwards Bach, according to a contemporary physician's report, suffered from 'accidental inflammation.'

tor's honorarium through the following half-year, the city accountant was smart enough to remember that Bach, when entering office 27 years previously, had received full payment for the first quarter, although he started work only in February; so the Council had the satisfaction of deducting 21 th.21 gr. from the relief-sum due to the widow.[1] The intractable Cantor was replaced by a man whose 'very quiet and accommodating nature' Count Brühl had emphasized, and the Council looked forward to a peaceful era at St. Thomas'.

1. Cf. Schering, *J.S.B. und das Musikleben Leipzigs*, p. 329 ff.

CONCLUSION: AFTER 1750

AFTER the Thomas Cantor's death his widow, aged forty-nine, declared her intention not to marry again,[1] a resolution one can well understand in a woman who for twenty-nine years had given all her devotion and loyalty to a Sebastian Bach. This decision Anna Magdalena took, although it was not unusual for a widow of her age to wed again, and she was aware that her financial position would be most insecure. Sebastian had, it is true, left an estate which, according to standards then prevailing among church musicians, was not inconsiderable; but there were nine children who claimed part of the property, and as no last will was available, one-third was allocated to the widow, and the other two-thirds evenly divided among the progeny. Before the official evaluation by the curators was undertaken, the two eldest sons took possession of that part of their father's music, books, and pictures which seemed useful to them, and the youngest, Christian, retained—against some opposition from his brothers—the three claviers his father had given him. The property to be divided was valued, after deduction of some debts, at 1007 thalers, and of it the widow received a mining share, some bonds from debtors, and various valuable instruments, silver, and jewelry. All the male members of the family moved away. Feeble-minded Gottfried stayed in Naumburg with his brother-in-law, Altnikol, while young Christian went to Berlin to join his half brother, Emanuel, who had offered him a home and further musical training. Four female Bachs remained in Leipzig: the widow, her unmarried stepdaughter, and her two young daughters, Caroline and Susanne. To provide for them proved anything but easy. The Leipzig authorities allowed the widow twice 21 thalers and 21 groschen, plus 11 thalers, 12 groschen for candles, and a certain

1. Cf. her letter dated October 21, 1750, to the University in which she expresses this determination and accordingly asks to be appointed guardian of her minor children. She furthermore suggests that J. G. Görner be appointed as co-guardian entrusted with the division of the property.

amount of grain. The apartment in the school had to be vacated by February 1751, and a desperate struggle ensued to make ends meet. Every vendible object had to be disposed of, and Magdalena sold what music of Sebastian's was still in her hands to the city council, which paid her for it 40 thalers, 'in view of her impoverished state.' The sons seem not to have contributed to her support, a shocking state of matters possibly due to the war that had broken out in 1756 and made communication to Leipzig from the towns where the sons resided almost impossible. Thus poor Magdalena had to subsist on the city's charity. When she died in 1760 at the age of 59, the Thomas Cantor's widow was as an "alms woman" given the lowest-class funeral.

It is with deep sadness that one learns of these facts. One feels strongly the ignominy of Magdalena's depending on the charity of the very same city council against which her husband, the Royal Polish and Electoral Saxon court composer, had stood up with so much spirit. The idea of Magdalena Bach as an alms woman strikes as discordant a note as the fact of the test performance offered by the new candidate for the Thomas Cantor's post one year before Sebastian's death.

What happened to her daughters afterwards is not known. We learn from Emanuel's letters to his publisher, Immanuel Breitkopf, that he regularly sent money to his sister, Elisabeth Altnikol, a widow since 1759, and it is possible that these payments were also meant for Catharina, Caroline, and Susanna Bach. The other brothers may have helped too, but no records to this effect have been found as yet. The darkness surrounding the fate of Sebastian's female offspring is only dispelled in 1800. By that time all of the Thomas Cantor's children had died, except the youngest, Susanna, then fifty-eight years old and apparently ailing and unable to work. Friedrich Rochlitz, editor of Breitkopf's *Allgemeine Musikalische Zeitung*, found out about her desperate situation and published a stirring appeal on her behalf, which yielded enough to grant Sebastian's daughter a modest security until her death in 1809.

Sebastian's surviving four sons, each an artist in his own right, had highly diversified careers.[1] Wilhelm Friedemann (1710-84), whom the family considered the most gifted among the young Bachs, met a tragic fate. While the father was alive, Friedemann had quite a sat-

1. Cf. K. Geiringer, *The Bach Family*, p. 303 ff.

isfactory career and won in 1746 the fine position of *director musices* in Halle (an appointment Sebastian himself had coveted in 1714). But after the Thomas Cantor's death, Friedemann seems to have been deprived of a moral support that was essential to him. Being unable to live in peace with his superiors he resigned, in a fit of temper, at the age of fifty-four, without having secured another position. Henceforth he led a wandering life, making a precarious living with organ recitals, teaching, and composition. He was acclaimed as one of Germany's foremost organ players; yet his eccentric behavior discouraged people from giving him a permanent position. After various failures in other towns, he settled down in Berlin, where he died in poverty at the age of seventy-four.

Witty and urbane C. P. Emanuel Bach (1714-88) was endowed with a realistic outlook on life and a steadfastness of purpose denied his elder brother. After serving twenty-eight years as accompanist to Frederick the Great, he was appointed music director in Hamburg, as successor of his godfather, G. P. Telemann. Here Emanuel discharged with great distinction his manifold duties as a conductor, composer, and administrator, and continued publishing his own works with eminent success. Influenced to a lesser extent than Friedemann by his father's model, he became the leading exponent of the idiom of sensibility in music and exercised a decisive influence on young composers like Joseph Haydn. It cannot be denied that in his lifetime Emanuel enjoyed fame and financial success—particularly as a composer of clavier music—such as was never granted to his great father.

Less colorful was the personality of J. C. Friedrich Bach (1732-95). He was the only one among the Thomas Cantor's sons to keep the same position throughout his professional life, serving from his eighteenth year to his death as concert-master at the small ducal court of Bückeburg. His feats as a performer on the clavier were acclaimed by his contemporaries. In his creative work he composed in most forms of music, revealing solid craftsmanship and pleasant melodic invention.

While this elder son of Magdalena Bach accepted with equanimity life in provincial Bückeburg, his younger brother J. Christian (1735-82) moved in Europe's music centers. Christian rebelled in significant ways against the family tradition. He was the only son of Sebastian to leave Germany, and he moved to Italy in order to study opera, the one musical form neglected by his father. In Milan he adopted the Catholic faith and earned success as a church composer; later he won laurels with his operas at the famous Teatro di San Carlo in Naples. Receiving a call from the Italian opera company in London, he settled down in the English capital, where he was prodigiously active in various fields of music, winning particular acclaim with a fine series of orchestral concerts he offered together with C. F. Abel. His fame spread beyond England, and he was commissioned to compose operas for Mannheim, capital of the German Palatinate, and for Paris. For about ten years Christian enjoyed a life of glamorous success. Then young newcomers began to undermine his position in London, and, worn out by intrigues and setbacks unavoidable in the capital's teeming musical life, he suffered a breakdown. He died at the age of forty-seven, leaving, despite his great income, sizable debts behind. As a composer Christian significantly prepared for the growth of the Viennese classical style. His graceful yet tender melodies exercised a decisive influence on young Mozart, who greatly admired the 'English Bach.'

Sebastian's four sons produced the last truly significant flowering on the family tree of the Bach musicians. In the following generation we find only two artists, both mediocre. Emanuel's son, Johann Sebastian II (1748-78), was a painter, while his cousin, Wilhelm Friedrich Ernst (1759-1845), a son of the Bückeburg Bach, followed the family tradition. Wilhelm Bach served through most of his career as a music instructor at the Prussian court in Berlin. In his younger years he was active as a composer too, contributing pleasant, though not very remarkable, works for piano, chamber music, and songs. After his two teachers, the father and the uncle in London, had died, he felt less incentive toward creative work and largely concentrated on teaching. Apparently he did not care for the life of a celebrity, for he led so secluded a life that Mendelssohn, while residing in Berlin, did not even know of his existence, although he was intensely interested in everything connected with Bach. Yet, in the 1840's fame came to Wilhelm Bach from an unexpected quarter. The town of Leipzig decided to make amends for its former attitude toward the genius it had harbored for twenty-seven years. A monument was erected to Johann Sebastian Bach, and the Thomas Cantor's grandson was invited to the solemn inauguration. Old Wilhelm was received with a graciousness and respect rarely accorded to his grandfather. The words Robert Schumann wrote after the ceremony expressed the general feeling in Leipzig: 'Let us honor the worthy head bearing so sacred a name!' This may have been the octogenarian's ultimate joyful experience. Two years later the last male Bach descended from Johann Sebastian passed away.

PART II

BACH'S ARTISTIC HERITAGE

BACH'S ARTISTIC HERITAGE

A BRIEF investigation of the soil from which Bach's music grew may contribute toward the understanding of his art.[1]

His sacred compositions received their decisive impulse from the Protestant church song, the *chorale*, as it is commonly called. Its basic significance for the new forms of worship was recognized by Luther himself. He realized that the chorale enabled the congregation actively to participate in the church service, and that it could be used, moreover, for domestic devotions.

Collections of chorale melodies appeared during the early stages of the Reformation, and in 1524 Johann Walter (1490-1570), Luther's musical adviser, offered a series of polyphonic arrangements of hymn tunes intended for trained musicians. Henceforth the church songs were presented both in simple settings for amateurs, and in various vocal and instrumental arrangements for professional artists.

The earliest Protestant chorales were as a rule not newly created. In translating and paraphrasing Latin liturgical texts, Luther and his associates produced German poems of great fervor and expressiveness. They preserved the curious mixture of Latin and German words ('macaronic' texts) in certain ancient songs, like the Christmas carol *In dulci jubilo, nun singet und seid froh* (In sweet jubilation, let us sing and be gay), and they treasured the valuable pre-Reformation German church songs, such as the Easter hymn *Christ ist erstanden* (Christ has risen). The old melodies to these texts were also kept in

1. Among the numerous reference works dealing with this subject the following might be singled out: G. Adler, *Handbuch der Musikgeschichte*, Berlin, 1930, in particular the articles by A. Schering (Die evangelische Kirchenmusik) and W. Fischer (Instrumentalmusik); E. Bücken, *Handbuch der Musikwissenschaft*, Potsdam, 1929 ff., in particular the volume by R. Haas (Musik des Barocks); M. F. Bukofzer, *Music in the Baroque Era*, New York, 1947; D. J. Grout, *A History of Western Music*, New York, 1960; F. Blume, *Geschichte der evangelischen Kirchenmusik*, Kassel, 1965.

use, though minor or even major adaptations were customary.[1] Moreover folksongs were used in church, and famous art songs of a secular
nature were given new sacred texts. Since a basic contrast between
secular and sacred music did not exist during the Renaissance and
Baroque periods, the 'parody technique'[2] (joining a new text to an
earlier composition) was customarily used in the creation of chorales.
Luther expressed this with his usual directness when he stated that the
devil ought not to keep all the beautiful melodies to himself. Thus
Heinrich Isaac's farewell song *Inspruck ich muss dich lassen* (Inns-
bruck I must leave thee) was transformed into the hymn *O Welt ich
muss dich lassen* (O world, I must leave thee), and similarly H. L.
Hassler's love song *Mein G'müt ist mir verwirret* (My soul is per-
turbed) into the Passion chorale *Herzlich thut mich verlangen* (My
heart is ever yearning for blessed death's release).[3]

At the end of the 16th century and, in particular, in the 17th, an
increasing number of chorales were newly invented. Great poets like
Johann Rist (1607-67), Paul Gerhardt (1607-76), the mystics Philipp
Nicolai (1556-1608) and Johann Franck (1618-77); composers such
as Johann Crüger (1598-1662), Johann Rudolph Ahle (1625-73),
and Johann Georg Ebeling (1637-76) made significant contributions.[4]
The great chorales they produced around the time of the Thirty Years'
War (1618-48) carried on the fine traditions of the past and were in
quality hardly inferior to the magnificent hymns written in Luther's
own time. The horrors of this period of devastation may have been
conducive to the creation of deeply felt religious music.

The number of chorales vastly increased all through the 17th cen-

1. Bach harmonized the tunes of these two songs and presented them also in various organ arrangements. Cf. BWV 368, 608, 729, and 751; 276, 627, and 746.

2. The term is here used without the satirical connotation frequently encountered.
A composition resulting from a 'parody' is sometimes designated as 'contrafactum.'

3. The two chorale melodies appear, for instance, repeatedly in the St. Matthew
Passion. Cf. Nos 16 and 44; 21, 23, 53, 63, 72.

4. Bach used chorale texts by Rist in his cantatas 11, 20, 43, 55, 60, 78, 105, 175,
and the Christmas Oratorio; texts by Gerhardt in cantatas 32, 40, 65, 74, 92, 103,
108, 153, 159, 176, 183, 195, and the Christmas Oratorio; texts by Nicolai in his
cantatas 1, 36, 37, 49, 61, 140, and 172; texts by Franck in cantatas 56, 64, 81, 180,
and the Christmas Oratorio; melodies by Crüger in the St. Matthew Passion and in
cantatas 79, 180, 192, the motet 'Jesu meine Freude,' the chorale arrangements
BWV 654, 657, 759, 610, 713, etc.; Ahle's chorale 'Es ist genug' in cantata 60;
Ebeling's chorale 'Warum sollt ich' in BWV 422.

tury. A little collection published at Erfurt in 1524 contained only twenty-six tunes, the Leipzig song book of 1697, more than 5000. J. S. Bach owned a copy of this monumental work[1] in eight volumes, and his stupendous knowledge of the chorale literature may partly have been derived from it.

Even before the year 1700 the great period of chorale writing had reached its end. In their new creations the poets and composers of the 18th century showed marked preference for the sacred 'aria,' a song with a more intimate and subjective character. For their devotions, however, the congregations still used the great texts and melodies of the past. Yet the rhythmic variety distinguishing so many tunes in earlier times largely disappeared. To meet the congregations' wishes, the 'isometric' structure, using notes of equal length, became the rule for chorale melodies. The composers of the time had to accept this, and it is fascinating to observe the ingenuity displayed by Bach in compensating through harmonic and polyphonic devices for the lack of rhythmic life in the ancient melodies.

The *church cantata*, which played so vital a part in Bach's output, was a typical product of the Baroque period. It grew out of the 'sacred concerto' with German text, a 17th-century form in which the age's fascination with the use of rivaling sound groups found full expression. Soloists competed with each other and with the chorus, singers with instrumentalists. The treatment of the human voices was often brilliant and offered ample opportunity for the display of technical skill; moreover a highly expressive interpretation of the text was encouraged. The instruments were given important tasks too, and a purely instrumental introduction to a sacred concerto was not unusual. The number of performers varied; concertos were written as vocal solos with one or more instruments, as dialogues, as compositions for three or four solo voices with or without chorus. Composers like Samuel Scheidt (1587-1654), Franz Tunder (1614-67), and Johann Pachelbel (1653-1706) based their concertos on church songs; other masters like Heinrich Schütz (1585-1672) and Dietrich Buxtehude (1637-1707) showed preference for free settings of Biblical texts.

Toward the end of the 17th century the over-all size of the con-

---

1. It is enumerated in the specification of his estate reproduced in Spitta, II, p. 961.

certos increased, and the individual sections presented varying numbers of performers as well as changes in rhythm, tempo, and key. The
church cantata which was thus developed assumed a firm place in the
Lutheran service. It resounded before the sermon, the general content
of which it anticipated. If the cantata consisted of two sections, the
second was performed after the sermon.

In the first half of the 18th century, when rationalism was making
great strides, it was felt that forceful new elements should be introduced into the cantata to preserve its vitality. A growing number of
'madrigalian' verses, paraphrasing the venerable texts from the past,
joined the Bible text and church song. Sharp contrasts between
clearly separated musical numbers became the rule. At the same time
two important new forms were added, both borrowed from the secular
cantata and the opera. They were the secco recitative accompanied by
organ and bass only and the da capo aria whose first section was repeated at the end of the second part. Thus once more sacred art was
enriched through the inclusion of secular elements. An orthodox Lutheran minister, Erdmann Neumeister (1671-1756), published five
sets of cantata texts in the new style, and leading composers such as
Johann Philipp Krieger (1649-1725), Georg Philipp Telemann (1681-
1767), and Johann Sebastian Bach carried the new form of the church
cantata to its highest development.

The *motet* of the Renaissance and Baroque periods was primarily
written for a group of singers, not for individual vocal soloists. Musical
instruments often provided reinforcement or support for them, but independent instrumental parts were not used. During the 17th century
the Latin motet gradually lost ground in the Lutheran church. It became customary to perform in the services motets written by earlier
composers, and cantors were thus reluctant to contribute new works to
the antiquated form. The German motet, on the other hand, remained
in general use, and was sung on specific occasions such as weddings or
funeral services. It seemed particularly fitting to honor the memory of
a deceased person through the performance of a piece in this venerable
form. Predilection was shown for eight-part motets employing two
four-part choirs or a quartet of four soloists opposed to a four-part
chorus. Chorale verses and Bible texts were given preference as texts.
Usually they were alternately employed; at times, however, simul-

taneous utterances took place, with different voices presenting different texts.

The Italian *secular cantata* was slow in gaining admittance to Germany. Even after its acceptance composers considered it advisable to deepen the worldly content through the addition of sacred elements. Around the middle of the 17th century, profane and religious works were presented in the same collection,[1] and Johann Christoph Bach (1642-1703), Sebastian's eminent relative, wrote a wedding cantata *Meine Freundin du bist schön* (My love thou art fair) based on words from the Song of Solomon, to which he added a running commentary which displayed a very earthy sense of humor. The secular cantata also began to borrow from the German opera and *singspiel,* forms enjoying a far greater popularity at that time. The dividing line between the two genres became at times quite thin, and apparently some of the 18th-century cantatas could also be represented on the stage. Johann Sebastian's secular cantatas clearly reveal these varied features. The fact that many movements from his compositions designed for secular celebrations could be used again in oratorios and church cantatas shows how closely these two worlds were linked. The theatrical character of some of the works Bach wrote in honor of illustrious Saxonians can hardly be overlooked, and it is significant that several of these compositions[2] were entitled *dramma per musica,* a designation frequently applied to 18th-century operas.

The presentation of Christ's *Passion* during Holy Week may be traced back to the Middle Ages. It was customary to have the Latin text from the Vulgate rendered by three priests who chanted it mostly on a single note. A cleric with a low-pitched voice represented Jesus, a singer in the middle range, the Evangelist, while the remaining characters were entrusted to a priest with a high voice. Later a small chorus was added to convey the utterances of groups of people, such as the disciples or the Jewish crowds (the so-called *turba* scenes). In this form the Passion was taken over by the Protestant liturgy. Johann Walter, Luther's friend, composed a Passion in German from the Gospel of St. Matthew, using unaccompanied recitatives and quite simple choruses. This work of 1550 was frequently imitated, and even more

1. For instance in Johann Rist's *Galathea, Sabbatische Seelenlust* of 1644.
2. They include BWV 205, 207, 207a, 213, 214, 215.

than a century later Heinrich Schütz produced his three Passions of 1666, which still use plain recitation for the soloists and forgo any kind of instrumental accompaniment. In earlier oratorios Schütz had adopted a less conservative attitude. His *Historie der freudenreichen Geburt Gottes* (Story of the joyful birth of God) of 1664 displays great variety in the use of voices and instruments. The part of the Evangelist, written for tenor, is accompanied by figured bass, and his lively parlando resembles more the recitative of an opera than the solemn narration used in church. Schütz's *Die sieben Worte Jesu am Kreuze* (The Seven Words of Jesus on the Cross) presents the utterances of the Saviour in the manner of an arioso,[1] accompanying them with the poignant sounds of string instruments, a poetical idea used again in Bach's St. Matthew Passion.

An important innovation can be observed in a rather insignificant composition. The St. Matthew Passion of 1663 by Johann Sebastiani (1622-83) interrupts the Gospel text to insert Lutheran chorales. This idea was taken up in 1673 by Johann Theile (1646-1724), and found increasing use with later composers.

A radical break with the traditions of the past was effected early in the 18th century. Hamburg, the city where German opera flourished, produced a form of oratorio imbued with the spirit of the theater. The Bible text was replaced by poems describing in a highly expressive manner characters and action of the drama. In 1704 Reinhard Keiser's Passion was performed using a libretto by C. F. Hunold, known under the pen name of Menantes. Apart from real persons, it introduced symbolical characters such as the daughter of Zion, whom we also meet in Bach's St. Matthew Passion. The author relied on his own poetical gifts and dispensed with Bible text or traditional church songs. Less revolutionary was a libretto written in 1712 by the Hamburg city councillor, B. H. Brockes. The poems of his Passion were partly modeled after Biblical texts, and chorale stanzas were introduced into the libretto. This book, which was not as theatrical as Hunold's, and superior from a literary point of view, had a tremendous success. Handel[2] and Telemann set it to music in 1716, Johann Mattheson (1681-

1. An arioso is an expressive recitative approaching the character of an aria and accompanied by several instruments.
2. Bach owned a copy of Handel's composition.

1764), two years later, and even Bach borrowed from the text for his St. John Passion.

Moreover, Bach's own artistic ideas were strengthened by the uninhibited directness in the interpretation of poetical situations which he encountered in these works, their boldly realistic choruses, and the gently contemplative arias, and these bore magnificent fruit in the works he contributed in this field.

In the Lutheran liturgical service the Latin Proper of the *Mass*, the section which changes from week to week according to the church calendar, was gradually replaced by German songs and cantatas. A different situation prevailed regarding the Ordinary, the section of the Mass which remained unchanged throughout the year. During the 16th century, musical settings of most of the Latin Ordinary were not infrequently contributed by Lutheran cantors. The Credo, however, was at times left out and replaced by a German song. Moreover in some of the Masses fragments of German texts were intermingled with the traditional Latin words, and Protestant chorale tunes introduced in the music.[1] A related procedure may be observed in the employment of the Latin Magnificat (Mary's song of praise), with interspersed German carols, at the Christmas Vespers service.

Gradually the Lutheran service became more and more uniformly German, though for specific festive occasions Latin texts remained in use. In particular the Latin 'Missa' or 'Missa brevis' (short Mass consisting of Kyrie and Gloria only) as well as the 'Sanctus,' reserved for the most solemn celebrations, were still employed. Cities like Nuremberg and Leipzig, where orthodox religious thinking prevailed, carried over this tradition into the 18th century.

Bach considered it a matter of course to adopt the ideas held in Leipzig. On the other hand he was also responsive to the trends toward Italian music predominant in nearby Dresden. He once decided to compose the entire Latin Ordinary of the Mass in the form of the 'Neapolitan Cantata Mass' cultivated at the Elector's Court. Thus he divided the liturgical text into brief sections shaped, alternatingly, as arias, duets, and choruses.

1. The Bachs seemed particularly fond of such a mixture. It can be observed in a Gloria by Johann Nicolaus Bach (1669-1753), a Kyrie and Gloria by Johann Ernst Bach (1722-77), and in the Kyrie of Sebastian's Mass in F (BWV 233).

The combination and fusion of various components, which are characteristic of Bach's art, manifest themselves with particular strength in his *music for the organ*. Italian and Dutch; north German, central German and south German; vocal and instrumental; Catholic and Protestant sources fed the majestic river of the Thomas Cantor's production for the 'king of instruments.'

Organ works of the 18th century can be divided into two groups: compositions based on a preconceived cantus and freely invented pieces. They both go back to forms developed before the beginning of the Baroque period. The freely composed works were derived from 16th-century Italian pieces which antedate the division of keyboard compositions into works for organ and for stringed claviers.

The *ricercar* was a fugue-like (cf. p. 118 f.) piece in several sections shaped after the sacred vocal motet of the Renaissance. Its name meant to 'search again,' thus referring to the polyphonic exploitation of themes customary in this form. Ricercars were based on brief themes in long note values bearing a vocal character. The great Venetian masters Giovanni Gabrieli (1557-1612) and Claudio Merulo (1533-1604) contributed such ricarcars, consisting of a chain of brief fugues introducing several musical subjects with an occasional reappearance of the initial one. Girolamo Frescobaldi (1583-1643), organist at St. Peter's in Rome, showed preference for another type, which made use of the variation technique. This variation ricercar employed a single theme which was altered rhythmically and melodically in the successive sections.

Closely related to the ricercar was the 16th-century keyboard *canzona*, a form derived from the secular vocal chanson. Its themes were somewhat lighter and gayer in character than those of the ricercar, and approached the instrumental idiom. The succession of polyphonic sections, each based on a new idea, was, however, similar to that of the ricercar. Gabrieli and Merulo were among the early authors of such canzonas. Frescobaldi, on the other hand, contributed variation canzonas in which—just as in his ricercars—a single subject was transformed in each successive section.

Jan Pieterszoon Sweelinck (1562-1621), the famous Amsterdam organist and teacher, wrote *fantasias* using elements of both ricercar and canzona. In these works a single main idea was used, to which changing countermelodies were added in successive sections. Swee-linck favored a monumental three-part form and themes of a typical and objective character.

Frescobaldi and Sweelinck exercised strongest influence on the German and Austrian organ music of the 17th century. Thus Johann Jakob Froberger (1616-67), court organist in Vienna, and a pupil of Frescobaldi, wrote variation ricercars and variation canzonas. Samuel Scheidt, on the other hand, who studied with Sweelinck and later became *director musices* in Halle, wrote pieces in the style of his teacher's fantasias. These imposing works making ample use of all devices of the polyphonic style, were entitled by their author *Fuge*, a designation widely used in Germany for works of a similar character.

Unlike the ricercar and canzona, which are derived from vocal forms, the *toccata* ('touch piece') is an improvisatory composition of instrumental origin. Andrea Gabrieli (1510-86) of Venice wrote a number of toccatas presenting chords, brief imitative sections, trills, and runs, of increasing rhythmic momentum, allotted to both hands. Claudio Merulo inserted ricercar-like sections separated by episodes between the improvisatory passages of his toccatas, thus imparting greater solidity to the form. Italian composers at the turn of the century, among them Frescobaldi, showed preference for the Gabrieli type. Sweelinck, on the other hand, made contributions to both the Gabrieli and the Merulo structures; his works of the second group display the elaboration of characteristic motives in the improvisatory sections, and fugue-like pieces in the center. Most Central European composers followed the latter trend. The Austrian Froberger wrote toccatas with one or more interspersed fugal sections usually displaying thematic interrelations between the fugal and the improvisatory sections.

During the second half of the 17th century, Germany assumed uncontested leadership in the field of organ music. This was partly due to the German propensity for the polyphonic style, and partly to the need for independent organ music in the Lutheran service, which far exceeded the demands made upon the instrument in the Catholic or the Calvinist churches. Among the great north German composers who exercised a direct influence on Bach were Matthias Weckmann (1619-74) and Jan Adams Reinken (1623-1722) in Hamburg, Dietrich Buxtehude (1637-1707) in Lübeck, and Georg Böhm (1661-1733) in

Lüneburg. In central Germany resided Johann Kuhnau (1660-1722), Bach's predecessor as Thomas Cantor in Leipzig, and Johann Pachelbel (1653-1706), with whom Sebastian's eldest brother and teacher studied. Pachelbel, who held positions in Vienna, Nuremberg, Eisenach, and Erfurt, thus formed a link between Italian-influenced southern Germany and the area occupied by the Bach musicians.

These composers and others of the time were responsible for transforming step by step the various polyphonic forms into the 18th-century fugue. Its main basis was the slowly emerging *equally-tempered system* of tuning keyboard instruments, which enabled performers freely to modulate within their fugues. An important document of this process was contributed by a German organist, Andreas Werckmeister (1645-1706), who published in 1686-87 a treatise entitled 'Musical Temperament or . . . mathematical instruction how to produce a well-tempered intonation on the clavier.' In this work the author advocated an improved method of tuning for all keyboard instruments. The earlier 'mean-tone system,' with its slightly flatted fifths, was satisfactory only as long as few sharps and flats were employed. Keys with many accidentals could not be used, and the possibilities of modulation were rather limited. In the 'equal temperament' of A. Werckmeister, the restrictions on the use of keys with many accidentals or on free modulations no longer existed. The octave was artificially divided into 12 half-tones which were exactly alike. Their sounds, though acoustically not quite correct, were acceptable. Each of the notes could serve as a tonic, and traffic between the keys presented no difficulties.

The 'well-tempered system' made both Sweelinck's introduction of new countersubjects and Frescobaldi's variations of the main subject unnecessary. Diversity provided in earlier compositions through thematic changes could be achieved in 18th-century fugues by modulatory alterations. The monothematic fugue based on the principle of free key changes came into its own.

Since fugues played a fundamental part in Bach's music, some of their characteristic features will be discussed here. A *fugue* is a contrapuntal composition with a fixed number of independent parts (voices). Fugues with three or four voices are most common, but compositions with two, five, or even six parts also occur. The fugue theme will usually start with the tonic or the dominant (the first or fifth note) and will avoid modulations so as to firmly establish the fugue's tonality. This 'subject'—as it is commonly called—is presented at the outset by one of the voices without any accompaniment. Then a second voice will state the same theme transposed a fifth up (or a fourth down). This altered entrance is known as 'answer.' The transposition of all the notes might be quite literal, the result being known as a 'real answer.' If, however, the fifth note of the scale appears near the beginning of the subject, the composer might prefer to transpose this particular note only a fourth up. Such a modification which is used to avoid a modulation at this early stage results in a 'tonal answer' of the fugue theme. While the second voice presents the answer, the first voice offers a rhythmically contrasting counterpoint. (Should this counterpoint appear frequently throughout the fugue, it might assume the significance of a 'counter subject'). Gradually, each of the fugue's voices enters, either with the subject or with the answer. Often there is an additional entrance to create the illusion of a larger number of voices. Thus the theme might be heard four times in a three-part fugue, five times in a four-part fugue, before the composition's first section, its 'exposition,' is concluded. (A miniature fugue, consisting of an exposition only, is often called a 'fugato.')

The middle section introduces modulations to related keys while simultaneously exploring the various contrapuntal possibilities of the theme. It may be introduced in 'augmentation' (the length of the notes increased) or 'diminution' (the length of the notes reduced), in 'inversion' or 'contrary motion' (every interval proceeding in a direction opposite to the model) or in 'retrograde motion' (the melody played backwards). There may be 'strettos' (overlapping entrances of the theme) and various combinations of all these devices. On the other hand the composers often interpolate passages which do not contain the subject and may only be loosely connected with it. These insertions, which are known as 'episodes,' separate the contrapuntal developments of the fugue theme. At the end the fugue returns to the initial key, and the composers like to achieve at this point a particularly striking contrapuntal effect.

Usually a fugue is based on a single main theme. There are also 'double fugues,' however, where two ideas are developed. They might be presented together, right from the start, or the second theme might make a later appearance to be eventually combined with the initial subject. Similarly compositions with three or four themes are known as 'triple fugues' or 'quadruple fugues.'

Related to the fugue is the *canon* known several centuries before Bach's time. This is a polyphonic composition in which one voice is strictly imitated by one or more other voices entering subsequently. The imitating voices come in at a certain distance from the original melody (one eighth note, or one measure, or several measures, etc.); they begin at the pitch of the first voice or at a certain interval from it (canon in unison, of the third, or fourth, or fifth, etc.). The imitating voices might present the original notes augmented, or diminished, or inverted or in retrograde motion. At times an accompanying voice is added which does not participate in the imitation. A great variety of canonic compositions can be found among Bach's works.

The gradual evolution of the late Baroque fugue left its imprint also on the development of the toccata. Particularly exciting were the large-scale works contributed to the genre by north German composers, headed by Dietrich Buxtehude. With their sharp contrasts between the individual sections, their dramatic recitatives borrowed from vocal compositions, and their outbursts of passion, they belong to the most subjective and fantastic utterances to be found in Baroque music. Fugue-like central sections were gradually inserted into this awe-inspiring form. It is interesting to observe that the polyphonic core in these pieces changed its structure in conformity with the alterations noticeable in the independent fugue forms of the period.

An apparently insignificant, though in the long run most important, development took place on Austrian soil. In the modest three-part toccata of Viennese composers the improvisatory final section degenerated and eventually disappeared altogether. At the same time the connection between the initial improvisatory section and the central fugal one was completely severed. The former ended with a full cadence, the latter started with a new theme, unrelated to the ideas of the first section. Thus around the year 1700 there appeared the new instrumental pair soon to be known as 'Prelude and Fugue.'

Bach's output in the free forms of organ music is not confined to the main types discussed here. In his *Passacaglia* he employed a kind of composition considered as old-fashioned in his time. The Munich organist Johann Kaspar Kerll (1627-93) and Buxtehude had written such variations on a recurring bass theme, but among Bach's contemporaries the form was little used.

In his *sonatas* for organ Bach transplanted the Trio Sonata for two melody instruments and bass (cf. p. 126) to the keyboard instrument. A form which seemed to have lost much of its vitality was successfully used here to infuse new blood into the output for the organ.

The development of *compositions based on a cantus firmus* is closely related to that of the free forms. They are mostly intended for liturgical use, and therefore meant for the organ. Both in quantity and quality the contributions of Protestant central and northern Germany are far more significant than those of Catholic Italy, Austria, or southern Germany. Once more Sweelinck showed the way to German organists. His arrangements display the favorite form of the time, the cycle of variations. The cantus firmus appears in long notes which are unchanged in each section. The set of variations begins with a bicinium (a composition in two voices), and the number of voices is gradually built up to three or four in the final section. The pupils of the 'organist maker,' as Sweelinck was often called, foremost among them S. Scheidt, followed their teacher's model. Scheidt's famous *Tabulatura nova* of 1624 contained numerous sets of chorale variations in which the cantus firmus was embedded in changing rhythmic patterns, the chorale melody being frequently entrusted to a two-foot or four-foot stop of the pedal.

The composers of the second half of the 17th century still cultivated such sets of variations, *chorale partitas* as they were usually called, clearly separating the individual sections through the insertion of double bars. In these partitas, which were also strongly indebted to vocal and instrumental forms of secular music, the number of variations frequently corresponded to the number of stanzas in the text. North German composers like Buxtehude added color to their compositions by altering the manner of variation within individual sections. Böhm, in Lüneburg, enriched the organ idiom through the introduction of ornaments and figurations borrowed from French clavier music. He liked to include bicinia in which the chorale melody was supported by the constantly recurring phrases of a ground bass, thus providing greater solidity to the form.

Central and north German composers also favored the polyphonic *chorale fantasia,* in which each phrase of the chorale melody was subjected to a different kind of contrapuntal treatment. The latter endowed the form with an improvisatory and brilliant character similar to that displayed in their free organ compositions.

The future did not belong to such outsize forms, however, but rather to the simpler and shorter *chorale preludes* played by the organist before the congregation intoned the hymn tune. It consisted of a single movement only, displaying at times a certain resemblance to a variation in a chorale partita or a section in a chorale fantasia. Sebastian's cousin once removed, J. Christoph Bach (1642-1703), used brief *chorale fughettas,* which begin with a fugato over the first phrase of the hymn tune and continue with the rest of the chorale in a more homophonic setting. Occasionally he worked with selected lines of the hymn tune only, or confined himself to the polyphonic elaboration of the chorale's initial phrase. Of greater significance than these patterns created under the influence of similar works by Pachelbel were the *cantus firmus chorale arrangements.* Here the hymn tune appeared in its entirety in the soprano or occasionally in the bass; rarely in one of the middle parts. The individual phrases were usually preceded and separated by short fugal sections based on the ensuing chorale line. These arrangements show some affinity to the vocal motet and are often referred to as *chorale motets.* Buxtehude preferred to ornament the cantus firmus in a strongly meaningful manner, and Böhm used French *agréments* in his arrangements.

In these works a growing subjectivity, an increasing concern with content and imagery of the text is becoming apparent. The dawn of programmatic aims might be observed, a tendency that achieved its consummation in the works of the Thomas Cantor.

Bach's predecessors in the field of *clavier music* are largely the men who also influenced his organ compositions, and some of the same forms are here employed. Nevertheless a number of new developments led to significant results of a different nature. J. Kuhnau transplanted the sonata for several instruments to the clavier. His work in this genre served as a direct model for a sonata by young Bach, and likewise as a starting point for the Cöthen conductor's sinfonias. Similarly short preludes by Kuhnau and by Johann Kaspar Ferdinand Fischer (1665?-1746) may have been models for some of Bach's small-sized clavier studies and for his two-part inventions.

During the Weimar years Bach became an ardent disciple of Italian composers. In particular concertos by the Venetian violinist Antonio Vivaldi (1678?-1741) and by other masters pursuing similar goals deeply impressed the German composer. Bach employed Vivaldi's concerto form (cf. p. 128) not only in his own concertos but also in his keyboard compositions, including some fugues where the entrances of the theme take the place of tutti, the episodes those of soli.

The development of the 'equally-tempered' system exercised a particularly strong influence on clavier composition. J. P. Treiber published in 1702 and 1704 two compositions which, according to his claim, employed 'all the keys and chords.' Of greater importance was J. K. F. Fischer's *Adriadne Musica . . . per XX Praeludia, totidem Fugas* (1710?) in which the composer, with the aid of the 'Ariadne thread' of modulation, guided his hearers through the labyrinth of the keys. In 1719 J. Mattheson presented in his *Exemplarische Organistenprobe* '24 easy and as many somewhat more difficult examples in all the keys,' and in 1722, the year of Bach's 'Well-tempered Clavier,' Friedrich Suppig, an organist in Dresden, wrote *Labyrinthus Musicus,* a 'fantasy through all the keys, 12 major and 12 minor.'[1]

Bach's 'Well-tempered Clavier I,' and, in particular, his second collection of 24 preludes and fugues for keyboard instruments, mark the last great flowering of prelude and fugue for clavier. He also made the decisive, final contribution to another form of keyboard music for domestic use, the *suite of dances.* A development of two centuries was crowned and concluded by the compositions Bach offered in this field.

The Renaissance period favored the combination of two related dances, the first in even, the second in triple time. As early as the 16th century this 'basic pair' was enlarged to three and, occasionally, even four dances. After 1600, French composers refined various types of dances and arranged them in loosely built collections. These *ordres* consisted of up to twenty, and even more, pieces, including several specimens of the same dance type, such as five allemandes, eleven

1. B. C. Weber's 'Well-tempered Clavier' with the forged date 1689 was not a model for Bach's work, merely a later imitation of it, probably written around 1750.

courantes, and four sarabandes, all in the same key. The German keyboard suite, on the other hand, included a small number of carefully selected pieces, each differing in character from the rest. To J. J. Froberger belongs the credit of establishing the standard sequence of four dances which served as a basis for the clavier suite of later generations. The first printed edition issued after the composer's death contained dance suites in this order: allemande–courante–sarabande–gigue. While these dances were no longer used in the ballroom, they provided delightful material for domestic music-making.

Composers of the 18th century liked enlarging this pattern. They often preceded the four main dances by an introductory movement without dance character, an innovation first developed in Italy. Moreover various 'optional dances,' originally cultivated at the French court, could be included. The minuets, bourrées, or gavottes thus added adopted a lighter mood and were closer to actual dance patterns than the highly stylized four main dances. These *Galanterien*, as the Germans liked to call them, found their place near the end of the suite, usually before the gigue.

The following are typical forms of the most frequently used dances:

THE BASIC DANCES:

Allemande: A 'German dance' in 4/4 time, with a brief upbeat and using a moderate, flowing motion. In the suite it often has the character of a prelude.

Courante: A somewhat faster French dance alternating between 6/4 and 3/2 rhythms. The Italian *corrente,* which occasionally takes its place, is a considerably livelier dance in 3/4 or 3/8 time.

Sarabande: Supposedly of Spanish-Oriental origin, the sarabande lost its vivid character to become the suite's slow and stately middle movement. It is usually in 3/2 time, with accents on the second beat.

Gigue: Probably of English origin, it uses dotted rhythms or a time signature which can be divided by three (12/8, 6/8, 3/8, 3/4). Simple fugal elaboration is customary at the outset of each part, and the second section often starts with the inversion of the first part's beginning.

THE OPTIONAL DANCES:

Minuet: A graceful, moderately fast dance in 3/4 time.

Gavotte: A moderately fast dance in ₵ time with an upbeat of two quarter notes.

Bourrée: A quick dance in ₵ time with an upbeat of a quarter note.

Passepied: A spirited piece in 3/8 or 6/8 time.

Air: A dance deviating from the established forms, or a composition without direct dance character.

Infrequently used are the *Loure,* a moderately fast dance with dotted notes in 6/4 time, the *Anglaise,* a brisk dance in ₵ time, and the *Polonaise* in moderate 3/4 time.

These optional dances often appear in pairs, with the first piece repeated after the presentation of the contrasting second one. This second piece is frequently designated as 'trio,' a remnant from the time when such compositions were written in three voices and played by three instruments. In the 18th and 19th centuries, however, the origin of this designation was usually ignored, and trios were written for any number of voices. While all the dances of a suite were in the same key, the trio sometimes provided an exception, as it adopted the parallel key in the opposite mode (A minor in an A major suite, G major in a G minor suite, etc.). A simple variation following a dance was designated as 'double.'

The main dances and the optional dances are constructed along similar lines. They are in two-part form with repeat signs at the end of each section. The first section modulates from the tonic to the dominant (in pieces in the minor mode the modulation occasionally reaches the relative major); the second returns from the dominant (or the relative major) over a related key to the tonic. The beginnings of the two sections usually resemble each other, the second often representing a transposition of the first. At times the second section is extended, and a cadence may subdivide it; such an enlarged two-part form approaches the features of a three-part form.

Introductory pieces are mostly extended compositions which shun dance rhythms. Neither in character nor in form do they follow any strict rule. Preludes, inventions, overtures, sinfonias, toccatas, concerto movements, etc. may be used for such purposes, whereby the names given to individual pieces by the composer often fail to convey the movement's true character.

Bach's *works for string and wind instruments* are based on favorite forms of the Baroque period. The 'Trio sonata' for two melody instruments and thorough bass had achieved a wide circulation since Salomone Rossi ('Il Ebreo') published 1607 the first work of this kind, scored for two violins and basso continuo. Italian masters and, before long, French, German and English composers contributed to the genre, offering works for violins, flutes, and various combinations of soprano instruments, with the support of the thorough bass. As a rule two persons presented the parts of the melody instruments and, in addition, one or two players the part of the thorough bass (also designated as figured bass or continuo). A plucked instrument (lute or theorbo) or a keyboard instrument (harpsichord or organ) together with a deep string or wind instrument were needed for the realization of the continuo. These players would perform the bass and improvise filling middle parts not directly prescribed by the composer. A low-pitched melody instrument, like the violoncello, bassoon, or even trombone, might further emphasize the bass line.

A reduction in the number of performers was attempted at an early date. In the absence of one of the two soprano instruments, the keyboard player added to his former duties the responsibility for the performance of one of the melodic lines. The subterfugue of earlier generations turned into a musical form of the highest significance for Bach. He systematically explored all the ramifications of the trio sonata executed by two performers or even just one (cf. p. 238).

The so-called 'solo sonata' for a single melody instrument and thorough bass was established soon after the trio sonata. In 1617 Biagio Marini included in his *Affetti Musicali* a sonata for violin and continuo, and a vast production in this field followed. Some of the composers went so far as to drop the supporting bass and to cultivate the true solo for unaccompanied violin. German masters in particular were attracted by this rather demanding form of composition. Thomas Baltzar (c. 1630-63), Heinrich Franz Biber (1644-1704), Georg Philipp Telemann (1681-1767) and Johann Georg Pisendel (1687-1755) belong to the artists active in this field. Bach likewise showed preference for the use of the unaccompanied violin. He also wrote solos for flute alone and for cello alone. Domenico Gabrielli's (1659-90) *Ricercari per violoncello solo* were among the significant compositions leading to the Cöthen conductor's works for the baritone instrument.

Bach's compositions for small or large groups of string and wind instruments are making wide use of the *sonata da chiesa* and its derivatives. As the name implies, the 'church sonata' (which grew out of the canzona for instrumental ensembles) was of Italian origin and employed in ecclesiastical services. In 1681 the great Arcangelo Corelli (1653-1713) published a set of 12 Sonate da chiesa, inspiring an extensive number of composers to write similar works. Basically the 'church sonata' consisted of the following four movements, although minor deviations occurred:

1. slow (homophonic or imitative)
2. fast (including a modest amount of fugal elaboration)
3. slow (homophonic, occasionally dance-like, often in triple rhythm and in the relative key)
4. fast (homophonic, occasionally dance-like; at times using a modest amount of fugal elaboration).

The Sonata da chiesa found such general acclaim that it was even used as an instrumental introduction to Italian operas. Alessandro Scarlatti (1660-1725), however, simplified the form for its use in the theater. He omitted the introductory slow movement and fashioned the first fast movement as a homophonic composition. The resulting Neapolitan *Sinfonia* was increasingly employed and proved of utmost significance for the development of 18th-century instrumental music. Its use was by no means confined to the theater. In orchestral and even in chamber music it likewise played an important part.

Jean-Baptiste Lully (1632-87), the founder of the French opera, proceeded along somewhat different lines. For the introductions to his operas he used the first two or three movements of the Sonata da chiesa. He started out with a 'Lentement,' usually in dotted rhythms, favoring trills and runs. There followed a fast section ('Vite' or 'Gay') with some loosely constructed fugal elaboration, mostly at the beginning. Frequently a second slow section ensued which was thematically related to the first Lentement. In Austria and Germany it became the custom to use *French overtures* as an introduction to a free succession of orchestral dances. The sequence of dances and short character pieces was kept independent of the strict arrangement used in the clavier suites, and the third section of the overture—if used at all—was often freed of its thematic reliance on the beginning. Composers like Georg

Muffat (1653-1704), Johann Philipp Krieger (1649-1725), Johann Joseph Fux (1660-1741), J. K. F. Fischer and the versatile G. P. Telemann wrote works of this kind.

J. S. Bach made use of each of these structural types. In his chamber music he employed the sonata da chiesa and sinfonia. Into his orchestral music he introduced the French overture with following suite and also included significant elements of the concerto. As the instrumental concerto occupied a central position within Bach's output, some of the main phases of its development ought to be outlined.

Solistic passages were occasionally inserted into instrumental canzonas in Italy during the first half of the 17th century. However, a systematic use of the concerto idea did not occur before the last quarter. Gradually three different forms developed. In the *concerto-symphony* (a term coined by A. Schering), groups of different instruments compete with each other, but there are no actual soloists. Composers of the Bologna school, like Giovanni Maria Bononcini (1642-78) and Giuseppe Torelli (1658-1709), cultivated this type. Of greater significance was the *concerto grosso,* in which a group of three or four soloists, the *concertino,* was opposed to a larger ensemble of instruments, the *ripieni* or *concerto grosso.* In the important *tutti* sections soloists and ripienists joined forces. Composers like A. Corelli, G. Muffat and, most of all, A. Vivaldi wrote works of this kind. The 'solo concerto' employed one principal instrument. This was the form to which the future was to belong, but during the Baroque period its development was only starting. Tommaso Albinoni (1671-1750), G. Torelli, and again A. Vivaldi belong to the leading composers of such concertos.

Among these composers, Vivaldi exercised the most powerful influence upon Bach. His style was animated, strongly rhythmical, and basically homophonic. During the first decade of the 18th century Vivaldi developed an architectonic structure of great solidity and beauty and adopted the tempo sequence fast-slow-fast of the Italian sinfonia. The first movement used a rondo-like arrangement of the musical material. It started and ended with a substantial tutti in the tonic key, which provided a solid foundation to the formal construction. Fragments of the tutti sections, mostly in related keys, were distributed over the whole movement, while contrasting episodes, in which the soloists were accompanied by only a few instruments, connected the entrances of the tutti. The graceful garlands of these solos provided the necessary modulations and frequently introduced new thematic material. This structural arrangement could also appear in the remaining two movements, but, as a rule, Vivaldi preferred a simpler construction or the use of ostinato basses for the slow movement, and a dance-like piece for the finale.

Bach made widest use of the Italian concerto form and, in particular, of the formal patterns developed by Vivaldi. For the German composer the rondo-like structure of Vivaldi's movements assumed a significance comparable to that of the sonata form in the works of Haydn and Mozart. But Bach was never satisfied simply to copy a model. He constantly experimented, trying out new combinations, allowing the various structural types to intermingle and to cross-fertilize each other. Thus, out of formal ideas provided by others, new artistic conceptions grew which bore the imprint of his own creative personality.

INTRODUCTION

IF an attempt were made to characterize the art of Johann Sebastian Bach in a single word, the word would have to be 'unification.' The most heterogeneous elements were welded together by him into a new entity, completely coherent in character.

Sebastian Bach was the greatest force in the unification of various regional and national styles. The sources of his art can be found in central, northern, and southern Germany alike. Of equal importance in the development of his style were the impulses his music received from the works of Italian and French composers. And Bach was almost as much indebted to Catholic composers as he was to the masters of his own faith. Out of a soil nurtured by the most diversified elements grew the gigantic structure of Sebastian's personal idiom.

Bach acted as a typically Baroque composer in recognizing no fundamental difference between sacred and secular music, nor even between vocal and instrumental composition. Nothing gave him greater joy than experimenting in the various media. He applied devices of the keyboard style to music for strings alone, and the technique of the violin to clavier compositions. Elements of the Italian concerto may be found in almost every form of his music, including the cantata. Bach constantly arranged and improved compositions by others or by himself, transforming orchestral works into clavier compositions, instrumental into vocal music, secular into sacred, and German into Latin church works. He retained something of the medieval conception in which music was undivided, and a tune could be sung or played, used for a dance round the village tree or for the praise of the Lord in church.

This attitude manifests itself with particular clarity in Bach's employment of chorale melodies. He never tired of presenting the time-honored tunes in new guises. He offered them in exquisite four-part

133

harmonizations,[1] in various types of canons, as a cantus firmus in plain, unadorned form, or surrounded with artful ornaments. These various types appeared in his vocal works and likewise in the organ chorales, without any change in the basic approach. The musical interpretation of the chorale text, one of the principal aims of his vocal compositions, was carried out with equal zeal in the instrumental arrangements. It is characteristic that near the end of his life Bach entrusted his pupil Schübler with the printing of various organ chorales which had originally appeared as vocal numbers in his cantatas. Throughout his work, voices and instruments dealt on equal terms with the hallowed melodies.

Bach's inexhaustible imagination created an immense variety of architectural forms. No two of his inventions, fugues, or cantatas, show exactly the same construction. Nevertheless there is a basic feature that recurs again and again both in his vocal and instrumental compositions. Bach was deeply concerned with symmetrical formal constructions built round a center with corresponding sections on each side. In their simplest version they are represented by the da capo form *a b a*, so often used by Bach; but also more complicated arrangements such as *a b c b a* or *a b c d c b a* are not unusual. The deeply religious composer may have found satisfaction in the thought that works in such a form have their visual equivalents in the structure of a cross, with two corresponding sidearms emerging from a middle beam, or in that of a church, with side transepts flanking a central nave.[2] Such correlations seemed quite natural to Baroque artists, and Bach was in this respect a true son of his time.

1. These harmonizations form not only part of the larger works we know. Bach seems to have written many additional chorale settings for four voices. Between 1784 and 1787 C. P. E. Bach and J. P. Kirnberger published four volumes of *J.S.B.s vierstimmige Choralgesänge* comprising 371 harmonizations, of which 162 only can be traced to larger Bach works such as cantatas, passions, oratorios, etc. If a few duplications are disregarded, the collection is found to contain no less than 186 magnificent arrangements (BWV 253-438) whose origin is unknown. They may have appeared in vocal works lost today, but so far no proof of this has been found. Even at a time when the work of Bach was very little known, these outstanding settings were greatly admired as examples of the master's incomparable art of harmonization and his impeccable scoring for four independent voices. Valuable editions of this collection with English text were presented by H. S. Drinker (Merion, Penna., 1944) and C. S. Terry (2nd ed. London, 1964).

2. The term 'chiastic' is occasionally used to designate these symmetric formal arrangements.

This accounts also for the tremendous importance which pictorial-ism assumed in Bach's vocabulary, as it did in that of his contempo-raries. High and low, long and short, bright and dark, were given in his music expressions typical of this era. From pictorialism Bach pro-ceeded to symbolism,[1] in which intellectual conceptions take the place of sensory impressions. In the cantata No. 12 *Weinen, Klagen,* for in-stance, the bass sings 'I follow Jesus Christ.' The *imitatio Christi* is expressed through strict imitation of the vocal melody in the string parts. Moreover, this tune is derived from the chorale melody 'What God does, is with reason done.' Thus Bach uses symbolism here in two different ways within the narrow space of two measures.

Of particular importance is the number symbolism, such as the use of an unlucky number in the 13 variations of the *Crucifixus* in the Mass in B minor. Moreover, substituting numbers for the letters of the alphabet was a common practice of the time, and one from which Bach derived great satisfaction. 14, for instance, is the number symbolizing Bach (cf. p. 94); inverted it turns into 41, which stands for J. S. Bach, as J is the ninth, S the eighteenth letter and 9 plus 18 plus 14 makes 41. In Bach's very last chorale arrangement this symbolic method is significantly used (cf. p. 256).

The composer's profound intellectualism made him adopt poly-phony as his favorite means of expression, and in this respect his work marks the summit of a magnificent development through several cen-turies. But while Bach, in his contrapuntal style, was firmly linked to the past, the harmonic idiom he employed was of a most progressive nature, opening up new realms of musical expression, to which even 19th-century harmony did not find much to add. No other composer succeeded in bringing polyphony and harmony to so complete a fusion. Bach's most intricate contrapuntal creations are always conceived on a strictly harmonic basis, while in his simple harmonizations of the chorale, the linear progression of the individual voices is superb. Ver-tical and horizontal elaboration are completely balanced and equally breathtaking.

The monolithic quality which we are apt to attribute to the music of Johann Sebastian Bach does not really exist. He was a genius, but also a very human person whose output changed and developed. He

1. Cf. A. Schering, *Das Symbol in der Musik,* Leipzig, 1941, and K. Geiringer, *Symbolism in the Music of Bach,* Washington, D.C., 1955.

never stood still, but he did not always proceed in the same direction. Bach liked to reverse his steps, and sharp reactions to the immediate past were not unusual with him. In his early thirties he had a different approach to music than in his late thirties. When he was forty-five his work took on an unexpected turn, to be reversed again as he was approaching his sixtieth year.

Bach's *first creative period*,[1] the period of youth, lasted up to his twenty-third year, that is, up to 1708. It was the time of his apprenticeship, including the important two appointments in Arnstadt and Mühlhausen. Bach eagerly absorbed the music of his contemporaries and predecessors by playing it, listening to it, and, above all, copying it. The number of works of others which he wrote down is substantial indeed. It comprises compositions by members of his own family and by masters from different countries adhering to different denominations. Like the young Mozart, he found himself by imitating others. In this first period the content of a work seemed of greater interest and importance to the composer than the form in which it was cast. The works are rich in ideas, imbued with ardent fervor and a tender, personal way of expression; they are colorful, and their emotional language is often of elemental strength. At the same time their technical immaturity is obvious. With some notable exceptions, they are overlong, vague in their formal construction, uncertain in their harmonic and polyphonic texture. It was a period of experimentation in which young Sebastian tried his hand at various types of composition, such as toccatas, capriccios, preludes and fugues, chorale preludes, and cantatas.

Bach's *second creative period*, the transition from youth to maturity, was spent in Weimar from his twenty-third to his thirty-second year, thus from 1708 to 1717. The nine years he served at the court of the Duke of Weimar were of supreme significance for Bach. Here he became acquainted with the simple beauty and plastic clarity of Italian music. He adapted concertos by Italian musicians for clavier or organ, and occasionally he used Italian themes as subjects for his own fugues. The magnificent logic, the superb balance of his works, is partly due to this powerful experience. In Weimar, Bach saw a primary goal of his

1. Cf. W. Gurlitt, *J. S. Bach*, Kassel, 1943. Here Bach's output is divided in a somewhat different manner.

art in the glorification of the Lord. He wrote a number of church cantatas intended for the Lutheran service. They combine elements of the sacred concerto and the Italian opera, thus presenting formal aspects later to be found in Bach's mature cantatas. However, their lyric warmth and subjective idiom point to an affinity with earlier works. Most of all he devoted his energy to the instrument that more than any other was meant for divine worship. In Weimar he developed into a magnificent organ player and the greatest organ composer of all times. The majority of his works for this instrument was completed, or at least conceived, in the little Saxonian duchy. Some of these organ works still display youthful exuberance and unbridled imagination; most of them reveal, however, the newly acquired mastery of contrapuntal form and well-balanced architecture.

A radical change in Bach's life and in his productivity occurred sooner than could have been expected. Suddenly Bach seemed unable to put up with the narrowness and restrictions at the small court. He felt he had to leave Weimar, or he would suffocate. And one of his greatest sets of compositions, the *Orgel-Büchlein* (Little Organ Book), remained a torso, for Bach deserted not only Weimar but his work in the field of sacred music.

In 1717, at the age of thirty-two, he became conductor in charge of all chamber music at the court of Cöthen. This appointment marked the beginning of his *third creative period* and, simultaneously, that of his artistic maturity. Bach's output in the field of secular music reached a climax in Cöthen. The organ was almost forgotten; harpsichord and clavichord were the keyboard instruments to which he turned. Organistic features can be found in his compositions for unaccompanied violin and cello, but true organ works were all but absent from his output. He wrote magnificent concertos and graceful dances, while the church cantata, which played a big part among his Weimar works, was not seriously cultivated. In his Cöthen compositions a perfect fusion of national styles may be observed. He not only mastered the Italian idiom in his concertos and sonatas, but handled the French style with equal perfection in his suites, imbuing all his compositions with his own powerful personality. His creative ability was so strong that he felt an urge to impart to others his own superior knowledge and to teach others the great art of music. The majority of the clavier works, such as the Inventions, the Sinfonias, and the 'Well-tempered Clavier,' written in this period, were meant for educational purposes. Far from being bored by the duties of a teacher, he composed instructive works on the highest level.

Although Bach was happy and prosperous in Cöthen, his attitude gradually underwent a change. He was not satisfied to carry on with the same kind of work year after year. The average musician of the Baroque era spent a lifetime in a single position, but to Bach changes in environment and occupation were essential. The Cöthen court had adopted the Calvinist creed, and Bach, a staunch Lutheran, could not contribute to the music made in his Prince's church. At the outset this had seemed of little consequence, since Bach was yearning for new tasks, but as the years passed he found it hard to bear. After he had completed a dazzling array of masterworks in the field of secular music, more and more he felt the urge to resume the creation of sacred compositions. He stayed for six years in Cöthen; then he resigned to accept an entirely different kind of work.

In 1723, at the age of thirty-eight, Bach became Thomas Cantor and *director musices* in Leipzig, thus assuming a central post within the Lutheran faith. This marked the beginning of his *fourth creative period*, which lasted to the year 1729. Inspired by his new duties his productivity broke forth with elemental force. In the fruitful first years he spent in Leipzig his output was mainly devoted to vocal compositions for the church. He created a breathtaking number of new sacred cantatas and revised his Weimar compositions in this field. The bulk of his church cantatas, overwhelming both as to quantity and quality, was completed in a comparatively short time. And when this gigantic output was tapering off, there followed one of his outstanding creations in the field of sacred vocal music. On Good Friday, 1729, the St. Matthew Passion was performed, an event that brought the fourth period to its glorious climax, but also to its conclusion.

The year 1730, when Bach's *fifth creative period* started, was marked by a crisis in his artistic career. The composer's magnificent achievements during the first years of his stay in Leipzig had been all but ignored by his employers who treated him with barely disguised enmity and contempt. But fortunately the composer managed at that time to find a new outlet for his creative urge. In the spring of 1729 he had taken over the direction of the Leipzig Collegium Musicum founded fifteen years earlier by Telemann. This position, which he held with interruptions to 1741, or possibly even 1744, gave him an opportunity to write music for an audience different in character from the congregations at St. Thomas' and St. Nicholas'. Bach now frequently composed works to celebrate festivities in the ruling electoral house. Other secular cantatas also originated in these years, such as the ribald 'Peasant Cantata' and the 'Coffee Cantata' which approach the spirit of the comic opera. Even a work intended for the church, the 'Christmas Oratorio' of 1734, was based on various secular cantatas. At that time Bach made repeated bids for public recognition, as he wanted to establish contacts with a larger circle of music lovers. He wrote harpsichord concertos for himself and his sons as suitable vehicles for public appearances. He saw to it that his works for clavier and organ most likely to win success should appear in print, to reach connoisseurs and amateurs outside Leipzig. Printing of the first part of the so-called *Clavier-Übung*, containing the six Partitas, was completed in 1731, that of the fourth and last part presenting the immortal 'Goldberg' Variations probably in 1742. At about the same time Bach also finished a large-scale collection of twenty-four preludes and fugues, known as the second part of the 'Well-tempered Clavier,' which he may have planned to publish at a later date.

Bach's works of this period, which lasted from his forty-fifth to his fifty-ninth year, belong to the very best he has written. But the quantity of the output produced in fourteen years seems modest when compared to the production of the previous period. There must have been weeks and even months in which creative work was at a standstill. The disagreements with the authorities certainly resulted in an uncongenial atmosphere; physical factors may also have contributed to the middle-aged artist's slowing up; yet it seems likely that also a certain mental malaise was responsible for this state of affairs. Bach must have felt that, despite his attempts to establish friendly relations with the university students and to win public recognition, the chasm between him and the younger generation of music lovers was widening rather than narrowing. The vicious attack of J. A. Scheibe in 1737 brought the trouble into the open, but it seems to have merely strengthened Bach's attitude. He refused to pay more than a token tribute to the demands of the time for light, melodious, and uncomplicated music, and he was unwilling to desist from the 'excess of art' which Scheibe so bitterly criticized.

Thus Bach finally decided to turn his back on the fashionable trends of his time and to write music that would give satisfaction to himself and to a small group of initiated. The year 1744 marks the beginning of his *sixth and last period* of composition which is decidedly retrospective in character. He felt that he was approaching the end of his life and the time had come to set his house in order. He enlarged a collection of fair copies made from selected vocal compositions of the past, and he issued in print the 'Schübler' Chorales, organ transcriptions of movements from sacred cantatas first conceived between 1724 and 1731. Most of his energy was devoted to revisions and collections of earlier works. He recast a substantial number of organ chorales from the Weimar period which count among his finest organ music. He added the missing sections to Mass movements written at an earlier time and thus produced the Mass in B minor, one of the sublime works of sacred art.

The aging composer felt closer to the distant past than to the present. His canonic variations on *Vom Himmel hoch* lead us back to the organ chorales of Scheidt, composed about a hundred years before Bach. In the 'Musical Offering' he revived archaic forms of canon composition, and in the 'Art of the Fugue' he presented an abstract course in the most exalted contrapuntal forms of earlier centuries. With these works the greatest genius in the field of strict polyphonic writing left an artistic testament not only of the skills of his own time but of those of a whole era. He knew that the days of Baroque grandeur were over, and he wanted to erect to it a monument that would last through the centuries.

I. WORKS FOR VOICES AND INSTRUMENTS

THE *church cantata* constitutes the core of Bach's vocal output;[1] the motets, oratorios, and Passions as well as the secular cantatas, are all closely connected to it. Thus, it seems advisable, in discussing the various aspects of Bach's music for voices, to begin with the church cantatas.[2] A few general remarks regarding performance practice and the methods used in dating scores might prove helpful for the understanding of these works.

The conception often held by amateurs that Bach played the organ in the Leipzig performances of his vocal works cannot be upheld. Maybe a picture to be found in J. G. Walther's *Music Lexicon* reflects conditions prevailing in the Leipzig churches. In this illustration the conductor is standing next to the organ and directing the performers with music rolls held in both hands. Another theory according to which a harpsichord was used for the accompaniment of solos, and the

---

1. Among the very extensive literature on this subject the following studies might be singled out: A. Schering, *J. S. B.s Leipziger Kirchenmusik*, Leipzig, 1936; W. Neumann, *J. S. B.s Chorfuge*, Leipzig, 1938; A Schering, *Über Kantaten J. S. B.s*, Leipzig, 1942; F. Smend, *J. S. B. Kirchenkantaten*, Berlin, 1947-49; A. Dürr, *Studien über die frühen Kantaten J. S. B.s*, Leipzig, 1951; W. Neumann, *Handbuch der Kantaten J. S. B.s*, Leipzig, 1953[2]; W. Neumann, *J. S. B. Sämtliche Kantatentexte*, Leipzig, 1956; L. F. Tagliavini, *Studi sui testi delle cantate sacre di J. S. B.*, Padua, 1956; A. Dürr, 'Zur Chronologie der Leipziger Vokalmusik J. S. B.s, *BJ*, 1957; G. v. Dadelsen, *Beiträge zur Chronologie der Werke J. S. B.s*, Tübinger Bach Studien 4/5, Trossingen, 1958; W. G. Whittaker, *The Cantatas of J. S. B.*, London, 1959; P. Mies, *Die geistlichen Kantaten J. S. B.s*, Wiesbaden, 1960.

2. The great number of sacred and secular *Songs for Solo Voice and Instrumental Bass* formerly attributed to Bach has shrunk considerably in view of recent research. Today only a few of the songs in Anna Magdalena's Notebook, such as the settings of *Gib dich zufrieden* (BWV 511-12, cf. p. 51) are considered as his own works. For Schemelli's *Gesangbuch* (BWV 439-507) of 1736 Bach provided the figuring of the basses, but again only three of the songs, namely *Dir, Dir Jehova will ich singen* (BWV 452), *Komm süsser Tod* (BWV 478), and *Vergiss mein nicht* (BWV 505) are known to be composed by Bach.

organ for that of the chorus,[1] seems likewise to be incorrect. As a rule, in both solo numbers and choral sections Bach had the figured bass executed only by the organ. As A. Mendel[2] pointed out, 'the registration used by the organist . . . was always quiet and discreet. The chords were played short and detached so that they really punctuated . . . the texture and did not obscure it.'

Bach's cantatas were performed by very small groups. As one learns from the old performing materials, one part each was, as a rule, written out for the wind instruments and the viola as well as for the singers of the soprano, alto, tenor, and bass parts; two parts each for the first and second violins; and three parts for the thorough bass (a figured one for the organ, two unfigured ones to be used by cello, bassoon, and double bass). Each of the singers' parts was meant for three vocalists. The soloist stood in the middle, the ripienists, employed in the choruses, at his two sides. The wind instruments' parts were used by one player each, those of the strings by two. On an ordinary Sunday, Bach had for his cantata performance an average of twenty-seven musicians at his disposal:[3] twelve singers and fifteen instrumentalists (eleven strings, three wind instruments, one organist). Occasionally trumpets and timpani were added. If he was able to obtain a larger number of musicians—for instance, for the Passions or for festive secular cantatas —he prescribed a five-part chorus or even double choruses and a correspondingly bigger orchestra. Thus the number of executants occasionally rose to forty, and for the St. Matthew Passion, with its special demands, he managed to get an even larger body of musicians together. The soloists were also utilized in the choruses, and all the vocalists were either boys or men, university students helping out occasionally. As a rule the number of instrumentalists balanced or slightly exceeded that of the vocalists, a fact present-day conductors might well bear in mind.

On only a few of Bach's works is a date provided by the composer himself. For the majority of the vocal compositions it seems, however, possible to remedy this state of affairs. References in old documents

---

1. Cf. M. Seiffert in *BJ* 1904, p. 65.
2. Cf. A. Mendel, 'Accompaniments to B.s Leipzig Church Music, *MQ*, 1950, p. 339 ff.
3. Cf. the document Bach submitted to the Council in 1730 (see p. 68 f.).

and dated libretti supply information. The church calendar helps us to allot certain cantatas to a specific year. Bach's instrumentation also varied in different periods. Thus, for instance, the divided viola parts customary in 17th-century music appear in Bach's early works; the (transverse) flute, on the other hand, not before 1718; the oboe d'amore only after 1719. Bach's method of transposing the parts of wind instruments and organ respectively also changed significantly. In Weimar the organ he used seems to have been tuned in the so-called *Chorton* (choir pitch), a minor third above the *tief Cammerton* (low chamber pitch) of the other instruments. The composer used the following, rather complicated device to cope with this difficulty. Usually he wrote for organ, vocalists, and strings in the same key,[1] and expected the string players to tune their instruments a third higher, according to the pitch of the organ. The wind instruments, on the other hand, could not change their pitch so easily; their parts were therefore written in the key in which they were to be played, namely, a third higher than that of the strings. Any manuscript notated in this way clearly belongs to Bach's Weimar period.[2] In Leipzig the composer used a simpler method. The organs of St. Thomas' and St. Nicholas' were tuned in the *Chorton,* which was one whole tone above the ordinary *Cammerton* employed by the other instruments. Here Bach merely transposed the figured bass part meant for the organ one whole tone down while all the other instruments were written in the key in which they played. The transposed organ part, combined with untransposed parts for all other musicians, is therefore characteristic of the music written in Leipzig.[3] The absolute pitch of the church works

1. An exception is to be found in the viola d'amore part of cantata No. 152, notated in the key of G minor and not, like the viola da gamba and continuo parts, in E minor.

2. Jauernig, p. 72, points out that the Weimar organ with the choir pitch described by G. A. Wette in 1737 was an instrument fundamentally reconstructed in 1719-20, i.e. after Bach's departure from Weimar. Yet the peculiar notation of cantatas that we know were performed in Weimar, offers ample evidence that the composer's instrument was tuned in the same way as that described by Wette.

3. When adapting Weimar cantatas for performance in Leipzig, Bach always modernized the notation. He endeavored, moreover, to achieve approximately the same absolute pitch as in Weimar. Since the *Cammerton* in Leipzig was at least a half-tone higher than the *tief Cammerton* in Weimar, a downward transposition had to take place. Thus cantata No. 185 which sounded in A minor in Weimar,

performed in Leipzig seems to have been approximately a=440, thus similar to the pitch in use today.[1]

The most significant results for the dating of the cantatas were obtained through the study of the handwriting and the paper to be found in the old manuscripts. Bach's own way of notation underwent changes in the course of the years, and, moreover, he employed in different periods different copyists whose handwriting we have learned to distinguish. There are also definite alterations in the watermarks on the paper used. A thorough study of this material undertaken in preparation for the new collected edition, brought about, around 1955, a revolution of the dating of Bach's vocal works. The chronology established by Spitta and, by and large, accepted by succeeding scholars could no longer be upheld, the dates of origin in many instances being changed by ten to fifteen years or even more. The resulting new picture is fully convincing in its basic concepts, and the editors of the new collected edition, especially A. Dürr, G. von Dadelsen, and W. Neumann,[2] deserve our gratitude for their significant achievements in this field.

According to the Obituary, Bach wrote five sets of church cantatas for all the Sundays and holydays of the ecclesiastical year. He therefore must have composed nearly 300. However, fewer than 200, that is, a little over three-fifths, have been preserved. For this tragic loss Bach's eldest son, Wilhelm Friedemann, may have been largely responsible. After Sebastian's death the cantata sets were divided among members of the family in such a way that—according to Forkel—Friedemann received the greatest number.[3] We know that at first he gave away some manuscripts of his father's, and later, when he was in financial straits, sold them.[4] Emanuel, on the other hand, seems to have

---

was—according to the testimony of the Leipzig parts—performed there in G minor. Similarly cantata No. 162 resounding in C minor at Weimar, was performed in B minor at Leipzig. Cf. A. Dürr, *Frühe Kantaten*, p. 64, and A. Mendel, 'On the Pitches in Use in B.s Time,' *MQ*, 1955, p. 332 ff., 466 ff.

1. Mendel, p. 479.

2. They made use in their research of the (unprinted) catalogue of watermarks to be found in Bach's manuscripts, as compiled by Wisso Weiss (cf. *BJ* 1957, p. 5).

3. See Dürr, *BJ* 1957, p. 10.

4. Cf. M. Falck, *Wilhelm Friedemann Bach*, Leipzig, 1913, p. 54.

preserved carefully the music handed over to him. A valuable catalogue of his holdings has survived, as the list of his estate was printed after his death.[1] At present the early scores and parts are mainly owned by the Berlin library and by the Thomas School in Leipzig. Parts of the Berlin property were housed at the end of World War II in Marburg and Tübingen. The Marburg collection was moved in 1965 to West Berlin where a new library is being erected. The MSS owned by the Thomas School are preserved in the Bach-Archiv, Leipzig.

Only about forty cantatas originated before Leipzig, and of these several were subsequently adapted by the Thomas Cantor. It seems that he wrote no cantata at Arnstadt. No. 15[2] which was previously ascribed to the year 1704, is no longer considered a genuine Bach composition (cf. pp. 169-70, footnote 1).

The number of cantatas written at Mühlhausen is not certain. The earliest appears to be No. 131, *Aus der Tiefe* (Out of the depths), which, as the autograph indicates, was composed at the instigation of Bach's friend, the Reverend G. C. Eilmar. To this group belongs also No. 71, *Gott ist mein König* (God is my king), performed on February 4, 1708, for the inauguration of the new city council, and perhaps No. 106, *Gottes Zeit* (God's own time),[3] the wedding cantata No. 196, and the Easter cantata No. 4. These early cantatas are strongly dependent on models provided by north and central German composers of the time. They are related to cantatas by older members of the family or those by Pachelbel, Böhm, and Buxtehude. Their librettos are almost exclusively based on Bible texts and on chorale verses, with emphasis on dramatic contrasts. The music too looks backward in some of its features. Usually the instrumental sinfonia is brief, and clearly separated from the vocal sections. The latter are often planned symmetrically, with a choral number at the beginning, the center, and the end. Short pieces, contrasting in tempo, time signature and number of voices, follow each other without any break. The 'concertato' principle

1. Reproduced by Miesner in *BJ* 1938, 1939, 1940-48.
2. In this chapter the customary system of numbering Bach's cantatas is adopted. It was started in the edition of the BG and taken over by BWV. The numbers do not indicate a chronological order.
3. It may have been intended for the commemorative service held for Bach's deceased uncle, Tobias Lämmerhirt (cf. p. 23).

rules the choruses, in which vocal groups of varying size compete with instrumental bodies. As a basis for the arias, ostinatos are frequently employed, repeating the same bass-phrase—sometimes in transposed form—over and over again, while the melodic line changes. Great importance is attached to the arioso, a melodious recitative, accompanied by instruments which interrupt the vocal part with independent *ritornelli;* the freely declamatory secco recitative, accompanied only by a figured bass, is not to be found in Bach's early cantatas.

The text of No. 131, *Aus der Tiefe* (Out of the depths), which deals with the contrast of sin and redemption, is based on Psalm 130 and two stanzas from a chorale. In this work coloraturas to be sung on a single syllable are frequently interspersed with rests, a mannerism by no means unusual in vocal works of the time, but as a rule avoided by Bach in later compositions. The final vocal fugue is so strongly instrumental in its design that it even slipped in with the composer's organ works in an arrangement by one of Bach's pupils (BWV 131a).

No. 71, *Gott ist mein König* (God is my king) is the only cantata by Bach printed during his lifetime that has been preserved.[1] In this *motetto,* as Bach himself called it, various instrumental groups—one brass choir with timpani; two recorders and cello; a trio of oboes and bassoon; strings and organo concertato—compete with one larger and one smaller vocal group in a manner recalling the splendor of Venetian art, as reflected in the cantatas of Buxtehude. The duet No. 2, *Ich bin nun achtzig Jahr* (Full fourscore years I am) entrusts an ornamented chorale tune to the contralto, while the tenor voice and an organ obbligato introduce counter melodies. The result is a vocal form somewhat reminiscent of an organ chorale. The concluding fugue, *Muss täglich von neuem,* shows a gradual buildup toward a magnificent climax in which all the voices and instruments collaborate, displaying the remarkable technical skill of the composer of twenty-three.[2]

One of the finest and most important among Bach's early cantatas is No. 106, *Gottes Zeit* (God's own time) known as the 'Actus tragicus.' Its text, likewise taken from the Bible and from church hymns, was

---

1. Cf. G. Kinsky, *Die Originalausgaben der Werke J. S. B.s,* Wien, 1937 p. 13 ff. Regarding B.s cantata printed in 1709, see p. 29, n. 1.

2. A detailed analysis of this chorus is offered by W. Neumann, *J. S. B.s Chorfuge,* p. 14 ff.

probably assembled by Bach himself, possibly with the Reverend G. C. Eilmar's assistance. The basic idea of this 'German Requiem'[1] is that Death's curse and punishment implied in the Old Testament were transformed through the intervention of Christ into promise and bliss. The cantata, which uses neither violins nor violas in its orchestra, begins with an instrumental introduction for recorders, viole da gamba,[2] and continuo, transporting the hearer to the land of the blessed souls, where there is no sorrow and pain. The first chorus starts with a folk-song-like melody (Ex. 1), such as Bach liked to use in his early works.

Ex. 1. Cantata 106

God's own time, God's own time, His own time is ev - er best, His time is ev - er best

Magnificent short ariosos by tenor and bass lead to the heart of the drama, the great middle chorus. In a ponderous fugue symbolizing the strictness of the Law, the three lower voices present the words of Ecclesiastes, *Es ist der alte Bund, Mensch du musst sterben* (For the covenant from the beginning is, Thou shalt die). In dramatic contrast the light voices of the boy sopranos frequently interrupt with a brief quotation from Revelation, *Ja komm, Herr Jesu* (Oh come, Lord Jesus). This invocation gains in intensity, and at the end the dark menace is completely vanquished, while the sopranos sing the last notes without any instrumental accompaniment. To emphasize the preponderance of the Christian spirit, Bach has the recorders supported by viole da gamba intone during this number the tune of the chorale *Ich hab' mein Sach' Gott heimgestellt* (My cause is God's). The words of the hymn were not needed to convey this message to a congregation familiar with Protestant church songs. In the following duet between contralto and bass we seem to hear the dialogue between the thief on the cross and the Redeemer, who promises the poor soul admission to paradise. A forceful chorale and a vigorous double fugue on the

1. The similarity both in content and architecture to Brahms's 'German Requiem' is quite striking (cf. Geiringer, *Brahms*, New York, 1947, p. 311). Brahms certainly knew Bach's cantata, which was first published in 1830 and was a favorite of his friend Julius Stockhausen.

2. Cello-like string instruments with six or more strings and a light, silvery tone.

hymn's last line form the conclusion. The musical architecture of this cantata is as simple and powerful as its meaning. Its modulatory basis displays a symmetrical arrangement:

F maj.-D min.-G min.-C min.-B♭ maj. (G min.)-D min.-F maj.[1]

The mighty Cantata No. 4, *Christ lag in Todesbanden* (Christ lay by death enshrouded), probably originated at this time, but was revised for a Leipzig performance in 1724. Rarely did Bach compose a work looking so decidedly into the past and at the same time showing features of a progressive nature. The text is confined to the words of Luther's powerful hymn and the music is based on his version of a 12th-century melody. The cantata consists of seven vocal movements, each using one stanza of Luther's chorale as a text and presenting a variation of the hymn tune. Even the introductory instrumental sinfonia in the style of Buxtehude employs the basic melody. The harsh modal harmonies and the doubled middle parts of the violas contribute to the very archaic nature of the composition, which assumes the character of a vocal interpretation of a chorale partita in the manner of Böhm or Pachelbel. But the dominating position which both the text and the melody of the hymn assume throughout the work also points to the chorale cantatas written by Bach in Leipzig. The structure of the cantata is once more completely symmetrical:

chorus	duet	aria	chorus	aria	duet	chorus
1	2	3	4	5	6	7

During the years Bach spent in Weimar he wrote about two dozen church cantatas, most of them basically different from his earlier works in this field. He adopted a new type of cantata texts which had been introduced by Pastor Erdmann Neumeister (cf. p. 49) who claimed 'it looked hardly different from a section of an opera.' The new librettos used 'madrigalian' texts as a basis for secco recitatives and da capo arias, which formed its core. The earlier arioso was but rarely employed, and the free choruses as well as chorale choruses were reduced in number and placed mainly at the beginning and the end of

1. The notation of the recorders reveals that in the performance the remaining parts had to be transposed one whole tone upwards. Thus it would seem better to print the cantata in the key of F, and not in E flat as it is usually done.

the works. The content of the texts was closely related to the pastor's sermon.

Bach wrote several of his Weimar cantatas to words by Neumeister, but he preferred librettos by Salomo Franck, secretary of the Protestant Consistory, court librarian, and accredited Weimar poet. Franck's texts were somewhat more conservative in character than Neumeister's as they avoided the new secco recitatives. What attracted Bach particularly was the deep mystic feeling pervading Franck's works.

Bach's earliest Weimar cantatas were written in 1714. In this year he composed five texts by Franck (Nos. 182, 12, 172, 21, 152[1]), two by Neumeister (Nos. 18, 61), and two (Nos. 54, 199) by C. C. Lehms.[2] These works exhibit a somewhat experimental character. Bach was clearly trying out new devices, and his study of Italian forms, especially those of Vivaldi's concertos, is reflected both in the melodic character and in the structure of his arias.

Cantata No. 21, *Ich hatte viel Bekümmernis* (I was sore distressed), which was subsequently revised for a performance in Leipzig, belongs to the comparatively few compositions by Bach in which his art meets with that of his greatest contemporary in the realm of music. Its final chorus, *Das Lamm, das erwürget ist* (The Lamb that was sacrificed), with its brilliant use of the trumpets, exhibits the grandiose al-fresco technique of Handel. On the other hand, it should be noted that the beginning of 'Worthy is the Lamb' in the *Messiah*, written a quarter of a century later, reveals a certain kinship with this chorus. The Sinfonia to the cantata's first part, with its long-held dissonant chords, and the oboe's outcry in the penultimate measure, is among the most passionate instrumental numbers Bach ever conceived, and it creates the right atmosphere for the feeling of desolation which predominates at the start of the opening chorus. The three ejaculations 'I, I, I' at the beginning of this number (*Ex. 2*) have been commented on in Bach's

Ex. 2. Cantata 21

8va - - - - - - -
I,   I,   I,   I had my heart . . .

1. Actually Franck's authorship is certain for No. 152 only, but it is most likely for Nos. 182, 172, 21, and 12 too.

2. Cf. Dürr, *Frühe Kantaten*, p. 54.

own time.[1] The repetition of the first word at the start of a composition is typical of 17th-century music, and in this particular case Bach may have reverted to it to stress the work's subjective character. Even more old-fashioned is the next chorus, with its emotional contrasts quickly succeeding one another, and the sudden changes between solo and tutti, fast and slow, forte and piano. On the other hand the solo numbers show how much the composer had learned from contemporary opera. The dialogue between the soul and Jesus, for instance, is a love duet of such sensuous beauty that it might well have shocked some members of the congregation. Pieces like this were responsible for the clause in Bach's Leipzig contract that his compositions 'should not make an operatic impression.'

A curious experiment was made by Bach in the first chorus of his cantata No. 61, *Nun komm der Heiden Heiland* (Come Thou of man the Saviour). It is a chorale setting in the form of a French overture. The movement begins with the traditional slow tempo and dotted rhythms of Lully's introductions, to which the voices intone the first two lines of the chorale 'Come Thou, of man the Saviour, Thou child of a Virgin born.' The time signature then changes, and Bach prescribes *Gai* as tempo. A fast and merry fugue on the third chorale-line 'Filled with wonder's the earth' forms the middle section, which leads to the slow conclusion using the last line 'At its Saviour's mortal birth.' A magnificent tour de force is here accomplished, such as we admire in the mature artist's cantatas Nos. 20, 97, and 119 (cf. p. 158). A striking instance of pictorialism can be found in the bass recitative No. 4, 'Look ye, I stand before the door and knock,' with the throbbing pizzicato motive (*Ex. 3*) and, even more stirringly, in the last

Ex. 3. Cantata 61

1. Mattheson, *Critica Musica* 1722-25, II, p. 368, derides it in a rather unfair manner.

chorus. Here the indefatigable runs of the violins, finally climbing up
to g''', a note felt to be of a dizzy height in Bach's time, symbolize
the heavenly abode from which the Saviour descended to dwell among
mortal beings.

More uniform in character than the cantatas of 1714 are those of
1715 and 1716. To 1715 belong Nos. 80a (first version of No. 80), 31,
165, 185, 161, 162, 163, 132, and maybe 72; to 1716 belong Nos. 155,
70a, 186a, 147a, and perhaps Nos. 168 and 164. All these works employ texts by Salomo Franck, and the similarity of the texts is matched
by a certain resemblance of the compositions. The rather dramatic character of the preceding works has given way to a more contemplative
attitude. Direct quotations from the Bible have disappeared and are
replaced by freely conceived recitatives. However, the 'concertato'
character of earlier works may still be observed in some of these cantatas. The concluding number is usually supplied by a simple chorale
harmonization.

This set comprises some of Bach's more personal cantatas. Now the
Jesusminne (love of Jesus), the all-consuming yearning for release
from earthly fetters, the welcoming of death as the gate of heavenly
bliss, assumed proportions unparalleled in the music of the time. While
the new form of the cantata was devised by orthodox ministers vigorously opposed to the ideas of Pietism, a mystic undercurrent in many
of the texts chosen by Bach, and tremendously strengthened by his intense music, brought these works perilously close to the controversial
doctrine, a fact Bach probably never admitted to himself.

A characteristic example is supplied by the Easter cantata No. 31,
Der Himmel lacht, die Erde jubilieret (The heavens laugh, the earth
exults in gladness).[1] The composition begins in a mood of rejoicing
and jubilation which soon turns to thoughts of death and suffering.
For Franck and Bach the idea of the resurrection was inextricably
bound up with that of decay and annihilation, and they saw in death a
goal to be sought eagerly by the Christian. Therefore it is not the
pompous introductory 'Sonata' in concerto form, nor the first jubilant
chorus that constitutes the climax of the work; it is the last aria *Letzte
Stunde, brich herein* (Hour of parting, come to me). Here a soprano,

---

1. A subsequent revision of the cantata by Bach may have been done as early as
1724 or in 1731.

assisted by oboe and instrumental bass, performs a trio in dance rhythm of irresistible sweetness, to which violins and violas add the venerable chorale tune *Wenn mein Stündlein vorhanden ist* (When finally my hour comes). This chorale is then taken up by the full chorus and orchestra, with the trumpet reaching the highest clarino registers, thus proclaiming the glory and bliss of death leading to the soul's reunion with Christ.

Even more transcendental is the character of No. 161, *Komm du süsse Todesstunde* (Come sweet death, thou blessed healer). Here the hymn *Herzlich tut mich verlangen* (My heart is ever yearning for blessed death's release), which was to play so important a part as Passion chorale in the St. Matthew Passion, constitutes the framework for the whole composition. In the first aria for contralto, in which the disembodied tune of the recorders seems to express a promise of eternal life, the organ intones this chorale, and it is taken up again at the end by the full chorus in a vision of trance-like bliss. Among the other numbers the recitative No. 4, accompanied by full orchestra, provides a deeply stirring illustration of sleep and awakening. In the singer's part the yearning for deliverance from earthly fetters reaches its ecstatic climax, while the recorders, with quickly repeated high notes, the strings with sombre pizzicati, and the basses with majestic octave leaps, sound a weird chorus of tolling death bells. (Ex. 4)

Ex. 4. Cantata 161

Cantata No. 80a was revised and thoroughly enlarged in Leipzig (cf. p. 167). The same is true of the last three cantatas Bach wrote in Weimar for the Advent season of 1716 (Nos. 70a, 186a, 147a). Originally they consisted of six numbers each: an introductory chorus, four arias (without recitatives), and a final chorale, but they were later expanded into extensive cantatas in two parts.

The church cantata played a rather insignificant part in Bach's output at Cöthen. But some secular works written there were subsequently transformed into sacred compositions while Bach served in Leipzig, and thus contributed to the awe-inspiring production the *director musices* achieved in his new position.

On February 7, 1723, he performed his 'test piece,' cantata No. 22. His regular work as Thomas Cantor started only on the first Sunday after Trinity (May 30) with the production of cantata No. 75. In an almost uninterrupted flow there followed sixty-odd cantatas within the first year ending at Trinity (June 4), 1724. Most are documented by the original scores, and to some extent by the old parts also, the whole material having been preserved through C. P. E. Bach.[1]

In using works that had originated in Cöthen (Nos. 134, 173, and 184) Bach had to make decisive changes in order to transform a secular work into a sacred one with a completely different text. But even the sacred works composed in Weimar were altered, mainly through transpositions, changes in the orchestration, and addition of new numbers.[2] Bach was not dismayed by the enormous volume of work he had undertaken. The set contains several very long cantatas consisting of 12 to 14 numbers and arranged in two parts (cf. Nos. 75, 76, and 194). Moreover, on some of the high holidays, Bach seems to have contributed two cantatas which were performed before and after the sermon or in different churches. On Easter Sunday he made the concession to use two previously composed cantatas (Nos. 4 and 31), since

---

1. According to Dürr (*BJ* 1957, p. 57 ff.), this first Leipzig set probably comprised the following works, enumerated here according to their sequence in the church year. Works adapted from earlier cantatas, written before Bach came to Leipzig, are underlined. If on the same day two cantatas were performed, their numbers are connected with a hyphen. 1723: Nos. 75, 76, 21, 24-185, 167, 147, 186, 136, 105, 46, 179-199?, BWV Anh. 20 (lost), 69a, 77, 25, 119, 138, 95, 148?, 48, 162, 109, 89, 194, 60, 90, 70, 61, 63-243a, 40, 64.
1724: Nos. 190, 153, 65, 154, 155, 73, 81, 83, 144, 181-18, 23?, 182, 4-31?, 66, 134, 67, 104, 12, 166, 86, 37, 44, 172-59, 173?, 184, 194, 165?

2. The Mühlhausen cantatas were as a rule not used in Leipzig because Bach considered their style as too old-fashioned.

the first performance of the St. John Passion, two days earlier, had required so much time and energy.

The cantatas which were newly written for Leipzig display a certain uniformity in the arrangement of their libretti, which in turn results in some structural affinities of the compositions. Bach shows marked preference for texts which start with a Bible quotation serving as a motto for the work, and conclude with a chorale, while the rest consists of freely invented recitatives and arias. The Bible quotation may be composed as an aria,[1] but mostly it is set as a mighty chorus.[2] In No. 60 the initial Bible motto is replaced by a chorale text with its tune, thus providing a second appearance of a hymn within the same work. Some cantatas also incorporate chorales in various arrangements in three places.[3] On the other hand a work, such as No. 181, without any chorale, is an exception.

The following six cantatas might serve as examples for the compositions written in 1723-24.

Johann Rist's awesome description of death and punishment, *O Ewigkeit du Donnerwort* (Eternity, thou thunder word), seems to have held a special fascination for Bach. He used the hymn in two of his cantatas, the first (No. 60 of 1723) being concise and rather free in its formal arrangement, the second (No. 20 of 1724), a 'strict chorale cantata' (cf. pp. 160-61) of mighty proportions based in all its movements on the old poem. Preference is generally given to the earlier version, which displays greater variety and brings a note of promise into the gloom conjured by Rist's text. Cantata No. 60, meant for the 24th Sunday after Trinity, is written in the form of a dialogue between the voice of 'Fear' (contralto) and that of 'Hope' (tenor). Such dialogues conducted between Biblical characters, or dealing with abstract concepts, were frequently used in 17th-century Protestant church music, and Bach felt tempted to experiment with the form. In the first movement of No. 60 the dialogue assumes the character of a chorale arrangement; here the contralto presents the text of the first stanza of Rist's poem with its unadorned melody, while simultaneously the

1. Cf. Nos. 166, 86, 89.
2. Cf. Nos. 136, 105, 46, 179, 69a, 25, 119, 148, 109, 40, 64, 190, 65, 144, 67, 104, 37, 44.
3. Cf. Nos. 138, 48, 153, 75.

tenor utters words from the Old Testament to a freely invented tune. The orchestra, consisting of strings, two oboi d'amore,[1] and a French horn, reflects the emotions expressed by the two protagonists. While the horn merely serves to reinforce the cantus firmus, the 'love oboes' with their gently slurred passages are designated as companions of 'Hope'; the strings, on the other hand, whose rapid note repetitions symbolize anguish and trembling, are obviously assigned to 'Fear.' The juxtaposition of these contrasting instrumental groups produces dramatic effects rare in this time. As 'Fear' feels more and more distressed, the musical expression in the second duet approaches terror. 'Hope' has no alternative but to withdraw from the struggle and to entrust its cause to a stronger power. A bass voice, in all likelihood representing Jesus,[2] is now heard announcing the message from Revelation: 'Blessed are the dead which die in the Lord, from henceforth.' Now at last 'Fear' is fully convinced that death leads to eternal life. In the chorale, presented to round off the cantata, Bach felt it advisable to replace Rist's threatening text by the powerful, yet consoling words of another 17th-century poet movingly set to music by J. G. Ahle. The hymn *Es ist genug, Herr* (It is enough, Lord) with its strangely exciting use of the whole tone scale in the first four notes, serves as a fitting conclusion for this story of anguish and divine consolation. It is noteworthy how minutely Bach expresses the content of the text within the narrow framework of a simple chorale harmonization. This is shown, for instance, in the phrase '*mein grosser Jammer bleibt darnieden*' (my great sorrow remains down here). An octave skip in the alto illustrates the word 'great,' the violently downward rushing middle parts at the cadence 'down here,' and the chromatic descending bass line the word 'sorrow' (*Ex. 5*). Throughout the chorale Bach uses bold melodic

Ex. 5. Cantata 60

1. Oboes with a pear-shaped bell tuned a third lower than the regular instrument.
2. The assumption of the BG, seeing in the bass voice a representation of the Holy Ghost, seems unconvincing. Cf. Schering, *Kantaten J. S. B.s*, p. 145.

leaps, harsh dissonances, an abundance of altered chords, passing tones, anticipations and retardations to create a Michelangelesque picture of the horrors of earthly existence and of the overwhelming longing for liberation from worldly bondage.

Alban Berg, writing in our time a concerto dedicated 'to the memory of an angel,' could not find a better climax for his 'requiem' than the sounds of this chorale, in Bach's harmonization, which loses none of its stirring power in the strange surroundings of modern serial technique.[1]

Cantatas No. 105 and No. 46 written for the ninth and tenth Sunday after Trinity, respectively, convey a similar message. The two cantatas deal once more with those extremes of Christian religious feeling, fear of damnation and hope for heavenly grace, but the musical treatment is quite different. The monumental first chorus of No. 105, *Herr, gehe nicht ins Gericht* (Lord, enter not into judgment), based on words from Psalm 143, starts with an adagio in G minor whose chromatic alterations and appoggiaturas, together with a ponderous bass, convey a frightening picture of anguish and guilt. For the second half of the text 'In Thy sight no man shall be justified' Bach uses a lively fugue in which the orchestra merely doubles the vocal parts. Thus the texture of an old-fashioned motet is used to emphasize that from time immemorial man could not measure up to the Lord's law. The mood of anxiety is further heightened by the next aria in which Bach omits the continuo part, as though to imply that the sinner has no solid ground under his feet. The piece is written as a trio for soprano voice, oboe and viola, the filling middle parts being provided by two violins. The atmosphere changes in the cantata's second half. A ray of hope is revealed to the guilty in a highly expressive bass recitative accompanied by strings. The ensuing tenor aria voices man's decision to forgo riches and elect Jesus as his companion. Here quickly sliding figures in the violins seem to indicate mammon slipping through the fingers, while the slower notes of the French horn might symbolize the security and steadiness afforded through Christ's assistance. In the final chorale, a harmonization of the hymn *Jesu, der du meine Seele* (Jesus, who delivered my soul), the accompanying strings

---

1. Cf. K. Geiringer, 'Es ist genug,' in G. Reese and R. Brandel, *The Commonwealth of Music*, New York, 1965, p. 283 ff.

provide a condensation of the whole cantata's mood. Beginning with anxiously wavering sixteenth-note repetitions, the motion gradually slows up until at the end quarter notes proclaim full trust in God's mercy. The poignant chromatic progressions in the final measures (*Ex.* 6)—Bach used them again at the beginning of cantata No. 78 based on

Ex. 6. Cantata 105

the same chorale—seem to emphasize that it was the Saviour's sacrifice that brought redemption to mankind.

On the following Sunday, in a typically didactic manner, Bach took up the same basic idea. The text of No. 46, *Schauet doch und sehet* (Look ye then and see), deals with the punishment meted out to the wicked and the reprieve granted to the faithful, a sharp contrast rather awkwardly interpreted by the unknown poet, yet inspiring the composer to one of his most moving creations. Gently sliding passages of two recorders serve as a brief introduction and lead to a monumental chorus based on the lamentations of Jeremiah (I/12), 'Look ye then and see if there be any sorrow like unto my sorrow.' This grief-stricken section, which was later used by Bach as a basis for the 'Qui tollis' of the B minor Mass, is followed by a five-part fugue filled with anguish and despair. It is noteworthy that in this fugue, only four parts are uttered by human voices, while the fifth is entrusted to the recorders playing in unison. Two arias preceded by recitatives form the work's middle section. The first offers an almost apocalyptic picture of fury and destruction to describe the Lord's 'storm of wrath.' Bach here uses a strange solo instrument, *tromba o corno da tirarsi*, a small brass instrument equipped with slides to change the pitch. Its harsh sounds must have increased the anguish in the hearts of the congregation. The threatening atmosphere prevails through the following recitative; then, however, the mood magically changes. (The sermon may have been inserted in this place.) A contralto aria lifts us into the realm of the blessed spirits. The weightless pastoral sounds of recorders and oboi da caccia,[1] without the support of strings or bass, mingle with the alto voice in its description of the good shepherd gathering the faithful. In the concluding chorale Bach refers back to the gentle recorder passages of the beginning. They are now used to connect the individual lines of the hymn and convey once more Bach's message: even in utter dejection man should be aware of God's loving grace.

It was customary in Leipzig to celebrate the inauguration of a new city council by a church service given special significance through the presentation of a cantata written for this occasion. Bach, who had composed the Mühlhausen cantata No. 71 (cf. p. 25) for a similar event, contributed several works of this kind.[2] The earliest of these, and one of the most remarkable, is No. 119, *Preise, Jerusalem, den Herrn* (Praise, Jerusalem, the Lord), performed in 1723. The initial chorus is imbued with a particularly festive mood. Bach chose an unusually large orchestra including two recorders, three oboes, four trumpets and timpani, and cast the piece into the form of a French overture. Its first and third sections, with the traditional dotted rhythms, are entrusted to the instruments, while in the middle part, presenting imitative passages, the chorus vigorously joins in, uttering words from Psalm 147 in jubilant praise of the Lord. The following two arias sung by an alto and tenor voice, respectively, are lyrical, almost pastoral in character, as they describe the importance of good government and the peaceful life of the citizens enjoying it. Oboi da caccia, apparently entrusted to the oboists of the first number, and recorders are used to accompany these amiable and idyllic compositions, in which Bach successfully frees himself of the shallow pomposity of the text. In the bass recitative connecting these arias Bach draws inspiration from the words *So herrlich stehst du, liebe Stadt* (How fair thou art, beloved town) and conjures with the help of trumpets and woodwind a powerful yet

1. Alto oboes, a fifth below the pitch of the regular oboe, and similar to the English horn. Cf. K. Geiringer, *Musical Instruments*, London, 1943, p. 171 ff., and C. S. Terry, *Bach's Orchestra*, London, 1932, p. 103 ff.

2. For such purposes Bach wrote his cantatas 29, 69, 119, 120, 193. No. 137 composed for the twelfth Sunday after Trinity was probably re-employed at such an occasion. The music to BWV Anh. 3 and 4 is lost. According to W. Neumann (*BJ* 1961, p. 52ff.) no less than 27 performances of 'inaugural' cantatas took place during Bach's service in Leipzig. Sizable losses among this output may therefore be assumed.

tender description of the city he had recently made his home. A second chorus displays broad da capo form. In its orchestration and festive character, as well as in the occasional use of dotted rhythms, it resembles the first number. The fugue subject introduced by the chorus alludes to the venerable hymn *Nun danket alle Gott* (Now let us all thank God) (*Ex. 7*) and thus expresses in simplest terms the work's

Ex. 7. Cantata 119

Now let us all thank God

The Lord is boun - ti - ful to us

fundamental idea. It is restated in the final chorale, fitting a powerful verse by Martin Luther to the melody of *Herr Gott, dich loben wir* (Lord God, we praise Thee).

No. 65, *Sie werden aus Saba alle kommen* (From Sheba shall many men be coming), was written for Epiphany of 1724 to words by an unknown author. The famous first chorus is a lofty piece of concerted music in which four groups of instruments—horns, recorders, oboi da caccia, and strings—compete with human voices to create a richly glowing picture of the stately procession leading camels laden with gold and incense as offerings to the Lord. Inexhaustible inspiration, unerring judgment in the combination of musical colors, and a highly emphatic declamation join forces to give the most powerful utterance to the prophecy of Isaiah (60:6). The remaining numbers—two simple chorales framing a bass and a tenor aria with preceding recitatives— are much less elaborate, as the composer wants to emphasize that gifts from the heart mean more to Jesus than luxurious presents.

No. 104, *Du Hirte Israel höre* (Give ear, O Shepherd of Israel) written for the second Sunday after Easter, 1724, conveys a pastoral atmosphere pervaded by deep seriousness. The first chorus, based on words from Psalm 80, begins with an instrumental introduction in which gently moving passages in triplets, long-held bass notes and the sounds of two oboes and oboi da caccia in the orchestra suggest the idea of a shepherd tending his flock. When the chorus sets in, homophonic sections alternate with animated fugatos, and thus a picture is conjured up of sheep milling around and in need of the herdman's steadying hand. A feeling of anxiety pervades the following B minor aria scored for tenor voice, two oboi d'amore and bass. Here creature's apprehension of getting lost in the desert finds stirring expression. Peace of mind is only restored in the bass aria in D major, an enchanting siciliano in 12/8 time (*Ex. 8*). The first and third parts of this pastorale express

Ex. 8. Cantata 104

Ye hap - py flocks whom Christ is keep-ing, ye hap - py flocks whom Christ is keep-ing,

the happiness of the sheep obtaining guidance, while the middle section movingly tells of the bliss awaiting the believer after his death. The final chorale to the melody *Allein Gott in der Höh' sei Ehr'* (To God on high alone be praise) uses as text a paraphrase of the poignant words from Psalm 23 'The Lord is my shepherd, I shall not want.' Maintaining the general character of this cantata, Bach also employs the reed instruments in this last number, thus endowing even the simple harmonization of the hymn tune with a pastoral quality.

The second set of Leipzig cantatas, reaching from the first Sunday after Trinity (June 11) 1724 to Trinity (May 27) 1725, is authenticated through parts largely acquired by the Thomas School in Leipzig and preserved in the Bach-Archiv as well as through scores various persons received from Wilhelm Friedemann Bach. It comprises a slightly smaller number of works than the first set; on the other hand, arrangements of earlier works are rare among the compositions of this group.[1]

Almost three-quarters of the cantatas display the same solid construction. Up to Annunciation day (March 25), 1725, Bach performed nearly exclusively a type of work which might be designated as 'strict

1. According to Dürr this second set probably comprised the following cantatas enumerated here in the order of the church calendar:

1724: 20, 2, 7, 135, 10, 93, 107, 178, 94, 101, 113, 33, 78, 99, 8, 130, 114, 96, 5, 180, 38, <u>80</u>?, <u>76</u> (part II)?, 115, 139, 26, 116, 62, 91, 121, 133, 122.

1725: 41, 123, 124, 3, 111, 92, 125, 126, 127, 1, 6, 4?, 42, 85, 103, 108, 87, 128, 183, 74, 68, 175, 176.

chorale cantata.' Each of them is based on a specific hymn, certain stanzas of the chorale text being quoted verbatim at the beginning and the end, and frequently also in the middle of the cantata, while the rest of the libretto consists of paraphrases of the remaining chorale stanzas. In general the literal quotations of chorale-stanzas occur twice or three times within one cantata, but there are exceptions, such as Nos. 92 and 178, where five stanzas are employed.[1] When the chorale text appears in its original form, it is usually combined with the original tune, while the freely paraphrased sections are as a rule composed by the Thomas Cantor.

Earlier Bach research assumed—mainly on the basis of Spitta's statements—that these 'strict chorale cantatas' originated between 1735 and 1744. Recent research, however, indicates[2] that these thirty-eight cantatas were composed at a much earlier date and in close succession, thus forming a solid unit within the composer's output.[3]

After Bach had exhausted all the possibilities of the 'strict chorale cantata,' he turned away from this form, showing preference once more for the cantata type of the first set by starting the compositions with a chorus based on the Bible, and concluding them with a chorale. While the librettists of the 'strict chorale cantatas' and of the works which immediately followed them are unknown this is not the case with the last ten cantatas of the set, whose texts were contributed by the successful 'imperial poetess' Mariane von Ziegler.[4] Here again one usually finds a Bible quotation at the beginning and a chorale at the end, but there are some significant variations. The Scripture texts are mostly from the Gospel of St. John, at times appearing only at the beginning (Nos. 103, 183); in other works at the beginning and in the middle (Nos. 108, 87, 175); in No. 74 even in three places. In Nos. 128 and 68 chorale choruses at the beginning replace the composition of Scrip-

1. In isolated cases Bach used an even stricter technique, quoting text and melody of the chorale in every number (cf. cantatas 4 and 137).

2. Some doubts against its validity were raised, however, by Chr. Wolff in *Festschrift für F. Smend*, Berlin, 1963, pp. 80-92.

3. The works listed on p. 160, footnote 1 between No. 20 and No. 1 are 'strict chorale cantatas' except for Nos. 80, 76, 107 and 113 in which certain deviations may be observed.

4. It is certain that the text for the last nine cantatas of the set were written by her; very likely this is also true of No. 85.

tural texts. Bach does not always entrust the quotation from the Bible to a chorus. If a solo voice is chosen, he likes to use the arioso form, the text being enunciated as carefully as in a recitative, while occasional word repetitions and a more elaborate treatment of the orchestra conjure up the technique employed in arias.

An analysis of six cantatas may help to clarify the picture of the second set.

No. 7, *Christ unser Herr zum Jordan kam* (To Jordan's stream came Christ our Lord), was written for St. John's day (June 24), 1724. The text closely follows Luther's poem describing the baptism of Christ and the sacrament's miraculous power over sin and death. The first and last stanzas are quoted literally and based on the hymn tune, while each of the intervening five verses was slightly paraphrased to produce the texts for three arias and two connecting recitatives which present freely invented music. In the initial chorus the tenor voice introduces the chorale melody in long notes, the rest of the singers surrounding it with countermelodies conceived independently. This vocal body is embedded in an instrumental framework of strikingly expressive power, which demonstrates the Baroque era's pleasure in tone paintings. With the help of strongly accented rhythms and gently slurred passages (*Ex. 9*), Bach creates here a pictorial masterpiece that

Ex. 9. Cantata 7

seems to foreshadow similar works in 19th-century music. He makes us see Jordan's rushing waters battling their way through rocky gorges. Somewhat different in character are the following five numbers. Each of the arias uses ostinato-like repetitions of certain bass passages, a technique the composer liked to employ in his earlier cantatas. Moreover the second of the arias displays surprising discrepancies between text and music, which caused Arnold Schering to suggest that the piece may have resulted from the 'parody' (cf. p. 110) of an older composition.[1] In the final number Bach returns not only to Luther's own

1. Cf. *Über Kantaten*, p. 163.

words and their tune, but also to the orchestration of the introductory chorus, rounding off his work with a monumental chorale harmonization.

No. 78, *Jesu, der du meine Seele* (Jesus, who delivered my soul) written for the fourteenth Sunday after Trinity (September 10), 1724, also consists of seven movements, which so frequently appear in Bach's sacred vocal works. All numbers are based on Johann Rist's hymn of 1641, the initial chorus presenting the text's first stanza, the concluding chorale its last stanza in unaltered form. Three arias present the poem in such a way that Nos. 2 and 6 offer free paraphrases of one stanza each, while No. 4 deals with two stanzas. Two recitatives inserted between the arias paraphrase three stanzas each; they incorporate some literal quotations from the original poem. The 17th-century tune, traditionally linked with Rist's hymn, is used not only in the cantata's first and last numbers; occasional allusions to it appear also in the two recitatives. The result is a strictly symmetrical, rondo-like construction of text and music which shows a certain resemblance to the Vivaldi concerto form so important for Bach's idiom. In the following table the parentheses surrounding Roman numerals indicate that the respective stanzas are used as the basis of a paraphrase while square brackets indicate that fragmentary literal quotations are intermingled with an 18th-century free rendering of the original text.

BACH:	1 Chorale Passacaglia	2 Aria (Duet)	3 Recitat. Allusions to chorale melody	4 Aria	5 Recitat. Allusions to chorale melody	6 Aria	7 Chorale harmonization
RIST:	I	(II)	[III-V]	(VI-VII)	[VIII-X]	(XI)	XII

The first movement is one of the loftiest exhibitions of contrapuntal art, outstanding even among Bach's works. It is a passacaglia on a chromatically descending bass (*Ex. 10*) such as Baroque masters liked

Ex. 10. Cantata 78

etc.

to use in their 'Lamentos,' and which Sebastian himself employed in the Crucifixus of his great Mass. In the course of the variations the woeful figure is raised to the upper voices; and it appears in transposition and in contrary motion. Into this highly artificial shell Bach built without any apparent effort fugal interpretations of the chorale in which the cantus firmus in the soprano is supported by the polyphonic web of the other voices. The result is an awe-inspiring description of the Lord's suffering. After this overwhelming chorus, scored for a large orchestra, there follows a delicate duet for soprano and contralto (We hasten with eager yet faltering footsteps), accompanied only by cello, organ, and a stringed bass 'staccato e pizzicato.' In its ingratiating melody, strong dance rhythm with accent on first and third beats, uncomplicated harmonies and frequent progressions in parallel thirds and sixths (*Ex. 11*) we discover a Bach with leanings toward folk-

Ex. 11. Cantata 78

song-like simplicity.[1] A joyful tenor aria and a dramatic bass aria are each preceded by significant recitatives. Particularly moving is the second one, accompanied by strings, which turns eventually into a fervent arioso for which Bach even prescribed 'con ardore.' The final chorale expresses the confidence of the faithful that they will be united with Jesus all through 'sweet eternity.' Thus the cantata overwhelmingly testifies to Bach's *Jesusminne* and to his abiding faith in salvation through Christ the Lord.

No. 92, *Ich hab in Gottes Herz und Sinn* (To God I give my heart and soul), written for Septuagesima Sunday (January 28), 1725, consists of nine numbers, three of which (Nos. 1, 4, 9) use the words of

1. It is curious to note that the piece bears a certain resemblance to the delightful duet 'Hark, Hark' in Purcell's *Masque to 'Timon of Athens.'* The possibility that Bach knew the score cannot be completely discarded.

Paul Gerhardt's 17th-century poem unchanged, while in the remaining sections the hymn text, completely quoted, is interspersed with words by an unknown 18th-century poet (Nos. 2, 7), or else altogether paraphrased (Nos. 3, 5, 6, 8). Bach uses the old French tune to which Gerhardt's poem is usually sung in more than half the numbers of the cantata, whenever he employs the original text. The following table might exemplify the relationship of the cantata to its sources:

BACH:	1. Chorale chorus	2. Chorale & Recit.	3. Aria	4. Chorale Aria	5. Recit.
GERHARDT:	I	[II]	(III-IV)	V	(VI-VIII)
BACH:	6. Aria	7. Chorale & Recit.	8. Aria	9. Chorale harmon.	
GERHARDT:	(IX)	[X]	(XI)	XII	

The introductory chorus is a powerful chorale arrangement with cantus firmus in the soprano, while the lower voices and the orchestra contribute to the interpretation of the text. In No. 2, *Recitativo e Corale,* we find most striking contrasts between the chorale lines, accompanied by consistently repeated bass figures, and the very dramatic recitatives inserted between them. The rapid succession of short and basically different sections, declamation alternating with singing, creates a strangely disturbing piece, typically Baroque in its expression. The following aria for tenor, which describes the breaking down and the destruction of everything not sustained by God, brings the wild excitement to a climax. Both the singer (whose part presents almost insurmountable difficulties) and the orchestra create a mood of fierce exultation. No. 4, in which chorale text and melody are presented by the contralto, is more objective in character. It resembles in its construction the chorale aria of cantata 140 *Wachet auf* (Sleepers wake; cf. p. 175). In No. 92 Bach inserts the individual lines of the hymn tune into a trio for two oboï d'amore and bass, a beautiful musical composition complete in itself. The last aria in 3/8 for soprano, with its oboe d'amore solo and pizzicato of strings, has almost the character of a serenade. It presents a picture of the paradisian joy experienced by a soul resting in Jesus. In the narrow confines of a cantata forming but one section of the service, Bach conjured up the whole wide world of Baroque Protestantism. His congregation had to pass through the horrors of the powers of darkness before the glory of salvation rose dazzlingly before them.

No. 1, *Wie schön leuchtet der Morgenstern* (How brightly shines the morning star), written for Annunciation day, 1725, is an unusually sunny and optimistic work. It might almost be designated as a dance cantata since allusions to familiar dance rhythms appear in most of its numbers. The score prescribes two solo violins apart from oboi da caccia, two French horns, and a group of accompanying strings. This orchestration limits the size of the chorus in modern performances to 18th-century proportions, since the two instrumental soloists would obviously not be a match for a large group of singers. *Wie schön leuchtet* is a 'strict chorale cantata' based on a well-known hymn which uses words Philipp Nicolai wrote in 1599. Again Bach's first and last movements employ the initial as well as the concluding stanzas from Nicolai's poem, together with the melody of the chorale. The middle section of the hymn (stanzas II-VI) was not used in its original form, but condensed and paraphrased by an unknown author so as to provide the texts for two pairs of recitative with following aria. Owing to the absence of literal text quotations, those four numbers do not refer to the old hymn-tune. The first movement is a radiant chorale chorus in which, after an orchestral introduction in soft-hued pastel colors, the sopranos present the hymn tune in long extended notes, while the lower-pitched voices and the instruments happily skip around, frequently borrowing from the material of the chorale. Equally serene is the mood in the soprano aria, with oboe da caccia and thorough bass accompanyment. A feeling of happy impatience pervades this trio, in which the joyful anticipation of the Saviour's coming finds expression. Even more jubilant is the brilliant, technically quite difficult, tenor aria containing some striking tone paintings. Here the two solo violins heard in the initial chorus reappear, greatly adding to the festive character of the piece. The last number, a chorale harmonization adorned by expressive countermelodies of the second horn, voices in simple, but powerful language mankind's trust in its final redemption.

Closely related to the 'strict chorale cantatas' is No. 80, *Ein feste Burg* (A mighty fortress), which may have resounded for the first time at the Reformation Festival of 1724. The work resulted from the enlargement of a cantata (80a) on a text by Salomo Franck composed 1715 in Weimar (cf. p. 152). The first number of the original cantata was a chorale arrangement in which the oboe intones as cantus firmus a stanza of Luther's 'A mighty fortress,' while the bass utters a counter-melody proclaiming the triumphant message *Alles, was von Gott geboren, ist zum Siegen auserkoren* (Every soul by God created is to win its battle fated). Two solo numbers with preceding recitatives followed, and a simple harmonization of Luther's chorale[1] concluded the cantata. In this version the work, consisting of chorale arrangement, recitative, aria, recitative, aria, chorale harmonization, displayed a symmetrical structure. In Leipzig two powerful chorale choruses based on Luther's hymn were added, one at the beginning and one in the middle, following the first aria. The cantata's fine proportions suffered through this addition, but its expressive power was immeasurably increased. A second adaptation seems to have been carried out by Friedemann Bach, who inserted trumpets and kettle-drums into the choruses, a reorchestration which so greatly enhances the effect that it has been generally adopted.

The first number of the definite version is a magnificent chorus which develops the individual chorale lines in freely constructed fugatos. They are framed by a canon presenting the hymn tune in long notes in the highest and lowest instrumental parts. The ultimate degree of contrapuntal artistry is displayed here to symbolize the rule of the divine law throughout the universe. In the second new chorus all four voices sing the hymn tune in powerful unison. Around them roars the wildly turbulent orchestra, the hymn's 'fiends ready to devour' (*Ex. 12*). Whoever hears this grandiose piece will realize that for the composer, just as for the author of the hymn text, the devil repre-

Ex. 12. Cantata 80

1. It was probably BWV 303 (cf. *BJ* 1940/48, p. 11).

sented a quite real power. The fight is over when we reach the concluding chorale harmonization; the hymn is heard now for the fourth
time, and the congregation expresses in simple sounds its faith in the
eternal rule of Christian law.

No. 6, *Bleib bei uns* (Abide with us), probably written for Easter
Monday, 1725,[1] returns to the arrangement of the text favored by
Bach in the first set of his Leipzig cantatas. The Scripture reading of
this day reports how Christ joined two disciples on the road to Emmaus
and they beseeched Him to stay with them. 'Abide with us,' they ex-
claim, 'for it is toward evening, and the day is far spent' (Luke 24 :
29). In Bach's setting this no longer seems to be the prayer of two
persons only; mankind implores the Lord to remain at their side when
darkness threatens. The first part of the chorus, which reappears as a
third section in modified and greatly condensed form, expresses vague
fears assailing the heart. Here Bach forms a trio of two oboes and oboe
da caccia, and a second trio of two violins and viola. While the woodwinds utter a sweetly sorrowful tune somewhat resembling the melody
in the final number of the St. Matthew Passion, the strings accompany
with low-pitched repeated notes expressing weary dejection. The middle section uses the same text, but intensifies it dramatically through
an artful contrapuntal treatment. Bach introduces three new subjects,
different in their emotional impact, to interpret the three lines of the
text. In a most exciting manner these ideas are juxtaposed and inter-
woven. The ending is particularly moving: the human voices unite in
the outcry 'Abide with us,' while the instruments utter the other two
melodies. The following aria for contralto begins and ends with the
same instrumental ritornel, but uses in its vocal section the unfamiliar
form *abb'*, a procedure caused by Bach's desire to emphasize especially
the second half of the aria's text, 'Be, oh be our shining light, through
the darkness of the night.' In No. 3, an aria for soprano, the voice
presents in extended notes the chorale 'Ach bleib bei uns, Herr Jesu
Christ' (Abide with us, our blessed Lord), while a violoncello piccolo (a five-stringed smaller type of cello) vigorously accompanies
with a melody drawn from the hymn itself. This piece of a more instrumental character was later arranged by Bach as an organ composi-

1. It is significant for the great changes in present Bach research that Dürr in his
KB to NBA, series I, vol. 10 (Kassel, 1956, p. 45), states that the work probably
originated in 1736 while he ascribes it to 1725 in *BJ* 1957 (p. 80).

tion and incorporated among the Schübler Chorales (cf. p. 254). The nervously excited tenor aria No. 5, in G minor, still expresses apprehension, and only at the end of the concluding chorale, based on words by Martin Luther, does Bach turn to the major mode and thus convey an upsurge of confidence in the human heart.

A kind of postscript to the second set is provided by the cantatas produced in 1725 after Trinity (May 27) and before Advent (December 2). To this group may have belonged No. 79, performed on Reformation day (October 31), the cantatas No. 168 and 164 which may have been written in Weimar, as well as cantata No. 137, which displays a surprisingly retrospective character, since—similarly to No. 4—it employs in all its numbers the unchanged chorale text together with the chorale melody in various arrangements. A systematic application to new composition is not noticeable in these six months. Maybe—as Dürr assumes—Bach wanted to start the new set at the beginning of the church year.

The third group of cantatas is mainly authenticated by scores and a few parts preserved by Philipp Emanuel Bach. It starts with a cantata performed on Christmas Day, 1725, and reaches up to Septuagesima Sunday (February 9), 1727. The feverish intensity of creative work has somewhat abated. The third set of cantatas covers almost fourteen months, as certain Sundays and holidays were bypassed by the composer. It is also remarkable that Sebastian included in this set seventeen or eighteen cantatas by another composer, his kinsman, the Meiningen court conductor, Johann Ludwig Bach (1677-1731). Beginning with the feast of the Purification of the Virgin Mary (February 2), 1726, Johann Ludwig Bach's cantatas appear frequently in the Leipzig church calendar, no less than eleven of his scores having been copied by the Thomas Cantor himself.[1]

1. According to Dürr, the third Leipzig set probably comprised the following cantatas listed here in the order of the church year. Works by Johann Ludwig Bach —as enumerated in BG, vol. 41, p. 275 ff.—are designated by an "L" before the figure.
1725: 110, 57, 151, 28.
1726: 16, 32, 13, 72, L 9, L 1, L 2, L 3, L 4, L 5, 34a?, 15, L 10, L 11, L 6, L 12, L 8?, L 14, 43, 194?, 39, L 17, L 13, 88, 170, L 7, 187, 45, 102, 193, L 15, 35, L 16, 17, 19, 27, 47, 169, 56, 49, 98, 55, 52, 36a.
1727: 58, 82, 83?, 157, 84.
1726 or 1727: 129.

Ludwig's cantatas, which often consist of two sections, show uniformity in their structure.[1] The first number is based on a text from the Old Testament which is composed as a short polyphonic chorus, a duet, or a simple arioso for one soloist, a few instrumental measures usually preceding the vocal entrance. The composer liked to repeat this instrumental portion in the last number, thus giving stronger cohesion to the whole work. The introductory piece is succeeded by a series of secco recitatives, arias (mostly in da capo form), and duets. The fourth of these numbers is always based on a text from the New Testament. The conclusion is formed by a larger number for chorus, frequently consisting of three sections: a rather polyphonic vocal piece, a short instrumental interlude, and a simply harmonized final chorale to which the energetically moving instruments supply a powerful accompaniment.

Scheide[2] pointed out that Ludwig's compositions exercised also a certain influence on the work of Sebastian Bach. The Thomas Cantor's third set includes seven cantatas,[3] performed partly between and partly after Ludwig's compositions, which use librettos similar to those employed by the Meiningen conductor. They consist of two sections, the first being based on a text from the Old Testament set as a polyphonic chorus or (as in No. 88) as an aria. There follow a number of recitatives and arias, the fourth of which, serving as a kind of motto, employs a text from the New Testament. In the usual manner a chorale harmonization forms the conclusion.

Although Bach employed two Bible texts in certain cantatas of the preceding second set based on words by Mariane von Ziegler, the marked contrast between Old and New Testament texts reveals the influence of the works of Johann Ludwig Bach and also evokes echoes of Sebastian's own Mühlhausen cantatas.

Arthur Mendel (*MQ*, 1955, p. 341 ff) first raised doubts regarding the authenticity of cantata No. 15 hitherto attributed to J. S. Bach. William H. Scheide (*BJ*, 1959, p. 65 ff.), proceeding along similar lines, expressed the well-founded assumption that this cantata, performed on Easter Sunday, 1726, and followed on Easter Monday by L 10, was actually composed by the Meiningen court conductor.

1. Cf. K. Geiringer, *The Bach Family*, New York, 1954, p. 108 ff., and W. H. Scheide 'J. S. B.s Sammlung von Kantaten seines Vetters Johann Ludwig Bach' in *BJ* 1961, p. 5 ff.

2. *BJ* 1961, p. 16 ff.

3. Nos. 43, 39, 88, 187, 45, 102, 17.

Both the recurrence of earlier features and the introduction of new ones are noticeable throughout the third set. The texts include libretti by Neumeister (No. 28) and Franck (No. 72). Several cantatas employ arrangements of two different chorales,[1] and the form of the dialogue occurs repeatedly,[2] usually between the soul (soprano) and Jesus (bass). Solo cantatas for a single voice, as a rule with a concluding chorale (probably sung by the congregation), are an important innovation. All voice ranges are represented here, Nos. 52 and 84 being for soprano, 35, 169, and 170 for contralto, 55 for tenor, 56 and 82 for bass.

After using in his earlier sets adaptations of previously composed vocal works, Bach in the third set frequently employed former instrumental compositions for his church cantatas. No. 169, for instance, introduces as sinfonia a composition known to us as the first movement of the E major Concerto for harpsichord and orchestra (BWV 1053). An aria in the same cantata appears as the slow movement of this concerto, great skill being displayed in the insertion of the vocal part into an instrumental composition.[3] On the other hand the finale of this concerto was used for the sinfonia to cantata No. 49.[4] In cantata No. 52 the sinfonia is based on the initial movement of the first Brandenburg Concerto; in cantata No. 110 the overture of the fourth orchestral Suite in D major has been transformed into the introductory chorus, the first and last Grave serving as instrumental prelude and postlude respectively, while a chorus is built into the middle section.

No. 19, *Es erhub sich ein Streit* (See how fiercely they fight), was written for St. Michael's day (September 29), 1726. The composer

1. Nos. 28, 19, 13, 16, 27.

2. Nos. 57, 32, 49, 58.

3. The cantata's two movements and the harpsichord concerto seem both to be derived from a concerto for oboe and orchestra, lost today.

4. Similarly in cantata No. 35 the sinfonias with organ obbligato introducing the first and second sections of the cantata seem to have resulted from the initial and last movements of a harpsichord concerto, largely lost today (only the first 9 measures of the score being preserved; cf. BWV 1059). The contralto aria No. 2 in the same cantata may be derived from the concerto's middle movement. A reconstruction of the harpsichord concerto's score was attempted by this author with the assistance of graduate students in music at the University of California, Santa Barbara. This version had its first performance at the English Bach Festival in Oxford, June 24, 1965. It seems likely that the composition with harpsichord in turn was based on an earlier violin concerto. G. Frotscher attempted to re-create this very first version of the score (Halle, 1951).

himself may have contributed the words, using as his model an earlier
libretto by his friend, C. F. Henrici, who published his poetic works
under the pen name of Picander. The text based on Revelation describes the war in Heaven, with Michael and his angels battling 'the
great dragon called Satan'; a subject that had also been set to music in
a masterly composition by Sebastian's great kinsman, Johann Christoph
Bach.[1] Without any introduction the basses intone the powerful melody of the battle (*Ex. 13*), which works its way upward through the

Ex. 13. Cantata 19

voices. Presently trumpets and timpani set in, leading the hearer right
into the heart of the furious fight. The combat reaches its climax at
the beginning of the passionate middle part, when the powers of darkness make a supreme effort to conquer Heaven. But Michael foils the
foe; victory is won, and the unison of three trumpets confirms the doom
of the horrible dragon. A composer who had a dramatic effect primarily
in mind would have ended his movement here; to Sebastian, however,
it seemed essential to round off the chorus, and give it a perfect form.
He therefore retraced his steps and started once more: 'See how fiercely
they fight.' Then he relinquished the description from Revelation and
proceeded to report in a partly lyrical, partly epic manner on the results of the victory. There is a tender da capo aria for soprano with two
oboi d'amore and a *recitativo accompagnato* referring to the loving
kindness of the Saviour, to which the full string body contributes a
kind of halo. In a moving tenor aria the soul prays *Bleibt ihr Engel*
(Bide ye angels bide with me), and to enhance the power of the sup-
plication, the trumpet intones the hymn *Herzlich lieb hab' ich dich*
(I love Thee, Lord, with all my heart), whereby Bach apparently referred to the text of its third stanza 'Lord, let Thy blessed angels come
. . . to take my soul to Abraham's bosom.' The same idea is expressed

1. The score of the work was published by this author in *Music of the Bach
Family*, Cambridge, Mass., 1955, p. 36 ff.

in the cantata's last chorale, in which the heavenly hosts are implored to assist mankind in the hour of final need. The orchestration here is the same as in the first movement, thus implying that Michael's victory prepared the way for the soul's eternal triumph.

It should be mentioned that the first page of the autograph bears the following title in Bach's hand: *J. J. Festo Michaelis Concerto a 14*. The first two letters stand for *Jesu Juva* (Jesus help), an abbreviation often employed by the composer at the beginning of a work. The fourteen voices are three trumpets, three oboes, three stringed parts, the vocal quartet, and thorough bass (as usual, the composer does not count the timpani). The author's name is not on the manuscript, although there would have been room enough to insert it, and as a rule Bach does write it on his scores. However, for those initiated in number symbolism 14 stood for Bach (cf. p. 94), and the composer evidently considered it unnecessary to write his name a second time in letters.

One of Bach's most beautiful compositions for a single voice in which vocal virtuosity is markedly stressed is No. 56, *Ich will den Kreuzstab gerne tragen* (I will my cross-staff gladly carry), a work of intimate chamber character, intended for the nineteenth Sunday after Trinity (October 27), 1726. The heartfelt cantata for bass voice, strings, oboes, and oboe da caccia has stirred not only church congregations but concert audiences as well. The work has no introduction and starts with a broadly conceived da capo aria. In its middle part the solo voice suddenly sings in triplets, while the instruments keep up the former movement in eighth notes. The resulting combination of different rhythms expresses the passionate yearning in the words *Da leg' ich den Kummer auf einmal ins Grab* (There will I entomb all my sorrows and sighs) (*Ex. 14*). In the following moving arioso, inspired by the words *Mein Wandel auf der Welt ist einer Schiffahrt gleich* (My journey through the world is like a trip at sea), Bach depicts the movement of the waves through a rocking motive given out by the cello. This accompaniment is suddenly discontinued as the weary traveler reaches heaven and leaves the ship. Of equal beauty is a recitative near the end of the cantata expressing the soul's readiness to receive its eternal reward from the hands of the Lord. Here the composer makes use of the sustained notes of the strings, which he also uses in the recitatives of the St. Matthew Passion to accompany the utterances of Christ. In

Ex. 14. Cantata 56

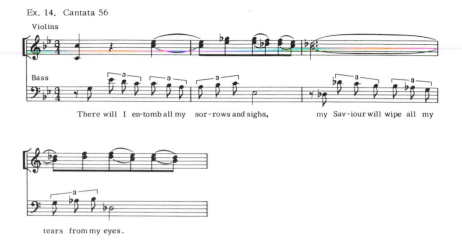

There will I en-tomb all my sor-rows and sighs,   my Sav-iour will wipe all my

tears from my eyes.

its second half the recitative very poetically turns into a quotation of the middle section of the first aria, thus creating a firm link between the initial and concluding solo numbers of the cantata. Even in a work so little suited to the inclusion of a hymn, Bach is loath to omit it, and he finishes his cantata with a simply harmonized four-part chorale.

About the character of the fourth set and, in particular, that of the fifth, very little is known, as most of these cantatas seem to be lost. More and more Bach relied on texts by the skillful amateur poet Picander. Dürr is probably justified in assuming that cantatas Nos. 120, 120a, 145, 149, 156, 159, 171, 174, 188, 197a, mostly on libretti by Picander, belonged to the fourth set and were produced in the second half of 1728 or in 1729.

In the two last decades of Bach's life his output in the field of the sacred cantata seems to have been quite small. Instrumental composition and secular cantatas absorbed his interest since 1729 when he had taken over the direction of the Collegium Musicum founded by Telemann. He also transformed secular cantatas into oratorios, which led to the production of the Christmas and the Ascension Oratorios written in 1734 and 1735. He often performed older sacred works unchanged or relied on adaptations of such compositions. The cantatas we know to have originated in this period are of superior value, but reveal no uniformity in their construction; almost all exhibit features discernible in former sets.

No. 140, *Wachet auf* (Sleepers wake), was written in 1731. Nicolai's beautiful hymn on which it is based deals with the parable of the wise and foolish virgins, and turns later to a description of heavenly Zion. In the first movement the chorale melody is presented in long notes by the soprano, under which the lower voices weave a vivid contrapuntal texture inspired by the words rather than by the hymn's melody. The orchestra adds a completely independent accompaniment picturing the approach of the heavenly bridegroom (a) and the eager anticipation of the maidens (b) (*Ex. 15*). Out of these various ele-

Ex. 15. Cantata 140

ments grows a sound combination of overwhelming sensuous beauty. In the magnificent second chorale arrangement (No. 4) the hymn tune intoned by the tenors is joined by a completely different violin melody of a caressing sweetness rarely to be found in Bach's cantatas; this depicts the graceful procession of the maidens going out to meet Jesus, the heavenly bridegroom (cf. p. 255). In the duets preceding and following this chorale arrangement the hymn tune is not used, and the pledges that Christ and the soul exchange sound not very different from those of earthly lovers. The first achieves a mood of sweet poignancy with the help of the bright cantilena intoned by a violino piccolo (a small violin tuned in Bach's scores a minor third higher than the parent instrument). The second, with its similarity of motives in both voices, points far into the future, to the duets between husband and wife in Haydn's *Creation* and Beethoven's *Fidelio*.

To the year 1731 also belongs No. 29, *Wir danken dir, Gott* (We thank Thee, Lord), written for the inauguration of a new city council. Because of the festive occasion Bach used trumpets and timpani in his orchestra. The introductory Sinfonia is an arrangement of the Preludio in the composer's Violin Partita No. 3 in E major (BWV 1006), a solo organ being entrusted with the brilliant part originally conceived for

the solo violin.[1] The structure of the seven vocal numbers that follow
is completely symmetrical. Two choral pieces using the full orchestra
surround three arias which are connected by two recitatives, the first
and third arias closely corresponding to each other. The initial chorus,
a fugue-like piece expressing feelings of gratitude to the Lord, was later
employed as the basis for the 'Gratias agimus' and 'Dona nobis' in
Bach's B minor Mass. The jubilant first and third arias use the text
Halleluja, Stärk' und Macht (Halleluja, strength and might). In their
musical content, too, they are almost identical; however, the third aria
is considerably shorter. It is transposed a fourth up, and Bach exchanged the original tenor voice for a contralto. Moreover the composer
replaced the violin solo of the tenor aria by an organ solo in the contralto piece, thus following the method employed in the introductory
Sinfonia. The tender soprano aria in between, the center of the whole
cantata, is cast in the form of a lilting siciliano, describing God's loving
mercy in a picture imbued with pastoral peace. Obviously Bach wanted
to convey here the feeling of security enjoyed by the citizens under the
new administration. There is a stirring episode at the end of the following secco recitative when the utterance of the contralto is interrupted
by a heartfelt 'Amen' sung by all the voices. The concluding plainly
harmonized hymn of thanks, with trumpets joining in at the end of the
chorale lines, is based on the melody of the hymn *Nun lob', mein' Seel',
den Herrn* (Now praise the Lord my soul). Thus throughout the composition gratitude to God is voiced, this mood being intensified by the
gentle joy radiating from the cantata's 'heart-piece.'

Related ideas find expression in quite a different way in No. 51,
Jauchzet Gott in allen Landen (Praise ye God throughout creation),
for solo soprano and orchestra, written about 1730. A singer of quite
outstanding abilities (boy soprano or student falsetto?) must have been
available to Bach, since the vocal part requires the skill of a virtuoso.
Bach also wrote almost as difficult a trumpet part for the cantata, thus

1. He transposed, however, the piece one tone down, as the key of D major was
better suited for the accompanying orchestra, and moreover the high e" with which
the violin prelude starts, was not available on the organ keyboard. While the original
composition, a kind of perpetuum mobile in constant sixteenth notes, was completely
idiomatic, the arrangement for the organ is less successful, as the fast passages are
not particularly effective on this instrument and are obscured whenever the accompanying trumpets raise their voices.

creating a kind of double concerto, unique in character. The composer himself may have been the author of the text, which expertly paraphrases verses from the Psalms. The first aria in resplendent C major presents the two soloists together with the accompanying orchestra of strings. The trumpet sets in full of joyful zest and is presently joined by the soprano jubilantly exhorting the whole creation to praise the Lord. Quite different from this piece of Baroque splendor is the second aria in A minor, in which only a figured bass accompanies the soprano. Its character is more intimate and prayerful, as the text addresses the loving father rather than the Lord of Glory. The sermon may have been inserted after this more sedate composition. As a concluding number, Bach used a chorale arrangement in C major by inserting into a richly polyphonic tricinium of two violins and bass the slightly ornamented chorale cantus firmus intoned by the soprano as a fourth voice. This piece reveals again that for Bach there was no basic difference between vocal and instrumental music, the chorale arrangement in this solo cantata being very similar to pieces Bach played on the organ. The last number reaches a climax in a mighty Alleluja, in which once more the trumpet and the full string ensemble join forces with the soprano. The breathless urgency of this somewhat theatrical piece, with its triads surging up like a flashing sword and its sweeping coloraturas (*Ex. 16*),

Ex. 16. Cantata 51

shows that Bach felt every means at his command ought to be used for the glorification of the Almighty.

In 1726 or 1728[1] Bach wrote the rather extensive wedding cantata No. 34a, *O ewiges Feuer, O Ursprung der Liebe* (Oh eternal fire, Oh

1. F. Hudson (in NBA I/33, KB, p. 46) considers it very likely that the work was first performed on November 8, 1728. Dürr assigns it to 1726.

source of love), which is not completely preserved.[1] Much later, possibly in the early 1740's, the composer remodeled this work into a sacred cantata for Pentecost, somewhat shortening the original score and rearranging its numbers. It was not necessary to alter the text very much, as Whitsuntide is a festival of love. The deep affection between husband and wife in the earlier work might be reinterpreted as burning love between mankind and its maker. Thus the new cantata No. 34 starts with a first chorus very similar to that of the model. It is a powerful piece in extended da capo form. Trumpets, timpani, and oboes are employed to increase the festive character, but at the same time the chorus is distinguished by remarkable fervor. The following aria for contralto *Wohl euch, ihr auserwählten Seelen* (Blessed ye souls whom God has chosen), scored for flutes and muted strings, displays a somewhat surprising pastoral character, which is motivated, however, by the text of the piece in the wedding cantata *Wohl euch, ihr auserwählten Schafe* (Blessed ye sheep whom God has chosen). Despite this slight incongruity, the aria, with the gentle charm of its orchestration and the sweet eloquence of its melodic language, is acknowledged as one of the most beautiful pieces Bach ever wrote. The last chorus *Friede über Israel* (Peace be unto Israel! Give ye thanks to God almighty) taking up the festive orchestration of the beginning, seems brief when compared to the imposing initial number. (In the model a less significant function was assigned to this piece; it marked the end of the cantata's first part.) But there is vigor, joy, and warm feeling in this utterance of a grateful heart, making it a fitting conclusion to one of Bach's most lovable cantatas.

Bach composed no Latin *motets*.[2] His office did not require him to

1. Apart from this sacred cantata written for a wedding service, Nos. 195, 196, 197, as well as the incompletely preserved 120a, were destined for such a purpose. Bach may also have employed at these occasions other, textually related, cantatas such as Nos. 97, 100, 9, 93, 99, 111 or wedding chorales (BWV, 250-52). Cf. Hudson, p. 7.

2. Among the extensive literature on B.s motets a few particularly significant articles should be singled out: B. F. Richter, 'Über die Motetten S.B.s,' *BJ* 1912, pp. 1-32; W. Luetge, 'B.s Motette, Jesu mein Freude,' *Musik und Kirche*, 1932, pp. 97-113; R. Gerber, 'Über Formstrukturen in B.s Motetten,' *Musikforschung*, 1930, pp. 177-89; K. Ameln, 'Zur Entstehungsgeschichte der Motette Singet dem Herrn ein neues Lied,' *BJ* 1961, pp. 25-34; U. Siegele, 'Bemerkungen zu B.s Motetten,' *BJ* 1962, pp. 33-57.

write works of this kind, and he was not interested in the genre, which he considered old-fashioned.[1] He did, however, produce six German motets for special occasions. One of them, *Lobet den Herrn, alle Heiden* (Praise the Lord all ye nations; BWV 230), was possibly completed before he came to Leipzig. The remaining five works—four destined for funerals, one probably for a birthday celebration—originated in the first decade of his service as Thomas Cantor. They are: *Jesu, meine Freude* (Jesus, dearest Master; BWV 227, comp. 1723), *Fürchte dich nicht* (Be not dismayed; BWV 228, comp. probably in 1726); *Der Geist hilft unsrer Schwachheit auf* (The Spirit also helpeth us; BWV 226, comp. 1729 and probably sung at the funeral of Rector Ernesti), *Komm, Jesu, komm* (Come, Jesus, come; BWV 229), and *Singet dem Herrn* (Sing unto the Lord; BWV 225), probably performed on May 12, 1727 as birthday celebration for the Elector Friedrich August 'the Strong' of Saxony.

In these motets Bach used the same kind of texts as in his early cantatas. The sources of his words are chorales and the Bible. His familiarity with the material, unusual even in religious circles, helped him compile deeply stirring and poetical texts.

The retrospective character of the motet form makes it understandable that Bach followed some of the methods employed by older members of his family. His second cousin, Johann Christoph Bach, too, wrote a motet *Fürchte dich nicht*, in which a Bible text is combined with a chorale text, and another kinsman, Johann Michael Bach, composed a motet *Jesu, meine Freude*, which is in E minor, like Sebastian's work of the same title. Nevertheless his main models for these compositions were not older German motets but his own cantatas. The melodic and the harmonic treatment of the voices, the rich polyphonic texture, and, most of all, the basic importance allotted to the chorale melodies, can be found here as in the cantatas. As a matter of fact Bach frequently wrote in his Weimar and early Leipzig cantatas motet-like choruses without independent instrumental parts.[2] On the other hand there are no arias or duets in the motets. Despite the lack of specific instrumental parts in the original scores, they were not performed only by voices. For the motet *Der Geist hilft unsrer Schwachheit auf*, the

1. A Latin Ode (BWV Anh. 20), which Bach wrote, is lost.
2. Cf. Nos. 182/7; 64/1; 38/1; 2/1; 28/2; 108/4; 243/11; 144/1; 4/5; 21/9; 68/5; 121/1; 179/1; 232/19, etc.

original set of string and wind instrument parts doubling the voices, as well as a figured bass, have been preserved. For *Lobet den Herrn*, too, Bach's continuo part exists. Real a cappella music was little heard at that time in Germany, and it seems certain that an organ or harpsichord, a string bass to reinforce the bass voice in the lower octave, and occasionally some additional instruments doubling the higher voices were used for performances of these motets.

The text of the four-part motet *Lobet den Herrn* consists of words from the short Psalm 117. This is the only motet without a chorale, and Bach also dispenses with a subdivision of the psalm text, which is composed as a grandiose double fugue with an extensive coda on the word 'Alleluja.'

Four motets (BWV 225-26, 228-29) are written for eight-part double chorus. Unlike earlier composers, Bach does not use a higher and a lower chorus, but prescribes two evenly balanced mixed vocal groups. At the performances he probably had only one to three singers for each voice.

In *Fürchte dich nicht* Bach sets to music two verses from Isaiah (41:10 and 43:1). The brisk alternation of the two choirs ends at the words 'I have redeemed thee,' and a fugue by the three lower voices ensues, in which the composer symbolizes Jesus' sacrifice with the help of a chromatically descending theme (*Ex. 17*), while the sopranos in-

Ex. 17. Motet: *Fürchte dich nicht*

I am He who has re - deemed_____ (thee)

tone the chorale 'Lord, my Shepherd, Fount of Gladness.'[1] The result is a work of strongest emotional impact which, because of its approach toward modal harmonization, displays a slightly archaic character. The motet has a remarkable symmetrical arrangement.[2] Its fugue begins in the 77th measure, thus dividing the 154 measures of the complete motet into two equal halves. Moreover there are certain breaks in measures 28 and 73 whereby three sections of 28 + 45 + 81 measures

1. It employs the eleventh and twelfth stanzas of Paul Gerhardt's hymn *Warum sollt ich mich denn grämen* (Why should I grieve?).

2. Cf. Peter Benary, 'Zum periodischen Prinzip bei J.S.B.' in *BJ* 1958, p. 91, and U. Siegele, p. 33 ff.

are created closely approaching the mathematical proportion 3:5:9.

Very different in mood is the eight-part motet *Singet dem Herrn*. Its extensive first movement employs the three first verses of Psalm 149 and assumes the form of a vocal prelude with ensuing fugue. The middle movement uses the third stanza of the chorale *Nun lob mein Seel* (Now bless my soul), based on Psalm 103, the individual hymn lines being interrupted by interludes quoting the first movement. The motet's third number again employs a psalm text (second verse of No. 150) and in conclusion a jubilant four-part fugue presents the psalm's sixth verse. Based on an unusually long theme in lively 3/8 time (*Ex. 18*) this piece bears a certain affinity to the *Pleni sunt coeli* of the

Ex. 18. Motet: *Singet dem Herrn*

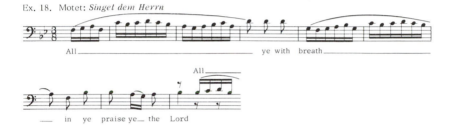

B minor Mass composed a few years earlier. One cannot admire enough Bach's art of achieving utmost clarity even in polyphonic numbers while putting the gigantic tonal masses into motion. The fugue is clearly divided into 32 + 4 + 40 + 4 + 32 measures thus creating the symmetrical construction *a-b-c-b-a*.[1]

Bach's only five-part motet, *Jesu meine Freude*, consists of eleven numbers, whereby six stanzas from Johann Franck's hymn alternate with five verses from the eighth chapter of the Epistle to the Romans. Interpretation and exegesis are offered after each verse by the appropriate quotation from the Bible. The first and sixth stanzas (Nos. 1 and 11) are presented in almost identical four-part harmonizations, while the stanzas in between are treated alternatingly as ornamentation or free setting of the chorale. To achieve greater formal symmetry Bach used closely related music for the first and fifth insertions (Nos. 2 and 10), while both the second and the fourth (Nos. 4 and 8) are the only numbers written in three parts. The centerpiece of the motet is the

1. Cf. Benary, p. 90.

big fugue No. 6, which is preceded by 209 and followed by 208 measures of music. The following over-all construction may be observed:[1]

1	2	3	4	5
4-part chorale harmoniz.	5-part Bible motet	5-part chorale ornament.	3-part Bible motet	5-part chorale free setting

		6		
		fugue 5-part		

7	8	9	10	11
4-part chorale ornament.	3-part Bible motet	4-part chorale free setting	5-part Bible motet	4-part chorale harmon.

This work, like all the other motets, can only be mastered by performers of the highest musicianship endowed with a tremendous voice range and a capacity for interpreting the countless shades of Bach's emotional palette. Such difficulties have not discouraged performers; in fact, the motets were almost the only vocal compositions by Bach never wholly forgotten. Zelter reports in a letter to Goethe how his singers loved to perform the motet *Singet dem Herrn,* and when Mozart heard the same work in 1789 in Leipzig 'his whole soul seemed to be in his ears' (Rochlitz). As early as 1803 five motets were made available in a printed collection.[2] This was not due only to the superb musical qualities of the motets; the deep abiding faith radiating from them brought to later generations a spiritual sustenance badly needed in periods of religious decline.

Among Bach's vocal compositions the *secular cantatas*[3] play a sig-

1. Cf. Siegele, p. 36.

2. The only one missing was *Lobet den Herrn alle Heiden.* Printed in its place was Johann Christoph Bach's *Ich lasse dich nicht,* then considered to be a work by Sebastian. It appeared in the Peters Edition up to 1949 with the erroneous attribution.

3. Important contributions to the research on Bach's secular cantatas were made by Friedrich Smend (*B. in Köthen,* Berlin, 1951) and Werner Neumann ('Das Bachische Collegium Musicum' in *BJ* 1960, p. 5-27, as well as in KB to NBA, vols. 36-38, Kassel, 1960-62).

nificant part. The composer wrote them for special occasions, such as weddings, birthdays, and namedays of important persons, or for events at the Leipzig University, many of them being first played by his Collegium Musicum. The dramatic power of Bach's art, an earthy sense of humor, and love of nature are strongly in evidence in the secular cantatas.

The exact number of these compositions is not known, but there may have been fifty or even more works of this kind. The thrifty composer did not cherish the idea of having some of his finest music performed only once. He used it over and over again, sometimes for other secular compositions, but frequently also for sacred works such as cantatas or oratorios. In Bach's time no one had any compunctions about doing this. Anything that stood artistically on a high level was suitable as a part of worship. Some of Bach's finest compositions were good 'parodies,' in which a secular work was raised to a higher spiritual level, without changing the prevailing mood. And in the process of adapting earlier compositions to new texts, Bach often made considerable alterations; he modified the instrumentation, adjusted the melodic line, and invented new counterpoints and modulations in order to achieve a better co-ordination of word and sound. Nevertheless it is true that at rare occasions a certain discrepancy occurred between the libretto and its musical setting.

In the Weimar period Bach produced cantata No. 208, *Was mir behagt, ist nur die muntre Jagd* ('The merry chase, the hunt is my delight'), written in all likelihood 1713 for the birthday of Duke Christian of Saxe-Weissenfels to words by Salomo Franck. In this allegorical work four mythological personages—the heavenly huntress Diana, the eager hunter Endymion, and the pastoral gods Pan and Pales—join forces to express to the prince, celebrating his birthday, the exaggerated flatteries common at the time. Bach bestowed the greatest care on the composition of this cantata, which consisted of no less than fifteen numbers. The delightful aria of Pales for two recorders and soprano *Schafe können sicher weiden* (Sheep may safely graze) ranks among the most intimate and amiable pastorales Bach ever wrote; it has become widely known through modern arrangements. The other solo numbers are hardly less inspired. It is not surprising that the composer again and again made use of the delightful work for specific occasions.

At Weimar he employed it—probably in 1716—for the birthday of
Prince Ernst August of Saxe-Weimar (in the score the name of Christian was simply changed to Ernst August). In Leipzig he performed
(in 1740 or 1742) the cantata in slightly altered form (BWV 208a)
with his Collegium Musicum for the nameday of the Elector Friedrich
August II of Saxony. In all likelihood it was also employed around
1729 with a different text for another festivity at the Weissenfels court.

Moreover Bach used it as a basis for sacred music. The bass aria
No. 7 and the soprano aria No. 13 were included in an extended and
revised form in the Pentecost cantata No. 68 performed in 1725. The
altered soprano aria employed the ostinato bass of the model (*Ex.
19*), to which a practically new melody was written, far exceeding the

Ex. 19. Cantata 208

original in warmth and beauty. Interestingly enough, this attractive
bass line occurs once more as the melody in an instrumental work for
violin, oboe, and continuo (BWV 1040). And finally the last chorus
in the 'Hunt' cantata was transformed into the opening chorus of cantata No. 149, written about 1728, and into the concluding chorus of
the cantata *Herrscher des Himmels, König der Ehren,* composed in
1740 in celebration of the newly elected city council and lost today.[1]

In Cöthen, Bach wrote a large number of secular cantatas. Smend[2]
lists more than a dozen of such works. Three are completely preserved,
while two are known to us from subsequent adaptations. Of the remaining pieces, however, the texts, or fragments of the music, employed in later arrangements, appear to be all that has survived. Yet the
scarce material available seems to point to a certain uniformity in
structure. These cantatas usually consisted of eight numbers, starting
with a recitative; they showed a preference for duets in which a solo
violin or obbligato woodwind instruments were used.

1. Cf. W. Neumann in *BJ* 1961, p. 52 ff.
2. Page 68 ff.

Of the three works that have come down to us in their entirety, the birthday cantata *Durchlaucht'ster Leopold* (Illustrious Leopold; BWV 173a) reappeared as the Pentecost cantata *Erhöhtes Fleisch und Blut* (Exalted flesh and blood; BWV 173), and the congratulatory cantata *Die Zeit, die Tag und Jahre macht* (The time creating days and years, BWV 134a) was adapted into the Easter cantata, *Ein Herz, das seinen Jesum lebend weiss* (A heart that knows his risen Lord; BWV 134). The secular wedding cantata *Weichet nur betrübte Schatten* (Vanish now, ye mournful shadows; BWV 202) exists in the original version only; apparently it did not lend itself to a transformation into a sacred work because of its light, often dance-like character. In this solo cantata for soprano, oboe, strings, and continuo Bach offered a singularly beautiful picture of youth and spring. The arpeggios at the beginning, describing the gently lifting wintry fog, would hardly seem amiss in the score of Haydn's *Seasons* (Ex. 20). In the second aria (No. 3) the

Ex. 20. Cantata 202

busily moving continuo seems to describe Phoebus' gayly prancing horses mentioned in the text. Aria No. 7 resembles a passepied dance (see p. 125) and the traditional final chorale of the church cantata is replaced here with a gay gavotte, in which all the instruments join the soprano to wish the best of luck to the newly married couple.

Of the secular cantatas preserved, the majority originated in Leipzig. On August 3, 1725, the 'dramma per musica' *Der zufriedengestellte Aeolus* (The pacified Aeolus; BWV 205) was performed in honor of the nameday of Dr. Augustus Müller, member of the faculty of Leipzig University. The libretto, based partly on Virgil, tells how Aeolus, the god of the winds, is planning to release the autumn gales. Zephyrus, the mild west wind, and Pomona, the fruit goddess, vainly implore him to wait; but when Pallas Athene, the goddess of wisdom, approaches him and tells him that she is preparing a celebration in honor of Dr. Müller, this impresses the god so strongly that he recalls his subjects. Bach's very striking music is unusually richly scored, with trumpets, French horns, flutes, various oboes and strings. The first chorus, *Zerreisset, zersprenget, zertrümmert die Gruft* (Come away ye tornadoes, break out from your cave), and the ensuing recitative present some of the wildest descriptions of turbulent elements that the composer ever wrote. Similar in expression is the second aria of Aeolus (bass), accompanied by trumpets, timpani, and horns, without any woodwind or strings. A most effective contrast is achieved by the aria of Zephyrus, whose gentle nature Bach portrays with the help of the silvery viola da gamba and the tender viola d'amore.[1]

Nine years later, the composer used the same music in honor of another man by the name of Augustus, when his Collegium Musicum celebrated the coronation of the Saxonian Elector, Friedrich August II, as king of Poland. The new text, probably written by Picander, substitutes Valour for Aeolus, Justice for Zephyrus, and Leniency for Pomona (BWV 205a). It cannot be said that the change is altogether successful. The text of the aria of Justice, for instance, with its shallow praise of the ruler, does not fit the peculiarly delicate instrumentation taken over from the original.

Der Streit zwischen Phoebus und Pan (No. 201; The contest between Phoebus and Pan), possibly performed as early as 1729, is a satiric burlesque by Picander, based on Ovid's *Metamorphoses,* in which Picander and Bach ridicule the new trends in music. Phoebus, representing tradition, has a singing competition with Pan, the representative of new-fangled notions. Among the judges, Tmolus is in favor of Phoebus, whereas Midas prefers Pan's foolish song, and in punishment for his faulty judgment is given long donkey's ears. In this work Bach had a chance to vent his contempt for the aesthetic views held by a younger generation, views that were soon to find an eloquent advocate in Johann Adolf Scheibe (see p. 89). The ill-advised Midas, in praising Pan's song,[1] which he could grasp and remember after a single hearing, and in criticizing Phoebus' art as too complex, only echoed what Bach had to hear time and again from

1. The viola d'amore is a string instrument equipped with metal strings below the fingerboard. They sound in sympathy with the fingered strings, thus producing a tender and slightly blurred tone quality. Regarding viola da gamba, see p. 147.

2. This song (No. 7) was also used by Bach with changed words in his 'Peasant Cantata,' No. 212.

younger musicians. The music to this satire is quite delightful. Phoebus' prize-song (No. 5), to an accompaniment of muted strings, oboe d'amore, and flute, exhibits great artistry in its intricate rhythmic differentiation and dynamic shading. Pan's aria is simple and rather crude, and is written in the form of a rustic dance. The ensuing aria of Tmolus (No. 9) exhibits remarkable dynamics. In its first measures the composer clearly asks for a crescendo, though employing a rather peculiar form of notation (Ex. 21). When Midas defends his opinion,

Ex. 21. Cantata 201

Bach indicates in the music that this was the judgment of a donkey, deserving his punishment of donkey ears. These long ears the singer describes, while the violins imitate the braying in a manner similar to Mendelssohn's Overture to 'Midsummer Night's Dream' (Ex. 22).

Ex. 22. Cantata 201

Of more general interest is another humorous work, the *Coffee Cantata* (BWV 211) performed between 1732 and 1735 by the Collegium Musicum. It employs three vocalists, strings, and flute. Picander's amusing text is composed in the manner of a comic oratorio. A 'historicus' (tenor), in the style of the Evangelist in the Passions, explains the plot at the beginning and again near the end. Also in this work two generations confront each other, but this time the younger one is victorious. Father Schlendrian (bass)[1] is worried because his daughter

1. Henry S. Drinker (*Texts of the Vocal Works of J.S.B.*, New York, 1942-43, vol. 3, p. 496) aptly translates his name as 'Old Stick-in-the-Mud.'

Liesgen (soprano) has fallen victim to the new craze for coffee drink-ing. All his attempts to lure her away from so detestable a habit by promises or threats have proved unsuccessful, until he offers her a hus-band as a bribe. This she enthusiastically accepts and the father rushes off to secure one. Picander's little poem ends at this point. Bach, how-ever, had learned only too well from his own family-life that it is not so easy to influence the young. He therefore added a recitative, in which Liesgen's plans are revealed: any man who wishes to wed her must consent to a clause in the marriage contract entitling her to drink coffee whenever she pleases. Finally, there is a short *coro* of the three singers accepting the coffee craze as something inevitable. With the help of masterly touches a little comedy is created that makes a charm-ing effect both in the concert hall and on the stage. The composer suc-ceeds in building up two characters who are very human indeed: a grumbling, boorish father and an obstinate, wily daughter. The carica-ture of the father is drawn with particular gusto. When the 'historicus' first mentions him, heavy dotted rhythms appear in the bass, with the prescription *con pompa,* while in the first aria the violins growl to indicate his vicious temper. When he later threatens to deprive Liesgen of her fashionable crinoline, Bach indicates its terrific width by the skip of a ninth (*Ex. 23*). Liesgen's aria (No. 4) in praise of coffee is a

Ex. 23. Cantata 211

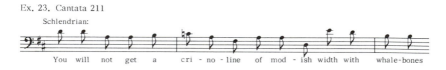

You will not get a cri - no - line of mod - ish width with whale-bones

little conventional in its musical diction, as though the composer wanted to hint that the girl had adopted coffee drinking merely to follow a fashion. In the second aria (No. 8), however, her enthusiasm for a prospective husband is not simulated. The joy she expresses in this folksong-like tune in dance rhythm is quite infectious and carries the listener away. There is even a bit of coarse humor. When Liesgen expresses her wish to find a 'husky lover' before going to bed, the violins and violas grow silent so as to make the audience understand every word of this rather outspoken statement. It is possible that the part of infatuated Liesgen was, in accordance with the prevailing custom, sung in falsetto by a male student, which would have further added to the comic effect of the work.

The congratulatory cantatas that Bach composed at about the same time for members of the ruling house, are best known today from subsequent adaptations. The allegorical cantata *Hercules auf dem Scheidewege* (Hercules at the crossroads; BWV 213), which was produced on September 5, 1733, in honor of the birthday of Prince Friedrich Christian of Saxony, was used for the Christmas Oratorio composed in the following year, only the recitatives and the final chorus being omitted. This chorus is, incidentally, based on one included in the Pentecost cantata No. 184 of 1724, which, in turn, is apparently a 'parody' from a Cöthen cantata not known to us today.[1] Likewise four movements (Nos. 1, 5, 7, 9) of the cantata *Tönet ihr Pauken, erschallet Trompeten!* (Sound ye drums, and blow ye trumpets!; BWV 214) performed on December 8, 1733, for the Electress's birthday, were included in the Christmas Oratorio. From the cantata *Preise dein Glück* (Praise thy good fortune, blessed Saxony; BWV 215), celebrating the anniversary of the Saxonian ruler's election as king of Poland on October 5, 1734, aria No. 7 was adapted for the same oratorio, while the first chorus of this cantata subsequently reappeared in a new adaptation in the Osanna of the B minor Mass.[2] *Auf schmetternde Töne* (Ring out all ye trumpets; BWV 207a) was played on August 3, 1735, in honor of the Elector's nameday. This is a 'parody' of the cantata *Vereinigte Zwietracht* (United discord; BWV 207) performed on December 11, 1726, to celebrate the appointment of Dr. Kortte as university professor. Its first chorus and the ritornel after aria No. 6 employ material from the first Brandenburg Concerto. The cantata *Schleicht, spielende Wellen* (Glide playful waves; BWV 206) played on October 7, 1736, in celebration of the Elector's birthday and a few years later for his nameday, is free from any 'parody.' Here four rivers, Pleisse (soprano), Danube (alto), Elbe (tenor), and Weichsel (bass), join forces to glorify the ruler and his wife, through whose territories they flow. In the composition each of the four is given a character of its own through the specific orchestration of the respective aria. The highlight of the

1. Cf. Smend, *B. Kirchenkantaten*, VI, p. 19.
2. Both BWV 215/7 and 232/22 seem to be derived from a lost congratulatory cantata, BWV Anh.11.

cantata is the first chorus, which presents a delightful, joyous portrayal of rushing and gently flowing waters.[1]

In a category of its own belongs Bach's latest congratulatory work, the so-called *Peasant Cantata* (BWV 212) which he wrote in 1742 in honor of Carl Heinrich von Dieskau, new lord of the manor of three villages near Leipzig. The text of this *Cantate en burlesque* is again by Picander; it is partly in Saxon dialect, and Bach has given each of the numbers the character of a then fashionable dance, such as bourrée, mazurka, and polonaise, while the overture is a medley of fragments from various folkdances. Three actual folksongs (*Ex. 24*) are even

Ex. 24. Cantata 212

Oh, may you get ten thou-sand duc - ats for ev - er - y day in the year.

inserted in the arias,[2] and Bach aimed at similar results with his own tunes. The orchestra, in true peasant manner, consists in most of the numbers of only one violin, one viola, and a double bass (continuo). Equally economical is the vocal apparatus: one soprano and one bass. The humorous plot, the very limited number of performers, and the unassuming, catchy musical idiom clearly indicate Bach's versatility. He showed that, although his main interest belonged to more intricate forms, he was quite willing at times to forsake his aloofness and write music so simple and appealing that even contemporary critics holding diametrically opposite views could find no fault with it.

Three sacred works of the Leipzig period destined for high holydays were designated by Bach as 'oratorios.' All are dependent on former secular compositions. The oldest is the Easter Oratorio (BWV 249),

1. The music to the following cantatas intended for the Saxonian court, is partly or completely lost, whereas the texts survive: *Entfernt euch* (BWV Anh.9) for the Elector's birthday, May 12, 1727; *Ihr Häuser* (BWV 193a) for his nameday, August 3, 1727; *Es lebe der König* (BWV Anh.11) for a similar occasion in 1732; *Frohes Volk* (BWV Anh.12) for the new Elector's nameday in 1733; *Willkommen, ihr herrschenden Götter* (BWV Anh.13) in honor of Friedrich August II, performed on April 28, 1738.

2. Nor did Bach hesitate to include a melody by Anton Seemann, conductor of Count Sporck, in Aria No. 16.

which was first performed on April 1, 1725. As Smend[1] proved, this is a 'parody' of the pastoral cantata No. 249a, *Entfliehet, verschwindet* (Take flight, disappear), on a text by Picander produced only five weeks earlier for Duke Christian of Saxe-Weissenfels's birthday on February 23, 1725. In the following year Picander transformed his poem, and Bach employed the music for the third time as a birthday cantata in honor of Count Flemming (August 25, 1726) entitled *Verjaget, zerstreuet* (Expel, disperse; BWV 249b). The similar meter and content in the three texts facilitated the procedure.

The most important and, at the same time, the most extensive of these three works is the second, the *Christmas Oratorio* (BWV 248) completed 1734. Basically this is a series of six cantatas, which were performed on the three Christmas days (December 25, 26, 27, 1734), New Year's day, the following Sunday, and Epiphany, 1735; yet it shows a certain unity in its construction. Sections from the New Testament (Luke 2:1,3-21; Matthew 2:1-12) are narrated by an 'Evangelist,' while the utterances of individual persons are entrusted to soloists, and those of a group to the chorus. The Biblical text is again and again interrupted by chorales and arias or recitative-like ariosos accompanied by the orchestra. The result is true church music, serving the purpose of edifying and uplifting the congregation. The sequence of keys and the orchestration give a kind of rondo-like character to the composition. Cantatas I, II, VI are in the main key of D major and are scored for a big orchestra (with trumpets, timpani, woodwind, strings); II, IV, and V, which are in the related keys of G, F, and A major, do not use trumpets.

The Christmas Oratorio offers us a chance to study the technique employed by Bach in his 'parodies.'[2] As model for one of its numbers he used an aria which in the cantata 'Hercules at the crossroads' Sensuality sings to the young Hercules (BWV 213, No. 3). It begins with the words, 'Sleep, my beloved, enjoy thou thy rest,' and accordingly the composer set it as a lullaby. Without compunction he could use it for

1. *Archiv für Musikforschung*, VII, 1941, p. 3 ff.

2. As mentioned previously the work is based on several secular cantatas. Nos. 4, 19, 29, 36, 39, 41 are taken from BWV 213; Nos. 1, 8, 15, 24 from BWV 214; No. 47 from BWV 215. Part VI seems to be derived from the sacred cantata 248a no longer in existence. For further information regarding the 'parodies' used in this work cf. KB to NBA II/6, p. 162 ff.

another lullaby in the Christmas Oratorio starting with the words
'Sleep, my beloved, and rest thee a while' (No. 19). But in the case of
the aria 'Prepare thyself Zion' of the Christmas Oratorio (No. 4) it is
rather different, as a comparison with the original text from 'Hercules'
(BWV 213, No. 9) will show.

HERCULES:	CHRISTMAS ORATORIO:
I will not regard thee	Prepare thyself, Zion,
but wholly discard thee,	with tender emotion
Contemptible pleasure,	The Fairest, the Dearest
I value thee not.	to welcome to thee.
Like the serpent	With what yearning
who attacked me in my cradle	must thy heart to-day be burning
Thee will I strangle	Welcome thy dear one
thou serpent, destroy thee.	with loving devotion.

To overcome the emotional disparity between the two texts, Bach
changed both the scoring and the phrasing. The original was for violin
I and II in unison, and continuo. In the oratorio he omitted the violin
II and replaced it by the tender oboe d'amore. At the same time the
bassoon was added to the bass. The threatening 'unisono e staccato' in
the secular cantata was, with the help of slurs and appoggiaturas, transformed into a caressing tune (Ex. 25). On the other hand the winding

Ex. 25.   *Hercules at the Crossroads*

Violin I

unisono e staccato

Christmas Oratorio

Oboe d'amore I
Violin I

line in the bass, used in 'Hercules' to portray the snake, was not con-
spicuous enough to call for a change. Thus Bach achieved a successful
adaptation with a minimum of effort.

    It is hard to single out individual numbers of this masterpiece. Al-
most all parts of the work start with a brilliant introductory chorus in a
gay dance-like triple time. The first begins in a rather unorthodox man-

ner with a festive timpani solo. Though the instrument was used because it had also been employed in the initial chorus to BWV 214, *Tönet ihr Pauken* (Resound ye timpani), which served as a basis for the 'parody,' it seems completely appropriate for the scintillating chorus of the Christmas Oratorio. In the second cantata the introductory chorus is replaced by a sinfonia, a siciliano of singular beauty, akin in character to the Pastoral Symphony in Handel's *Messiah,* but definitely deviating from it in its more intricate texture and orchestration, with alternating groups of woodwinds and strings. The treatment of the chorales is highly significant. Three times Bach employs the tune *Vom Himmel hoch, da komm' ich her* (From heaven above to earth I come): at the end of the first cantata, in the middle, and at the end of the second. The last time the chorus sings the sweet melody the orchestra concludes each line with a quotation from the blissful pastorale of the sinfonia, thus tying together the cantata's beginning and end. Although the general mood of the oratorio is one of exultation, the thought of Christ's sacrifice also plays an important role. The Passion hymn *Herzlich tut mich verlangen* (My heart is ever yearning) appears both as the first and as the ultimate chorale of the whole oratorio, thus emphasizing that only through the death of Jesus did the birth of the heavenly child result in the salvation of mankind.

Bach's oratorio for Ascension day, *Lobet Gott in seinen Reichen* (Praise God in His Kingdom; BWV 11) was first performed on May 19, 1735. The narration of episodes from the New Testament through a tenor (Evangelist), and the inclusion of accompanied recitatives and arias voicing observations of the faithful, may account for the designation 'oratorio' for a composition which on the whole resembles a church cantata, and was included by the Bachgesellschaft among these works. It appears likely that some of the main pieces of the composition (1, 4, 10) result from the 'parody' of earlier secular compositions no longer in existence.[1] A broadly contoured chorus in ternary form scored for trumpets, timpani, flutes, oboes, and strings serves as the jubilant introductory piece. Following this powerful song of praise the story of Christ's farewell and His ascension into heaven unfolds. There is a moving bass recitative (No. 3), in which dropping staccato passages

1. Cf. A. Pirro, *L'Esthétique de B.,* Paris, 1907, p. 349, and F. Smend, 'B.s Himmelfahrtsoratorium,' in K. Matthaei, *B. Gedenkschrift 1950,* Zürich, 1950, p. 42 ff.

express the bitter tears of man, soon to be separated from his Saviour. Even stronger emotions are expressed in the following aria for contralto. Sorrow and despair reach a climax here and it is characteristic that at a later date Bach took up this poignant number in the 'Agnus Dei' of his Mass in B minor. According to the narrator's report, Christ now rises to Heaven. The chorale in the center displays a serene, detached, almost dance-like quality to show that all sorrow and anguish have been left behind. Thereupon successive recitatives lead to an aria for soprano voicing the soul's longing to follow Christ. This piece is scored for high-pitched woodwind and strings without basses, to symbolize freedom from terrestrial fetters. The concluding number is a mighty chorale arrangement. Embedded in a brilliant concerto of the full orchestra are the utterances of the chorus, consisting of the choi melody *Von Gott will ich nicht lassen* (God I won't relinquish), presented in long notes in the soprano and accompanied by exultant passages of the lower voices. While the text expresses the timid question 'when will the hour be when I may see my Saviour,' the music seems to give the triumphant answer that the time is close at hand.

According to the Obituary, Bach wrote five Passions, as he is reported to have contributed five sets of church cantatas. Two of them have been completely preserved, the Passion according to St. John and that according to St. Matthew.[1] Of the Passion according to St. Mark, most of the music is lost. The Passion according to St. Luke preserved in a Leipzig manuscript, partly written by Bach himself, is so weak a composition that we are justified in considering it as the work of a minor contemporary, which Bach copied for the purpose of performing it. About the fifth Passion nothing is known. Spitta[2] suggests that Bach

---

1. Among the very extensive literature dealing with B.s Passions the following studies might be singled out: W. Werker, *Die Matthäuspassion*, Bachstudien II, Leipzig, 1923; F. Smend, 'Die Johannespassion von B.,' *BJ* 1926, p. 105 ff.; F. Smend, 'B.s Matthäuspassion,' *BJ* 1928, p. 1 ff.; H. Abert, 'B.s Matthäuspassion,' (*Gesammelte Schriften*), Halle, 1929; K. Ziebler, 'Aufbau und Gliederung der Matthäuspassion von J.S.B.,' *Musik und Kirche*, IV, 1932, p. 145 ff.; M. Schneider, 'Revisionsbericht zur Urtextausgabe der Matthäuspassion,' BG, IV (new revision 1935); F. Smend, 'B.s Markuspassion,' *BJ* 1940/48, p. 1 ff.; W. Serauky, 'Die Johannes-Passion von J.S.B. und ihr Vorbild,' *BJ* 1954, p. 29 ff.; J. Chailley, *Les Passions de J.S.B.*, Paris, 1963.
2. Vol. II p. 335.

may have set to music a text which Picander published in 1725; Smend,[1] on the other hand, conjectures that the work was based on the Gospel of St. Matthew and composed for a single chorus, unlike the St. Matthew Passion we know.

The *St. John Passion* (BWV 245) was first performed on Good Friday, 1724, but, according to recent research,[2] its origin may go back to the Weimar years. For four subsequent presentations under Bach's direction the composer made various alterations. Basically the work shows the construction to be found in the later Passion and in the Christmas Oratorio. The main part of the text is Biblical, in this case taken from St. John 18-19 (with short insertions from St. Matthew). The narration is done in recitative form by a tenor, the Evangelist, accompanied only by the organ and bass instruments; individual characters, including Christ, are sung by soloists, utterances of several persons and of the crowds, by the chorus. Ariosos and arias inserted in between express the reaction of the individual to the events described, the chorales, that of the whole congregation. The work is in two sections, to be performed before and after the sermon. It seems that Bach himself was responsible for the selection of the chorales, and that he also provided the texts for the arias. In these he often followed the model of the widely known text by Hamburg Councillor Barthold Heinrich Brockes, *Der für die Sünden dieser Welt gemarterte und sterbende Jesus* (Jesus tortured and dying for the sins of this world). But even in these pieces Bach never copied Brockes literally, and, in particular, he did not adopt the poet's rhymed paraphrases of the Bible text. Moreover, he included some words from J. G. Postel's 'St. John Passion,' which Handel had set to music at the age of nineteen. Bach apparently knew this score, as there are a few slight analogies between the two works.

An interesting peculiarity of Bach's composition[3] is the repeated use of the same music for various short choruses of the crowds. Some pieces

---

1. *Kirchenkantaten*, II, p. 14.

2. Cf. A. Mendel, 'Traces of the Pre-History of B.s St. John and St. Matthew Passions,' in W. Gerstenberg, *Festschrift O. E. Deutsch*, Kassel, 1963, p. 31 ff., and A. Mendel, 'Documentary Evidence concerning the Aria "Ich folge dir gleichfalls" from B.s St. John Passion' in *College Music Symposium*, New Brunswick, Fall 1965, p. 63 ff.

3. A revised edition of the work was presented by A. Mendel, New York, 1951.

are employed twice; one, with little variations, as often as five times (Nos. 3, 5, 25, 29, 46). It has been suggested that lack of time in preparing the score for the first performance caused Bach to adopt this method. Had this been the case, the composer could easily have remedied this deficiency when he subsequently revised the work. Actually, these repetitions are indispensable for the architectural plan as Bach had conceived it. In order to achieve a symmetrical arrangement he distributed related choruses in widely separated sections of his score. Take, for instance, the 'heart-piece'[1] of the second part: Here the choruses No. 29 and 34 (separated by the solos 31-32) form a unit that recurs with similar music in the choruses No. 46 and 50 (separated by the solo No. 48). In the center of the section is a chorale (No. 40), just as chorales (Nos. 27 and 52) frame the whole 'heart-piece.' Therefore this is the over-all arrangement:

A	B	C	D	E	D	C	B	A
27	29,31/2,34	36	38	40	42	44	46,48,50	52

(The numbers missing in this table refer to recitatives in which the Bible text is uttered by the Evangelist.)

Both the regular alternation of tutti choruses with solo recitatives and arias and the strictly symmetrical construction in this section produce a form reminiscent of Bach's concertos, a fact not surprising in view of the close relationship between Bach's instrumental and vocal works and between his sacred and secular music.

The choruses of the Jews in the St. John Passion demonstrate a strangely wild, passionate, and disturbing character. They produce a weird picture of human masses gone out of control. These scenes go well with the intensely dramatic, almost violent recitatives. How stirring, for instance, is the recitative No. 18 which turns into an arioso depicting Peter's tears, and the ensuing tenor aria in F sharp minor expressing mankind's confusion and desolation! By and large the great arias in this Passion are among the most impressive pieces of the score. Particularly dramatic is the bass aria No. 48, in which excited exclamations of the chorus again and again interrupt the utterances of the soloist. There is a counterpart in No. 60, where the bass joins forces

1. Cf. Smend in *BJ* 1926 and in *B. in Köthen,* p. 112.

with the chorus which intones a simply harmonized chorale. Hymn tunes, mostly in plain four-part setting, play a very important part in the score and strike a tender, warmly human note otherwise not prevailing in this work. It is characteristic that both sections of the St. John Passion end with straight chorale harmonizations. This was not the case in the second version of 1725 where an intricate chorus concluded the work.[1] In the course of a revision Bach replaced it by the simple visionary chorale *Ach Herr, lass dein lieb' Engelein* (Lord Jesus, Thy dear angel send). Other important changes took place before the composition achieved its definite form. The tender chorale arrangement which formed the beginning of the St. John Passion[2] was replaced by a monumental chorus depicting in grandiose manner the basic idea of the Passion: heavenly power as opposed to earthly suffering. Bach also eliminated the aria 'Do not writhe tormented souls' (BWV 245c) and replaced it by one of the highlights of the score, the arioso No. 31 with following aria. In the accompaniment of the arioso the mellow two viole d'amore and the lute help to conjure up a vision of celestial bliss rising out of physical pain. In the aria No. 32 Bach was inspired by the text's reference to a rainbow to express overwhelmingly in music the idea of salvation. In making this change he achieved an overpowering contrast between the crude picture of tortured Jesus and the unearthly joy derived from His sacrifice. The two pieces reveal, with an intensity rarely equaled in Bach's works, the composer's innermost faith.

Bach performed his *St. Matthew Passion* (BWV 244) on Good Friday, 1729.[3] We do not know how long he was engaged in the tremendous task of its composition. It seems that while he was working on the Passion news reached him that on November 19, 1728, his beloved former patron, Prince Leopold of Anhalt-Cöthen, had suddenly died,

---

1. It was inserted as final chorus into the cantata No. 23.

2. It was transplanted into the St. Matthew Passion to conclude its first part.

3. Schering's theory that the performance of the St. Matthew Passion did not take place until 1731 and that the St. Mark Passion was played in 1729 (cf. *BJ*, 1939) can no longer be upheld, in spite of the many psychological reasons which seem to corroborate the later date. Smend pointed out in *BJ*, 1940-48, that Zelter, in the program notes to the first Berlin performance of the St. Matthew Passion in 1829, referred to the 'old church text,' evidently the church program of the Passion in his possession, which was clearly dated 1729. However, Zelter emphasized that it was not certain whether this was the first performance of the work. A performance as early as 1727 is not impossible, although unlikely (cf. footnote p. 65).

and that he was expected to supply and perform music for a memorial
service the following spring. Nothing appeared more appropriate than
to use parts of his sublime new work for this purpose, and so Picander,
the librettist of the St. Matthew Passion, was requested to paraphrase
the text of ten pieces.[1] The funeral cantata *Klagt, Kinder* (Lament,
O children; BWV 244a)[2] was played on March 24, 1729, at Cöthen.
Shortly afterwards, on April 15, the mighty Passion itself resounded at
St. Thomas'.

The St. Matthew Passion represents the climax of Bach's music for
the Protestant Church. His own conception of its importance is clearly
revealed in the exquisite score he made of it for a subsequent performance, a score which is unique even among his many beautiful manuscripts. He worked on it with ruler and compass, and he used red ink
for the utterances (recitatives) of the Evangelist to distinguish the divine message from the rest of the text. The composer wanted this
Passion to be of general appeal, and indeed there is in this work a
simplicity and directness not often to be found in Bach's larger compositions. The motto Beethoven placed in front of his 'Missa Solemnis'
—'It comes from the heart—may it go to the heart'—can well be applied
to this work also.

The text of the St. Matthew Passion appears in the second part of
Picander's *Ernst-Schertzhaffte und Satyrische Gedichte*, published in
1729. Spitta pointed out[3] that the author merely reproduced the madrigalian poems while omitting both the Bible words and the chorale
texts. This may indicate that Bach himself was responsible for the selection of the sacred texts, and he may also have exerted some influence
on Picander's own idiom, as the libretto contains some allusions to
poems by Salomo Franck. Thus the text that emerged fully conformed
to the composer's wishes.

The work's construction is related to that of the St. John Passion.
Here again the words of the gospel (St. Matthew, 26-27) are the basis,
with the addition of Picander's madrigalian texts, which in ariosos,

---

1. They are Nos. 10, 12, 47, 58, 66, 29, 26, 75, 19, 78.

2. Smend in *B. in Köthen*, p. 86 ff. proved from the Cöthen account books that
not one, but two funeral cantatas were performed on this occasion, one on March 23
at night and *Klagt, Kinder* on March 24. Of the first no trace has yet been found, but
it is evidently the work to which Forkel alluded in his Bach biography, praising its
'double choruses of uncommon magnificence.'

3. Vol. II, p. 367.

arias, and choruses convey the emotions of the faithful watching the unfolding of the imposing drama. Bruno Walter[1] aptly compared these devout characters to the figures of the sponsors at the fringe of religious paintings. A third group is provided by the chorales expressing the reaction of the Christian congregation. These three spheres are, however, by no means sharply separated. They are in constant movement and at times they mingle.

Despite their structural relationship Bach's two Passions are very different in character. The later composition radiates tenderness and love; harsh contrasts are toned down, and a heart-stirring blend of bliss and grief, such as only Bach could create, prevails throughout. According to the gospel, the Christ of the St. John Passion was endowed with sublime calm and remoteness. The gospel of St. Matthew, however, allowed Bach to express his own fervent *Jesusminne* (devotion to Jesus). Here no unbridgeable gap exists between the human and the divine; the Lord in his suffering approaches mankind, and mankind suffers with him. While in the earlier Passion the utterances of Christ are presented in recitatives accompanied only by the organ, the St. Matthew Passion, following the example of Schütz and Telemann, uses a string quartet to surround the personality of the Lord with a kind of halo.[2] This recitative is transformed into an arioso only once: when at the last supper Jesus explains the mystic significance of bread and wine. And the accompanying strings are silenced only once: when Christ in agony cries out 'My God, why hast thou forsaken me?'—the halo is extinguished.

One indication of the great importance Bach attached to the work is the vast musical forces needed to perform it. They far exceed those in the St. John Passion; indeed they exceeded those of virtually all his other compositions. In its definitive form the St. Matthew Passion employs two mixed choruses, two orchestras, and another group of boy-singers for the cantus firmus of the first chorus. If there are no independent parts for each of the eight voices of the two choirs, Bach prescribed which choir should perform an individual number, or whether they should join forces.

The composer's predilection for mingling stylistic elements is amply

1. *Von der Musik*, Frankfurt, 1957, p. 206.
2. This very apt designation was first used by C. v. Winterfeld in his *Evangelischer Kirchengesang*, Leipzig, 1843-47.

demonstrated in this work. The recitatives of the Evangelist, accompanied by basses and organ only, speak an exciting tonal language. For certain occasions, as in the crying of Peter, the recitative changes to a melisma[1] of deep intensity (No. 46). At times the bass accompaniment matches the highly dramatic narration; for instance, in the famous description of the rending of the temple veil and the earthquake after the death of Christ (No. 73). Among the gems of the score are the accompanied recitatives preceding the arias. These brief ariosos contain some of the most exquisite music that Bach ever wrote, such as No. 9, in which a motive intoned by two flutes conveys the gentle flow of tears; No. 60, giving a realistic description of Jesus' flagellation; No. 69, the daughter's of Zion heart-stirring lament, accompanied by two oboi da caccia; or No. 74, 'At even, sweet, cool hour of rest,' which, quite in the romantic manner, links the stillness of evening with the peace achieved through Jesus' death. In two cases recitatives are combined with choral numbers. In No. 25, 'Ah woe, how trembles the tormented heart,' an accompanied recitative alternates with verses from a chorale, a technique Bach occasionally employed in his chorale cantatas. Similarly in No. 77, 'And now the Lord is led to rest,' each of the four soloists in a brief arioso says a tender farewell to the Master, and in between the chorus sings a heart-stirring refrain.

The arias are mostly in da capo form and, as in the cantatas, are often conceived as a kind of duet between a singer and an instrument of approximately the same range. No. 58, for instance, is scored for soprano voice and solo flute, and, to enhance its poignant character, the accompaniment is provided by two oboi da caccia without any strings or organ. Similarly the deeply moving B minor aria, No. 47, is composed as a fervent prayer for contralto and solo violin, and the bass aria, No. 66, written in free three-part form, presents a dialogue between the bass voice and a viola da gamba. The combination of solo voice and chorus, which Bach had already used in the St. John Passion, occurs again in the later work. At the beginning of the second section a contralto solo (the daughter of Zion) expresses her grief over having lost the Saviour, and the chorus using words from the 'Song of Songs' offers to help her in her search. In aria No. 26 for tenor solo and chorus, there is a characteristic move into the realm of numbers.[2] The tenor,

1. A succession of expressive notes sung to a single syllable.
2. Cf. M. Jansen in *BJ* 1937, p. 96 ff.

representing Peter, sings 'Yea, I will watch with Jesus gladly.' The chorus adds the refrain, 'So all our sins have gone to sleep' ten times, once for each of the remaining disciples (except the absent Judas) who are gradually succumbing to sleep. Similarly, the duet with chorus (No. 33) after Christ's capture can be interpreted as the expression of grief by two distressed disciples, who are being interrupted by nine (three times three) brief ejaculations of the chorus 'Loose Him—Halt ye —Bind him not,' one for each of the remaining followers of the Lord. This leads us finally to the well-known chorus 'Lord, not I?' (No. 15), after Jesus has said that one of His disciples will betray Him. The same question is asked eleven times, and Bach thus implies that each of the disciples, except Judas, raises his voice.

In the St. Matthew Passion the composer avoids the repetition of choruses that played so important a part in the structure of the St. John Passion. The variety in the music devoted to the crowd scenes is quite overwhelming. Callous slander could hardly have been better portrayed than in the canon (No. 39), in which one false witness slavishly repeats every word of the other witness's accusation. How stunning are (No. 54) the three powerful chords used at the word 'Barabbam'; the senseless fury of the crowd in 'Let Him be crucified' (No. 59), ending abruptly in an unexpected key; and the increasing vigor in the eight-part chorus (No. 67) 'Saviour was he of others,' in which the two choruses at first respond each other, then join forces, and end in a weird unison, accusing Jesus of blasphemy for having said 'I am God's own son' (Ex. 26). There are also madrigalian choruses of singularly

Ex. 26.

This man has said: "I   am   God's own   son."

expressive power. At the end of No. 33 we find the eight-part double chorus 'Ye lightnings, ye thunders,' one of the most violent and grandiose descriptions of unloosened passion produced in the Baroque era. The last number of the work is mankind's deeply moving farewell song to the dead Saviour. It is a delicate lament that assumes the character

of a nostalgic lullaby and thus conveys the idea that the end also means
another beginning.

Chorale tunes are frequently repeated in this work. Bach's favorite
'Oh sacred Head now wounded' appears no less than five times in
different places (Nos. 21, 23, 53, 63, 72), with words and harmonization superbly matching the mood of the moment. In the selection of
the hallowed tunes and texts, and in the choice of their appropriate
position within the score, Bach showed a poetic power and insight
given only to one who was the descendant of generations of Protestant
church musicians. Particularly beautiful are the intricate chorale arrangements which serve as a frame to the Passion's first part. At the
end of it he placed the four-part chorale setting, 'Oh man, bewail thy
sin so great,' taken from the St. John Passion. The adorned hymn is
presented by the soprano to the accompaniment of free countermelodies intoned by the three other vocal parts, while the orchestra, used
quite independently, utters a solemn lament. In the initial number
Bach introduced a chorale melody as cantus firmus. It was played by
the organ in the first performance, but was later taken over by a separate boys' choir. This is the most elaborate piece of the whole composition. Two wildly excited groups confront each other with terse
questions and sorrowful answers, against a background of floods of
tears, suggested by the heaving and milling orchestra. Above the passionate grief of humanity thus depicted rises the crystal-clear, serene
church tune,[1] thus setting the stage for this work on mortal frailty and
divine strength.

Of the St. Mark Passion (BWV 247), performed for the first time
on Good Friday 1731, we have only Picander's libretto which was published in the third part of his *Ernst-Schertzhaffte und Satyrische Gedichte* (Leipzig, 1732). Interestingly enough, this time the entire
libretto, including the quotations from the gospel and the chorale texts,
is reproduced, which may point to Picander's having had a larger share
in the formulation of the text than in the St. Matthew Passion. Though
both the score and the parts are lost, the composition may be partly

---

1. Chailley (p. 268) emphasizes the ambivalent tonal character which this piece
assumes since the chorale tune in a major mode is built into a chorus in minor. Such
'bitonality' is not rare in B.s compositions. It occurs repeatedly in BWV 4 and, as
W. Neumann pointed out, also in BWV 161/1 and 137/4.

reconstructed from other works.[1] The introductory and the concluding chorus as well as arias No. 27, 49, and 59 were recognized as 'parodies' of numbers 1, 10, 5, 3, 8 of the funeral ode *Lass Fürstin* (BWV 198) performed on October 17, 1727, in memory of the Electress Christiane Eberhardine. Aria No. 53 *Falsche Welt* may be preserved in the Weimar cantata *Widerstehe doch der Sünde* (BWV 54), while the music to the chorus No. 114 seems to have survived in the chorus No. 45, 'Where is he that is born king of the Jews' in the Christmas Oratorio.[2] Some chorales of the St. Mark Passion may possibly have been included in C. P. E. Bach's collection of his father's hymn arrangements. However, when compared with the 132 numbers of the original score, the amount of fragments preserved is rather pitiful.

There exists only a small number of Bach compositions on Latin texts. Next to the B minor Mass, the *Magnificat* is the most significant of them. In Leipzig it was customary to perform an elaborate Latin Magnificat at the Vespers service on important holy days. For such purposes Bach liked to employ works by other composers, but he himself set also the Latin text to music. One of these (BWV 243) has survived, and is available in two versions. The original one of 1723 was destined for Christmas. To the text of Mary's hymn from the Vulgate (Luke 1:46-55) ending with the doxology 'Gloria Patri,' Bach added four independent pieces destined specifically for Christmas and based partly on German, partly on Latin, texts he found in a Christmas cantata by Johann Kuhnau, his predecessor in Leipzig.

About 1730 he thoroughly revised his work. The key of E flat was changed to D, more suitable for trumpets; flutes were added and the four additional pieces removed. The result was a uniformly constructed work employing Latin words throughout and usable at Easter or Pentecost as well as at Christmas.

In its final version the Magnificat is one of Bach's most compact compositions, imbued with joy and exultation, and radiating the same

1. A reconstruction of sections of the work was attempted by Diethard Hellmann, Stuttgart, 1964; its English premiere took place in Oxford, July 1965.
2. Cf. Smend in *BJ* 1940-48, p. 9 ff.

happy optimism which found so irresistible an expression in the Brandenburg Concertos. The brief movements (lasting an average of three
minutes each) are clearly united in three groups starting with an aria
and ending with a full chorus (2-4, 5-7, 8-11). The individual sections
are framed by the mighty initial Magnificat chorus and the concluding
Gloria, which, at the words *Sicut erat in principio* (As it was in the
beginning), quotes the music of the first number. Each individual
piece, in spite of its brevity, has its own clearly defined emotional character. The first movement, scored for full orchestra (trumpets, timpani, woodwind, strings, organ) and five-part chorus, carries us along
with its brilliance and exuberance. An overwhelming effect is produced
later, in the aria for soprano solo, *Quia respexit* ('For he hath regarded
the low estate of his handmaiden'), when at the words *omnes genera-
tiones* ('all generations shall call me blessed') the full chorus suddenly
cuts the solo voice short. There is transcendent beauty in the trio for
two sopranos and alto, *Suscepit Israel* ('He hath holpen his servant
Israel'), to which the two oboes intone in unison, like a cantus firmus,
the venerable Magnificat tune. Only Sebastian Bach could write a
composition so strict in form and yet so tender and ethereal. To the
following *Sicut locutus est* ('As he spake to our fathers') the composer
gave an archaic motet character by writing a vocal fugue, accompanied by the continuo, to stress the connection with the past. After
this austere piece, the re-entrance of the orchestra in the ensuing
Gloria is all the more dazzling. Twice the voices rise in a mighty arc
to glorify the Father and the Son. At the words *et Spiritui sancto* the
melodic line is inverted to symbolize the descent of the Holy Ghost.
Here the entrance of the trumpets leads to the climax of the work,
triumphantly proclaiming in its music, 'My soul doth magnify the
Lord.'

It is regrettable that the attractive four interpolations (which in 1723
followed the numbers 2, 5, 7, 9) are generally omitted in modern performances. They are imbued with the Christmas spirit and through
their contrasting structure bring the monumental character of the main
work into full relief. The first is a brief four-part motet on a tune cherished by Bach: the Lutheran Christmas song 'From Heaven above.' In
long notes the soprano intones the venerable tune, the other voices accompanying with excited counter melodies, the material of which is

taken from the cantus firmus. No. 2 is a gay song, *Freut euch und jubiliert* (Rejoice and jubilate), set for two sopranos, alto, and tenor; the instrumental bass accompanies these voices with a jocular ostinato-like figure, a sequence of 'inverted mordents' (*Ex. 27*). No. 3 em-

Ex. 27.

ploys the liturgical text *Gloria in excelsis Deo*,[1] set for five-part chorus, strings, and oboes. The last number is again in Latin, a duet for soprano and bass, *Virga Jesse floruit* (The branch of Jesse flowered) which unfortunately breaks off after thirty bars, for the last page of the score is lost. However, the number can be reconstructed, as Bach employed the music in his Christmas Cantata, No. 110.[2] If the four pieces are performed by a separately placed small group of singers and instrumentalists, a delightful effect can be achieved, the spatial separation helping to stress the stylistic contrast.

In the Lutheran services of the Baroque period parts of the Latin Ordinary of the Mass were occasionally used in a polyphonic setting. The Kyrie was played on the first Sunday of Advent, the Gloria at Christmas, the Sanctus on the highest holidays. Bach took an interest in Catholic church music—he copied and arranged Latin works by Palestrina, Pergolesi, Lotti, Caldara, and others—and contributed four short Masses (BWV 233-36) which probably originated after 1735. It may be doubted, however, that these works were intended for Leipzig; they were probably destined for Count Franz Anton von Sporck of Lissa, Bohemia. They are mainly adaptations of church cantatas as the following table will show:

		based on:
Mass in F major (BWV 233)	No. 1 Kyrie (chorus) and No. 2 Gloria (chorus) newly composed	
	No. 3 Domine Deus (aria)	cantata BWV. Anh. 18 (?)
	No. 4,5 Qui tollis, and Quoniam (arias)	cantata 102/3 and 5
	No. 6 Cum sancto (chorus)	” 40/1

1. Following Kuhnau's example Bach, however, continued with the words *et in terra pax hominibus, bona voluntas.*
2. Cf. the edition by A. Dürr in *Hortus Musicus*, No. 80, Kassel, 1951.

Mass in A major (BWV 234)	No. 1 Kyrie (chorus) and No. 3 "Domine" (aria) newly invented		
	No. 2 Gloria (chorus)	cantata	67/6
	No. 4 Qui tollis (aria)	"	179/5
	No. 5 Quoniam (aria)	"	79/2
	No. 6 Cum sancto (chorus)	"	136/1
Mass in G minor (BWV 235)	No. 1 Kyrie (chorus)	cantata	102/1
	No. 2 Gloria (chorus)	"	72/1
	Nos. 3-6 (3 arias and 1 chorus)	"	187/4,3,5,1
Mass in G major (BWV 236)	No. 1 Kyrie (chorus)	cantata	179/1
	No. 2 Gloria (chorus)	"	79/1
	No. 3 Gratias agimus (aria)	"	138/5
	No. 4 Domine Deus (duet)	"	79/5
	No. 5 Quoniam (aria)	"	179/3
	No. 6 Cum sancto (chorus)	"	17/1

Thus all four Masses start with a chorus on the Kyrie text and are followed by a Gloria in which choruses at the beginning and end frame a number of arias. The F major Mass contains the smallest number of 'parodies,' whereas those in G minor and G major consist exclusively of such adaptations. Particularly interesting is the *Kyrie* of the F major Mass. Here the vocal bass introduces as cantus firmus the *Kyrie eleison, Christe eleison, Kyrie eleison* of the Litany and simultaneously horns and oboes intone the Protestant hymn tune *Christe du Lamm Gottes*. The insertion of Protestant chorale melodies into the Latin *Ordinarium Missae*, not too rare in Bach's time, represents a remarkable attempt to fuse diverse liturgical elements into an artistic whole.[1]

Of incomparably greater significance than these short masses is a gigantic work, the *Mass in B minor*[1] (BWV 232), which occupied Bach intermittently for nearly twenty-five years. It seems that in 1733 he composed a Kyrie in B minor for the commemorative service held for the deceased elector, Friedrich August I 'the Strong,' as well as a Gloria in D major to celebrate the new elector's ascension to the throne (cf. p. 81). A Sanctus in D major had possibly preceded these compositions in 1724 to be performed on Christmas day. In the last years

---

1. The five 'Sancti' which are preserved in Bach's own hand (BWV 237-41) seem to be mainly arrangements of works by other composers.

2. Cf. R. Gerber in *BJ* 1932, p. 119 ff.; A Schering in *BJ* 1936, p. 1 ff.; F. Smend in *BJ* 1937, p. 1 ff.; W. Blankenburg, *Einführung in B.s H-moll Messe*, Kassel, 1950.

of his life, perhaps as late as 1747, Bach conceived the idea of adding to these individual movements. His aim was to create, through the inclusion of a Credo and of the concluding sections from Osanna onwards, a grandiose complete composition.[1] The resulting work was not intended for the Roman Catholic service. It is far too extensive; the text does not follow the exact wording of the Catholic Mass,[2] and Bach did not observe the grouping in five sections (Kyrie, Gloria, Credo, Sanctus, Agnus) customary in this liturgy. Nor did he expect it would be used in the Protestant service. While the individual sections may be employed in the Lutheran church, the setting of the entire ordinary of the Mass does not lend itself to inclusion in the Protestant liturgy. The Mass in B minor is an abstract composition of monumental dimensions, a gigantic edifice conceived by the composer as the crowning glory of his life-work in the field of sacred music. Its completion might well indicate a mellowing in the aged master's attitude, a deviation from belligerent Lutheran orthodoxy toward a more ecumenical attitude.

The majestic work abounds in forms of intricate technical mastery: a superb passacaglia, highly artistic fugues with stretti, augmentations, and other devices of the strict contrapuntal style. There is an objective character to this composition, and only when the text refers to Jesus, does the musical idiom assume a more personal and intimate character. Thus the duet *Christe Eleison* (No. 2)[3] radiates ethereal bliss and ecstatic longing, in marked contrast to the first and second *Kyrie eleison*, which address God the Father and God the Holy Ghost in a spirit of solemn veneration. Similarly the two choruses *Qui tollis peccata mundi* (No. 8) and *Et incarnatus est* (No. 15) are both simple, heart-stirring compositions, fervently expressing Bach's *Jesusminne*.

Here again the composer did not hesitate to include in the Mass numerous 'parodies' of movements from church cantatas related in con-

1. The origin of the Mass is outlined here in accordance with the assumptions of G. v. Dadelsen (*Beiträge zur Chronologie der Werke J.S.B.s*, Trossingen, 1958, p. 143 ff.). They diverge in various respects from the statements made by F. Smend (KB to NBA II/1, Kassel, 1956).

2. There are deviations in the 'Domine Deus' and the 'Sanctus.'

3. W. Blankenburg, p. 17, points out that the various references to Christ, the second member of the Holy Trinity, are in the form of duets (cf. No. 2, No. 7, *Domine Deus*, and No. 14, *Et in unum Dominum Jesum Christum*).

tent. These adaptations are not mechanically done; indeed, each of them shows a higher degree of perfection than its model. No. 20, *Et expecto resurrectionem mortuorum,* is taken from cantata No. 120, *Gott man lobet,* using the second movement, 'Shout ye, all ye joyful voices.' While the original contained a four-part chorus, Bach, with supreme mastery, added a fifth obbligato part, which in a completely natural way enriches the polyphonic texture. The *Crucifixus* (No. 16) is based on a passacaglia from cantata 12, *Weinen, Klagen,* and was given its exquisite ending, modulating from minor to major, only in the Mass.[1] In making this addition, Bach not only prepared for the glory of the *Et resurrexit* (No. 17), which immediately follows; he had thirteen variations instead of the original twelve and so symbolized the tragedy by that ill-fated number.[2]

Since Bach was going back in this work to a time when the Christian church in the West was as yet undivided, he felt it was appropriate to include archaic forms. Thus the first and the last sections of the *Credo* use the melodies of the Gregorian chant (well known in the Protestant liturgy too) in grandiose fugues of a definitely antiquated motet character. The Mixolydian mode[3] also makes its appearance here. Moreover, the frequent five-part choruses and the old-fashioned alla breve rhythms (4/2) in several sections enhance the retrospective character of this music.

But there is no lack of contemporary forms either. The Mass contains arias equipped with the coloraturas of the Italian opera, and superb duets in the style of Agostino Steffani. These numbers, too, afford a deep insight into Bach's mentality. In the duet *Et in unum Dominum Jesum Christum filium Dei unigenitum* (No. 14) the mystic unity of the Father and His Son Jesus Christ is symbolized by an imitation in unison which presently turns into a canon at the fourth.

1. Other noteworthy 'parodies' are: No. 6, *Gratias* and No. 25, *Dona nobis* based on BWV 29/2; No. 8, *Qui tollis* on BWV 46/1: No. 13, *Patrem omnipotentem* on BWV 171/1; No. 22, *Osanna* on BWV 215/1, or rather on its model, the congratulatory cantata BWV Anh.11, lost today. Some measures from BWV 198/1 were included in the adagio introduction to the *Kyrie.*

2. Smend (*Kirchen-Kantaten,* III/20) points out that with the help of the number alphabet the word 'Credo' can be expressed as 43, and that in the Credo movement of Bach's Mass the word 'Credo' appears 43 times.

3. An archaic key in which the seventh note of the major scale is lowered by half a step.

The gentle duet of the oboi d'amore in aria No. 18 for bass, with its reference to *unam sanctam Catholicam et apostolicam Ecclesiam*, is particularly beautiful. Since this forms part of the Creed accepted by all Christian denominations, it might well be that the peaceful dialogue of the two 'love oboes' is intended to signify harmony and understanding between Catholics and Protestants.

Following the model of the Italian cantata-mass the work consists of no less than twenty-five substantial numbers. They are arranged in four sections of uneven length. The composer inscribed as *Missa*, the *Kyrie* and *Gloria* which he handed to Friedrich August II, Elector of Saxony. The *Credo* bears in the autograph the designation *Symbolum Nicenum*. The third section is the *Sanctus*, and the fourth comprises the remaining movements: *Osanna, Benedictus, Agnus Dei, Dona nobis pacem*. Each of these sections has a well-balanced structure. The *Kyrie* is, in accordance with the text, in ternary form: two choruses surround a duet. The *Gloria* starts with a monumental introductory chorus, which is followed by seven numbers. The center of this group is formed by the reference to the Saviour (No. 8, *Qui tollis peccata mundi*). On either side we find a number for solo voices (No. 7, *Domine Deus* and No. 9, *Qui sedes*). The beginning as well as the end is formed by a pair of movements, an aria preceding a chorus (No. 5, *Laudamus*—No. 6, *Gratias agimus*; No. 10, *Quoniam*—No. 11, *Cum sancto*). The *Symbolum Nicenum* consists of seven sections with emphasis on Jesus' sacrifice in the 'heart-piece' (No. 16, *Crucifixus*). It is preceded and followed by a chorus (No. 15, *Et incarnatus est*; No. 17, *Et resurrexit*). These three numbers are flanked by solo pieces; a duet (No. 14) and an aria (No. 18), respectively. At the beginning of the *Symbolum*, and at the end, are the mighty double pillars of connected choruses (Nos. 12, 13; 19, 20), in each of which Gregorian chants form the melodies of the first half. The *Sanctus* (No. 21), the shortest of the work's sections, consists of a pair of interconnected choruses only, the majestic *Sanctus* proper serving as a kind of introduction to the jubilant *Pleni sunt coeli*. The concluding section comprises four numbers. Two choruses (No. 22, *Osanna*—No. 25, *Dona nobis*) surround two arias for tenor and alto respectively (No. 23, *Benedictus*, No. 24, *Agnus*).

Looking at the work as a whole, we find that the name of Mass in

B minor generally used in modern times is not justified. The composition comprises more than twice as many movements in D major as in B minor. D is the key of the jubilant, resplendent *Gloria* and of the majestic *Credo*. The dazzling Easter-piece of the *Resurrexit* is also in D, as is the awe-inspiring *Sanctus* in which Heaven and Earth seem to resound with the praise of the Lord. (The six voices used in this chorus may have been inspired by the six wings of the Seraphims in Isaiah 6.) The predominance of this brilliant key holds the individual sections firmly together. To this should be added the fact that the last number, *Dona nobis pacem* (No. 25), uses the same music as the chorus *Gratias agimus tibi* (No. 6), which stands at the very center of the *Gloria*. This connection is of more than musical significance. Bach felt that he did not have to implore his maker for peace, and instead thanked Him for granting it to the true believer. In this way the composer also concluded his Mass with the expression of gratitude traditional in the Lutheran service.

In our time we are privileged to hear frequent concert performances of the lofty work, which we have learned to consider as one of the greatest manifestations of the religious spirit. Together with Beethoven's *Missa solemnis*, it belongs to the immortal documents of man's quest for the eternal truths.

II. WORKS FOR ORGAN SOLO

OUR time sees in Bach the unmatched master of organ composition.[1] We are aware that in his works for the 'king of instruments' Baroque music reached a peak which later generations hardly
succeeded in ascending. Bach's contemporaries, however, considered
him primarily as a stupendous organ virtuoso and an expert in the field
of organ construction. The Obituary states that he was able to execute
with his two feet passages which some, by no means unskilled, clavierists could hardly play with five fingers. Even Johann Adolph Scheibe,
while attacking Bach's compositions, admitted that it was amazing how
the Thomas Cantor managed to perform with his hands as well as with
his feet the widest skips without ever striking a wrong note or contort-
ing his body.[2] The composer was quite willing to exhibit his improvisatory skill, and Forkel has left us a vivid account of the unparalleled
artistry displayed in such demonstrations (cf. p. 33).

Bach played in his lifetime on a great number of organs, most of
them of merely average quality. They all were built according to individual specifications, and differed from each other. Some displayed

1. Among the numerous works devoted to B.s organ music the following studies
might be singled out: A. Pirro, *L'Orgue de B.*, Paris, 1895, English version, New
York, 1902; H. Luedtke, 'J.S.B.s Choralvorspiele,' *BJ* 1918, p. 1 ff.; H. Grace, *The
Organ Works of B.*, London, 1922; F. Dietrich, 'B.s Orgelchoral und seine geschichtlichen Wurzeln,' *BJ* 1929; H. Klotz, *Über die Orgelkunst der Gotik, der Renaissance
und des Barock*, Kassel, 1934; G. Frotscher, *Geschichte des Orgelspiels*, Berlin,
1935, II, p. 849 ff.; F. Florand, *J.S.B. L'oeuvre d'orgue*, Paris, 1946; H. Keller, *Die
Orgelwerke B.s*, Leipzig, 1948; F. Germani, *Guida illustrativa alle composizioni per
organo di J.S.B.*, Roma, 1949; N. Dufourcq, *J.S.B., le maître de l'orgue*, Paris, 1948;
H. Klotz, 'B.s Orgeln und seine Orgelmusik,' *Musikforschung*, III, 1950; P. Aldrich,
Ornamentation in J.S.B.'s Organ Works, New York, 1951; W. Emery, *Notes on
B.'s Organ Works*, London, 1952 ff.; W. Tell, *B.s Orgelwerke für den Hörer
erläutert*, Leipzig, 1955; W. L. Sumner, 'The Organ of B.,' *Hinrichsen Musical Year
Book*, VIII, 1956; R. L. Tusler, *The Style of J.S.B.'s Chorale Preludes*, Berkeley,
1956.

2. *Der critische Musicus*, May 14, 1737.

the richness and versatility introduced into north German organ building by Arp Schnitger (1648-1719), others the simple and more unified construction prevailing in the instruments produced in Saxony by Gottfried Silbermann (1683-1753). A discussion of basic technical features in the German organs of Bach's time may supply the background for an understanding of his organ compositions.

The core of the organ was formed by the pipes of the diapason or *Prinzipal* family. It consisted of open cylindrical flue pipes of medium bore, usually made of tin, which emitted a full-bodied, vigorous tone. They appeared mostly as an 8' register,[1] although registers of larger or smaller pipes were also employed. Next in importance was another group of flue pipes, which could be open or stopped (closed at the upper end) and likewise appeared in various sizes. They were often made of wood and produced a light and clear tone. Closely related were the string-type registers, like 'gamba' or 'violin,' only occasionally used, which were distinguished by a warm and luminous sound. A limited number of reed stops was added to enrich the instrument's coloristic potentialities. They frequently imitated the character of the orchestra's brass and reed sections and were named accordingly. Mixtures combining pipes of various sizes (primarily octave and fifth) were common and contributed to the organ's brilliance and vitality.

Different organ registers were grouped into units and connected with one of the instrument's manuals. The most important stops were enclosed in the *Hauptwerk* (main organ); below it were the pipes of the *Brustwerk* (breast organ), above it those of the *Oberwerk* (upper organ); behind the organist was the *Rückpositiv* (back organ), and special sets of pipes, located at the sides, were provided for the pedals. Couplers enabled the organist to combine pipes of different keyboards.

It should be noted, however, that all the divisions mentioned above were rarely found in the same organ. Bach's instruments were usually equipped with two or three manuals and a pedal; four manuals were uncommon.

Wind pressure was low, allowing a bright and brilliant, yet never

---

1. The designations 8' (8 foot), 16' (16 foot), 32' (32 foot) are customary to indicate the pitch of organ pipes. In an 8' stop of pipes each pipe sounds at the pitch of the corresponding key. In a 16' stop each pipe sounds one octave lower than the related key, in a 32' pipe two octaves lower. On the other hand 4' pipes sound one octave higher, 2' pipes two octaves higher than the corresponding keys.

explosive, tone quality. The dynamic range was smaller than in 19th-century instruments, sharp contrasts between extremely soft and very loud sounds being neither possible nor desired. It was difficult for a player—unless he had an assistant—to change the register stops during his performance. Usually the selection of stops remained unaltered throughout a movement. On the other hand alternation between various manuals was quite common. The 'terrace dynamics' of the Baroque period resulted from such an arrangement.

The organist had to apply increasing pressure on the keys if he simultaneously used several organ registers. This was particularly true if *organo pleno,* a combination of a sizable number of voices, was prescribed. A fast tempo or rich ornamentation of the melodic line was rendered difficult under such conditions.

The Baroque organ had tracker action. Wooden rods, levers, and wires provided the connection between the keys and the pipes. The instrument's mechanical equipment was simple, and the organist was able to influence directly the creation of the sound. To a certain extent the touch of his fingers controlled the tone quality, and careful phrasing was made easy. Thus Bach's organ was an intimate and highly responsive instrument that compared favorably with the overdeveloped electro-pneumatic products of a later period.

Repeatedly Bach was invited to pass judgment on organs and to make recommendations for their improvement. He examined critically instruments in Arnstadt, Mühlhausen, Dresden, Altenburg, Halle, Erfurt, Naumburg, Kassel, Gera, Leipzig, and neighboring places. A unique opportunity was offered to him in Mühlhausen in 1708 and 1709, when the organ in St. Blasius' was rebuilt according to his specifications. Bach wanted the instrument both strengthened and enriched. He demanded that the bellows be reinforced, a powerful sub-bass (32') stop added, and the existing trombone bass (16') enlarged. Most of all he recommended the production of a completely new set of pipes, a *Brustwerk,* with seven stops and a new manual as well as additional bellows. The young composer's memorandum shows how fully capable he was to cope with the technical side of the project as well as the artistic.

Organ music occupied Bach throughout his whole life. Among his earliest compositions were works for this instrument, and one of the last pieces that absorbed the interest of the master, then nearly blind, was an organ chorale. Since an important aim of Bach's art was to magnify the Lord, the organ offered him the most direct way to pursue this goal, without the co-operation of other musicians. Most of the approximately 250 works he wrote for the organ were designed for liturgical purposes.

As in other fields of Bach's creative output, it is impossible to determine the exact date of composition of most of his organ works. Nevertheless, stylistic features enable us to establish certain significant patterns for each of his creative periods. The situation is somewhat complicated by the fact that Bach often revised and rewrote organ compositions many years after their first conception. If such works reflect the features of the period in which they received their final form, they will be discussed with the compositions of that phase.

The works of the *first creative period* are typical of those of a young composer who is trying to find himself and to master the intricacies of his craft. Bach was always eager to learn from others, but, naturally, this tendency was more apparent in the works of his youth. The incipient organist studied the works of his own clan, especially the compositions of his second cousin, Johann Christoph Bach of Eisenach. Moreover the great masters of keyboard music in Italy and southern, central, and, most of all, northern Germany were his models. He copied and imitated their music, sometimes barely approaching their level, although occasionally surpassing it. His musical language is often voluble, his harmonic and polyphonic technique immature, his sense of balance and form not yet fully developed. It is typical of the uneven character of Bach's early organ works that, while some contain very difficult and brilliant pedal parts, others dispense with the pedal altogether. Nevertheless these works of the young Bach are by no means unattractive. They are highly emotional, exuberant, and, in their subjective expressiveness, typical products of a young genius. Bach's first period shows a definite resemblance to that of Brahms, whose early compositions compensate for their lack of formal perfection by their stirring and passionate content.

Bach's organ works fall into two main groups: those freely invented, and those based on a chorale. The former reflect the brilliant and rhapsodic art of north German masters such as Dietrich Buxtehude,

Vincent Lübeck, and Georg Böhm. Central German influences are also noticeable. Passages with fast moving parallel thirds and sixths seem to follow the example of Johann Pachelbel, teacher of Bach's brother Johann Christoph, who in turn taught young Sebastian. Good examples are furnished by the *Preludes and Fugues in A minor and C minor* (P. III:9 and IV:5;[1] BWV 551, 549), which might possibly still belong to Bach's Lüneburg period (1700-1702). The work in A minor is a kind of toccata, a showpiece, containing in its middle part two rather superficially constructed fugal sections. The brief first fugue, consisting of seventeen bars, uses a gaily rambling theme of the Buxtehude type, without any attempt at serious elaboration. The second fugue seems to employ a new theme, but this subject is accompanied by a running countermelody which, as the piece proceeds, gains in importance and, at the same time, increasingly resembles the theme of the first fugue. Thus there is an attempt to unify the different sections of the composition.

The work in C minor is composed of three sections: a rhapsodic introduction, a fugue, and a freely improvisatory coda. The broadly contoured theme of the fugue is developed from a motive presented in the initial toccata section. Nevertheless, Bach clearly distinguishes between these two parts, separating them by a full cadence. There is verve and spirit in the lively composition, and the occasional fast passages entrusted to the pedal contribute to its brilliant character.

An effective thematic interrelation between three successive movements is achieved in the *Fantasia in G major*[2] (P. IX:4; BWV 571). Clearly modeled after north German compositions, the work begins with a rather nondescript initial piece, but gradually increases in sig-

---

1. To facilitate the identification of organ works references are given to their location in the nine-volume edition of C. F. Peters, the abbreviation P. standing for Peters.

2. The authenticity of this composition has been doubted. By and large the composer's organ music still presents unsolved problems in this respect. Some of the works the 19th century accepted as compositions by Johann Sebastian are recognized today as the works of others, while in several cases the question is as yet unanswered. The organ chorales *Ach Gott und Herr* (BWV 692/93), for instance, are works by J. G. Walther. The chorale partita on *Allein Gott in der Höh* (BWV 771) which A. E. Hull considered one of the finest works by young Bach, is in all likelihood by A. N. Vetter, while the Trio in C minor (BWV 585) is probably by J. Tobias Krebs (cf. the edition of J. T. Krebs's works in *Die Orgel*, II, No. 18, Leipzig, 1963).

nificance. It achieves its culmination in the final section, which introduces an 'ostinato' figure consisting of six stepwise descending notes.
They appear not only in the bass but also in the soprano and alto parts,
both in their original and in transposed form. This is an early and
modest example of Bach's use of a technique that was to reach its
magnificent climax in the great Passacaglia in C minor (cf. p. 227).

To a somewhat later period, possibly the year 1707, belongs the *Toccata in E major,* known also in a version in C major (P. III:7; BWV
566). Once more two fugues are preceded and separated by free improvisatory sections. The introductory toccata and the two contrapuntal
movements—the first in 4/4, the second in triple time—display a close
relationship as Bach creates the main ideas with the help of thematic
variation (*Ex.* 28). Particularly attractive are the festive, sparkling be-

Ex. 28. *BWV* 566

ginning and the solemn and brilliant effect produced at the end by
contrapuntal elaboration.

A number of organ works seem to stand on the borderline between
Bach's first and second creative periods. They display retrospective fea-
tures and signs of immaturity but also the hand of a skilled craftsman.
Bach may have written them prior to his departure for Weimar.

The *Prelude and Fugue in G minor* (P. III:5; BWV 535) is a
toccata-like composition with an improvisatory coda corresponding to
the introductory section, thematic interrelations between prelude and
fugue, and the tone repetitions favored by Buxtehude in the themes of
his fugues. Bach's powerful fugue increases in intensity until at its climax an impressive pedal solo leads to the Baroque grandeur of the final
measures.

A toccata character also prevails in the *Prelude and Fugue in G
major* (P. IV:2; BWV 550). Again the two pieces are thematically
related and a short transition, north German in character, ties them
together. The somewhat ostentatious character of the prelude, which

includes a pedal solo of more than a hundred notes, and the rather primitive, primarily harmonic, character of the fugue, point to the first period, but a certain elegance and logic of elaboration forecast Bach's later organ works.[1]

The *Prelude and Fugue in D major* (P. IV:3; BWV 532) is conceived on a particularly large scale. The prelude consists of three sections: an impetuous and brilliant introduction, a serene and sedate 'Alla breve,' reminding us with its slowly shifting harmonies of Frescobaldi's *durezze e ligature* (dissonances and tied notes), and a dramatic Adagio, concluding with recitative-like passages. The brilliant fugue, in which Bach seems influenced by both Pachelbel and Buxtehude,[2] is based on an extensive, rambling theme with a striking rest in the middle. As the fugal elaboration unfolds, it is effectively filled in by other voices. This brisk, though somewhat superficial, piece provides an effective contrast to the more substantial and serious-minded prelude.

The *'Little' Prelude and Fugue in E minor* (P. III:10; BWV 533), on the other hand, is particularly short and concise. Careless youthful mistakes like parallel octaves may be observed in this work, but organists admire it as one of the most sensitive and expressive compositions written for the instrument, an exquisite miniature in which the emotional content surpasses the technical elaboration. André Pirro[3] assumes that the work was played in Mühlhausen at the inauguration of the organ rebuilt according to Bach's specifications.

The *'Short' Fugue in G minor* (P. IV:7; BWV 578) has come down to us without a prelude. This frequently played composition is characterized by one of those tuneful, easily remembered themes which often distinguish the works of the young genius (*Ex. 29*). The com-

1. Keller (p. 78) indicates that the work prescribes in the pedal the unusual note e' (a third above middle c) which we find also in the Vivaldi-Bach Organ Concerto in A minor (cf. p. 222) written in Weimar. Similarly Klotz (p. 194) stresses the use of C sharp (two octaves below middle c) in the pedal part of the Toccata in D minor (cf. p. 218), a note not available on Bach's Arnstadt or Mühlhausen organs, but used in certain works obviously written in Weimar. This induces the scholars to assign the two compositions to the Weimar period. However, the possibility should not be disregarded that these showy works were composed by the virtuoso Bach for special exhibitions of his technical skill on organs outside his residence. This could well account for the employment of unusual notes in works of the first period.

2. Cf. Pachelbel's Fugue in D major (*Denkmäler der Tonkunst in Bayern*, IV: 1, 1903, p. 43) and Buxtehude's Fugue in F major (Collected Edition, Klecken, 1925, I, p. 83).

3. 'L'Art des organistes,' *Encyclopédie Lavignac*, II, Paris, 1926, book 2, p. 1352.

Ex. 29. *BWV* 578

poser himself was apparently infatuated with the tune, as he made no great effort to develop it. The texture is loose and the contrapuntal elaboration superficial, but the reappearance of the main theme never fails to charm the listener with its light grace.

Possibly the most striking and best-known organ work from Bach's youth, is the *Toccata in D minor* (P. IV:4; BWV 565). Strongly rhapsodic sections start and conclude the work. The freely flowing fugue in the center is loosely constructed, with runs and broken chord episodes separating the different entrances of the theme. Obviously Bach wished to maintain the predominant character of brilliant improvisation even in the middle section. The theme seems to be inspired by the violinistic technique of playing in quick alternation on two neighboring strings, a device Bach was often to employ in his music for keyboard instruments. The toccata's torrents of sound and dazzling fireworks create a tone poem of passionate subjectivity; yet there is a masterly craftsmanship underlying all this outpouring of emotion. The work was written by an organist with so deep an insight into the possibilities of the instrument that he was able to produce the most powerful effects without unduly taxing the player's technical abilities. In its intensity and exuberance this is clearly a product of Bach's youth, but there is no groping and uncertainty in it.

The BWV lists 173 *organ chorales* by Bach. Of these at least fifteen, but possibly considerably more, were wrongly attributed to Bach or are of doubtful authenticity (cf. p. 215, n. 2). Over ninety of the remaining works were incorporated by Bach into various collections established in Weimar, Cöthen, and Leipzig respectively. The balance of some fifty items consists of separate pieces, the greater part of which originated in Weimar, while only a limited number may be ascribed to the preceding period. The comparative scarcity of chorale arrangements produced in

Arnstadt may reflect the young organist's resentment against the nar-
row-minded rulings laid down by the authorities with regard to his performance in the church service (cf. p. 21).

In spite of the uncongenial atmosphere in which he spent some of
his most important formative years, Bach's inquisitive mind explored
at least three different forms of the organ chorale. In his first period
Bach turned to the chorale partita (chorale variation), the chorale fantasia, and the cantus firmus chorale arrangement.[1]

It is significant for the development not only of Bach's artistry but
for organ music in general that Bach began with widely extended
forms and then proceeded to brief and concise structures. The *Partite
Diverse,* written in Lüneburg, are among the longest chorale arrangements he produced. For these works, consisting of seven to eleven numbers each, he seemed to use compositions by Georg Böhm and by Sebastian's kinsman, the Weimar organist Johann Bernhard Bach, as
models. *Christ, der du bist der helle Tag* (Christ who art the light of
day; P. V:60, BWV 766) consists of seven pieces, corresponding to the
seven stanzas of the hymn. Only in the finale is the pedal introduced,
but even there it is ad libitum. In *O Gott, du frommer Gott* (Oh God,
Thou Holy God; P. V:68; BWV 767) the initial harmonization of the
chorale melody is rather clumsy, with frequent repetitions of tonic and
dominant, and heavy five- and six-part chords on the weak beat (*Ex.
30*). Böhm's influence is particularly noticeable in the second piece, a

Ex. 30. *O Gott, du frommer Gott (BWV 767)*

---

1. Bach's systematic use of the chorale fughetta seems to have started in Weimar,
but he may have experimented with the form at a very early age. *Herr Jesu Christ,
dich zu uns wend* (Lord Jesus Christ, oh turn to us; BWV 749) which treats the
hymn tune partly as a fugal subject and partly as a basis for free imitations, is obviously fashioned after the arrangement of the same chorale by Johann Christoph
Bach. Similarly, *Herr Jesu Christ, mein's Lebens Licht* (Lord Jesus Christ, light of
my life; BWV 750) is the awkward product of a beginner. Bach's authorship of these
works is not proved.

sensitive bicinium which accompanies the chorale tune with a constantly restated bass ostinato. *Sei gegrüsset, Jesu gütig* (Thee I greet, oh merciful Jesus; P. V:76; BWV 768) shows unmistakable traces of subsequent revisions. It displays the youthful fervor of the other sets, but not their amateurish weaknesses. The highly competent four-part harmonization of the chorale at the beginning of the Partita is obviously of later origin, and, likewise, the independent pedal part in the last five variations which is handled with masterly skill. Particularly attractive is No. 10, in which the cantus firmus is presented in long notes in the soprano, each line being preceded by its lyric paraphrase.

In the *chorale fantasia*[1] *Christ lag in Todesbanden* (Christ lay in death's dark prison; P. VI:15; BWV 718), each phrase of the chorale is differently treated. The direct model of Sebastian's work was a fantasia by Georg Böhm on the same melody;[2] however, it is also easy to detect references to the style of two masters from Lübeck. Sebastian starts with a richly ornamented treatment of the first two lines of the chorale; the third line he develops as a brief fugato, the fourth as a kind of gigue in 12/8 time in imitation of similar movements by Buxtehude, and in the fifth line he uses the mystical echo-like effects so dear to Buxtehude's father-in-law, Franz Tunder. The over-all effect of the work is as attractive as it is unusual.

Bach also tried his hand on *cantus firmus chorale arrangements*. In the motet-like *Vom Himmel hoch* (From heaven above; P. VII:55; BWV 700), which introduces the cantus firmus in the bass, doubling the left hand with the organ pedal, Bach followed very closely in the footsteps of Pachelbel. However, in *Wo soll ich fliehen hin* (Whither shall I flee; P. IX:25; BWV 694), a three-part composition with the hymn tune in the bass, Bach attempted to free himself from Pachelbel's technique and to introduce counterpoints independent of the chorale tune. The experiment was hardly a success. The composition is uninspired and repetitious. Nevertheless the composer returned to it at a much later date, using material from this early venture for the masterly arrangement of the same hymn tune he included in his Schübler Cho-

---

1. Bach used the term 'Fantasia' occasionally with a different meaning to designate an extended cantus firmus chorale arrangement, usually with the hymn tune in the bass.

2. *Sämtliche Werke*, Leipzig, 1927, II, p. 98.

rales (cf. p. 254). *Ach Gott vom Himmel* (Oh God from heaven;
P. IX: 13; BWV 741) displays a different character. Bach conceived it
in four parts, with the cantus firmus in the bass. A fifth part is added
near the end when the chorale melody is introduced in a bold stretto
of the double pedal. The piece also has a striking chromatic idiom. Yet
its daring inspiration is marred by technical incompetence.[1] Quite obviously the young genius overreached himself here.

During the nine years the composer spent in Weimar (1708-17), he
was primarily an organist, and many of his organ compositions were
written or at least conceived there. This *second creative period* started
as a typical transition phase. Bach's output comprised a substantial
number of studies and transcriptions, which served him as a means of
widening his artistic horizon and allowed him to become fully conversant with new types of musical expression. But toward the end of
this period the composer achieved stylistic perfection and wrote organ
compositions which rank among the best he produced.

In Weimar, Bach was at first a student of the Italians. In Lüneburg
and Arnstadt their works had reached him only in versions transformed
and remodeled by German composers. In Weimar he had the chance
of a direct study of their compositions. The effect on Bach was somewhat similar to the effect Italian art exercised on the foremost German
painter, Albrecht Dürer. Serene and well-balanced works from the
Adriatic peninsula helped the two masters to find themselves. They
discarded the excessive harshness and angularity of the North, and
replaced it by a plastic clarity, transparency, and simple structure.
Eventually Bach completely assimilated Italian music, and, by fusing
it with his own contrapuntal heritage and the Northern idiom, he
created what we now regard as the typical Bach style.

The transcriptions and studies of the Weimar period begin with a
number of *arrangements of concertos for violin and orchestra*, both for
the clavier and for the organ. Apparently Bach was inspired to do this
work by studying similar arrangements which his friend and kinsman,
the organist Gottfried Walther, made about that time in Weimar. Bach

1. Ernst Naumann complained about its numerous 'musical impossibilities . . .
the occasional awkward and angular progressions of the voices.' (Preface of BG edition, vol. 40, p. xlvi)

transcribed for the organ one concerto and a separate movement (P. VIII:1, 4; BWV 592, 595) written by the talented Prince Johann Ernst of Weimar, who was a faithful disciple of the Italians, as well as three concerti by Vivaldi (P. VIII:2, 3, and No. 3002; BWV 593, 594, 596). For a long time there was confusion about the authorship of the third of these transcriptions, the Concerto in D minor (BWV 596). Although Sebastian's autograph is preserved it bears in Friedemann's hand the inscription 'di W. F. Bach, manu mei patris descript.' (by W. F. Bach, copied by my father). In 1911 Max Schneider clarified the facts,[1] and explained that the organ work, which had been considered as one of Friedemann's most inspired compositions, was actually an arrangement his father had made of a concerto for violin and orchestra by Vivaldi.

Bach was strongly impressed by the natural grace of the Italian style and fascinated by the results that could be achieved by using Vivaldi's concerto form in compositions for solo organ. Work on these transcriptions also confirmed his conviction that the violin idiom could be employed to good advantage in keyboard compositions. The Concerto in A minor (BWV 593) appears, for instance, as a genuine organ work. Violinistic figures are cleverly adapted to the keyboard, and in the last movement challenging double stops for the pedal are prescribed, the two feet being at times one and a half or even two octaves apart. By and large these transcriptions reveal that Bach had no intention of mechanically transferring into his works every note of the model. His new versions strengthen the harmony and introduce, particularly in the middle parts and the bass, small rhythmical and contrapuntal details which add significance to the composition.[2] The transcription of the D minor Concerto was done with particular care, and the single movement (BWV 595) by Prince Johann Ernst even arranged twice. Bach adapted it first for clavier, then for organ, and in so doing increased the length of the piece by almost one-fourth.

It is most significant that throughout these transcriptions the change of manuals is carefully indicated by the arranger, which was not done very often in Bach's organ works. The concertos are all written 'a 2

1. *BJ* 1911, p. 23 ff.
2. Some of the deviations of Bach's versions from the original are due, however, to the fact that the arranger did not use the printed edition as basis for his work. Cf. R. Eller in *Kongressbericht*, Hamburg, 1956, p. 81 ff.

Clav. con Pedale,' and the two manuals are usually designated as *Oberwerk* and *Rückpositiv* with occasional references to *organo pleno* (cf. p. 213).[1]

Other works which followed Italian models were the *Allabreve* (P. VIII:6; BWV 589) and particularly the *Canzona* (P. IV:10; BWV 588). These compositions may reflect the influence of the great Italian organ master Frescobaldi, whose *Fiori musicali* Bach acquired in 1714. Both the quiet, dignified, and solemn mood of the *Allabreve* and the principle of thematic variation employed in the *Canzona* seem to be inspired by the Roman composer. In the latter work each of its two sections presents a four-part fugue. Their quietly singing themes are interrelated, and chromatically descending countersubjects appear in both fugues. While the harmonic and melodic limitations of the composition may be ascribed to the old canzona tradition, Bach's ample use of chromaticism produces a peculiar, soul-stirring quality.

The first movement of the well-known *Pastorale* (P. I:8; BWV 590) reflects the spirit that can be found in countless Italian musical descriptions of the nativity. With its gentle, rocking motion, its extended pedal points, and the 12/8 siciliano rhythm, it resembles Christmas compositions by Frescobaldi, Corelli, Schiassi, and many others. The main movement is followed by three shorter pieces of a dance-like character, written for the manual only. A brisk movement in 6/8 time, anticipating in its principal theme the finale of the Brandenburg Concerto No. 3, concludes the little suite.

In both clavier and organ compositions of this period Bach occasionally used Italian themes. A *Fugue in C minor* (P. IV:6; BWV 574) has the title 'Thema Legrenzianum, elaboratum . . . per J. S. Bach.'[2] while his *Fugue in B minor* (P. IV:8, BWV 579) makes use of a theme by Corelli.[3] Bach's composition is almost three times as long as Corelli's and employs four parts instead of the three in the model.

---

1. In the D minor Concerto, *Oberwerk*, *Brustwerk*, and in the finale *Rückpositiv* (but not *Brustwerk*) are prescribed. This could indicate that Bach had three manuals in mind. In all likelihood, however, he did not deviate from the two manuals of the whole set, the expressions *Rückpositiv* and *Brustwerk* being used interchangeably.

2. Keller, p. 51, suggests that this is a work from Bach's youth. Although the technical weakness of the piece is obvious, the use of a theme of Italian origin indicates the Weimar period. Bach's actual source has not yet been ascertained.

3. The Corelli arrangement is based on the second movement of the composer's op. III/4, of 1689.

Nevertheless it is easily understandable that the simple and plastic theme of the Roman master (*Ex.* 31) fascinated the young composer.

Ex. 31. *BWV* 579

Through his mastery of such music Bach was able to develop the expressive character of his later fugue themes.

As to works which are neither transcriptions nor based on a specific model, the first results of Bach's study of Italian music may be detected in a number of compositions which contain Southern and Northern elements in close juxtaposition.

The *Toccata in C major* (P. III:8; BWV 564) combines the style of the German toccata with that of the Italian concerto. An adagio following the bravura passages of the introductory toccata contains one of the sweetest and most poignant cantilenas Bach ever wrote. Apparently he visualized a long drawn-out violin solo of the kind to be found as a second movement in a concerto. The third section, a spirited fugue, has the character of a scherzo. Its skipping theme is interspersed with amusing rests (*Ex.* 32), setting the stage for the light-hearted game

Ex. 32. *BWV* 564

enacted here. Occasional awkward progressions may be considered as part of the fun, and amidst the merry uproar the entertainer suddenly disappears, without bothering properly to take his leave.

A similar combination of divergent styles may be observed in the *Prelude and Fugue in F minor* (P. II:5; BWV 534) and the *Fantasia and Fugue in C minor* (P. III:6; BWV 537). In the introductory movements a well-proportioned Italian two-part form is combined with Germanic elements: thorough imitative work in the fantasia and a poignant toccata ending in the prelude. Likewise the two fugues display certain experimental features. While the F minor piece is marred by technical imperfections, the C minor work skillfully shapes the fugue into a three-part form. Its middle section develops a new, chromatically ascending theme, whereupon, in a kind of da capo, the first fugue section is restated. In later years Bach again took up this combination of aria and fugue construction.

It is not easy to follow up the various results of Bach's study of Italian models. The composer revised in Cöthen, and, in particular in Leipzig, works he had first conceived in Weimar, changing and remodeling them, and even reallocating certain pieces to new sets. In some cases various versions of the same work are preserved, but often only the finished product is available, making it most difficult to assign the composition to a particular year.

A handful of organ pieces, however, do not seem to pose this problem. Apparently they were written at the end of Bach's stay in Weimar, and some may well have been finished in Cöthen.

The process of simplification that occurred in Bach's music as a result of his encounter with Italian masters is revealed in the so-called *Dorian Toccata and Fugue*[1] (P. III:3; BWV 538). The introductory movement does not show the dramatic contrasts prevailing in north German toccatas. The whole powerful piece grows out of a simple motive which is stated in the first half-measure. The well-planned modulations and Bach's art of melodic evolution protect the work from any possibility of monotony. It builds up to a blaze of glory in the fugue, which is based on a beautifully shaped theme. This subject slowly rises and then descends within the range of an octave. Schweitzer aptly describes the magnificent piece, with its impressive strettos, as a 'miracle of juxtaposed and superimposed vaulted arches.'[2]

Similar in character is the *Toccata and Fugue in F major* (P. III:2; BWV 540). The germ cell, out of which this toccata grows, is again a simple, brief, and fast-moving motive; all fantastic and improvisatory elements are discarded. There is an introductory passage over an organ

1. The designation is due to the fact that this composition in D minor has, according to the Dorian mode, no flat in its signature. It is interesting that for this toccata instructions regarding the use of the manuals were preserved. Deviating from the nomenclature in the organ concertos, the main manual is referred to as *Oberwerk*, the second manual as *Positiv*.

2. Cf. A. Schweitzer, *J.S.B.*, Leipzig, 1937[13], p. 253.

point followed by a long-drawn-out pedal solo; the whole section is then restated and transposed to the dominant, thus bringing the exposition to an end. The following section, a sort of development, is clearly comprised of four corresponding subdivisions. A third part, resembling a restatement of the first section, leads to another organ point supporting a figuration in which the ascending motive of the beginning is inverted. In spite of its gigantic dimensions—the toccata consists of 438 measures—the disposition of the material is unusually lucid. The work displays a logical, well-balanced construction, and is, at the same time, of dazzling brilliance. Mendelssohn, when performing it in 1831, exclaimed: 'It sounded as if it would bring the church down.' The following fugue is based on two themes contrasting in character. Bach used each of them separately and then both of them together in a highly attractive manner, thus revealing different aspects of a complex idea.

The gradual shaping of Bach's work is graphically illustrated by the *Prelude and Fugue in A minor* (P. II:8; BWV 543). An earlier and a later version of the prelude are known; the fugue resembles a composition for clavier (BWV 944) and recurs in not too different form, as an organ piece. In its original form the prelude rather crudely emphasized a chromatically descending melodic line; only later was the elegant shape of the impetuously rushing tune achieved. Bach felt the need to solidify the clavier fugue when arranging it for the organ. Its theme was adapted to conform to the requirements of the pedal technique, and the polyphonic texture was strengthened. Despite the separate origin of the two components, they are intimately connected, the fugue bringing the drama initiated in the first section to its inexorable conclusion.

The *Fantasia and Fugue in G minor* (P. II:4, BWV 542) is traditionally associated with the visit Bach paid in 1720 to old Reinken in Hamburg. It seems unlikely, however, that the composer played the piece at that time, as the fantasia prescribes one high, as well as three low, notes not available on the organ of St. Catherine's, over which Reinken presided. On the other hand the fugue (sometimes called the 'Great' G minor Fugue) exists in a copy by J. T. Krebs, who was a pupil of Walther and Bach in Weimar, an indication that the piece may have been written before 1717. The fantasia is an improvisatory toccata with brief polyphonic insertions. Bach makes systematic use of the chromatic idiom, effectively employing it in modulations. The ensuing fugue has a gay theme closely related to an old Dutch folksong[1] and, at the same time, to a piece by Reinken (*Hortus Musicus*, Sonata V). Despite its great dimensions the work is admirably organized and proportioned. The cascades of pedal passages and the sequence of more than 30 broken chords presented in a tornado of sixteenth notes make it a brilliant virtuoso piece. In its happy and powerful character it voices the exuberance of a genius in its early manhood.

Likewise the final version of the *Prelude and Fugue in G major* (P. II:2, BWV 541) was attributed to Bach's period of maturity. A re-examination of the watermark in the autograph by A. Dürr revealed, however, that the composition was probably completed in Weimar around 1716 or earlier.[2] The work starts with a fast-moving, very energetic introductory movement which leads to a cheerful fugue. Near the end Bach has a special surprise in store. A homophonic episode within the fugue is followed by a group of dramatic, sharp dissonances. But the mood of the beginning is restored in the concluding stretto. Thus the swiftly passing clouds served only to underline the movement's optimistic character. Bach considered inserting between the prelude and the fugue a movement which now serves as the finale in the fourth organ sonata. He realized, however, that such a procedure would destroy the unity of the composition, whereas his purpose was better served through the *durezze* of the fugue.

Probably the best known of the organ works of the second period is the *Passacaglia in C minor* (P. I:7; BWV 582),[3] a set of variations on a ground bass. Bach might have found the first half of the theme in the *Trio en Passacaille* by the French organ master, André Raison (1650?-1719), and the model for its form in similar works by Buxtehude. The idea of using mathematical patterns as a basis for music construction was a familiar one to the Baroque period. Despite such

---

1. Cf. J. Röntgen in *Scheurleer-Gedenkboek,* Den Haag, 1925, p. 265 ff.

2. Cf. W. Emery, in Program Book of the English Bach Festival 1965, p. 53 ff.

3. The former conception that this work was originally written for a clavier equipped with a pedal can no longer be upheld. Cf. G. Kinsky, 'Pedalklavier oder Orgel bei B.,' *Acta Musicologica*, VIII, 1936, p. 158 ff.

easily traceable relationships, Bach's work is unique. Its theme, comprising eight measures instead of the traditional four, shows a dignity, strength, and intensity which make it admirably suited for further treatment. The twenty variations of the set are divided into two groups of ten. A decisive break is established after var. 10, as in var. 11 the theme leaves the bass for the first time and moves to the soprano. Each group of ten variations shows in its turn a clear separation into subgroups of five. A quietly flowing 16th motion is initially established in var. 6, and in var. 16 the theme returns to the bass, after having appeared in the upper voices from var. 11 through var. 15. Even within the subgroups a further organization may be observed. As a rule the first two of the five variations are rhythmically connected, forming a pair, and the same is true of the last two, while the third variation stands alone. Only the fourth subgroup (var. 16-20) presents a slightly different aspect. It appears to be a condensed recapitulation of the first ten variations. No. 16 is reminiscent of No. 1, while No. 18 is rhythmically related to No. 4; the contrasting No. 17 helps to reproduce the three-sectional organization of the first subgroup. Nos. 19 and 20 are rhythmically related to the variations of the second subgroup. The over-all structure is therefore as follows:

A	B	C	A	B
1,2-3-4,5	6,7-8-9,10	11,12-13-14,15	16,17,18 -	19,20

Thus the passacaglia as a whole displays the same tripartite construction found within each subgroup. With the majestic ending of No. 20, Bach exhausted all possibilities of the variation form, but instead of concluding he decided to carry on in a different manner. In the fugue following the passacaglia he employed only the first four measures of the theme, but he adorned Raison's melody with a counterpoint that remains the subject's faithful companion throughout the fugue. As always, Bach drew the strongest possible inspiration from the apparently barren soil of self-imposed restrictions and limitations. What in the hands of a smaller mind might have developed into a sterile mathematical tour de force, was transformed by him into an immortal creation; the technical mastery is as nothing compared to the power and magnificence of Bach's inspiration.

The uncongenial atmosphere in Arnstadt and Mühlhausen had, as we noticed, curtailed the number of organ chorales Bach produced in his first creative period. In Weimar the situation was very different; the need to supply new works for church service presented a permanent challenge to his productive genius.

In Weimar, Bach turned largely to new forms of the organ chorale. He was no longer interested in the lengthy chorale partita, better suited for domestic worship than for the church service; likewise, he gradually neglected the extensive and disorganized chorale fantasia. By and large he gave preference to stricter and more concise forms, exploring the following types:

> the chorale harmonization with interludes;
> the chorale fughetta, which occasionally grows into a substantial chorale fugue;
> the cantus firmus chorale (appearing in three different forms);
> the melody chorale;
> the chorale canon.

Of even greater importance than the formal development of the chorale arrangements was the gradual change that took place in their content. In the Weimar years Bach displayed increasing interest in the meaning of the hymn text. He was not satisfied merely to elaborate the chorale melody in an objective, purely musical manner; he attempted to express subjectively the message of the hymn. His arrangements, though works of abstract art, communicated a specific poetic meaning.

The *chorale harmonization with interludes* graphically illustrates the transition from the simple harmonization of a hymn tune to its interpretation on the organ.[1] The most rudimentary stage is represented by a few chorale settings which Bach apparently used to accompany the singing of the congregation. Only two voices are written down: the melody and a carefully figured bass (cf. *Christ lag in Todesbanden*, Christ lay by death enshrouded; P. VI: 16; BWV 695/2 and *Wer nur den lieben Gott lässt walten*, Who so will suffer God to guide him,

---

1. The primitive character of these arrangements induced Keller (p. 141) to ascribe them to the Arnstadt period. Their manuscripts prove, however, that they are products of the Weimar years (cf. NBA IV: 3, KB p. 11).

P. V:53; BWV 690/2).[1] According to the custom of the time Bach often separated the individual chorale lines by short improvisatory passages. These arrangements were preserved in their original two-part version, consisting of chorale melody and figured bass, and in a more finished form, with fully realized middle parts. (Cf. *Gelobet seist du, We praise thee*; P. V:suppl. 1; BWV 722a and 722.) Gradually Bach proceeded to a freer and more flexible idiom, allowing passages and phrases from the interludes to penetrate into the accompaniment of the chorale lines (cf. *In dulci jubilo*, P. V:suppl. 3; BWV 729; and *Lobt Gott*, Praise the Lord, P. V:suppl. 6; BWV 732). Eventually a homogeneous structure was achieved (cf. *Vom Himmel hoch*, From heaven above; P. V:suppl. 7; BWV 738).

Bach used the light and gay form of the *chorale fughetta* to interpret several chorales destined for Advent and Christmas. In these arrangements individual phrases from chorale melodies are subjected to fugal elaboration. *Herr Christ, der einig Gottes Sohn* (Lord Christ, by God engendered; P. V:23; BWV 698) is in three voices. Bach begins with a development of the first chorale phrase. He then combines it with the second phrase (b. 11), ending up (b. 15) by paraphrasing both lines. The microcosm of the fughetta deals with each of the first two lines in two ways, in accordance with the repetition of these essential phrases in the original hymn.

The five-part *Chorale Fugue sopra il Magnificat* (P. VII:41; BWV 733), which consists of 136 measures, might be considered the crowning glory of the Advent and Christmas fughettas. The composition is based on the Holy Virgin's song of praise from Luke I:46-47. Bach introduced the same tune as cantus firmus in the ninth movement of his *Magnificat*. The very freely constructed organ fugue bases its theme on the first phrase of this hymn. The piece achieves its stirring climax near the end when the pedal sets in, majestically intoning in long notes the entire hymn 'My soul doth magnify the Lord—And my spirit hath rejoiced in God my Saviour.'

Three different types of *cantus firmus chorales* occur in the Weimar compositions.

---

1. In the manuscripts these harmonizations follow more elaborate settings.—These and several of the following chorale arrangements were also presented in critical new revisions in NBA IV:3.

The *motet type* (or 'chorale-motet') presents the unadorned cantus firmus in extended notes. The individual chorale lines are introduced by fugatos in shorter notes, using as theme the tune of the following chorale line. In *Vater unser im Himmelreich* (Our Father in the kingdom of heaven; P. VII:53; BWV 737), this type is offered in a condensed and somewhat freer form. The entrances of the chorale phrases in the cantus firmus follow each other too closely to allow for introductory fugatos. These are replaced by mere references to the chorale melody or even by short episodes free of thematic material. The organ chorale is written in four voices and uses the pedal. The cantus firmus lies in the soprano, its sedate motion in 4/2 time producing an archaic, monumental character. *Vater unser im Himmelreich* resembles a motet performed without words; yet the basic idea of Luther's powerful prayer is evident.

In the *paraphrase type* the countermelody, accompanying the cantus firmus, paraphrases the chorale. As the hymn tune is joined by its own variation, the fugal elaboration is reduced or completely abolished. *Nun freut euch, lieben Christen G'mein* (Now rejoice, ye Christian throng; P. VII:44; BWV 734) is written for three voices with the cantus firmus in the tenor. No separate pedal part is prescribed.[1] The soprano voice presents a busily rushing melody in sixteenth notes which outlines the main melody of the chorale and expresses jubilant happiness. In accordance with the subtitle of the arrangement, *Es ist gewisslich an der Zeit* (Verily the time has come), a note of joyful impatience is mingled in.

In the *ornamented type* the cantus firmus is more or less embellished, while the countermelodies may paraphrase the hymn melody. *Wir glauben all' an einen Gott* (We all believe in one God; P. VII:62; BWV 740) and *An Wasserflüssen Babylon* (Beside the streams of Babylon; P. VI:12a; BWV 653b) may be used as examples. The two pieces show a certain affinity. They are both in five parts to be performed on two manuals and double pedal. The slightly ornamented cantus firmus is presented by the soprano voice. In *Wir glauben all'* the chorale phrases are usually anticipated by the upper voice of the pedal. A bizarre passage in thirty-second notes, which provides a

---

1. The notation for manual and pedal in BG 40/84 deviates from the manuscript, and was not used in NBA IV:3, p. 70.

cadenza-like ending, shows that the north German idiom had not lost its attraction for the Weimar composer. In *An Wasserflüssen* the second soprano intones the two initial phrases of the hymn before they appear in the cantus firmus. The same voice then repeats those two phrases over and over again with poignant monotony through the full length of the piece. The pitch is occasionally changed to adapt this strange ostinato to the continuation of the hymn in the cantus firmus, but the basic melodic line remains unaltered. Throughout, mourners seem to repeat their deep grief: 'When we remember Zion, we never cease from weeping.'[1] In later years the practical-minded composer produced two simplified four-part versions with single pedal of this difficult piece. The second one (BWV 653) was incorporated in his 17 Chorales (cf. p. 250).

Ein feste Burg (A mighty fortress; P. VI:22; BWV 720) is a chorale fantasia combining two different types of cantus firmus chorales. In this composition, which was written at the beginning of the Weimar years, certain phrases of the cantus firmus appear in their original form, while others are presented in an ornamented manner. The hymn tune is at times entrusted to the right hand, then again to the left, and in two phrases to the pedal. The number of voices increases from two to three, and finally to four. For the execution Bach prescribed no less than three manuals and pedal. The composition is colorful and very brilliant, but the young genius did not fully succeed in unifying its varied elements. Spitta points out[2] that Bach probably performed this piece in 1709 to demonstrate all the possibilities of the Mühlhausen organ to best advantage after it had been rebuilt according to his specifications.[3]

---

1. Spitta, I:606 establishes a connection between this arrangement and Bach's famous interpretation in Reinken's presence (cf. p. 48). Hans Klotz (NBA IV:2, KB. p. 68) states, however, that this work was written for Weissenfels and not for Hamburg, since only the pedal of the Weissenfels organ was equipped with the notes e flat and e, above middle c.

2. I/394.

3. Unique among Bach's organ chorales is the arrangement of *Herr Gott, dich loben wir* (We praise Thee, o God; P:VI:26, BWV 725). Apparently the composer intended to provide a five-part accompaniment to congregational singing. However, Bach could not resist the temptation to interpret details of the text; thus he frequently changed the type of setting he used. The result is a fantasia-like composition of large proportions (208 measures) which is of little practical value.

After Bach had composed many separate chorale arrangements, he embarked on a greater venture. The result, one of the most important works in the field of organ music, was given the unassuming title *Orgel-Büchlein* (Little Organ Book) by its author. It seems that Bach was engaged in this extensive composition during the last years he spent in Weimar; but it was unfinished when he moved to Cöthen. Bach had originally planned this work on a very large scale. It was to comprise 164 chorales, the names of which the composer wrote at the top of the empty pages, arranging them in the order they were to be employed during the liturgical year. However, more than two-thirds of the sheets remained unused, since Bach discontinued his work after completing 45 arrangements[1]: 4 for Advent, 13 for Christmas and New Year, 13 for Holy Week and Easter, and 15 for other events of the church year.

The title of the work, written in Bach's own hand, reads in an English translation:

LITTLE ORGAN BOOK

wherein an organ student is instructed how to develop
in sundry ways a chorale and, at the same time, gain
experience in the use of the pedal which in each of
these chorales is treated as entirely obbligato.
To the Glory of God in the Heights,
and the instruction of the fellow-man
by Johann Sebastian Bach
pro tempore conductor of His Highness,
the Prince of Anhalt-Cöthen.

At that time Bach had several gifted pupils, and he was becoming more and more concerned with the problem of how to pass on his craft to others. The Orgel-Büchlein (P. V; BWV 599-644) is the earliest in a long row of important educational keyboard compositions.

Most pieces in this collection are *melody chorales*. The hymns are presented in a simple and concise manner; introductions or interludes are dispensed with, and, as a rule, the soprano offers an unadorned

1. There are actually 46 chorales. However, *Liebster Jesus* (Dearest Jesus; P.V:37; BWV 633, 634) appears twice, in versions which closely resemble each other.

version of the chorale melody, which is supported by the three lower
voices with consummate contrapuntal mastery. Usually the same rhythmical pattern is maintained throughout each arrangement; thus Bach
obtains a form resembling an individual variation in a chorale partita.
A characteristic feature of these melody chorales is the highly subjective
manner in which the hymn tunes are interpreted. Bach often expresses
in the three lower parts a fervor and intensity of feeling, of which only
the young are capable. On the other hand, the extreme economy of the
musical language—so different from the inexperienced organist's volubility that perplexed his Arnstadt congregation—and the superb craftsmanship, displayed in the strict polyphonic treatment of the lower
voices, show the composer to be close to his period of maturity. Within
the limited space available (some of the arrangements are only eight or
nine measures long), he succeeds both in presenting the chorale melody and in interpreting the emotional content inherent in the text.

Johann Gotthilf Ziegler (1686-1747), who studied with Bach in
Weimar, recorded a very significant piece of advice his master gave him
as to how to perform chorales: the pupil should not merely play the
hymns in an offhand manner, but ought also to express the 'affect' (the
symbolical and emotional content) of the text. The Orgel-Büchlein
clearly illustrates what Bach had in mind. The running triplets of *In
dulci jubilo* (P. V:35; BWV 608) and the dance character of *In dir ist
Freude* (In thee is joy; P. V:34; BWV 615) express happiness and
rapture. Similarly, the animated rhythm of *Mit Fried' und Freud' ich
fahr dahin* (In peace and joy I go my way; P. V:41; BWV 616) voices
glad confidence. In *Christ ist erstanden* (Christ has risen; P. V:4;
BWV 627), Bach is so engrossed in his task of announcing the Lord's
resurrection that he sets all three verses of the hymn to music, each in a
slightly different manner, thus creating a kind of miniature chorale
partita. On the other hand the succession of 'sighs' (descending appoggiaturas) in *O Lamm Gottes* (O Lamb of God; P. V:44; BWV 618)
creates an atmosphere of poignant sadness, while the perpetuum mo-
bile-like rushing figures in *Herr Gott, nun schleuss den Himmel auf*
(O God, unlock the Heavens; P. V:24; BWV 617) convey a picture of
the anxiety and restlessness of man on earth.

In three arrangements the melody is almost obliterated by rich ornamentation, which establishes a mood of utter dejection, as though a

mourner was hiding his face. *Das alte Jahr vergangen ist* (The old year is past; P. V:10; BWV 614) describes the dangers and fears through which mankind has gone. Equally stirring is *O Mensch, bewein' dein' Sünde gross* (O man, thy grievous sin bemoan; P. V:45; BWV 622), in which Bach, near the end, inspired by the final words of the text 'In sacrifice miraculous He shed His precious blood for us, upon the cross suspended,' unfolds both the drama of Golgotha and its message of redemption (*Ex*. 33). *Wenn wir in höchsten Nöten sein* (When we

Ex. 33. *BWV* 622

are troubled through and through; P. V:51; BWV 641) is of special significance, as Bach took it up again shortly before his death.

Particularly striking is a chorale in which, at first sight, Bach seems to have misinterpreted the text. In *Alle Menschen müssen sterben* (Every mortal must perish; P. V:2; BWV 643) the dance-like rhythm of the bass produces a serene mood, which is only explained by the vision of eternal life evoked near the end of the text: 'There the faithful souls will see God's transcendent majesty.'

Frequently Bach evokes pictorial motives out of references in the text. In three successive Christmas chorales,[1] ascending and descending runs depict in traditional manner the rapid motion of angels between heaven and earth. A fourth Christmas chorale, *Der Tag, der ist so freudenreich* (This day, so rich in joy; P. V:11; BWV 605), describes, with the help of a swaying rhythm in the middle parts (*Ex*. 34), the

Ex. 34. *BWV* 605

1. *Vom Himmel hoch da komm ich her* (From Heaven above to earth I come; P.V:49; BWV 606), *Vom Himmel kam der Engel Schar* (From Heaven came the host of angels; P.V:50; BWV 607), *In dulci jubilo.*

gently rocking motion of the cradle. In the Easter hymn *Erstanden ist der heil'ge Christ* (Risen is Holy Christ; P. V:14; BWV 628) upsurging figures point to the resurrection. The complex symbolism in the chorale arrangement *Durch Adams Fall* (Old Adam's fall; P. V:13; BWV 637) is famous; the interval of a descending diminished seventh in the bass describes the sinful fall, the alternation between major and minor (f sharp and f natural) mankind's vacillation, while an undulating alto voice portrays the snake in paradise (*Ex. 35*).

Ex. 35. *BWV 637*

(Tenor voice omitted)

Nine of the finest arrangements are treated canonically, among them five at the interval of an octave and four at that of a fifth. Symbolism was responsible here for the use of *chorale canons*. It is most clearly apparent in *In dulci jubilo*, where the canon is inspired by the words 'trahe me post te' (draw me after Thee) in the second verse. Similarly in the chorale *Hilf Gott, dass mir's geling'* (Lord, help me to succeed; P. V:29; BWV 624) the imitation of Christ is symbolized through a canon of the fifth, while in *Erschienen ist der herrliche Tag* (Now dawns for us the glorious day; P. V:15; BWV 629) the canon between the soprano and the pedal bass, two octaves lower, shows Christ triumphantly leading his captive foes.

Dies sind die heil'gen zehn Gebot (These are the holy ten commandments; P. V:12; BWV 635) belongs to the few chorales in the Orgel-Büchlein in which the counterpoint to the hymn tune is not freely invented, but, following the earlier chorale tradition, is derived from the melody of the cantus firmus. It is characteristic of the pleasure Bach took in numerical symbolism that the motive of the counterpoint appears exactly ten times in this organ chorale. The intervals of the first statement are carefully preserved throughout; only the very last statement in the pedal bass is slightly changed so as to produce the final cadence.

Apart from the chorale canons and the melody chorales incorporated in the Orgel-Büchlein, very few arrangements that survive display a similar character. Among these isolated pieces is *Herzlich tut mich verlangen* (My heart is ever yearning for blessed death's release; P. V:27; BWV 727). Here Bach delicately ornamented the Passion hymn and created a melody chorale of exquisite beauty, equal to the outstanding settings of the piece he included in his vocal music.

Looking at Bach's later contributions in the field of the chorale arrangement, we notice that he continued to cultivate in Leipzig most of the forms treated in Weimar. The melody chorale, however, no longer appeared. The subjective, unassuming treatment of the sacred tune presented in the soprano may later have seemed too intimate to him. Possibly this was one of the reasons why the Orgel-Büchlein was left unfinished. Bach's way of giving to the melodies a uniform accompaniment which expressed the meaning of the text was to be taken up, however, in the romantic *Lied* of the following century.

After Bach's departure from Weimar his organ composition came more or less to a standstill. In Cöthen secular music was his main interest, while in the first Leipzig years sacred vocal music absorbed most of his time. Although it is possible that some of the works discussed above received their definite form in Cöthen, hardly any organ composition can be assigned with certainty to his *third and fourth creative periods*, the dozen years between 1717 and 1729.

The *Prelude and Fugue in D minor* (P. III:4; BWV 539) shows a direct connection with a work which originated in Cöthen. Around 1720 Bach composed his sonatas and partitas for unaccompanied violin, and the fugue from the Violin Sonata in G minor has been preserved in a D minor version for organ.[1] In this form it is preceded by a concise prelude written for the manual only. Although the style of the violin fugue is completely idiomatic and displays the deepest insight into the possibilities of the string instrument, the essence of the original composition is preserved in this transcription; only such additions were made as appeared necessary to transform the work into an organ fugue. To

---

1. B.s authorship of this arrangement has, not quite convincingly, been questioned. Cf. D. Kilian in *Musikforschung*, 1961, p. 323 ff. The same fugue exists also in a version for lute (BWV 1000; cf. p. 311).

this end the harmonic and polyphonic texture is intensified (*Ex.* 36): there are new entrances of the theme, a bass part is supplemented, and

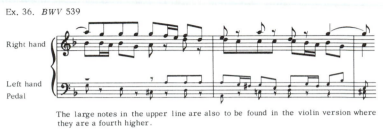

Ex. 36. *BWV* 539

Right hand

Left hand
Pedal

The large notes in the upper line are also to be found in the violin version where they are a fourth higher.
The small notes in the lower line are additions of the organ arrangement.

mock imitations of the original are replaced by real imitations.

According to Forkel, a set of six Sonatas for two claviers and pedal (P. I: 1-6; BWV 525-530) was intended for the instruction of Bach's eldest son, Wilhelm Friedemann. With these works Bach continued an earlier experiment investigating the various potentialities inherent in the trio sonata for two melody instruments and bass. He had come to the conclusion that a significant new form could be derived from the traditional combination, if the part of one of the melody instruments was assigned to the right hand of a harpsichordist and the bass to his left hand. Thus the basic components of the trio were maintained, but one player eliminated (cf. p. 312). In the Leipzig Sonatas, Bach went even further with the process of simplification. On a keyboard instrument equipped with two manuals and a pedal a complete trio could be performed by a single person, if the musician played the parts of the two melody instruments with his hands and those of the bass with his feet. Even the crossing of the two melody parts, common in the Baroque trio sonata, presented no difficulty on separate manuals.

Bach may have completed these sonatas around 1729, but he appears to have started work at a much earlier time. Three different movements were finished in 1715 and earlier versions of Sonatas III and V written before 1729. It is not quite certain whether Bach primarily considered the organ or a pedal clavier with two manuals (harpsichord or clavichord) for the execution of the sonatas. His designation 'for 2 claviers and pedal' is somewhat ambiguous, but as the same inscription is used in many of the large chorale arrangements of the

Clavier-Übung, part III (cf. p. 242), it would seem that he intended an organ to be used.[1] Nevertheless the lack of a truly idiomatic organ style is quite obvious in these compositions. The thematic elaboration is that of the trio sonata, the basic three parts never being augmented or reduced. The sonatas use the three movements fast-slow-fast of the concerto, and the rondo-like structure of individual concerto movements quite often appears. These movements start and end with an impressive, often quite extended statement in the tonic, while parts of it, transposed into related keys, are distributed throughout the piece. Contrasting episodes performing the necessary modulations connect the various entrances of the main idea.

It is hardly surprising that several pieces in these sonatas were used by Bach in different contexts. The poignant 'Adagio e dolce' of the third sonata appears in a transposed form in his Concerto in A minor for flute, violin, and harpsichord (BWV 1044). Similarly, the first movement of the fourth Sonata, a spirited Vivace preceded by four measures in tempo Adagio, is borrowed from Cantata No. 76, where it is scored for oboe d'amore, viola da gamba and continuo. Sonata IV also points to another experiment formerly undertaken by Bach. Apparently he attempted (in BWV 541) to separate an organ prelude from its fugue through the insertion of a middle movement, thus reviving a form previously tried out in BWV 564 (cf. p. 224). This middle movement was, however, not included in the definite version of the work and appears as the finale of Sonata IV.

These six Sonatas are undoubtedly among the most cheerful and entertaining works Bach wrote for the organ. The spring-like mood in Sonata I, in E flat major, with its gay initial movement, the Adagio resembling a siciliano, and the energetic final Allegro; the powerful C minor Vivace in II, its tender Largo, and the vigorous concluding Allegro which skillfully combines elements of the fugue and concerto forms; the noble Andante in B minor of IV; and the magnificent V, in C major, which in its merry, high-spirited character resembles the fourth Brandenburg Concerto—all prove that in writing these pieces Bach tenderly envisioned the young student for whom they were destined.

1. Cf. W. Schrammek, Die musikgeschichtliche Stellung der Orgeltriosonaten von J.S.B.,' *BJ* 1954, p. 7ff.

The peculiar nature of this set induced various musicians to restore the character of the trio sonata through arrangements for several instruments.[1] Interesting though these arrangements are, they destroy the composer's true intentions. Bach wanted to offer trios which could be performed by a single person. His attempt was completely successful. The Sonatas make superb exercises for developing precision and complete independence of the organist's two hands and feet. Through the introduction of new stylistic devices Bach offered here a challenge which the true organ virtuoso will be eager to accept.

The number of preludes and fugues for the organ Bach wrote in Leipzig was very small. Approximately half a dozen works of this kind seem to have been completed during the composer's *fifth creative period*.

These preludes and fugues exhibit the composer's tendency to combine various stylistic elements within the realm of keyboard music. They are highly significant, and some of them belong to the best works Bach ever wrote.

It can be seen from the *Prelude and Fugue in C major* (P. II:1; BWV 545) how important it was for Bach to round off his musical forms. The first draft of the prelude was shorter than the ultimate version. In the final arrangement, made in or before 1730, Bach added a little introduction which he restated at the end of the movement, thus enhancing the solidity of the formal construction. This festive and stately prelude is followed by a simple and straightforward fugue which ends—in the manner of some of Bach's early fugues—with a harmonization of the theme presented in the top voice.

Similar in character is a second *Prelude and Fugue in C major* (P. II:7; BWV 547). The broadly contoured prelude is brimming over with joy. Bach balances its mightily surging main theme by a descending pedal arpeggio in rocking motion. In the manner of a ground bass this arpeggio is repeated over and over again and provides the move-

1. A setting of the 'Adagio e dolce' of the third Sonata for violin, viola, and cello is attributed to Mozart (K. 404a). Sonatas I and VI were arranged by H. Engel for 2 violins, cello, and clavier. R. Tody edited all six sonatas in a version for violin, viola and clavier. Naumann and David adapted them for violin and clavier. H. Keller presented I and VI in arrangements for 2 claviers.

ment's energetic ending. The second movement, which is based on a very concise theme, seems to be almost a brief study-course in fugal technique. The theme is first developed in its original form, then in inversion, and finally in various strettos, including the augmentation of the main idea. Bach starts this piece in the manual and gives it the appearance of a fugue in four voices. Only in the last third of the fugue does the pedal come in, with the fifth voice[1] powerfully intoning the main theme in extended notes.

The fugues in the minor mode are of even greater significance. In the *Prelude and Fugue in C minor* (P. II:6; BWV 546) the first movement is most remarkable. It employs the concerto form, the first ritornello of twenty-four measures being literally restated at the movement's end. Episodes of equal length follow the first and precede the last of these imposing, block-like sections. The center of the prelude is occupied by a statement of the transposed ritornello with an interpolated episode. As a result the following, symmetrical arrangement of the 144 (12 × 12) measures may be observed:[2]

RITORNELLO	EPISODE	TRANSPOSED RITORNELLO	EPISODE	RITORNELLO
		with interpolated episode		
24 meas.	24 meas.	48 meas.	24 meas.	24 meas.

The following five-part fugue, whose theme rhythmically interprets a sequence of arpeggios, is far less imposing. Spitta[3] assumed that this movement was written in Weimar. However, the return of the fugue's coda to the chords appearing at the beginning of the prelude seems to indicate that the two pieces were conceived at the same time.

The first movement of the *Prelude and Fugue in B minor* (P. II:10; BWV 544) presents a structure similar to that in the C minor Prelude. In its melodic idiom this tender and poignant piece assumes, however, the character of an aria imbued with gentle nostalgia. The fugue fittingly conveys a mood of quiet restraint. Even the display of contrapuntal skill is limited. Only toward the end does the composition discard its reticence and move to an imposing climax.

1. Exactly in meas. 49 of a piece 72 meas. long.
2. Cf. also Keller, p. 115.
3. I:581 ff.

The *Prelude and Fugue in E minor* (P. II:9; BWV 548) belongs to
Bach's most powerful and extensive organ compositions. Rightly Spitta
calls it an 'organ symphony in two movements.'[1] The mighty prelude
is again indebted to the concerto form, but as the main material of the
episodes grows out of the main ritornello, the cohesion of all sections
is particularly strong. The fugue is known in English-speaking countries as 'the wedge,' since the beginning of its theme, containing one
ascending and one descending line, gradually widens from the interval
of a third to that of an octave (*Ex.* 37). The huge and extremely diffi-

Ex. 37. *BWV* 548

cult movement introduces, after a brilliant contrapuntal development
of the theme, a strongly contrasting section. Here free passages and
runs are presented, while the 'wedge' theme appears only occasionally.
In conclusion the fugal part from the beginning is literally restated,
and it reveals the working of Bach's mind that the middle section is
almost exactly as long as the two outer parts together. In this magnificent work, full of vigor, verve, and brilliance, elements of the concerto,
the toccata, and the da capo aria are fused together with singular
success.

Bach's earliest organ work to appear in print was published in 1739
under the title 'Third part of the *Clavier-Übung*[2] (keyboard exercise),
consisting of sundry [chorale] preludes on the catechism and other
hymns for the organ written for the enjoyment of amateurs and in particular for connoisseurs of such work.' The majority of the twenty-seven
pieces contained in this collection exists only in the single version preserved in print, in which respect they differ from Bach's '17 Chorales'
completed at a later date (cf. p. 249). Although the composer mainly
used forms he had previously employed, the new pieces display the
technical perfection, the monumental conception, and the spiritual

1. II:690.
2. The other parts of this work which are written for harpsichord are discussed
on p. 290 ff.

depth we are wont to expect from Bach at the peak of his creative output.

The solid, logically organized structure of the whole work is indicated by the fact that its first and last numbers are interrelated. The collection begins with an extended Prelude in E flat major (P. III:1; BWV 552), which is clearly connected with the so-called *St. Anne*[1] or *Trinity Fugue* printed in the same volume as its mighty ultimate piece. Although twenty-one organ chorales and four 'duettos' separate the two movements, they are linked together by the symbolic emphasis on the number three, employed as a reference to the Holy Trinity. Both the prelude and the fugue prescribe *three* flats, and each consists of *three* main sections and uses *three* themes. In between the two powerful tutti of the beginning and the end, the prelude introduces two different subjects, which are presented alternately with the main idea. In the fugue, one of the most dazzling works of the kind Bach ever wrote, thematic variation plays a big role. Each of the three sections in this movement has a subject of its own, but the second and third sections employ in addition a rhythmic alteration of the first theme (*Ex.* 38) in contrapuntal combination with their own ideas.

Ex. 38. *BWV* 552

Theme

Alteration I

Alteration II

Perhaps the clearest expression of the symbolic meaning in the 'Trinity' fugue can be found in the three versions of the same main theme used here.

1. The designation *St. Anne Fugue* is customary in the English-speaking countries. It is due to the coincidence that Bach's fugue theme uses the same intervals as the 'St. Anne tune' of an early English hymn. Both melodies have a folksong-like quality which may account for their similarity. A direct connection probably did not exist.

The collection of chorale preludes contained in the *Clavier-Übung* (P. III, V, VI, VII; BWV 669-689) supplements in a way the earlier one of the Orgel-Büchlein. Whereas the Weimar preludes dealt with chorales for the different holydays of the church year, the *Clavier-Übung* contains arrangements of German hymns used in the first half of the Lutheran Mass and connected with Luther's catechism. The series starts with the German versions of Kyrie and Gloria, and continues with Luther's songs on the Ten Commandments, the Creed, the Lord's Prayer, Baptism, Penitence, and Communion. As Luther compiled two versions of the catechism, a large and a small one, so Bach wrote two versions of each chorale, a more elaborate one for 'connoisseurs' and a simpler and briefer version without pedal for 'amateurs.' For the German Gloria he even supplied three arrangements (one large and two small ones) possibly as an additional allusion to the Holy Trinity to which—apart from the prelude and fugue—the three-partite Kyrie had referred.

Four pieces without a pedal part which appear near the end of the collection (P. No. 4465; BWV 802-805), are written in the style of two-part inventions. Their only heading is 'Duetto' with no specific reference to any chorale melody. Klaus Ehricht proved,[1] however, that there is a direct melodic relationship between these duets and some of the smaller chorale arrangements of the collection. The duets belong to the group of small chorale preludes without pedal which could be used outside the church in the homes of the faithful. Thus the third part of the *Clavier-Übung* consists of the 'large catechism,' made up of 12 numbers with pedal (10 large organ chorales preceded by the E flat major Prelude and concluded by the 'Trinity' Fugue), and the 'small catechism,' made up of 15 numbers without pedal (11 small chorales and 4 duets).[2] The old printed edition somewhat obscures this organi-

---

1. *BJ* 1949/50 p. 40 ff. The author convincingly refutes the contention of earlier authorities like Schweitzer, Keller, Kirkpatrick, that the four duets are clavier pieces, unconnected with the rest of the numbers of *Clavier-Übung* III. The symbolic meaning of these four compositions was explored by G. Friedemann, *B. zeichnet das Kreuz*, Pinneberg, 1963.

2. The organist who wishes to perform the *Clavier-Übung* in a concert will have to choose between the 'large catechism' and the 'small catechism.' The former can be played in the order in which the arrangements appear in the original edition. More complicated is the rendition of the 'small catechism,' as it contains two settings

zation, as it usually pairs those arrangements based on the same hymn tune.

The majority of the large arrangements uses the form of the cantus firmus chorale. The 'motet type' can be found in four numbers. In the first *Kyrie* (P. VII: 39a; BWV 669) the chorale appears in extended notes in the soprano; the following *Christe* (P. VII:39b; BWV 670) entrusts it to the tenor; the second *Kyrie* (P. VII:39c; BWV 671), a monumental piece in five parts, presents it in the bass.[1] It seems hardly possible to surpass the grandeur of this setting, but Bach succeeds in doing so in the only six-part organ composition he ever wrote, the arrangement of the penitential chorale, *Aus tiefer Not schrei' ich zu dir* (Out of the depth I cry to Thee; P. VI:13; BWV 686). This setting in the Phrygian mode, which prescribes a double pedal, displays a richness of contrapuntal elaboration, outstanding even among the Thomas Cantor's works. The music succeeds in rising from the feeling of contrition and penitence to trust in the Lord's mercy.

Bach used the 'paraphrase type' three times. The German 'Gloria' (*Allein Gott in der Höh' sei Ehr'*: To God in the Highest alone be glory; P. VI:6; BWV 676) is based on an earlier version which the composer revised and greatly enlarged for the *Clavier-Übung*. This is a strict *tricinium* with sections of the cantus firmus alternately appearing in all three voices. They are joined by a briskly moving paraphrase of the same tune, evidently depicting the motion of the angels' wings. In the baptismal hymn, *Christ unser Herr zum Jordan kam* (Christ our Lord to Jordan came; P. VI:17; BWV 684), the swiftly moving sixteenth notes in the bass voice which are derived from the cantus firmus (*Ex. 39*) seem to conjure up the flow of water in the Jordan river, and

Ex. 39. *BWV 684*

---

of the *Gloria* and four duets. Klaus Ehricht, p. 56, suggests the following order, which has been successfully tried out in performances: BWV 802, 672, 673, 674, 677, 804, 679, 681, 683, 805, 685, 687, 689, 803, 675.

1. In these three arrangements the material for the contrapuntal introductions and accompaniments to all the lines of the chorale tunes is taken from the first hymn line only. This increases the cohesive character of the pieces.

also the stream of Christ's blood cleansing us of our sins.[1] Vastly different is the five-part arrangement of the Lord's Prayer, *Vater unser im
Himmelreich* (Our Father who art in heaven, P. VII: 52; BWV 682).
Here the hymn tune is introduced as a canon between soprano and
alto. A complete trio sonata with its typical bass and imitative upper
parts which paraphrase the chorale melody is added to this strict form.
The work presents almost unsurmountable difficulties to the organist,
who attempts to keep each of the two basic elements of the piece dis-
tinctly audible. Wilhelm Weismann offers a sensitive interpretation
of the prelude,[2] the symbolical meaning of which is particularly difficult for us to grasp. Following Luther's text Weismann explains the
canon as the symbol of man obeying God's commands, while the
strangely tortured counterpoints of the trio sonata signify the world's
suffering and its obstruction of the divine will.

In two of his cantus firmus arrangements Bach employed a device he
had not used hitherto. It might be termed the 'independent type' of
organ chorales. In these pieces the cantus firmus is joined by a new
melody unrelated to the hymn tune, a dualistic element thus being introduced into the form. The communion chorale *Jesus Christus unser
Heiland* (Jesus Christ our Saviour; P. VI: 30; BWV 688) entrusts the
pedal with the cantus firmus, while the manuals execute a turbulent
two-part invention. The arrangement might depict the 'wrath of God'
and the 'hellish pain,' mentioned by Luther, from which we were saved
through Christ's intervention.[3] In the setting of *Dies sind die heil'gen
zehn Gebot'* (These are the holy ten commandments; P. VI: 19; BWV
678) a two-part canon of the chorale melody is again surrounded by a
trio of voices. Bach simplified the technical problem, however, by en-
trusting to the organist's right hand two freely invented parts and to
his left hand the two cantus firmus voices. This prelude not only displays the symbolic use of the canon technique, which signifies the ob-
servation of God's laws; it is also subdivided into ten periods and shows
a kind of binary construction, referring to the two tablets on which the
ten Commandments were inscribed.[4]

1. Cf. Spitta II/695.
2. *BJ* 1949/50, p. 57 ff.
3. Keller's attempt (p. 209) to find references to the chorale tune in the upper
voices of this arrangement seems too contrived.
4. Cf. Dietrich in *BJ* 1929, p. 80.

A kind of 'chorale fugue' is used for the hymn of the Creed, *Wir glauben all' an einen Gott* (We all believe in one God; P. VII:60; BWV 680). Bach fashioned the chorale's first line into a theme for a three-part fugue, which he entrusted to the manuals. It is supported by an ostinato bass in the pedal whose constant repetition of the same phrase seems to symbolize the firmness of our faith in God. The chorale's middle section is left out, but its last line appears near the end in the tenor voice. The hymn's initial and ultimate phrases are used here to represent the whole song.

A contrapuntal form based on the chorale's first line appears in most of the arrangements in the small catechism. A full-fledged four-part chorale fugue in the Dorian mode attempts to express the unfathomable mystery of communion (P. VI:33; BWV 689). Brief, yet technically brilliant and exquisitely expressive chorale fughettas are supplied for seven numbers (the three Kyrie pieces, P. VII:40a-c; BWV 672-674; the last Gloria, P. VI:10; BWV 677; the Ten Commandments, P. VI:20; BWV 679; the Creed, P. VII:61; BWV 681; Baptism, P. VI:18; BWV 685). Number symbolism again appears in the Ten Commandments. As Dietrich pointed out, the theme of the little fughetta has a compass of 10 half tones (g to f') and it is used ten times within the composition. In the Baptism fughetta the theme is introduced three times, each statement being followed by its inversion. Keller interprets this[1] as symbolic references to the three immersions of Christ. Bach's habit of enriching his music through the introduction of idioms developed in other media of expression is noticeable in the Creed chorale; with its dotted rhythms it resembles the introductory movement to a French overture (*Ex.* 40).

Ex. 40. *BWV 681*

A simple and unadorned melody chorale of the kind employed in the Orgel-Büchlein is used for the Lord's Prayer (P. V:47; BWV 683). In the original edition it is preceded by one of the most intricate pieces

1. Page 207.

of the set, sharing with it the same chorale melody. This dramatically illustrates the variety that exists in this collection.

In two arrangements the composer showed that the cantus firmus technique can also be used for compositions employing the manual only. The Penitential chorale (P. VI: 14; BWV 687) in the Phrygian mode is set as a four-part composition using the motet style in its strict form, the hymn tune being presented in the soprano. In the first of the Gloria arrangements (P. VI: 5; BWV 675) the cantus firmus in the alto is surrounded by two gaily rambling voices which paraphrase the hymn and seem to carry the listener into heavenly spheres.

Thus Bach's first organ work to appear in print presents a perfect picture of its author's supreme technical mastery, intellectual power, and religious fervor.

The organ works of Bach's *last period of composition* consist exclusively of chorale arrangements. It seems likely that Bach intended to have them published, but only a comparatively small number was actually printed in his lifetime. Like other works written in the last Leipzig years, the chorales display for the most part a retrospective character; yet a few point the way to future stylistic developments.

The twenty-five compositions we have to consider here, may be divided into four groups:

    a. 17 chorales[1] (P. VI, VII; BWV 651-667)
    b. Canonic variations on the Christmas song, *Vom Himmel hoch* (P. V: 92; BWV 769)
    c. 'Schübler' Chorales (P. VI and VII; BWV 645-650)
    d. *Vor deinen Thron* (Before Thy throne; P. VII: 58; BWV 668)

The *17 Chorales* are in a way the earliest of these works, reaching back to the Weimar years. Bach conceived them independently of each other. Toward the end of his life, possibly as late as 1749, he revised and collected them, improving their texture and ornamentation, and

---

1. Usually the works enumerated under (a) and (d) are referred to as a single collection embracing '18 Chorales.' However, the original manuscript presents first the '17 Chorales,' then the 'Canonic Variations' and finally *Vor deinen Thron*, thus clearly separating BWV 668 from BWV 651-667. In other respects too the single arrangement appears different from the '17 Chorales' and it seems therefore appropriate to consider it separately (cf. Klotz in KB to NBA IV: 2, p. 13).

enlarging some of them.[1] Bach may have had an over-all structure for the whole set in mind when he assembled his Leipzig manuscript. It is impossible to tell its exact nature,[2] however, for the composer's failing health seems to have prevented him from completing the work. The last two numbers are not in Bach's own hand but in that of his subsequent son-in-law, Altnikol.

In the arrangements of the collection seven chorale melodies appear once, two in two different versions, and two in three settings. Basically Bach used two kinds of technical devices in the individual arrangements, the paraphrase and the ornamented type, modifying and adapting them to specific requirements in a most ingenious manner. The *paraphrase* type can be found both in three-part and in four-part settings. *Herr Jesu Christ, dich zu uns wend'* (Lord Jesus Christ, turn to us; P. VI:27; BWV 655) and *Allein Gott in der Höh'* (To God on high alone be praise; P. VI:7; BWV 664) are fast-moving, lively trios stressing the independence of the voices, like the organ sonatas. In both pieces the paraphrase of the hymn is dominating, while the cantus firmus in the pedal is introduced only near the end. In BWV 664, a sparkling and luminous setting of the German Gloria, the cantus firmus proper is confined to meas. 85-90. Obviously Bach's main concern was to convey the Christmas spirit; the presentation of the unadorned hymn tune hardly mattered. In the four-part arrangement of *Nun danket alle Gott* (Now thank we all our God; P. VII:43; BWV 657) the fugatos preceding the entrance of the individual hymn lines in the soprano approach the idiom of Pachelbel in their simplicity. The purity and strength of an early woodcut seems to be recaptured here.

In *O Lamm Gottes* (O lamb of God; P. VII:48; BWV 656) Bach

1. Vol. IV/2 of the NBA presents both the Weimar and the Leipzig versions of the chorales thus offering an opportunity for easy comparison. An enlargement of the compositions may be observed in BWV 652, 653, 656, and in particular in 651. The notation was clarified through doubling of the length of the notes in BWV 656 (3rd stanza) and 661.

2. Hans Luedtke's attempt (*BJ* 1918) to prove that the collection forms a unit from the liturgical point of view is not fully convincing. Klotz (p. 59) emphasizes that both the first and the last of the '17 Chorales' contain invocations of the Holy Ghost. He points out, moreover, that the first, eleventh, and seventeenth pieces of the collection were inscribed *organo pleno*. Thus the first and the last arrangement were singled out, and possibly also what the composer had considered as the centerpiece of the set. In this case Bach would have planned a collection of twenty-one organ chorales of which four are missing.

adapts three verses of the chorale melody. The first and second stanzas are set for the manual only, with the cantus firmus in soprano and alto respectively. Then the hymn tune glides down to the pedal, achieving a glorious climax in the third stanza, which expresses man's triumph over death through Christ's sacrifice. The monumental first setting of *Jesus Christus unser Heiland* (Jesus Christ our Saviour; P. VI:31; BWV 665) is designated for use at the communion. The cantus firmus is in the bass, and each line is preceded by fragmentary entrances of the melody in tenor and alto, and followed by the soprano, the whole composition being fused through a gently flowing allemande rhythm. Varying countermelodies interpret the meaning of the text. In the third line Christ's 'anguish sore' is described through chromatic descending progressions, while the concluding line conveys the redemption from the 'pains of Hell.' Equally impressive is the opening number of the set, the *Fantasia super Komm, heiliger Geist* (Come, Holy Ghost; P. VII:36; BWV 651), which employs Luther's version of the Latin hymn, *Veni Sancte Spiritus.* This monumental piece of more than a hundred measures is a festive toccata based on a paraphrase of the melody's first line and supported by widely spaced entrances of the cantus firmus in the pedal. Bach headed this piece with 'J.J.' (*Jesu juva,* Help Jesus), and every measure of the composition seems to express his confidence that divine assistance was being granted.

In contrast to *Clavier-Übung,* part III, the '17 Chorales' make ample use of the *ornamented* type of chorale arrangement. The five-part version with double pedal of *An Wasserflüssen Babylon* was previously discussed (cf. p. 232). Bach rearranged the piece into a four-part version with single pedal, transferring the ornamented cantus firmus from the soprano to the tenor voice. Subsequently this arrangement was revised again, the rhythm receiving a keener and more interesting character (*Ex.* 41) before it found its place among the '17 Chorales,' where

Ex. 41. *An Wasserflüssen Babylon*

BWV 653a (Weimar)

BWV 653 (Leipzig)

it constitutes one of the gems of the set (P. VI:12b; BWV 653). An arrangement of *Nun komm der Heiden Heiland* (Come now, Saviour of men; P. VII:45; BWV 659)—in which the soprano presents the cantus firmus surrounded by coloratura—produces a mysterious and fantastic piece of poignant beauty. A second setting of the same tune (P. VII:46; BWV 660), a trio for soprano and two accompanying basses offers a puzzling aspect. Keller suggests that Bach might have intended to describe Christ's descent to Hell in this unusually dark-hued piece. In the first version of *Allein Gott in der Höh'* (P. VI:9; BWV 662) the ornamented hymn tune is again entrusted to the soprano, while the other voices develop an idea derived from the chorale's first line. The mood is jubilant, almost ecstatic. The second setting of the same chorale (P. VI:8; BWV 663), which may be regarded as an early work, influenced by north German models, places the cantus firmus in the tenor and ornaments it so profusely that the melodic substance is all but obscured. Fortunately the other voices, and in particular the simple statements of the pedal, help to clarify the content. Possibly the most famous of the '17 Chorales' is *Schmücke dich, o liebe Seele* (Deck thyself bright my soul; P. VII:49; BWV 654). Bach used here a poignant sarabande melody developed from the first two lines of the hymn tune as a companion to the ornamented cantus firmus. Schumann was deeply impressed by the 'state of bliss' conveyed in this setting, and he quoted Mendelssohn's remark that, if life had robbed him of all hope and faith, Bach's unique chorale would restore them to him.[1]

The last two pieces of the set seem to belong to a special category. *Jesus Christus, unser Heiland* (Jesus Christ, our Redeemer; P. VI:32; BWV 666), with the hymn tune in the soprano, is the only arrangement written almost exclusively for the manual.[2] The piece is technically primitive and lacking in stronger inspiration. The first part of *Komm Gott Schöpfer, heiliger Geist* (Come Creator, Holy Ghost; P. VII:35; BWV 667) is borrowed from a chorale of the Orgel-Büchlein, where the melody is in the soprano. In the new version a second stanza is added with the cantus firmus in the pedal, and the connection of the two sections does not appear to be quite organic. Is it a mere coincidence

---

1. *Gesammelte Schriften*, Leipzig, 1854, I/219.
2. The pedal enters with a single note, three measures from the end, a sparing use not uncommon among Bach's early organ works.

that these inferior pieces were entered into the manuscript by Altnikol and not by Bach? Would the composer have kept them in the collection, had he been able to complete this magnificent torso?

During the earlier Leipzig years Bach showed little interest in the canonic elaboration of chorale melodies. This attitude changed toward the end of his life, when he became absorbed in reviving the strict contrapuntal techniques of the past. During his last period of composition he wrote *Einige canonische Veränderungen über das Weihnachtslied: Vom Himmel hoch, da komm' ich her* (A few canonic variations on the Christmas song, From Heaven above to earth I come; P. V:92; BWV 769) as a kind of companion piece to the 'Musical Offering' and the 'Art of the Fugue.' This set is related to the organ partitas written in Bach's youth, but it resembles even more the chorale cycles of Scheidt.

The story of the composition is somewhat enigmatic. In June 1747 Bach joined the *Mizler'sche Societät* (cf. p. 93 f) and submitted the 'Canonic Variations' as a proof of his technical skill. Later the work was printed[1] in an edition which emphasized the author's scholarly approach. Only the initial notes of the imitating voices are provided in three of the variations, while the rest has to be supplied by the reader. A fourth variation, the canon 'per augmentationem,' is offered in open score on four lines, with a different clef for each of the voices. The manner of presentation is similar to that employed in the 'Musical Offering,' and the abstract notation is certainly not meant for the direct use of performers.

Bach, however, left the 'Canonic Variations' in another version that presents no such difficulties to the player. An autograph of the work has been preserved in which the imitating voices are completely written out and the canon 'per augmentationem' is notated in the customary manner on three lines, using two clefs only. In other respects, too, this manuscript deviates from the printed edition. All the variations— in particular the one with the indication 'alla settima'—are somewhat changed, and the order of the pieces is altered. The monumental finale of the print forms the autograph's centerpiece, the result being a completely different structure of the whole composition.

Both versions, the one printed in Bach's lifetime as well as the other

---

1. By Balthasar Schmidt in Nuremberg.

preserved in his own handwriting, reflect the master's intentions.[1] Bach scholars have expressed different opinions regarding their aesthetic merits, but as the order of the manuscript appears more logical and convincing from a structural point of view, it was chosen as a basis for the following analysis.

The five movements of this set combine cantus firmus technique with canonic elaboration. The first two variations are three-part arrangements with the c.f. in the pedal. The hymn tune is accompanied by two voices, which are connected by strict canonic imitation. In the first variation the interval of an octave separates the imitating voices, in the second that of a fifth. They use thematic material often borrowed from the church song itself which increases the melodic uniformity of the music. The fourth and the concluding fifth variations correspond to the first two numbers. Bach introduces in each of these variations, however, a freely invented fourth voice which does not participate in the canonic elaboration. The next to last variation offers a canon of the seventh, the last one a canon of the augmentation in which notes presented by the soprano are uttered in double length by the tenor. Like a painter Bach attached his name to the finished work. Four measures from the end of the fifth variation, the alto voice introduces after a brief rest the notes B flat (in German designated as 'B'), A, C, and B natural (in German designated as 'H'), thus presenting the composer's name in music.

The third variation offers a remarkable contrast to the pieces which precede and follow it. The chorale itself is offered in canonic elaboration, and the imitation is always inverted. This 'heart-piece' of the whole set consists of four sections, each of which uses a different interval of imitation. The first two sections (with imitations at the interval of a third and sixth) are in three parts and correspond to the two pre-

1. Musicologists differ sharply on the question whether the autograph preceded the printed edition or represents a later revision. Wilhelm Rust (Preface to BG XXV:2, p. xx), Friedrich Smend (BJ 1933, p. 1 ff.), and Hans Klotz (KB to NBA IV:2, p. 86 ff) contend that the printed edition came first, while Ernst Naumann (Preface to BG XL, p. xli) and recently Walter Emery (*Musical Times,* Jan. 1963) consider the printed edition as the later form of the work. There is likewise no uniformity in the publications of the music. P. as well as BG (vol. XL, p. 137 ff.) present the variations in the order of the first edition. The edition of the Neue Bach-Gesellschaft (vol. XXIV:2), on the other hand, is based on the autograph. The NBA (vol. IV:2) offers both versions.

ceding three-part variations. The last two sections (with imitations at
the interval of a second and ninth) are in four parts and thus aptly
prepare for the following four-part variations. At the end of variation
3 Bach offers a special tour de force. In an awe-inspiring stretto he
presents all four lines of the hymn tune together, and finally the letters
of his name (*Ex. 42*) appear again.[1]

Ex. 42. *BWV* 769

(The filling voices are left out)

Thus the autograph of the 'Canonic Variations' displays the following completely symmetrical organization:

I and II	III		IV and V
2 variations	2 sections	2 sections	2 variations
in three parts.	in three parts.	in four parts.	in four parts.
C.f. accompanied	C.f. with its inverted canonic		C.f. accompanied
by canonic imitat.	imitation		by canonic imitation

Despite the formidable display of logic and consummate learning,
this work is basically a piece of lyric music filled with the spirit of
Christmas. In the very first variation the gaily running voices in canonic imitation seem to represent angels merrily chasing each other,
and the happy mood is maintained throughout this work by the bright
key of C major. Once more the contrapuntal forms offered Bach an
opportunity to create music imbued with expressive beauty.

Another organ work printed at approximately the same time provides
a curious contrast to the 'Canonic Variations.' The Six Chorales of
Various Sorts were published during the last years of Bach's life, in
1746 or afterwards. Printing was done by Bach's pupil, J. G. Schübler,
and they are usually referred to as *Schübler Chorales*. While the 'Vari-

1. The whole set offers canonic imitation in most intervals up to the ninth, similar to Bach's 'Goldberg Variations.'

ations' appear as a highly sophisticated composition intended for the expert and scholar, Bach meant the 'Chorales' to be popular works. This is music easy to understand and to enjoy. It is obviously written for the amateur; there are rather elementary hints for selecting register stops, which the professional organist might have resented.

The 'Schübler Chorales' present organ arrangements of vocal numbers in Bach's cantatas. Five of these are based on chorale solos or chorale duets in church cantatas, mostly from the first years of his stay in Leipzig. The source of one piece is unknown; it may have originated in a cantata lost today. The arrangements are derived from the following works:

Wachet auf (P. VII:57; BWV 645), based on No. 4, tenor aria, in cantata 140 of 1731;

Wo soll ich fliehen hin (Whither shall I flee; P. VII:63; BWV 646), source unknown;

Wer nur den lieben Gott (Who-so will suffer God; P. VII:59; BWV 647), based on No. 4, soprano and alto duet in cantata 93 of 1724;

Meine Selle erhebet den Herren (My soul magnifies the Lord; P. VII:42; BWV 648), based on No. 5, alto and tenor duet in cantata 10 of 1724;

Ach bleib' bei uns (Abide with us; P. VI:2; BWV 649), based on No. 3, soprano aria in cantata 6 of 1725;

Kommst du nun, Jesu (Art Thou coming, Jesu; P. VII:38; BWV 650), based on No. 2, alto aria in cantata 137 of 1725.

All six settings belong to the cantus firmus type. Yet polyphonic treatment is almost completely abandoned, and the chorale melody is escorted by broadly flowing melodies. These accompanying voices are sometimes paraphrasing the chorale melody (as in BWV 647 or 649); sometimes they are largely independent of it (BWV 645). It is interesting to note that the vocal versions were taken over without major changes. Bach transplanted the basic three or four parts of the original to the organ and made no provision for the realization of the filling continuo which was obviously used in the cantatas. It seems likely that he considered the sound of the organ rich enough so that no padding was required.

We may well imagine that in former years Bach had presented some of these arrangements in his own organ recitals and that the settings had met with the enthusiastic response of the audience. Such melodious and uncomplicated music was certainly in keeping with the prevalent taste of the time. In the last years of his life he remembered these earlier pieces, and it may have seemed a good idea to put them in print. They certainly reveal a side of Bach's artistic personality completely hidden to students of the formidable 'Canonic Variations' and the 'Musical Offering.'

The success of the 'Schübler Chorales' was probably not as immediate as Bach had hoped, but it was long lasting. The work was widely imitated by Bach's pupils and became a model for organ chorale composition in the second half of the eighteenth century. Thus the old composer not only brought the ancient craft of polyphony to a climax, but at the same time heralded future developments of his art.

Among Bach's final organ compositions was a highly significant arrangement of *Wenn wir in höchsten Nöten sein* (P. VII:58; BWV 668). In his Orgel-Büchlein he had presented the hymn tune in a richly ornamented version (P. V:51, BWV 641). Later he simplified the melodic contour of the chorale, reducing the ornamentation until the tune comprised exactly the number of notes required to express Bach's symbolic intentions, viz. 14 in the first line standing for 'Bach' and 41 in the whole cantus firmus standing for 'J. S. Bach' (cf. p. 135). Moreover, in the new arrangement each line of the hymn was preceded by a little fugato in which phrases of the chorale melody were skillfully combined with their own inversions. Like the 'Canonic Variations' this work has come down to us in two slightly diverging texts, a printed and a written one, both of which can be considered authentic. One shows the piece in open score and is to be found as the concluding number in the posthumous edition which C. P. E. Bach prepared of the 'Art of the Fugue.' The source for this edition is no longer known. The second version appears in normal keyboard notation in the important original manuscript that contains the '17 Chorales' and the 'Canonic Variations.' As his eyesight was failing Bach seems to have dictated the organ chorale[1] and a copy of the dictated piece was inserted into the volume. This copy bears the significant heading *Vor deinen Thron tret'*

---

1. The identity of the scribe is unknown. The traditional view that Altnikol was the writer, which is based on a remark by Forkel, was refuted by Dadelsen (*Beiträge zur Chronologie der Werke J. S. Bachs,* Trossingen, 1958, pp. 63 and 114).

ich (Before Thy throne I step, O Lord). It breaks off in the 26th measure, as if death had prevented the composer from completing his dictation. Significantly enough, this piece, which seems to have occupied Bach's mind in the last days he dwelt on earth, reverts to the 'motet type' of chorale arrangement which had been important to him since the days of his youth.

III. WORKS FOR CLAVIER SOLO

AMONG the few works Bach had printed in his lifetime, compositions for keyboard instruments took up the greatest space. Apparently he thought highly of them and felt that they would particularly appeal to the musical public. The generations that followed him likewise knew him best as a composer for the 'clavier.'

The term 'clavier' (from Latin *clavis*, a key) was used in Bach's time to indicate any kind of keyboard instrument. The first, second, and fourth parts of Bach's *Clavier-Übung* (keyboard exercise), for instance, contain works for stringed keyboard instruments, while the third part is for organ. Similarly works for the organ are often inscribed as compositions for 'two claviers and a pedal.' But the term was also used in a more limited sense. Quite often 'clavier' denotes only one of the three main types of stringed keyboard instruments known to musicians in the Baroque period:[1]

(1) harpsichord (Italian *cembalo*, French *clavecin*), furnished with one or two manuals, different register stops and several sets of strings, plucked by pieces of quill or leather;

(2) spinet or virginal, with a single manual, usually no register stops, and one set of strings, plucked by pieces of quill or leather;

(3) clavichord, with a single manual, no register stops and one set of strings, struck by thin metal tangents.

The pianoforte, although in existence before the middle of the century and known to Bach, was hardly used by him.[2]

In a few isolated cases, such as the 'Goldberg Variations' or the 'Ital-

---

1. For a discussion of the instruments' construction cf. C. Sachs, *The History of Musical Instruments,* New York, 1940, p. 330 ff., and K. Geiringer, *Musical Instruments,* London, 1943, pp. 124 ff., 167 ff.
2. Cf. F. Ernst in *BJ* 1961, p. 61ff.

ian Concerto,' Bach indicated that a harpsichord ought to be employed. But as a rule he did not express any preference, and only by analyzing each specific composition can we discover whether Bach intended it to be played on the harpsichord, with its crisp tone and its capacity for undergoing sudden changes in color and strength, the spinet, with its brilliant yet unbending sound, or the clavichord, with its highly flexible, though extremely soft tone. Pieces without rests, for example, would not allow a harpsichord player to change his register stops, which in Bach's time were always operated by hand. On the other hand pieces that required sharp dynamic changes, the so-called 'terrace dynamics,' particularly noticeable in compositions in concerto form, with their contrasts between solo and tutti, could be achieved only on the two manuals of this instrument; while melodic lines of a singing character would best be interpreted on a clavichord.

We may assume, for instance, that for the vigorous and fiery 'English Suites' Bach had the harpsichord in mind, while he would have preferred the clavichord for the delicate and intimate 'French Suites.' Likewise the clavichord was probably used in the 'Inventions' and 'Sinfonias,' for Bach stated in the preface that the work's main purpose was to train performers in a singing style of playing.

In the second half of the 18th century the meaning of 'clavier' was gradually narrowed down to clavichord. This accounts for the faulty translation of *Das wohl temperirte Clavier* widely used in English-speaking countries. The English designation of 'The Well-tempered Clavichord' would imply that Bach had only a single instrument in mind for his work, whereas the composer did not in fact indicate any such preference.[1]

In the absence of specific evidence it must be assumed that during Bach's lifetime the term 'clavier' could mean any keyboard instrument, and in particular one equipped with strings. In this narrower sense—

1. Forkel's statement that Bach liked best to play upon the clavichord need not be taken literally. The author received much information from Emanuel Bach, the foremost exponent of clavichord playing. It is quite likely that the Hamburg composer attributed to his father an attitude which was basically his own. Equally unconvincing is the attempt of Hans Brandts-Buys (*Het wohltemperirte Clavir*, Arnhem, 1944) to prove that Bach's famous 48 preludes and fugues were all written for the organ. Although individual pieces lend themselves to a performance on this instrument, the scholar's sweeping statement is not convincing.

embracing harpsichord, clavichord and spinet—the expression will be
used in this chapter.[1]

The clavier works from Bach's *first period of composition* were primarily dependent on models provided by masters from central and
southern Germany. North German influences, which were of so great
an importance for Bach as an organ composer, are far less in evidence
here. A *Fugue in E minor* (BWV 945), obviously one of the composer's earliest works, attempts to imitate Pachelbel. It is an awkward
composition, completely lacking in modulations, and written against
rather than for the clavier. For devotees of number symbolism it is
interesting to note that the fugue subject appears 14 times in this work
(cf. p. 94). This might also indicate that the fugue is authentic Bach,
an attribution that has been questioned. A *Sonata in D major* (BWV
963), probably written around 1704,[2] is still influenced by Johann
Kuhnau, who was the first to write sonatas in several movements for
the clavier. The last movement has the heading 'Thema all'Imitatio
Gallina Cucca,' which is apparently intended to mean: 'Theme imitating hen and cuckoo'; these two birds can in fact be heard merrily
raising their voices all through the movement (*Ex.* 43). The Austrian

Ex. 43. *BWV* 963

Poglietti's *Capriccio über das Henner und Hannergeschrey* (Capriccio
on the cries of hens and roosters) and the cuckoo-calls in works by the

1. Among the numerous works dedicated to Bach's clavier music the following
studies might be singled out: M. Seiffert, *Geschichte der Klaviermusik*, Leipzig, 1899
(3rd ed. of C. F. Weitzmann, *Geschichte das Klavierspiels*); W. Apel, *Masters of the
Keyboard*, Cambridge, Mass., 1947; N. Dufourcq, *Le Clavecin*, Paris, 1949; H. Keller,
Die Klavierwerke B.s, Leipzig, 1950; C. Auerbach, *Die deutsche Clavichordkunst des
18. Jhdts.*, Kassel, 1953[2]; E. Bodky, *The Interpretation of B.'s Keyboard Works*, Cambridge, Mass., 1960; J. Gillespie, *Five Centuries of Keyboard Music*, Belmont, Cal.,
1965. Additional literature is listed in connection with individual compositions.

2. It was obviously intended for a clavier equipped with a pedal keyboard. (Cf.
the transition from the Sonata's first to its second movement.)

Bavarian Kerll may have acted as godfathers to this gay composition. South German sources can also be seen in the name *Capriccio,* which Bach gave to a kind of toccata-fugue in E major (BWV 993) with the interesting inscription: *In honorem Joh. Christoph. Bachii (Ohrdruf).* The rather insignificant work dedicated to Sebastian's eldest brother and teacher is based on a theme breathing youthful exuberance in its excessive range of close to two octaves.

Inspiration flowed much more freely in a clavier piece which the young composer wrote for another member of his family. It is the humorous *Capriccio sopra la lontananza del suo fratello dilettissimo* (Capriccio on the departure of his most beloved brother; BWV 992), written in 1706 when Johann Jacob Bach (b. 1682) decided to join the army of Charles XII, king of Sweden.[1] This delightful work is a jocose interpretation of devices introduced six years before by Kuhnau in his 'Biblical Sonatas.' Young Sebastian employed the technique which the older master had applied to the description of incidents from the Old Testament in depicting some tender and amusing domestic scenes. Each of the six movements has its own heading, which quaintly expresses, partly in German and partly in Italian, the composer's programmatic intentions:

(1) Arioso. Adagio. Blandishments of his friends not to undertake this journey.
(2) [Andante] A portrayal of the kinds of accidents that can happen to him in foreign lands.
(3) Adagissimo. A general lament by his friends.
(4) His friends see that they cannot stop him, and so they come to bid him farewell.
(5) Aria di Postiglione. Adagio poco.
(6) Fuga all'imitazione della cornetta di postiglione (fugue imitating the sound of the posthorn).

The most varied devices are used to convey the different emotions. The 'blandishments' of the friends are described by means of a wide array of cajoling French ornaments. Modulations into distant keys are employed to depict the dangers that might befall the traveler in foreign lands. The 'general lament' introduces the chromatically descending

1. Cf. A. Protz in *Die Musikforschung,* vol. 10, 1957, p. 405 ff.

bass figure, which Baroque composers used as a vehicle for the expression of supreme grief. (Purcell employed it in the death-song of Dido, and Bach himself in the *Crucifixus* of the B minor Mass—to mention only two out of a very large number of examples.) Here the composer temporarily relinquishes the clavier style proper; the 'lament' takes the form of a solo for a melody instrument and figured bass to which the performer has to add filling parts not contained in the manuscript. The 'Aria of the postilion' introduces the gay octave jump, which was produced by the tiny posthorns of the 18th century. This simple motive returns as a persistent counterpoint to the march-like theme (*Ex.* 44) of the concluding fugue, where the young composer displays

Ex. 44. *BWV* 992

quite a respectable degree of technical skill.

Among the works Bach produced in his formative years, a fantasia and a group of toccatas deserve mention. He felt particularly attracted to the free and rhapsodic character of these forms, which offered good opportunity for dramatic contrasts between individual sections. The iron logic and well-balanced proportions of later compositions are missing in most of these pieces, but they do display the ardor and rich imagination characteristic of the youthful genius.

The *Fantasia (Präludium) in A minor* (BWV 922) resembles a series of short preludes, each based on a single motive. When writing it, the composer had not yet learned the wisdom of restraint, and so he did not hesitate to repeat the same brilliant, though somewhat shallow, ideas over and over. But though moderation and self-discipline were not yet Bach's goal, he knew how to create a most rewarding virtuoso piece. In particular the twenty measures of the coda are remarkable.

The *Toccata in D minor* (BWV 913) bears in an early manuscript the heading 'Toccata Prima,' and it appeared as the first number in the edition of Bach's clavier works published in 1801. The sequence of different movements in this work was maintained in several of the other toccatas as well. After free rhapsodic passages, Bach continues with an expressive arioso section. This in turn is followed by a rather unorthodox fugue in common time, in which Bach introduces his theme in two slightly different versions; they alternate repeatedly and so provide the unassuming piece with a strangely restless quality. A richly modulating Adagio, stirring in its subjective language, ensues, and the work reaches its climax and conclusion in a more extensive fugue in triple time. It is interesting to note that this second fugue is thematically related to the first (a device frequently used by Froberger), and in this manner a certain cohesion is achieved within the work. The highlights are, however, not provided by the two polyphonic movements, but rather by the arioso-like sections, which are imbued with strong emotion.

The *Toccata in G minor* (BWV 915) is built along similar lines. A turbulent passage in triplets starts and concludes the work. The rhapsodic introduction is followed by a lofty adagio section, and then the artist's high spirits reassert themselves in a short double fugue employing a lively theme. Another pensive arioso ensues, and then comes an extensive fugue of more than a hundred bars, which abounds in vigor and vitality. The variety of mood in this work provides the performer with splendid opportunities and we can imagine Bach himself at the clavier keeping his listeners entranced while he improvised works of this kind.

The *Toccata in E minor* (BWV 914) deviates somewhat from the preceding works because it lacks the arioso episode near the beginning. A compact double fugue forms the core of the piece; it is followed by an Adagio assuming the character of a recitative intermingled with free improvisations. The concluding fugue written for three voices is based on a rushing theme made up of continuous sixteenth notes. The composer establishes a thematic relationship not only between the subjects of the two fugues but with the rhapsodic beginning as well. Yet, here again Bach is more concerned with expression than with form. Philipp Spitta describes the toccata[1] as 'one of those pieces steeped in melancholy and deep yearning which Bach alone could write. . . . The last

---

1. Vol. I, p. 437.

movement can only be fully appreciated by those who, experienced in sorrow, have lived through the whole cycle of grief.'

In Bach's *second period of composition* we notice his systematic application to the solution of specific clavieristic problems. He concentrated his effort on arranging violin concertos for the organ and the clavier (cf. p. 221). His discovery of such works, particularly those of young Vivaldi, would decisively shape his whole creative output.

The exact number of Bach's arrangements of Vivaldi's violin concertos is not yet known. The forty-second volume of the Bach Gesellschaft, issued in 1894, contains '16 concertos after Vivaldi' (BWV 972-87). It has been proved, primarily by Arnold Schering,[1] that of these works three (Nos. 11, 13,[2] and 16) were based on concertos by Duke Johann Ernst of Weimar, one (No. 14) on a violin concerto by Georg Philipp Telemann, and one (No. 3) on an oboe concerto by Alessandro Marcello.[3] Of the remainder, six (Nos. 1, 2, 4, 5, 7, 9) have been identified as works by Vivaldi.[4] The sources for the other concertos have not yet been found, but it seems likely that there are some more compositions by Vivaldi, Marcello, and Telemann among them.

Bach did not transfer the string parts to the keyboard instrument in a mechanical fashion. Wherever it seemed necessary, he gave greater flexibility to the bass line, filled in middle parts, enriched the polyphonic texture, and ornamented the melodic lines, so that the sustained tone of strings would be adapted to the transient sound of the clavier (*Ex. 45*). Bach made these arrangements primarily for his own use. They satisfied his zest for experimenting, and they also served the purpose of supplying good clavier music for his performances.[5]

1. Cf. *Sammelbände der internationalen Musikgesellschaft*, IV, p. 234 ff. and V, p. 565 ff.
2. The first movement of Concerto No. 13 was also arranged by Bach for the organ.
3. This concerto, too, is occasionally attributed to Vivaldi.
4. Individual movements seem to have been exchanged, however, before Bach made his keyboard reductions. Cf. R. Eller in *Kongressbericht*, Hamburg 1956, p. 80 ff.
5. Clavier adaptations of works by the Hamburg organist Jan Adams Reinken and by the Freiberg organist Johann Christoph Erselius are also attributed to Bach. Reinken's *Hortus Musicus* was originally conceived as a set of trio sonatas for two violins, viola da gamba, and continuo. Of this work the complete first sonata (BWV 965), 4 movements from the third sonata (BWV 966), and the fugue of the second

Ex. 45. Vivaldi, Concerto, Op. 7^{II} No. 2

Bach's arrangement for clavier, *BWV* 973

Bach's own compositions during this period reveal the strong interest he took in the music of Italy. A piece that resulted from such preoccupation is the *Aria variata alla maniera italiana* (BWV 989) which resembles a duet between violin and cello. The variation technique is of the Italian type; the melodic line of the tuneful air is ornamented and transformed in a rather superficial manner, in contrast to Bach's later variations, which were much more intricate. In the same category is the *Toccata in G major* (BWV 916) in the three movements of an Italian concerto. It begins with a piece which resembles one of Bach's clavier arrangements of the initial movement in a Vivaldi concerto. Bach presents an energetic tutti which is repeated several times in various keys, with modulating solo episodes serving as connecting links. The original character of the toccata is maintained only in the rhapsodic passage work which precedes the powerful chords of the tutti theme. The beautiful Adagio that follows 'moves us by its very simplicity' (Schweitzer).[1] The elegiac piece brings into full relief the following bright and cheer-

sonata (BWV 954) have been preserved in arrangements which, particularly in the fugues, widely modify and enrich the original. Staying much closer to the model is the Fugue in B flat major (BWV 955) based on an organ fugue by Erselius in G major. It seems more like a transposed and improved copy than an independent arrangement.

1. P. 317.

ful fugue which is somewhat reminiscent of a gigue. Its subject, like
that of the first movement, exudes youthful joy and vigor.

The *Toccata in D major* (BWV 912) starts with a surging motive
which Bach also used in his Organ Prelude in D major (BWV 532).
The improvisatory first ten measures prepare for an allegro, which
again has the features of a concerto movement, although the treatment
is neither as logical nor as skillful as in the G major Toccata. Next
comes a strange movement in which two recitative-like sections, at
some points overemphatic in their highly expressive language, surround
a short fugue that employs no less than three closely connected themes.
In the second of the recitative-like sections we find the unusual prescription 'con discrezione,' indicating that this piece may be played in
a free manner at the performer's discretion. The concluding fugue, a
light and gay perpetuum mobile, is based on a theme which might have
been inspired by the finale of a violin concerto arranged by Bach for
the harpsichord (*Ex. 46*).

Ex. 46. *BWV 912*

The magnificent *Prelude and Fugue in A minor* (BWV 894) has
likewise the brilliant character of a concerto. Later (possibly after
1730) Bach actually orchestrated the work with consummate skill and
by so doing transformed the initial and concluding movements into a
real concerto for flute, violin, harpsichord, and accompanying string
orchestra (BWV 1044). The middle movement was borrowed from
the third of his organ sonatas (BWV 527). Bach's arrangement of the
prelude and fugue was done in a most ingenious manner. He dissected
the original material, entrusted it to the solo instruments, and added
new tutti sections, which he placed at the beginning and end as well as
at strategic points in the middle of the movements.[1] Accordingly the
prelude was enlarged from 98 to 149 measures and the fugue from 153
to 245 measures. The original length was left practically unchanged
in the middle movement, which Bach set just for the solo instruments;
thus no tutti sections were added. Despite the superb craftsmanship dis-

1. Cf. H. Boettcher, 'B.s Kunst der Bearbeitung dargestellt am Tripelkonzert a
moll,' in *Festschrift Peter Raabe*, Leipzig, 1942.

played in the fashioning of the triple concerto, the simpler, more coherent, prelude and fugue may well hold its own with its more pretentious brother.

Two *Fugues in A major and B minor* (BWV 950-51), based on trio sonatas for two violins, 'cello, and keyboard instrument by Tomaso Albinoni (1671-1750), would seem to belong to the master's arrangements. Actually Bach changed so much and preserved so little that it is justifiable to consider them as independent works inspired by Italian models. Bach was particularly impressed by the plastic themes of the Italian composer,[1] but their elaboration did not satisfy him. As a matter of fact, the Fugue in B minor exists in two versions: one fairly close to the Italian work, and another from a later period which is considerably longer. The latter exhausts the contrapuntal potentialities of the theme far beyond its original composer's intent, and it imbues the fugue with an intensity of feeling quite different from the calm serenity of Albinoni's music.

In certain clavier compositions written in Weimar, or possibly at the beginning of Bach's stay in Cöthen, the Italian influence is completely sublimated. These superbly proportioned pieces, beautifully worked out in every detail, could not have been conceived if Sebastian had not gone through a period of the most intense study of Southern art; but there is no direct reference to Italian sources, and it almost seems as if Bach were retracing his steps. In the *Toccata in F sharp minor* (BWV 910) the composer establishes the traditional thematic interrelation by evolving the subject of his concluding four-part fugue from a chromatic melody employed in the slow section (*Ex. 47*). The toccata's rhapsodic

Ex. 47. *BWV* 910

beginning is far removed from mere technical display and serves to express true emotion. Equally stirring is the fugue imbued with pathos

2. Cf. the use of themes by Legrenzi and Corelli in Bach's organ works of the period (p. 223).

and grief and concluding in a spirit of resignation. The mighty *Toccata in C minor* (BWV 911) has a similar character. Its introduction and the following Adagio conjure up a mood of lament and longing. The atmosphere changes with the beginning of the fugue, a masterpiece both in structure and substance. We are carried away by its irresistible strains, which Spitta aptly compared to a 'proud and handsome youth swimming on the full tide of life, and never weary of the delightful consciousness of strength.'[1] After forty-eight bars the fugal work is momentarily interrupted by a recitative-like passage, whereupon Bach introduces a second subject and proceeds to develop a splendid double fugue. The mighty ending in an adagio passage rises to a fortissimo chord and then quickly fades away in the bass. In these two works which are among the finest clavier pieces contributed in Bach's earlier years, the composer returns again to the traditional toccata form and the variation technique of Froberger, and imbues them with a new sense of cohesion.

The Bach of the Cöthen years was by inclination and vocation a teacher. Unlike the majority of great composers, he considered instructing others not a tedious chore but a stimulating experience. Keyboard instruments were particularly well suited to teaching purposes, and Bach wrote a great number of works which are primarily intended as technical studies, yet developed under the master's hands into creations of superior craftsmanship and great beauty. They are by no means mere études written for his personal pupils, but collections devised on the largest possible scale and intended for students and music-lovers alike.

The title 'Orgel-Büchlein' (Cf. p. 233), with its reference to the 'beginning organist' and the 'instruction of the fellow musician,' clearly reveals a pedagogical purpose. This purpose is just as obvious in a work of a different nature started on January 22, 1720, for Sebastian's eldest son, Wilhelm Friedemann, then nine years and two months old. This *Clavier-Büchlein* (Little Clavier Book), written partly by Bach himself and partly by the little boy,[2] starts out as a manual well adapted to

1. I, p. 644.
2. The original manuscript of the work belongs to the Library of the School of Music, Yale University. In 1959 the Yale University Press offered a facsimile edi-

the needs of a beginner. Gradually, however, the father pays less heed to the original purpose of training the young pupil as a performer and composer. Despite the child's attempts to preserve his rights, Sebastian is eventually carried away by his creative urge. The pages of the *Clavier-Büchlein* are finally transformed into worksheets of a genius who impatiently brushes away the limitations imposed upon him by body and mind of a young, though highly talented pupil. Thus it affords an insight into a situation which seems to have occurred repeatedly, when Bach's aims as a teacher clashed with his aims as a composer.

On the first page Bach offers a very thorough explanation of notes and clefs. Right from the beginning he expects Friedemann to familiarize himself with a range of four octaves and no less than eight different clefs (violin, soprano, mezzo soprano, alto, tenor, and three kinds of bass clefs). Then follows the famous explanation of ornaments (Pl. VI), which the composer seems to have adapted from the table in d'Anglebert's *Pièces de clavecin*, an indication that Bach's use of embellishments was influenced by the study of French models.[1] The next page, headed by 'I.N.J.' (In nomine Jesu), offers the *Applicatio* (BWV 994), a short piece for the clavier, which is completely fingered, a rarity among Bach's keyboard compositions. Here we find a bold innovation in the use of the thumb (which had hitherto not been employed much on the clavier), but there is also the old-fashioned method of crossing the third finger over the fourth (*Ex. 48*). As so often, Bach

Ex. 48. *BWV 994*

tion of the work with a sensitive preface by Ralph Kirkpatrick. The NBA presented the collection 1963 in Series V, vol. 5, edited by Wolfgang Plath, who also contributed a thorough KB. Dr. Plath distinguishes between the handwriting of father and son which, in many respects, show a close resemblance, and he establishes a chronology of the various entries. The present analysis is based on the results of this study.

1. Cf. the thorough discussion of this problem in W. Emery, *B.'s Ornaments,* London, 1953.

systematically combined traditional and new devices, relinquishing little that came to him from the past, but rather improving it along the way.

The first *Praeambulum* (prelude) in C major (BWV 924) looks deceptively simple. But the embellishments prescribed in the left hand are not really easy to perform, and it is significant that Friedemann later rewrote the piece in a shortened version, omitting all the ornaments.[1] Next the father inserted two chorale preludes, obviously intended for domestic worship (BWV 691a, 753), and separated them by a little *Praeludium* in D minor (BWV 926). The second chorale is not completed, as the boy apparently clamored to make a contribution. Started on his task and supervised by the patient teacher, he inserted two Allemandes (BWV 836, 837) probably of his own composition. The second is incomplete, as a sheet has been cut out of the booklet at this spot. Next comes one of Sebastian's preludes (BWV 927), copied by the son,[2] and two more compositions of the same kind entered by Sebastian himself (BWV 930, 928). A minuet in Friedemann's hand (BWV 841)[3] shows the child's taste asserting itself again, and once more the father acceded to his wishes. A second minuet (BWV 842) was jointly written, a third (BWV 843) by Sebastian alone.

At this point the rather haphazard arrangement of the material gave way to a systematic application to a single task. With the help of his father, who also inserted corrections, Friedemann copied no less than eleven of the preludes which were later to be used in the 'Well-tempered Clavier' (Nos. 1, 2, 6, 5, 10, 9, 11, 3, 4, 8, 12). It is noteworthy that the versions of the *Clavier-Büchlein* frequently deviate from the finished product included in the complete set. The C major, C minor, D minor, and E minor preludes are considerably shorter in Friedemann's copies, and the last mentioned moreover is lacking the impressive melodic line of the right hand. These seem to be earlier versions of the compositions, but it is also conceivable that in some cases the pieces were simplified for the child's use. Four of the preludes from the 'Well-tempered Clavier' (Nos. 5, 11, 8, 12) break off at the end of a page without reaching a conclusion. This may have been due to the writer's impatience, but it seems more likely that Friedemann wanted to avoid

1. Fol. 30 r. of the MS.
2. According to Plath, KB p. 59, BWV 927 was inserted at a somewhat later date.
3. The piece appeared later also in the *Clavier-Büchlein* of 1722.

turning pages near the end of a composition. Unfortunately his hand-writing was comparatively large and awkward, and he depended on his father's superior skill in being able to squeeze in the missing measures at the bottom of the page. Sebastian willingly obliged, as long as it was a question of fitting in one or two measures (this he did in Preludes 6 and 4), but he balked when he was expected to do the same with 4 or 5 measures. Thus several numbers throughout the collection remained a torso (unless the missing bars were written on separate scraps of paper which are not preserved).

Eventually the child seems to have tired of the task, and Sebastian tried to recapture his interest with a new group of pieces, a series of fifteen interrelated *Praeambula*. The first two and the last eight of this group were written by Sebastian, Nos. 3-7 by Friedemann. This is the earliest manuscript of a collection known to-day as Bach's Two-part Inventions. The individual pieces follow each other first in an ascend-ing, then in a descending order of keys: C major, D minor, E minor, F major, G major, A minor, B minor, B flat major, A major, G minor, F minor, E major, E flat major, D major, C minor. Friedemann's share of the copying work was arranged in such a manner that he did not have to cope with more than one flat or two sharps. Maybe he had com-plained about the excessive difficulty of handling keys with 6 flats or 7 sharps, as was required of him in the preludes from the 'Well-tempered Clavier.' In the case of the Two-part Inventions Sebastian did not go to such extremes; keys with more than four flats or four sharps are avoided altogether.

The son was allowed a further excursion into a more popular type of music. Three dances, probably works by Telemann, and a suite by Stoelzel followed in Friedemann's hand. The father merely contributed a Trio (BWV 929) to Stoelzel's Minuet. The end of the booklet con-tains fourteen *Fantasias* written by Sebastian. These short composi-tions, which were arranged in the same order of keys as the Two-part Inventions, represent the initial copy of the so-called Sinfonias or Three-part Inventions.[1] The last group of the 'Praeambula' had al-ready shown that Bach was still engaged in fashioning these composi-tions while he committed them to paper. To an even greater degree this

---

1. Plath p. 9 assumes that the *Clavier-Büchlein* originally contained all 15 Fan-tasias, two sheets (comprising the second half of No. 14 and all of No. 15) having been lost.

was true of the 'Fantasias.' Bach wrote hastily and made repeated corrections, at times even endangering the manuscript's legibility. Friedemann was no longer allowed to help. There was no manuscript from which he could copy, and quite likely the father, in the heat of the creative process, had forgotten the music book's original scope. Eventually, though, the son seems to have reasserted his rights. Once more he appropriated the book and filled pages in the middle of the little volume that had been left empty. He amused himself with an Allemande and a Courante by J. C. Richter and four little preludes (including BWV 924a, the simplified version of BWV 924), in which he tried to imitate his father's style. Sebastian himself inserted one final contribution, a briskly moving three-part fugue (BWV 953) primarily intended to develop technical skills.

Among the numerous pieces in the *Clavier-Büchlein* which are designated as 'Praeambulum' or 'Praeludium,' one finds six independent musical vignettes (BWV 924^1-28 and 930). They are brief and unassuming compositions, valuable both as elementary studies and for the enjoyment they gave the young pupil. These pieces were published around the middle of the last century, together with the Trio Bach added to the Minuet by Stoelzel (BWV 929) and five other numbers (BWV 939-42, 999) preserved by Bach's friend, Johann Peter Kellner, as *Zwölf kleine Praeludien* (12 Little Preludes). The editor, F. K. Griepenkerl, arranged the numbers in an ascending order of keys, starting with C major and ending in A minor. Despite their very concise structure and the limited demands they make on the performer's technical proficiency, the preludes do not lack variety. No. 3 in C minor (BWV 999), with its broken chords, has the character of a lute improvisation; Nos. 8 and 9 in F major (BWV 927, 928), on the other hand, develop the independence of the two hands, while introducing the novice to the problems of a more polyphonic texture. No. 11 in G minor (BWV 930) is completely fingered by Bach himself, and the original version therefore could be consulted profitably by present-day keyboard players. Unfortunately most contemporary editions ignore the interesting instructions Bach gave.

1. The authenticity of BWV 925 in D major is doubtful. It may have been written under Sebastian's supervision by Friedemann Bach (cf. NBA Serie V, vol. 5, No. 27).

A set of *Six Preludes à l'usage des Commençants* (BWV 933-38) was first edited by the Bach biographer, Johann Nikolaus Forkel. In spite of the reference to beginners, these pieces are more elaborate than the 12 Little Preludes and make use throughout of the two-part form Bach employed in his sonatas and suites. In No. 1 in C major (BWV 933) the character of a tiny concerto movement is achieved, as four-measure tutti seem to alternate with four-measure solos. Similarly No. 3 in D minor (BWV 935) is a musical vignette where Bach appears to try out melodic material he was to use in the monumental Toccata in F major for organ (BWV 540). A separate Prelude in C major (BWV 943) has been considered as an organ composition for the manual only. It foreshadows, however, the intricate Sinfonias for clavier and should therefore be counted among the studies for stringed keyboard instruments. These pieces (BWV 933-43, and 999) are not contained in the *Clavier-Büchlein,* and the autograph is no longer in existence.

The largest group of entries in the *Clavier-Büchlein* is formed by the 15 Praeambula and 14 Fantasias, which make up the second half of the manual.[1] Bach must have used these compositions a great deal, since they also exist in a second autograph. This final copy deviates, however, in certain respects from the original draft. The headings of the individual pieces are altered from Praeambulum to Inventio and from Fantasia to Sinfonia. The order of the numbers is likewise changed. Both the Inventions and the Sinfonias are presented in the ascending order of keys: C major, C minor, D major, D minor, E flat major, E major, E minor, F major, F minor, G major, G minor, A major, A minor, B flat major, B minor. The unfinished 14th Fantasia (BWV 789) is now completed, and the missing 15th Fantasia (BWV 788) added; moreover minor improvements and changes are made throughout the set.[2]

1. Among the numerous articles and books dealing with this set we might single out: R. Oppel, 'Die neuen deutschen Ausgaben der zwei- und dreistimmigen Inventionen,' *BJ* 1907, p. 89 ff.; F. Jöde, *Die Kunst B.s,* Wolfenbüttel, 1926; L. Landshoff, *Revisionsbericht zur Urtextausgabe von J.S.B.s Inventionen und Sinfonien,* Leipzig, 1933; J. N. David, *Die zweistimmigen Inventionen von J.S.B.,* Göttingen, 1957; J. N. David, *Die dreistimmigen Inventionen von J.S.B.,* Göttingen, 1959.

2. In particular two measures are inserted in the Praeambulum in E minor (BWV 778) and four measures each in the Praeambula in F major and A minor (BWV 779, 784).

A characteristic inscription is to be found on the title page of the final copy, which reads in English translation:

Honest Guide

by which lovers of the clavier, and particularly those desirous of learning, are shown a plain way not only (1) to play neatly in two parts, but also, as they progress, (2) to treat three obbligato parts correctly and well, and, at the same time, to acquire good ideas and properly to elaborate them, and most of all to learn a singing style of playing, and simultaneously to obtain a strong foretaste of composition.

Executed by
Joh. Seb. Bach
Capellmeister of His Serene Highness, the Prince of Anhalt-Cöthen
Anno Christi, 1723.

The title again indicates the educational purpose of the compositions. These thirty pieces (BWV 772-801) are meant as studies for the performer and for the budding composer, two activities which Bach considered inseparable. The reference to the singing style of playing seems to indicate that the little compositions were intended to be performed on the clavichord (cf. p. 259). It is easy to trace the works which served as a starting point for Bach's compositions. The Two-Part Inventions are derived from preludes by Johann Kuhnau and J. Kaspar Ferdinand Fischer. Bach may have found the unusual designation in Bonporti's *Invenzioni* for violin and bass, written in 1712, pieces which even slipped into the critical edition of the BG[1] as works attributed to the German master. The vivid dialogue between soprano and bass which unfolds in the *Invenzioni* might have induced Bach to adopt this designation for his own pieces in lieu of the vague 'Praeambulum' he had originally used.

What Bach created out of such varied elements was basically new. Using all the devices of the contrapuntal vocabulary, he evolved characteristic compositions out of a single idea stated at the beginning. No other composer had hitherto imbued clavier works of such small dimensions with a content of such significance. There are studies in independent part writing using all the devices of fugue, canon, and double counterpoint, but without strict adherence to any of them. Bach freely blends all known techniques, and creates forms which are held to-

1. Vol. XLV, p. 172 ff.

gether by the logic, and the iron consistency, of his musical thoughts. For instance in the very first of the Two-Part Inventions the simple initial idea (*Ex.* 49a), together with its inversion (*Ex.* 49b), dominates

Ex. 49a   Ex. 49b

the whole composition. Apart from the cadences, there is not one measure that does not contain either one or both of them. The piece is divided into five sections (b. 1-6, 7-10, 11-14, 15-18, 19-22), all approximately of the same length, and there is a marked relationship between the first and last section, as well as between the second and fourth. The arrangement of the modulations is likewise symmetrical. In section I the tonic is established, whereupon a rise to the dominant ensues; there follows in II a descent to the supertonic, in III a further descent to the relative minor, in IV a return to the tonic and in V a firm re-establishment of the tonic.

Like this piece, the inventions 3 (D major), 4 (D minor), 7 (E minor), 13 (A minor) and 14 (B flat major) develop the initial idea with the help of voice exchange, sequences, and thematic inversion. In the contemplative No. 2 (C minor) there is an interesting adaptation of a canon. During the first ten measures the left hand strictly imitates the melodic line in the right hand. Thereupon the game is transferred to the dominant, with the bass in the lead and the soprano following (b. 11-20). An abbreviated recapitulation in the tonic (b. 23-27) concludes the piece. Canonic elements also dominate in No. 8 (F major), one of the most ebullient and merry pieces of the set. The gay and high-spirited No. 15 (B minor) has the character of a two-part fugue, although, contrary to tradition, the first entrance of the subject is supported by brief notes in the bass. No. 10 in G major is a fugue whose main subject consists of broken chords, providing the invention with a basically harmonic character. A kind of double fugue, in which theme and countermelody usually appear together, can be observed in several inventions, such as Nos. 5 (E flat major), 9 (F minor), 11 (G minor), and the technically rather demanding 12 (A major). Yet, in accordance with the general character of the set, the fugue technique is lightly treated, and there is no slavish following of tradition. In No. 6 (E major) the contrapuntal character even retreats to the background. The

Invention uses simultaneously ascending and descending melodic lines which seem to 'approach each other as in a contredance and to recede again after a graceful bow' (Keller). Bach chose for this expressive Invention the three-part song form; repeat signs appear at the end of the first and third parts, and exposition, development, and recapitulation are practically of the same length (20-22-20 measures). Tenderness and warmth radiate from this peaceful composition. Bach handles the exchange of voices with playful virtuosity, but at the same time he trains the player's fingers in the execution of mordents, for the figure appears throughout the piece. In a typical Bach way, the performer's mind, heart and hands are all profiting from the little master–piece.

At the end of the Inventions Bach's definite autograph states: *Sequuntur adhuc 15 Sinfoniae tribus vocibus obligatis* (there follow now fifteen Sinfonias with three obbligato voices). The student examining the thirty compositions cannot help but realize that the use of the same tonalities does not constitute the only link between the two sets. An early manuscript, formerly owned by Friedemann Bach and for a long time considered as Sebastian's autograph, presents the numbers in such order that each three-part composition follows the two-part piece in the same key. There is a similarity of mood between certain numbers in the same tonality (cf. Nos. 1 in C major, 6 in E major, and 12 in A major), and sometimes a thematic relationship as well (*Ex. 50*). Above

Ex. 50. Inventio 15

Sinfonia 15

all, both the Inventions and the Sinfonias (often referred to as 'Three-Part Inventions') have the same artistic and technical aim, although the Sinfonias are more demanding and presuppose the two-part compositions.

In considering the Sinfonias as a separate unit, we again see the striking variety in expression and structure which exists between the individual numbers. New artistic vistas seem to be revealed in each succeeding piece.

No. 2 in C minor, with its chordal melodies and busily moving sixteenth runs, has the character of a lute composition. No. 5 (E flat major) has the form of a tender duet of two voices accompanied by an ostinato bass which keeps repeating the same provocative figure. The rhythmic structure of dances is strong in No. 11 (G minor) and No. 13 (A minor). They are both in 3/8 time, the former displaying a lilting, song-like character, the latter, with its prevailing 4-measure periods, resembling a passepied. No. 15 (B minor), the last of the Sinfonias, seems to re-establish the contact with the earlier set. It is basically a two-part composition in which the third voice is used as an occasional filler.

In the remaining Sinfonias the fugue form becomes the construction's backbone. Bach modifies the pattern by adding the supporting bass to the first two entrances of the theme (subject and answer). Then the bass presents the subject, and afterwards assumes an integral part in the polyphonic web. No. 1 (C major) grows out of one main theme, which furnishes the basic material for the whole composition. In this respect it clearly resembles other polyphonic composition in C major, like the first Invention or the first fugue in the 'Well-tempered Clavier.' Similarly in No. 14 (B flat major), the counterpoints are derived from the initial theme, which gives the whole piece a monolithic quality. The vigorous No. 12 (A major) is divided into five sections, a structure which Bach favors. The theme's entrances at the beginning, in the middle, and at the end (b. 1-8, 15-16, 24-31) are separated by two episodes of equal length (8-14, and 17-23). In the Triple Fugue No. 9 (F minor) strong effects are achieved by a masterly handling of melodic contrasts. Here the intricate polyphonic interpretation of the three subjects creates an atmosphere of sinister pathos, which Bach hardly ever surpassed in dramatic power. The piece was greatly admired in Bach's time, and Friedemann imitated it in a clavier fugue written in the same key.[1]

1. Friedemann's composition, together with seven other fugues, was dedicated in 1778 to Princess Amelia of Prussia. (Reprinted in Peters Edition.) An arrangement for string trio with an added new prelude is ascribed to Mozart (K.404a).

The Sinfonias are works of striking beauty and originality. It may be doubted, however, whether they are accorded the recognition today that they deserve. The student who has mastered Bach's Little Preludes and Inventions is apt to bypass them in his impatience to proceed to the clavier suites and the fugues of the 'Well-tempered Clavier'; and the concert artist hardly ever bothers to explore the rich possibilities of this many-faceted cycle.

The most important keyboard composition of the Cöthen years, the *Well-tempered Clavier*,[1] Part I, was composed in 1722. This is a collection of 24 preludes with following fugues (BWV 846-69). Each pair is in a different key, and they are again presented in ascending order. This time, however, all the keys, including those with five and six sharps or flats, are used. After the start in C major, there follow pairs in C minor, C sharp major, C sharp minor, D major, D minor, ending with the prelude and fugue in B minor.

Bach seems to have worked on this collection for quite some time. It contains a number of earlier compositions, among them the eleven preludes which appeared in simpler and abbreviated form in Friedemann Bach's *Clavier-Büchlein*. The author's own title of the work reads in an English translation:

The Well-tempered Clavier, or preludes and fugues in all the tones and semitones, both with the major third, or 'Ut, Re, Mi' and with the minor third or 'Re, Mi, Fa'.[2] For the use and profit of young musicians who are eager to learn, as well as for the entertainment of those who are already expert in the art.

The unusual name Bach chose for his collection was inspired by the development of the 'equally tempered' system which took place at the turn of the 17th century (cf. p. 123). He was not the first composer to

1. Among the numerous studies dealing with this composition, we might single out: H. Riemann, *Katechismus der Fugenkomposition*, Leipzig (2nd ed.), 1906; W. Werker, *Studien über die Symmetrie im Bau der Fugen. von J.S.B.*, Leipzig, 1922; C. Gray, *The 48 Preludes and Fugues of J.S.B.*, London, 1938; H. Brandts-Buys, l.c.; L. Czaczkes, *Analyse des wohltemperierten Klaviers*, Wien, 1956-65; J. N. David, *Das wohltemperierte Klavier*, Göttingen, 1962.

2. In the ancient system of solmisation Mi-Fa indicated a half-tone step, while Ut-Re and Re-Mi stood for whole-tone progressions. Thus Ut-Re-Mi implies the major mode, Re-Mi-Fa the minor mode. The expressions 'major' and 'minor' were not well known in Bach's time.

profit from the improved method of tuning, but his work surpasses in every respect the achievements of his predecessors. Bach explored all the possibilities of the new system with a thoroughness no other composer had attempted.[1] Loosely built fugues with a certain amount of modulation had often been used in both chamber and orchestral music. In Bach's work they are transferred to the clavier, where they take on the greater solidity of texture peculiar to keyboard music. Even the material of the episodes is usually derived from the main theme or the counterpoints which escort it, thus producing uniformity of substance within the individual fugues. As a rule, full cadences or general rests are avoided; the different sections are carefully interlinked so that the feeling of unbroken solidity conveyed by this music is enhanced.

The prevailing unity within the individual fugues is counterbalanced by sizable differences between the various numbers of the set. No two preludes or fugues resemble each other in mood; each of them represents a particular frame of mind, and a similar variety may be observed in the formal construction and the technical devices used in the various pieces. Particularly strong is the differentiation among the *Preludes*. The famous first one imitates a lute improvisation. Broken chords serve also as the basis of the texture in other preludes (Nos. 6 and 15), and at times they take on an etude-like (No. 2, 5) or toccata-like (No. 21) character. No. 10 shows a striking transformation. In its primitive form it appeared in the *Clavier-Büchlein;* the final version adds a cantilena in the right hand, attaching, however, a new presto section which reaffirms the earlier piece's improvisatory character. The Two-part Inventions obviously exert an influence in Nos. 3, 11, and 13; and a certain dependence on the Inventions may still be detected in Nos. 14, 17, 20, although they deviate from a strict observance of the two-part style. The Three-part Sinfonias have left their imprint on Nos. 9, 18, 19, and 23. Aria-like pieces and compositions resembling the slow movement of a 'church sonata' appear in Nos. 4, 8, 16, and 22. No. 24 is a trio for two voices supported by a steadily moving bass. No. 7 starts out with a brief improvisatory section and leads to a miniature double fugue, which in turn provides a rather incongruous intro-

1. Cf. J. M. Barbour, 'B. and the Art of Temperament,' *MQ*, 1947, p. 64 ff; H. Kelletat, *Zur musikalischen Temperatur*, Kassel, 1960; H. Kelletat, 'Zur Tonordnung im Werke J.S.B.s,' *Annales Universitatis Saraviensis*, vol. IX/1, 1960, pp. 19-26.

duction to the main fugue that follows. In No. 12 broken chords and
the features of an invention and aria are fused into an unfamiliar, yet
highly attractive combination.

Likewise the formal construction of the *Fugues* displays a fascinating
variety. There are pieces not only with three voices (Nos. 2, 3, 6-9, 11,
13, 15, 19, and 21) and four voices (Nos. 1, 5, 12, 14, 16-18, 20, 23,
and 24), but also with two (No. 10) and five (Nos. 4 and 22). While
the themes usually establish a firm tonality, chromatic and modulating
fugue subjects (Nos. 7, 10, 18, and 24) are also present. In some pieces
a melody paired with the fugue theme assumes such significance that
it may be considered a countersubject (Nos. 7, 9, 10, 13-16, 23, and
24). Several fugues even use two countersubjects (Nos. 2, 3, 12, 18,
and 21) and No. 4 is a triple fugue with three subjects of almost equal
importance. It is particularly difficult to single out individual pieces in
this superb collection. The mighty opening fugue No. 1, a piece of unusual firmness and coherence, develops the main theme in strettos of
various kinds and forgoes all distracting episodes. (Students of numer-
ology will notice that in this introductory composition the theme consists of fourteen notes, the symbol of the name Bach.) No. 6 has a
similar character. The theme is developed very logically, partly in its
original form and partly in inversion. On the other hand, a light, almost
popular character is to be found in No. 2. The main theme and the
countersubjects are repeatedly stated—in the tonic, in related keys, and
once more in the tonic—and the forthright composition concludes with
a simple harmonization of the principal idea. In No. 3 the performer
has to overcome considerable technical difficulties to be able to express
properly the composition's light, almost playful nature. This piece is
clearly divided into three sections, a kind of recapitulation starting in
b. 42. No. 4, with the extended notes of its main theme, reverts to the
old-fashioned ricercar type of Froberger. No. 5, a great favorite of keyboard players, is rather loosely constructed and closer to Handel in its
over-all character, than to Bach. A climax is reached with No. 8, one
of the most striking pieces of the set.[1] The theme, its inversion, aug-

---

1. While Bach notated the Prelude of No. 8 in E flat minor, he wrote the Fugue
in D sharp minor. He may have wanted to demonstrate the possibilities of enharmonic exchanges of notes. More likely is, however, that he composed the Fugue in
D minor, and changed the key signature afterwards.

mentation, and double augmentation, are here developed in two- and three-part strettos of breathtaking complexity. Goethe's idea of 'eternal harmony conversing with itself,' seems to have found realization in this awe-inspiring piece. No. 10, on the other hand, displays improvisatory features. Its two parts at times move in carefree parallel octaves, progressions never tolerated in a tradition-bound fugue. The first half of the set is concluded by the mighty four-part fugue No. 12. It is based on a highly chromatic theme opposed to two strictly diatonic counter-subjects; a conflict between the forces of darkness and of light seems to be expressed here. A serene and peaceful character pervades No. 13, one of the gentlest and most amiable pieces of the set. Stately and dignified No. 17 is imbued with fervent feeling. An upward skip of a minor ninth produces an outcry in the theme of No. 22. Near the end of the fugue the effect of this exclamation is magnificently stressed when no less than five entrances of subject and answer are piled on top of one another in a masterly stretto (*Ex. 51*).

Ex. 51. W.T.C., Fugue XXII, meas. 67-72

(Notation in the original on two staves)

But there is no lack of the gay and carefree element in the set. In No. 15 the sprightly theme is first presented by the three voices in its original form, and immediately afterwards by all of them in inversion, the exposition now standing saucily on its head (b. 20-31). In No. 19 the theme starts with a brief signal, which is followed immediately by a puzzling rest before a busily upward-climbing motion ensues. The second voice is too impatient to await its turn, and it rudely breaks in with the answer of the theme, before the first has had its full say. (*Ex. 52*). A carefree dance character is established in the scintillating No.

Ex. 52. W.T.C., Fugue XIX

21. No. 24 seems to revert to the character of No. 12, but it also fore-shadows future musical developments. Its vigorously modulating theme comprises all twelve notes of the chromatic scale. While the composer uses restraint in the display of polyphonic artistry, he boldly employs a harsh harmonic idiom and angular melodic lines imbued with ardent expression. In this 'crown of thorns,' as Spitta calls the piece, Bach establishes a bridge to the idiom of the 19th century and even to that of the 20th century.[1]

In general there is an inner relationship between the two members of each pair of prelude and fugue in the same key, since the prelude effectively prepares for the ensuing fugue. In rare cases there is even an actual thematic bond, as Wilhelm Werker proved. Thus the inter-vals of the fugue theme in No. 3 are anticipated by the melodic pro-gressions, both in the right hand and in the left hand, of the prelude. Similarly in No. 1 the top notes of the arpeggios in the first 7 measures state the main notes of the following fugal subject (*Ex. 53*). The two

Ex. 53.

members of No. 14 have diametrically opposed contents; yet, they dis-play a thematic relationship. In No. 7 prelude and fugue seem to be completely incompatible, for the little double fugue in the prelude clashes with the following principal fugue. To Richard Wagner this conflict appeared, however, as the real meaning of the two pieces. He

1. The somewhat pedantic and overextended fugue No. 20 appears like a foreign body in the set. Unlike the other numbers, this piece requires a keyboard instrument (organ or harpsichord) equipped with a pedal, as the last measures cannot be per-formed with only two hands.

compared the prelude to Wotan, the ferocious leader of the Germanic gods, and the ensuing fugue to the wife who soothes her husband.[1]

Besides the *Clavier-Büchlein* for Friedemann, Sebastian began two other works of a similar nature. The first, inscribed to Anna Magdalena in 1722, and probably meant for the entertainment of members of the household, shows in most of its entries the hand of the master himself. It contains the first five French suites (BWV 812-16) as well as some fragments and insignificant little pieces. The binding of this *Clavier-Büchlein*[2] deteriorated through the centuries and some sheets are missing altogether, yet it still gives a good idea of the kind of music Bach liked to have performed in his own home. In much better condition is the second *Clavier-Büchlein* for Anna Magdalena, which her husband presented to her in 1725. He personally inserted his Partitas III and VI and five small pieces,[3] but the remaining pages were given to his wife to do with as she pleased. The book contains a number of little dances (minuets, polonaises, marches, a musette), which were not composed by Sebastian and may not even reflect the taste of Magdalena, who entered them in the book. These pleasant and technically very simple representatives of the *style galant* were probably meant for the little hands of Emanuel, aged eleven, and for the younger children. They were also well suited for use in the dancing lessons which, according to the custom of the time, every growing boy and girl had to take. There is some doubt whether Bach produced such anonymous works as the philistine air 'Elevating Thoughts of a Tobacco Smoker' (BWV 515) and the rather crude wedding poem.[4] Likewise a little love song, *Willst du dein Herz mir schenken* by Giovannini, a Rondeau by Couperin, and a Minuet by Böhm slipped into the collection.

1. Hans von Wolzogen, *Erinnerungen an Richard Wagner*. Leipzig, 1891, p. 27.
2. Cf. NBA, Series V, vol. 4, and KB to this volume by Georg von Dadelsen. Kassel, 1957.
3. This early manuscript of the two Partitas deviates in some respects from the definite version subsequently printed. In particular the Scherzo from BWV 827 and the Air from BWV 830 are still missing.
4. According to a statement by von Dadelsen (KB, pp. 92 and 124) the tender aria *Bist du bei mir* (BWV 508) may have G. H. Stölzel as author. Up to 1945 the Berlin Singakademie owned a MS. entitled *Airs divers comp. par M. Stöltzel*. This volume which is lost today contained the aria *Bist du bei mir* in a version for soprano, strings, and bass with the melody which appears also in the *Clavier-Büchlein*.

The composer Sebastian is not represented in this family music book as often as one would expect. Besides the two Partitas, it again contains two 'French Suites' (BWV 812 and part of 813), the first prelude from the 'Well-tempered Clavier' Part I, and some chorales and arias. Altogether the *Clavier-Büchlein* presents a rather amusing medley with contributions not only by father and mother Bach, but occasionally also by the children (those entered by Philipp Emanuel were probably also composed by him). It appears that Sebastian wanted in addition to provide for his sons a systematic course in the realization of a figured bass. After the fifteenth rule, however, the teacher gave up, with the excuse that 'the rest could be better explained orally.'

The two *Clavier-Büchlein* introduce a new form of composition which became very important to Bach in the Cöthen years: the dance suite. Between 1720 and 1724 the composer completed two different sets of this kind, a group of larger works, known as the 'English Suites' (BWV 806-11) and another of smaller proportions called 'French Suites' (BWV 812-17).[1]

No one yet has been able to establish beyond doubt the reasons for these names, but it seems certain that Bach himself was not responsible for the designations. The use of several French dance types and of French titles for all the pieces may account for the heading 'French Suites.' The title 'English Suites' is far more puzzling, even though it does seem that it was used as early as the 18th century. On a copy of the set probably produced by a relative or pupil of the composer, there is written 'Fait pour les Anglois,' and Forkel states in his Bach biography that the work was composed for a distinguished Englishman. Another more probable theory is that his study of suites of Dieupart, who lived in London as a teacher and composer, stimulated Bach to write this collection. Actually Sebastian made a copy of Dieupart's Clavier Suite in F minor and used this composer's Gigue in A major as a model for the Prélude in his own English Suite in the same key.[2] There are

---

1. Cf. E. Kurth, *Grundlagen des linearen Kontrapunkts*, Bern, 1927[3]; W. Fischer, 'Zur Chronologie der Klaviersuiten J. S. B.s,' in *Musikwissenschaftlicher Kongress, Basel*, Leipzig, 1925; G. Oberst, 'J. S. B.s Englische und französische Suiten,' in *Gedenkschrift für H. Abert*, Halle, 1928.
2. Cf. E. Dannreuther, *Musical Ornamentation*, London, 1893-95, vol. I, p. 138.

also obvious connections with the eight keyboard suites by Handel published in 1720.

A great variety of stylistic elements are contained in the *English Suites*. They make direct references to other composers' music of the kind to be found in Bach's first two creative periods. Apart from the re-lationship to Dieupart's work there is a resemblance between the theme starting the Prélude to No. II and the fugue subject of Corelli's op. III No. 4[1] while the Gigue of No. VI seems to be fashioned after an organ composition by Buxtehude.[2] Moreover, the spirit of Bach's earlier works is revived in some of the turbulent Gigues of the set, and occasionally a certain youthful volubility is noticeable in the Alle-mandes. On the other hand, the didactic thoroughness with which the composer elaborates on the execution of the *agréments* (ornaments) in the Sarabandes of Suites II and III reflects the pedagogic Bach of the Cöthen period; he wrote out every detail and took no chance of being misunderstood by an incompetent performer. The descending order of keys (A major, A minor, G minor, F major, E minor, D minor) used for the English Suites directly parallels the procedure employed in the Inventions, while the Sarabande in No. III, with its extensive modula-tions and use of even an enharmonic change (*Ex. 54*) might have been

Ex. 54.

written at the same time as the 'Well-tempered Clavier.' By and large, the English Suites display a rather confusing combination of earlier and later features, and the logical inference is that the composer was occupied with them for quite some time.

The core of the collection is formed by the four main dances, Alle-mande, Courante, Sarabande, and Gigue, used in Germany since the

1. Cf. M. Seiffert in *Jahrbuch Peters,* 1904. The same theme was also used by Bach as a basis for an organ fugue (cf. p. 223).
2. Collected Organ Works, ed. by M. Seiffert, Leipzig, 1903-4, I/94.

days of Froberger. Moreover a pair of optional dances (*Galanterien*) is regularly inserted between Sarabande and Gigue, and an introductory movement placed at the head of each suite.

This introduction always bears the same rather nondescript title of Prélude. The first of these pieces is a kind of fantasia based on the rhythm of the gigue. The remaining five introductions display interesting combinations of concerto and fugue forms, which makes them resemble monumental clavier reductions of movements in a concerto grosso.[1] The contrast between tutti ritornels and solo episodes can be demonstrated on the cembalo with the help of manual changes. These introductory movements significantly forecast the greatest composition Bach wrote in this idiom, his Italian Concerto. In Suite VI the concerto movement proper is even preceded by a slow introduction, which results in an extended double movement that effectively balances the ensuing six dances.

The basic pattern of the four main dances is occasionally enlarged in the English Suites. In No. I there are two Courantes and the second is followed by two Doubles. It is not quite clear whether the performer is supposed to play all four pieces or to make a selection between them. Similarly the Sarabande of the sixth Suite is followed by a Double. The Sarabandes of Nos. II and III are first presented in lightly ornamented form, then with a wealth of *agréments*. It seems that the composer meant to demonstrate the best manner of adorning the repetitions in a slowly moving dance. Attractive modifications of the customary type occur in some Gigues. No. II assumes the character of a high-spirited Italian dance, while No. VI presents it in the guise of a turbulent virtuoso piece. Sizable demands are made on the performer's technical skill, for he has to play both a trill and the notes of a second voice with one hand.

The 'Optional Dances' have the most direct appeal. In the two Bourrées of No. II a gentle dance alternates with a gay and vigorous scene. In Nos. III and VI humorous Gavottes are followed by Musettes imitating the sound of bagpipes. No. IV presents two Minuets, the

---

1. Following a suggestion by this author, the Préludes to the suites III and IV were arranged by students of Boston University for three solo instruments (violin, oboe, bassoon) accompanied by strings and harpsichord. Professor Clayton Wilson of the University of California, Santa Barbara, transcribed the Prélude to No. III as a concerto grosso for wind instruments only.

second appearing for once in the relative minor instead of the customary parallel key. The effervescent Passepieds of No. V offer impish character-pieces in rondo form. In every suite a lighter mood appears before the grand finale of the gigue.

The six *French Suites* are shorter, simpler, and easier to play than the pieces in the English set. They use the same four basic dances, as well as a number of *Galanterien*, but the Prélude is missing, each suite starting with the Allemande.

It is obvious that the production of the French Suites, like that of the English Suites, extended over a prolonged period. Bach rewrote and revised individual numbers of the set, and it required time before the definite order of the suites emerged. In an old manuscript, probably copied in 1723, two other suites (BWV 818, 819) were inserted instead of the fifth and sixth of the French Suites.[1]

The numerous changes were in every respect satisfactory, the result being a strongly cohesive set. The first three suites have a more serious character and they are written in the minor mode; they are followed by three serene and even joyful pieces in major keys. Nos. I-IV are in six movements,[2] No. V has seven, and No. VI has eight movements. It appears that the sequence of the suites may even correspond to the chronological order. Nos. I and II might have been written earlier than the rest. The thematic interrelation between the beginnings of the different dances in Suite I recalls 'variation suites' in 17th-century music, a style that Bach subsequently abandoned. On the other hand Nos. V and VI are the latecomers in this collection. They bring the set to a climactic conclusion, for they belong to Bach's finest clavier music.

As introductory movements are missing, Bach emphasizes the prefatory character of the Allemandes. In Suites III and IV in particular they have all but shed the last remnants of a dance character. The Courantes appear in two different shapes. In Nos. II, IV, V, VI they do not follow the slow and deliberate French type, but rather have the vivacity of the fast-moving Italian *corrente* in 3/4 time. Supple Italianized melodies enhance the Southern character of these pieces. Likewise there are several kinds of Gigues, which vary in rhythm and character. No. I

1. Dadelsen, *Chronologie*, p. 99 ff., assumes that No. V was started in 1723 and concluded at least 18 months later.
2. An additional Minuet in No. IV (BWV 815a) seems to be of later origin.

uses dotted rhythms, characteristic of the stately slow sections of French overtures. Little of the habitually gay character of the finale appears in this solemn piece. In No. II, on the other hand, the composer employs the joyfully skipping rhythm of the French *canarie* (*Ex. 55*). No. III

Ex. 55. French Suite II, Gigue

contains a smoothly flowing Italian *giga,* while the remaining end-dances conform with traditional patterns. Especially the bright and spirited finale of No. V presents one of the most attractive Gigues Bach has written. The composer has fashioned finely wrought masterpieces out of the interspersed *Galanterien.* He shows special fondness for the graceful, at times ceremonious, Minuet. The Airs in II and IV remind us of an old French custom, for they are not only dance music but are very singable as well. Among the Gavottes the ingratiating pieces in No. V and VI are especially noteworthy. The rarely used Loure appears in delicate and sensitive form in No. V. By and large the definite version of the French Suites represents the most compact and, in a way, the most perfect keyboard suites Bach wrote. In another set published in Leipzig new elements are incorporated into the form, breaking up its traditional shape.

Three shorter clavier compositions have to be discussed before the final big collections are analyzed. Cöthen seems to have witnessed the composition of another clavier work which may have received its final shape only after Bach arrived in Leipzig. It is the *Chromatic Fantasia and Fugue in D minor* (BWV 903), a brilliant virtuoso piece in the grand style. Not surprisingly it is among the few clavier works of Bach that have found their way into 20th-century concert halls. In spite of its emotional intensity the Fantasia has a logical construction. Its first section (b. 1-48) is toccata-like, using runs, broken chords, and arpeggios. The second (b. 49-61) introduces a recitative, imbued with Baroque expressiveness, while the third (b. 61-79) effectively combines these two elements. Exciting chromatic and enharmonic progressions occur in this highly dramatic composition (*Ex. 56*) testifying to Bach's

Ex. 56. *Chromatic Fantasia*

urge to explore boldly the possibilities of the well-tempered system. The following fugue is likewise based on a theme which makes ample use of chromatic progressions. It starts in strict contrapuntal style, but gradually loosens up as the composition progresses, moving at the same time from the basic key of D minor as far afield as E minor and B minor (b. 79-83). Some aspects of the rhapsodic, improvisatory style of the Fantasia are still preserved here. There are numerous episodes, some of them with toccata-like passages; full chords with up to eight notes are introduced, and powerful octaves in the bass lead to the climactic ending. One would like to think that Bach used a work of this type to hold the Dresden audience spellbound after Marchand had evaded a contest with him.[1]

A second *Fantasia and Fugue in A minor* (BWV 904) may have been composed in Leipzig around 1725. It consists of a dignified introductory movement, which, with its slowly shifting chords, recaptures the idiom of Frescobaldi. Its structure resembles that of the Préludes in the English Suites. A massive subject of twelve measures appears at the beginning and end, and, transposed to related keys, twice in the middle (b. 1, 31, 69, 100). Its different entrances are connected by modulating sections in three or four voices. A magnificent double fugue follows in which Bach develops first an extended and energetic theme, then a brief and mournful, chromatically descending second subject (b. 37). The final juxtaposition of these sharply contrasting ideas produces an imposing combination. This work may be performed on any keyboard instrument; it is as suitable for the organ as it is for an instrument equipped with strings.

The single *Fantasia in C minor* (BWV 906) apparently belongs to a later period; it may have been written in 1738. Despite its very small

1. The first notes of the fugue theme are, according to the German designation, A-B-H-C. These letters make up the name of the composer, although in a different order. The same notes were used by Bach in the final fugue of his 'Art of the Fugue' (cf. p. 344).

dimensions this vigorous piece significantly heralds the newly emerging sonata form. An exposition, sixteen measures in length, introduces a fiercely flashing first theme and also a more sedate and lyrical second subject, in which the left hand, following the example of Scarlatti, crosses over the right hand. A slightly extended middle section transposes and develops these two ideas, whereupon a contracted recapitulation restates the exposition's first half. Bach felt unable to match this stirring piece with a fugue of equal significance. Actually such a composition was started, but after a few boldly conceived measures it disintegrated and finally broke off, leaving the fantasia as a masterfully fashioned composition in its own right.

Bach's third collection of clavier suites (BWV 825-30) occupies a special place within his output, as it was the first work published (and possibly also engraved) by the composer himself. Sebastian was forty-one when the suite No. 1 was printed in 1726; additional pieces appeared in the following years, until by 1731 the whole set of six was available and designated as his opus I. He called this collection *Clavier-Übung* (keyboard exercise) and each individual suite, Partita. Johann Kuhnau, Bach's predecessor as Thomas Cantor, had won great success with two sets of clavier works (published in 1689 and 1692) which he entitled *Clavier-Übung*; each of these sets comprises a number of suites he likewise inscribed as Partitas. Bach was encouraged to present these Leipzig suites in the same manner. Such works, he knew, would also serve very well for the numerous gifted pupils he was instructing there.[1]

In the same year, 1731, Sebastian's son, Carl Philipp Emanuel, then seventeen, also presented an opus I in print, a minuet for clavier he had engraved himself. It seems quite possible that Emanuel, who had mastered the craft of engraving music, helped his father with the production of the *Clavier-Übung* and, by cutting expenses, induced the thrifty composer to undertake this publication.

Like the English Suites, each Partita starts with an introductory

1. Bach's concern for the musical education of his pupils induced him also to dictate rules for the realization of the thorough-bass. J. P. Kellner preserved this manuscript of 1738 which seems to have been copied by a pupil of Bach. It elaborates on the instruction given in concise form in Anna Magdalena's Clavier-Büchlein of 1725 and offers excerpts from contemporary texts and compositions (cf. Spitta II, p. 599 ff and 913 ff; *Bach-Reader*, p. 389 ff).

movement. On the other hand there is no lack of progressive features anticipating developments of a later era. Bach increasingly employed simple phrases of 4, 8, 12, and 16 measures, such as were to be favored by the classic composers, while the structure of individual dances heralds the sonata form. The sequence of dances is occasionally changed and their original character sometimes obliterated.

Each of the introductory movements differs in name and character from the rest. The *Praeludium* in No. I is a comparatively short and simple piece, resembling a three-part invention. Its gentle melodic idiom so greatly stirred Sebastian's youngest son, Johann Christian, that he quoted the beginning in one of his violin sonatas.[1] No. II starts with a *Sinfonia*. Here the fusion of styles, so characteristic of Bach's work, is in full evidence. The composition begins with the majestic slow section of the French overture and ends with its fast fugue, but inserts in the middle a cantabile section reminiscent of the slow movement in an Italian 'sinfonia.' Thus the tempo is twice accelerated, and contrapuntal devices in the third section produce an increase of intensity toward the end. No. III begins with a *Fantasia*. Bach had previously designated three-part inventions with this term. Here he uses it for a two-part invention which displays a very logical and strict construction, being clearly subdivided into four sections of about equal length (b. 1-30, 31-65, 66-89, 90-120). The IVth Partita uses a French *Ouverture* as introduction. It consists in the traditional manner of a Grave leading to a fugue. No. V is headed by a *Praeambulum*. This movement, with its runs and arpeggios, somewhat resembles a brilliant toccata. In its formal construction it recalls, however, the keyboard arrangements of a concerto like those Bach uses in the Préludes to the English Suites. Related to it is the introduction to No. VI which bears also the heading *Toccata*. The majestic piece has embedded in its middle section a fugue using a subject derived from the beginning of the movement. This imposing composition, with its beautifully balanced structure, was the last toccata Bach wrote.

The dances in the Partitas also present a many-faceted picture. The quietly flowing Allemande of earlier suites is superseded in No. VI by a dramatic composition with dotted rhythms. In addition to the French Courante (Nos. II, IV), the Italian Corrente type (Nos. I, III, V, VI)

1. Op. 10, No. 1, in B flat major.

is also used, while the Sarabandes in Nos. III and V have discarded their original stately character. The richly ornamented Sarabande in No. IV is imbued with sadness and pathos; in its expressiveness it seems to anticipate the melodic idiom of Philipp Emanuel Bach, one of the protagonists of the emotion-filled style which stirred music lovers in the era of sensibility. This Sarabande also contains progressive features. The movement displays important elements of a condensed sonata form: exposition with initial and concluding subject, richly modulating development, and complete recapitulation. Although each section is on the smallest possible scale, the rudiments of the future form can be easily observed. The influence of Italian music, so strongly noticeable in this set, manifests itself with particular clarity in the Gigue of No. I. This is a completely homophonic virtuoso piece making continuous use of Scarlatti's favorite device—crossing of the hands. In No. II the Gigue is replaced by an energetic and brilliant 'Capriccio' which only in its general construction approaches the character of the traditional concluding dance. The Gigue in No. IV employs the unusual time signature of 9/16. Its second part surprisingly starts with a new theme, but Bach quickly clears up the confusion by combining this second idea with the main subject. The superb gigue of No. VI uses a theme which assumes an audacious character through the employment of diminished sevenths. In the second part the listener witnesses, as Hermann Keller aptly remarks, 'an outburst of the irascible composer who suddenly resolves to let the whole structure stand on its head, the bass assuming the place of the top voice.' A remarkable ending for this most impressive of the six Partitas!

In this set the *Galanterien* do not always keep to their customary place. Nos. IV and VI present optional dances not only between Sarabande and Gigue but also between Courante and Sarabande. The composer fully realized that his dances did not always conform to the customary pattern, and accordingly he stressed in the heading that he had only observed the traditional tempo (cf. 'Tempo di Minuetto' in No. V, and 'Tempo di Gavotta' in VI). New names also appear in the set. The 'Burlesca' in No. III might be considered as a kind of minuet, while the 'Scherzo' in the same suite seems to replace a gavotte. The heading 'Rondeau' in No. II refers to the form of the sprightly piece. Four times the main theme appears either in its original shape or with

slight changes, and in between Bach presents short contrasting episodes. This witty and lively composition in 3/8 meter somewhat resembles a gigue, and this may have induced Bach to dispense with a
piece of this kind for the conclusion of the suite.

The first part of the *Clavier-Übung* represents the culmination of
Bach's treatment of the keyboard suite, which under his masterly hands
assumed a unique grandeur and significance. But it also marks an ending, since the form as created in the 17th century was beginning to
dissolve. The single piece of the kind that Bach later contributed
illuminates with particular clarity this process of gradual disintegration.

The publication of Bach's opus I seems to have met with considerable success. According to Forkel 'this work made in its time a great
noise in the musical world.' Such excellent compositions for the clavier
had never been seen and heard before. Accordingly the second part of
the *Clavier-Übung,* published in 1735, contains a new partita, or *Overture nach Französischer Art* (Overture in the French style; BWV 831)
as Bach called it. The composer used the unfamiliar name because
he was attempting to infuse new life into the structure of the partita.
As his model he employed the popular form of the orchestral dance
suite preceded by a French overture. Following the example of Georg
Böhm,[1] he transplanted it to the harpsichord. An experiment of this
kind had already been made in Bach's Partita No. IV; the later work
turns, however, more decisively toward the idiom of the orchestral suite.
The Overture, the powerful initial movement, to which the whole work
owes its name, consists of three substantial sections, slow-fast-slow.
After this extensive piece an additional introduction is not needed, and
the Allemande is altogether omitted. There is an obvious preponderance of the modern-type *Galanterien* in this suite. They are inserted
both before and after the Sarabande and even after the Gigue. The
whole work conveys the impression of an orchestral ballet, and we
seem to hear various groups of instruments conversing with each other.
To achieve a maximum of coloristic variety Bach prescribed a harpsichord with two manuals. Repeated indications of 'forte' and 'piano,'
particularly in the first and last movements, clearly indicate where
Bach expected changes from the fuller sounding to the softer keyboard.
The Sarabande uses a solid four-part texture; the transparency of the

1. *Sämtliche Werke,* edited by J. Wolgast, Leipzig, 1927, Vol. I.

other dances rather brings Watteau's softly-hued canvases to mind. Among the highlights one should like to single out the exquisite Gavottes, a tender Passepied in the airy key of B major, the impish Gigue based on the skipping rhythm of the canaric, and the delightfully humorous 'Echo' at the end. In this Overture a gossamer structure imbued with French elegance is erected on a solid Germanic foundation.

In the original edition, the 'Overture in the French style' was preceded by a *Concerto nach Italiaenischen Gusto* (Concerto in the Italian taste; BWV 971). Thus Bach bowed in the same collection to the two nations which in his time exercised the strongest influence on German music, representing each of them with a characteristic form of orchestral composition he had transcribed for the harpsichord. With the 'Concerto' for unaccompanied clavier Bach seems to revert to his Weimar clavier arrangements of works for violin solo and orchestra. Unlike the préludes to the English Suites, which are based on the idea of adapting a concerto grosso with several solo instruments to the keyboard, the 'Concerto in the Italian taste' represents the clavier arrangement of an orchestral work with a single soloist, the exact model of which exists in the composer's imagination only. Vivaldi's concerto form is clearly recognizable in the brilliant first movement,[1] with a solid tutti section in the tonic serving both as introduction and conclusion. Fragments of this basic idea occur at regular intervals and are connected by thematically contrasting and modulating solo passages. The lofty middle movement sounds like a broadly extended violin solo accompanied by strings. Particularly effective is Bach's method of suggesting in the accompaniment a pedal point of the string basses (*Ex. 57*). In the dashing finale, which has a form similar to that of the ini-

Ex. 57.

tial movement, some of the phrases in the main tutti seem to result from the adaptation of violin passages (cf. b. 5-8, 17-22).

1. The beginning displays a striking resemblance to the theme of a *Sinfonia* in Georg Muffat's *Florilegium Primum* (1695).

Despite this mock realism, which keeps up the pretense that the composition is an arrangement, the work is extremely well suited to the clavier. The composer once again gives directions for the use of the harpsichord's two manuals. He even likes to indicate 'forte' in one hand and simultaneously 'piano' in the other. Probably two or even three strings in unison or octaves should sound on the 'forte' manual and single strings on the 'piano' clavier. Usually the tutti sections are to be played by both hands in 'forte,' while in solos melody and accompaniment are presented on different manuals. But there are very attractive deviations from this rule, showing that Bach was not averse to a dynamically diversified style which conjures up the variety of colors in an orchestral composition.

The Italian Concerto, as it is commonly called, fully deserves the affection and admiration music lovers have always felt for it. With its perfect equilibrium between emotional content and musical form, it radiates an accomplished master's serenity and joy in supreme craftsmanship.

The third part of the *Clavier-Übung* includes only organ works (cf. p. 242). The fourth part, which was published between 1742 and 1745 is again written for the harpsichord. It contains a single work *Aria mit verschiedenen Veraenderungen* (Aria with sundry variations; BWV 988), which had been commissioned by Count Keyserlingk, a great admirer of Bach, who lived in Dresden as Russian ambassador to the electoral court of Saxony. Bach's pupil, Johann Theophilus Goldberg, a very brilliant young harpsichord virtuoso, was entrusted with the performance. He had to play the work over and over again for the music-loving Count, who was suffering from insomnia, and thus evolved the designation 'Goldberg Variations.'

In this set Bach draws on a lifetime of composition in various fields of clavier music. Canon, fugue, dance-elements, études, and character-pieces of various kinds are here combined in a monumental composition of striking compactness. The 18th century produced nothing in the field of clavier variations that could stand comparison with this gigantic work, which demonstrates both the soaring imagination and the consummate technical skill of its composer. Educational aims are here of lesser significance as Bach meant to write a true virtuoso piece of steadily increasing brilliance.

The work is once more designated for a harpsichord with two manuals. Contrary to *Clavier-Übung II,* the composer no longer prescribes, however, 'piano' or 'forte.' He simply states at the beginning of each variation whether it is to be performed on a single manual or on two, and he occasionally leaves the choice to the performer ('a 1 ovvero 2 Clav.'). The pieces designated for two manuals by and large offer particular opportunities for the performer to display his technical mastery.

The 'Aria' which forms the theme of the set possibly was not written by Bach himself. This tender sarabande in the French style appeared also in the *Clavier-Büchlein* for Anna Magdalena Bach from 1725, which contains several pieces by other composers. Bach may have chosen the Aria for its lucidity of form. It consists of two sixteen-measure periods, each subdivided into eight-measure phrases. A single chord forms the harmonic basis of each measure, the first sixteen bars modulating from the tonic to the dominant, the next sixteen bars from the dominant to the relative minor and back to the tonic. There are repeat sings at the end of each period.

This simple, yet forceful structure forms a fitting basis for the set of thirty variations. Here the composer no longer uses the simple technique applied in his early variations in the Italian manner. He shows little concern for the richly ornamented tune of the sarabande. The formal construction and the harmonic progressions derived from the Aria's bass line are the elements joining theme and variations together. Bach's technique is inspired by passacaglia and chaconne, the basic principles of which are here redesigned on a larger scale.

Like the theme, most variations consist of 16 + 16 measures. Four variations only (Nos. 3, 9, 21, 30) use 8 + 8 measures, contracting two bars of the model into a single one. In No. 16, on the other hand, the process is partly reversed. Here Bach keeps in the first section the model's sixteen measures, while the second consists of thirty-two, each bar of the sarabande being replaced by two brief bars in the variation's second half. The theme's key of G major and its harmonic skeleton are preserved in most variations. Only three (Nos. 15, 21, 25) offer a welcome contrast by using G minor instead.

Without ever deviating from the basic structure of the theme, the composer presents in this set nine different kinds of canon, one in every third variation. There is a canon at the unison in No. 3, one of the second in No. 6, of the third in No. 9. Each time the interval of the imitation is augmented by one tone, until variation 27 ends up with the canon of the ninth. In the first eight of these canons a bass voice, following the outline of the sarabande's bass, supports the two imitative voices. The canons of the fourth and fifth (Nos. 12 and 15) are not in straight imitation, but in inversion; possibly to indicate the approach to the center of the composition. The second half of the set is introduced through a French Overture forming Variation 16. Its stately slow section with dotted rhythms corresponds to the theme's first section, the ensuing fugue to its second part. No. 30, the final variation, is a roguish *Quodlibet* which fits melodic phrases taken from two folksongs into the framework of the variations (*Ex.* 58). The com-

Ex. 58. *Goldberg Variations*

poser here revives the humorous custom of singing several tunes simultaneously, a favorite pastime at the family reunions of the Bach clan. In this *Quodlibet* the songs incorporated begin with the following texts: *Ich bin so lang nicht bei dir g'west* (Long have I been away from you) and *Kraut und Rüben haben mich vertrieben* (Cabbage and turnips have put me to flight). It has been suggested that these two quotations were used as a comical device to herald the imminent reappearance of the theme which concludes the set. The sarabande seems to blame its protracted absence (throughout the set of thirty variations the tune did not make an appearance) on the lowly 'cabbage and turnips' the composer's imagination had provided. Bach was bound to enjoy such a little joke made at his own expense.

The nine canons, the Overture and the *Quodlibet* give the set a firm formal structure. They are interspersed with a number of highly diversified character-pieces, which are making increasing demands on the player's technical abilities. We might single out the gay and vigorous No. 4, the gracefully skipping No. 7, the strictly constructed fughetta No. 10 (with eight entrances of the fugue subject, one in every fourth measure), the tender and soulful No. 13, followed by the brilliant No. 14, the passepied-like No. 19, the high-spirited No. 23, the deeply moving chromatic No. 25, and finally the magnificent Nos. 28 and 29, with various kinds of trills in both hands, anticipating technical devices in 19th-century piano music (*Ex. 59*). The mixture of

Ex. 59.

strictest logic with imaginative freedom of expression that manifests itself in this gigantic work places it among the greatest manifestations of Bach's genius.

At about the same time Bach turned once more to a systematic treatment of one of his favorite forms of composition, prelude and fugue for a keyboard instrument. In or before 1742 he completed[1] a collection of twenty-four pairs of pieces in all the major and minor keys. It is commonly referred to as 'The Well-tempered Clavier, Part II' (BWV 870-893), although the composer himself did not give it this designation. The title seems justified in view of the obvious similarities between the two sets. As in the first part, a thematic relationship between the two members of a pair may often be observed. With more or less clarity it appears in about half the pairs (cf. Nos. 2, 5, 10, 12, 14, 15, 17-21, 23). Surprising thematic connections between pieces of the same key in the first and second parts may even be detected (*Ex. 60; cf. also Nos. 5-7, 15*).[2]

Ex. 60. Prelude XXII

W.T.C. I

W.T.C. II

1. Cf. Walter Emery in *Music and Letters* 34, 1953, p. 106 ff., and Dadelsen *Chronologie*, p. 108 f.

2. J. N. David stresses this aspect in his monograph quoted above.

The set reveals clear signs of its growth through an extended period of time. Several pieces seem to have originated in the Cöthen years. Of the Prelude and Fugue No. 1, two primitive and far less inspiring versions exist. Pair No. 3 was originally conceived in C major. It received its final shape only later when it was transposed to C sharp major. There is a simpler and shorter version of the prelude to No. 6; the fugues No. 15 and 17 also exist in an earlier form, where they are, moreover, combined with different preludes.

Consequently the set displays a variety of forms unusual even among the multifaceted collections Bach has presented. The *Preludes* deviate in many instances from those of the first book. There is only a single arpeggio piece (No. 3), and it breaks off in its twenty-fourth measure, the second half of the prelude being formed by a brief fugato. Similarly No. 22 resembles a three-part fugue. Contrary to this procedure, in which fugue-like pieces are employed as introductions to fugues, Bach presents preludes in a luxuriant al fresco style which most effectively prepare for the ensuing contrapuntal creations (Nos. 1, 16). Pieces inspired by two-part inventions (Nos. 2, 8, 10, 20, 24) or three-part sinfonias (Nos. 4, 19) often occur. It is significant, however, that, unlike the earlier pieces, most of the invention-like preludes are clearly divided into two sections, with repeat signs at either end. The concerto form is used in the broadly contoured No. 17 and in No. 13, which also has the character of the introduction to a French overture. A slow middle movement in a concerto is conjured up by the expressively singing, tender No. 14. There are even pieces in a kind of sonata form, with a regular recapitulation, though lacking a contrasting second subject. To this category belong the sparkling, dance-like No. 21; No. 5, which seems inspired by the rhythms of the gigue; and Nos. 12 and 18, which display the affectionate and sensitive idiom of Sebastian's second son, Carl Philipp Emanuel. Several great preludes in this set can no longer be considered as mere introductions, for they equal or even surpass the significance of the following fugue.

On the surface the twenty-four *Fugues* of the second book appear more homogeneous than those of the first. The later collection contains only compositions with three or four voices and avoids those with two or five. Likewise chromatic themes are missing here. A closer investigation reveals, however, considerable stylistic divergencies.

There are many fugues which display the greatest polyphonic intricacy. The new collection contains contrapuntal masterpieces which foreshadow the supreme achievements in the 'Art of the Fugue.' No. 5 is a stretto fugue par excellence, exploring over and over again the various possibilities of overlapping entrances of the theme. The countersubject also grows out of related material, the result being an unusually compact composition with hardly a chink in its solid armor. Similarly, No. 9 employs various types of stretto, including the augmentation and diminution of the theme. Bach returns to the spirit of early vocal polyphony by offering a piece which appears to be almost a keyboard reduction of an a cappella motet. No. 22 is one of the most imposing fugues Bach ever wrote. It is based on a highly expressive theme which is gradually joined by two counterpoints imbued with passion and strength. With the help of strettos and inversion, a magnificent edifice is erected which is remarkable, even among the works of Bach. Yet it seems hardly possible to do justice to this mighty creation with the modest resources of 18th-century claviers. One cannot help but remember in this connection Beethoven's contemptuous retort to a musician who was complaining about the composer's inconsiderate manner of writing: 'Do you think I care about your wretched instrument when the spirit seizes me?'

Deviations from traditional fugue standards, however, do occur frequently in this set, which was written at a time when fugue composition had begun to lose its standing among German musicians. The homophonic element intrudes in some of these late compositions, where greater emphasis is put on the content than on the form of the piece. No. 12 interrupts the flow of the polyphonic developments by inserting homophonic episodes. No. 20 is a fiery, wild, and turbulent character-piece; yet as a fugue it does not offer too much interest. Both numbers maintain the same mood throughout and end with a minor chord, contrary to Bach's previous custom of concluding pieces in minor with a major chord ('Picardy third'). Bach's feeling for modern tonality has overcome this remnant of the ancient church modes. In No. 15 the extended subject is at first based only on broken chords. These arpeggios, though producing a charming composition, do not form a suitable basis for contrapuntal elaboration.

A few additional fugues from this outstanding set might be mentioned. No. 2 appears to be an ordinary three-part fugue for more than half its length; but ten measures before the end the fourth voice comes in with the augmentation of the theme, adding a new dimension to the piece's finely wrought texture. No. 13 displays a completely symmetrical construction rarely found in Bach's earlier fugues. Five thematic developments, alternately long and short, are separated by two types of episodes which likewise alternate. The resulting form schedule is:

THEME	EPISODE	THEME	EPISODE	THEME	EPISODE	THEME	EPISODE	THEME
long	A	short	B	long	A	short	B	long
1-13	14-20	20-23	24-31	31-44	45-51	51-56	56-63	63-84

In the double fugue No. 23 the set reaches its climax. The powerful first theme is later joined by a gently moving second idea (b. 28), conveying a spirit of determination tinged with slight nostalgia. The high-spirited and mischievous No. 24 rather forms an appendix to the whole set. In this carefree rococo dance Bach seems to bow to the precepts of a younger generation.

IV. WORKS FOR STRING AND
WIND INSTRUMENTS; CONCERTOS

BACH'S superb craftsmanship, exquisite in the most minute detail, lent itself especially to the filigree style of chamber music.[1] Some of his works in this field belong to the most inspired compositions he ever wrote. The majority owe their conception to the last Weimar years or to Bach's activity in Cöthen, where he was able to develop his instrumental style to supreme mastery. Significantly enough, it was not the *sonata for a solo instrument and thorough bass,* so widely used in his time, that really interested him, for it did not present any particular challenge to his ingenuity. The few compositions he wrote in the form reveal a somewhat aloof attitude toward this kind of music.

The E minor Sonata for violin and thorough bass (BWV 1023) shows in structure and melodic language the influence of compositions by Corelli and Vivaldi, thus suggesting that the work was written in Weimar, possibly between 1714 and 1717.[2] The Sonata starts with a spirited toccata of 29 measures supported by the single bass note E. Such an extended pedal point seems to call for the organ as accompanying instrument, and we are reminded of a statement made by

---

1. The list of chamber music works attributed to J. S. Bach had to be drastically revised and curtailed in recent years. Of the pieces listed in BWV the following are of doubtful authenticity:
BWV 1020 Sonata in G minor for violin and clavier
BWV 1022 Sonata in F major for violin and clavier (by C. P. E. Bach?)
BWV 1024 Sonata in C minor for violin and figured bass
BWV 1025 Suite in A major for violin and clavier
BWV 1026 Fugue in G minor for violin and clavier
BWV 1031 Sonata in E flat major for flute and clavier
BWV 1033 Sonata in C major for flute and figured bass
BWV 1036 Sonata in D minor for two violins and clavier
BWV 1037 Sonata in C major for violin and clavier (by J. T. Goldberg?)
BWV 1038 Sonata in G major for flute, violin, and figured bass (by C. P. E. Bach?)
2. Cf. G. Hausswald and R. Gerber in KB to NBA, Series VI, vol. I. Kassel, 1958, p. 134.

Forkel: 'In his time, it was usual to play in the church, during the communion, a concerto or solo upon some instrument. He often wrote such pieces himself and always contrived them so that his performers could, by their means, improve upon their instruments.'[1] The fugue that we expect as a sequence to the toccata is replaced in the sonata by a tender Adagio that makes effective use of languorous progressions in the bass. The second half of the work consists of an Allemande and a Gigue. Thus an introduction is followed by dance movements, a combination frequently used in Bach's later suites. The Sonata in G major for violin and thorough[2] bass (BWV 1021) displays the regular tempo sequence slow-fast-slow-fast, common in *sonate da chiesa*. Italian elements may again be observed both in the bass line and in the melody, but the technical perfection and elegance of diction suggest that the work originated later than the E minor Sonata, probably during the early Cöthen years.[3]

To the same period the Sonatas for flute and continuo in E minor (BWV 1034) and in E major (BWV 1035) apparently belong. As in BWV 1021, they use the four-movement form of the *sonata da chiesa* and start with an adagio section. The outgoing, cheerful Allegros of the E minor Sonata surround an Andante supported by a dignified ostinato bass. The E major Sonata starts with a tender cantilena, and a graceful 'Siciliano' precedes the energetic finale. BWV 1034 must have enjoyed great popularity, since a comparatively large number of manuscript copies have survived.[4] BWV 1035 was taken by Bach to Pots-

---

1. Cf. Translation by A. C. Kollmann in *Bach Reader*, p. 346.

2. Cf. F. Blume, 'Eine unbekannte Violinsonate von J. S. B.,' in *BJ* 1928, p. 96 ff.

3. The finely wrought bass line of the sonata seems to have been considered as a suitable starting point for composition assignments Bach gave to his pupils. A Sonata in G major for violin, flute, and continuo (BWV 1038) uses the same bass as BWV 1021, while the string and wind instrument have completely new melodies. U. Siegele suggests (*Kompositionsweise . . . in der Instrumentalmusik J. S. B.s*, dissertation, Tübingen, 1957) that C. P. E. Bach was the author of this trio sonata. This theory would also explain why the father, proud of his son's achievement, copied the piece in his own hand, since neither the style nor the quality of the composition point to Sebastian's authorship. Strangely enough this adaptation was later rearranged. It was transposed to F major and the flute part entrusted to the right hand of the keyboard player. The result was a sonata for cembalo obbligato with the accompaniment of a violin (BWV 1022). Possibly it was again C. P. E. Bach who tried thus to modernize his earlier attempt.

4. Cf. H. P. Schmitz, KB to NBA, series VI, vol. 3, Kassel, 1963, p. 14.

dam in 1741 or 1747, and given to M. G. Fredersdorf, the private secretary of King Frederick the Great. It is due to this visit that the
attractive composition survived.

It seems almost paradoxical that the further development of the
sonata for a solo instrument and thorough bass resulted from a process
of elimination. Bach dispensed with the support of the continuo, thus
creating a new freedom and new possibilities for the solo instrument,
but also sizable difficulties. More than a dozen compositions of this
kind were written in the Cöthen years, between 1718 and 1723.

One of the *works for an unaccompanied melody instrument* is the
Partita in A minor for flute solo (BWV 1013). While Bach's later solo
suites and sonatas magnificently explore the technical potentialities of
the instrument for which they are written, the language of the Partita
is not altogether idiomatic. The introductory Allemande, for instance,
with its uninterrupted flow of sixteenth notes, would seem better suited
for a string instrument than for a flute, as the performer is forced to
insert pauses to breathe. A gay Italian Corrente and a poignant Sarabande ensue, and the work is concluded by a scintillating piece entitled
'Bourrée anglaise,' the most captivating number of the little suite.

On quite a different level are the *Six Suites for violoncello solo*
(BWV 1007-12). Here Bach uses with supreme skill the sonorous,
organ-like tone qualities of the large string instrument. His ability to
create melodic lines which imply harmonic progressions and even a
polyphonic texture is revealed at its best here. Double stops and full
chords are deftly added to solidify the musical web. Bach's rejection of
any additional instrument does not give the appearance of an artificial
restriction to the composition. He demonstrates the cello's self-suffi-
ciency by freeing its sound from distracting additions.

Each of the six cello suites starts with a 'Prélude,' which is followed
by Allemande, Courante, Sarabande, two *Galanterien,* and a Gigue.
Bach used the same arrangement in his English Suites for clavier,
which may have been written at about the same time. Yet the string
compositions seem to be imbued with a more optimistic spirit. Four of
the cello suites are in the major mode and only two in the minor, a
relationship the composer reversed in the clavier suites.

To enlarge the coloristic and technical possibilities Bach prescribed that in the 5th Suite in C minor the top string ought to be tuned to g instead of a.[1] The Sixth Suite in D major was written for a somewhat enigmatic instrument which added a fifth string tuned to e' to the cello's customary four strings.[2] The tessitura of the piece is accordingly higher than that of the other suites, which lends the tone a peculiar countertenor quality.

The introductory Préludes may be considered as the most important movements in the set. They offer many examples of Bach's ingenious use of the cello's resources. A favorite device is to alternate the tone of an open string with notes played on a neighboring string (*Ex. 61*).

Ex. 61. Cello Suite No. 1

The introduction to No. 4 creates the illusion of a pedal-point serving as a foundation for slowly gliding harmonies. The contrast between quietly moving and excitedly rushing passages produces both here and in the Prélude to No. 6 a concerto-like effect. In the initial movement to No. 5 Bach offers a French overture, including even the fugal entries in the fast section.

The Allemandes of the collection are mostly slow and pensive pieces of great beauty, quite different in character from the nimble Courantes which reveal the strong influence exercised by the lively Correntes. The poetical Sarabandes offer a last opportunity for quiet introspection before the gay final section starts. Bach offers in this set three different kinds of *Galanterien*. The first two suites present pairs of Minuets, the next two, pairs of Bourrées, and the final two, pairs of Gavottes. Some of these contain folk tunes of great charm. In particular the first Bourrée to No. 3 well deserves the great popularity that has been accorded it. A light and cheerful, occasionally quite brilliant, Gigue serves as effective endpiece for all the suites.

1. The 5th Suite was also arranged for lute by Bach. This version (BWV 995) which is preserved in the composer's own hand is in the key of G minor. (cf. p. 310)

2. This *violoncello a cinque corde* was not the *viola pomposa*, a claim generally made in the Bach literature. C. Sachs who rectified this error (*Musical Instruments*, New York, 1940, p. 362 and 367 ff.) also questions the myth that Bach invented the viola pomposa.

There is a widely held belief that Bach wrote the six suites for Christian Ferdinand Abel, viola da gamba player and cellist of the Prince of Cöthen. If this man was able to do justice to the music, he must have been quite a master of his instrument. It might be interesting to speculate, moreover, on whether the forthright and affirmative character of the set reflects Bach's state of mind in those days or rather that of the performer for whom it was intended.

Bach's compositions for unaccompanied melody instruments reach their climax in the *three Sonatas and three Partitas for violin solo* (BWV 1001-1006), completed in 1720, which stand among the most powerful manifestations of his genius. Although the violin had been treated polyphonically in Italy, and particularly in Germany, before Bach's time—H. Biber, J. P. Westhoff, and J. J. Walther having made significant contributions—Bach's achievement is unique. No other composer has written in this field works of similar grandeur and magnificence.

Bach's deep insight into the violin's potentialities was part of his heritage, for both his father and grandfather had been successful violinists. As a child he studied the instrument with his father,[1] and at Weimar he was appointed as violinist. In the congenial atmosphere of Cöthen he had an opportunity to write works displaying his outstanding ability on the instrument. He used it not only as a carrier of a singing melody but also as the interpreter of harmonic expression. Bach, a born fighter who exulted in overcoming apparently unsurmountable difficulties, succeeded in doing the nearly impossible: to write four-part fugues and polyphonic variations for an instrument whose very nature seems to exclude such devices.[2]

The violin of Bach's time had a flatter bridge than the modern instrument, and its bow was differently constructed. Nevertheless it seems highly doubtful that violinists could sound four notes of a chord simultaneously.[3] Anyway, Bach does not seem to have expected this.

---

1. Cf. J. Pulver, 'J. S. B. as Violinist,' *Monthly Musical Record*, London, 1926, p. 35, and K. Geiringer, *The Bach Family*, pp. 19 and 72.

2. Cf. G. Hausswald, 'Zur Stilistik von J. S. B.s Sonaten und Partiten für Violine allein,' *Archiv f. Musikwissenschaft*, 1957, p. 304 ff.

3. A. Schering (*BJ* 1904, p. 105) and subsequently A. Schweitzer (p. 361 ff.) claimed that the German players of Bach's time could produce, thanks to a loosely strung bow, full chords, without resorting to arpeggios. This theory can no longer be

His score abounds in chords obviously meant to be performed as arpeggios or by holding the notes for a shorter duration than prescribed. Again and again one of the strings or one of the fingers involved was required for the production of new notes before the original chord had resounded for the full length of time indicated by the composer[1] (*Ex.* 62). Bach assumed, however, that arpeggios of three and four notes,

Ex. 62.   Violin Sonata III, Fuga

and even successions of notes, would be understood as harmonic unities. The sonatas and partitas are thus typical not only of Bach's personality but of the artistic conceptions of the Baroque era. At that time the walls of houses were occasionally decorated with paintings simulating vistas of wide colonnades and formal gardens. Such embellishments require the working of the inner eye, just as the implied polyphony and rich harmonic texture in Bach's compositions require the co-operation of the inner ear.

In addition, the composer's joy in experimenting and adapting certain stylistic devices to changed conditions was given a wide scope in these works. Previously he had liked to use features of violin technique in his keyboard compositions; now the process was reversed, and he adopted basic designs of keyboard technique in his violin music. It is therefore not surprising that several movements from the violin sonatas and partitas were subsequently transcribed for keyboard instruments,

---

upheld. (Cf. G. Beckmann, *Das Violinspiel in Deutschland vor 1700*, Berlin, 1918; A. Moser in *BJ* 1920, p. 30 ff.; D. D. Boyden, 'The Violin and Its Technique in the 18th Century', *MQ*, Jan. 1950; E. Melkus, 'Zur Frage des B. Bogens,' *Öster-reichische Musikzeitschrift*, 1956, p. 99; W. Rabey, 'Der Originaltext der B.schen Soloviolinsonaten,' *BJ* 1963-64, p. 23 ff.) Nevertheless attempts were made to build for the performance of Bach's music curved bows with a device attached to the frog allowing the player quickly to tighten or loosen the hair of the bow (cf. Schweitzer in *Bach-Gedenkschrift*, 1950, p. 75 ff., and the recorded performances by R. Schrö-der and E. Telmányi). It is evident that a highly mechanized bow of this nature did not exist in Bach's time. Moreover the smooth, organ-like tone resulting from per-formances with this modern curved bow lacks the Baroque passion and fire inherent in B.'s music.

1. Cf. Rabey, p. 29ff.

the implied contrapuntal writing of the original being changed with ease into real polyphony. The fugue in the first sonata in G minor was transcribed for the organ (BWV 539, cf. p. 237), and the whole second sonata in A minor, as well as the first movement of the third sonata in C major, was arranged for the clavier (BWV 964 and 968). The 'Preludio' to the third Partita was adapted by the composer for the organ and equipped with an orchestral accompaniment. In this form he used it as introduction to cantatas No. 120a and 29.[1]

In their formal construction the three sonatas show great similarity. They all use the four movements of the *sonata da chiesa* (slow-fast-slow-fast), with a fugue in the second place and the slow third movement as the only movement in a different key. Particularly stirring are the two slow movements of the first sonata, the majestic introductory Adagio and the tender Siciliano that conjures up an idyllic nativity scene. The fugue in the second sonata won fame even in Bach's lifetime. Johann Mattheson quoted its theme in his treatise, *Kern melodischer Wissenschafft*[2] and remarked: 'Who would believe that these . . . short notes would be so fruitful as to bring forth a counterpoint of more than a whole sheet of music paper, without unusual extension and quite naturally? And yet the skilled Bach who is particularly gifted in this form, has set just this before the world; indeed he has also introduced the subject here and there in inversion.' The joyfully affirmative fugue of the C major sonata, No. 3, is a gigantic piece of 354 bars, approaching in its majesty and power the *Ciacona* of the D minor Partita. Its subject is one of Bach's favorite tunes, a quotation from the Pentecost antiphon, *Veni Sancte Spiritus* (Come Holy Ghost), which the composer also used in other instrumental and vocal works.[3] This magnificent piece, like the rest of the sonatas for violin solo, was probably intended for performance in church.

Contrary to these strictly conceived works, the three partitas, which in the autograph alternate with the sonatas, show a great variety of forms. The first partita in B minor consists of four dances, each fol-

1. There is also a version for lute (BWV 1000) of the fugue from the G minor Sonata (cf. p. 311) and a transcription for harp of the E Major Partita (BWV 1006a).

2. Hamburg 1737, p. 147.

3. The organ chorales BWV 651 and 652, Cantatas 59 and 175, the Motet BWV 226.

lowed by a Double, an étude-like variation. There is an Allemanda, an Italian Corrente, a Sarabande, and, in conclusion, a 'Tempo di Borea.' The traditional gigue, with its fugal elements, did not lend itself so well to variation work. Bach therefore replaced it by a gay and effervescent bourrée-like piece, a procedure adopted also in the suite for flute solo. The third Partita in E major drops completely the pattern of the clavier suite and replaces it by the free arrangement of pieces customary in an orchestral suite. It starts with a lively Preludio, a kind of perpetuum mobile, distinguished by an unusual wealth of dynamic signs. The most substantial among the following six dances is a rollicking 'Gavotte en Rondeau,' which presents the main ritornel five times, interrupted by sparkling episodes. A Bourrée with puckish echo-effects and a cheerful Gigue provide a fitting ending to the light-spirited work. The 'heart-piece' of the set is formed by the second Partita in D minor, which starts out with the traditional sequence Allemanda, Corrente, Sarabanda, and Giga.[1] These four numbers appear, however, to be a mere introduction to the final movement, the monumental *Ciaccona*. This is a gigantic set of interconnected variations on a harmonic pattern derived from a simple, four-measure bass. The variations usually appear in pairs, the second one subtly enhancing the content of the first. In the middle of the movement Bach changes from D minor to D major, but he reverts to the original key near the end. Philipp Spitta wrote as follows about this unique masterwork:[2] 'From the grave majesty of the beginning to the thirty-second notes which rush up and down like the very demons; from the tremulous arpeggios that hang almost motionless, like veiling clouds above a dark ravine . . . to the devotional beauty of the D major section where the evening sun sets in a peaceful valley: the spirit of the master urges the instrument to incredible utterances. At the end of the major section it sounds like an organ and sometimes a whole band of violins seem to be playing. . . .This *Ciaccona* is a triumph of spirit over matter such as even Bach never repeated in a more brilliant manner.'

1. Bach's use of the dance names alternates in this set between Italian and French forms. In the second partita Italian designations are exclusively used. In the first partita there is a 'Sarabande' while the remaining names are in Italian. In the third partita, on the other hand, 'Preludio' is followed by French dance-titles. Cf. NBA, vol. VI/1.

2. I/705 f.

Related to Bach's compositions for unaccompanied cello and violin are a handful of works he wrote for the *lute*.[1] In the 18th century the instrument, after a brilliant career during the Renaissance period, was reaching the end of its life-span. Yet Bach seems to have been quite interested in it. He established contacts with leading lutenists of the time, such as the famous virtuosos, S. L. Weiss and J. Kropfgans of Dresden, and E. G. Baron, the instrument's historian, who studied in Leipzig. At least two of Bach's pupils, J. L. Krebs and R. Straube, played the lute and composed for it. Bach himself employed it as a solo instrument and in ensembles,[2] and we may deduce from the nature of these compositions that he was fully conversant with its technique and possibly a lute player himself.

Bach seems to have been active in this field primarily in the Leipzig years. The most impressive of his solos for the lute is the *Suite in G minor* (BWV 995), which has been preserved in the composer's autograph with a dedication to a 'Monsieur Schouster,' about whom nothing further is known. This is an arrangement of Bach's fifth Suite for unaccompanied cello (BWV 1011). The adaptation, with its occasional changes of passages or additions of a new bass line, is so skilfully done that it appears to be an independent composition, hardly inferior to the outstanding model. No doubt such stylized dances, ingeniously set for the plucked instrument, suit the lute very well.

The well-known little *Prelude in C minor* (BWV 999) seems to be a natural outgrowth of the lute's possibilities. Although the old manuscript which is the source for the tiny composition clearly bears the designation 'pour la lute,' F. K. Griepenkerl began using it as a work

1. Cf. H. Neemann in *BJ* 1931, p. 72 ff., and in *Archiv für Musikforschung*, 1939, p. 167 ff.; C. S. Terry, *B.'s Orchestra*, London, 1932, p. 141ff.; N. Carrell in Program Book of the English Bach Festival, 1965, p. 85.

2. In Bach's funeral music for Queen Christiane Eberhardine (BWV 198), written in 1727, two lutes are used. With hollow sounds they describe in the recitative No. 4 the tolling of death bells. In other numbers of the work they reinforce the bass and act as filling continuo instruments. The Arioso No. 31 of the St. John Passion (BWV 245) entrusts two viole d'amore, a lute, and continuo with the accompaniment of a vocal solo. The poignant melancholy of the scene it fittingly expressed with the help of the lute's soft, mournful sound. However, Bach may have encountered difficulties in finding the proper person to perform these eighteen measures. Eventually he seems to have settled for more easily available instruments as the autograph part of this number is headed 'Organo ó Cembalo.'

of educational keyboard music. As No. 3 of the set of the '12 Little Preludes' assembled by him (cf. p. 272), it has been studied by generations of budding clavierists.

Bach indicated that either lute or harpsichord could perform the rather abbreviated *Sonata in E flat major* (BWV 998), consisting of a prelude, a toccata-like fugue, and a brisk final allegro. The first and last movements, which are predominantly in two parts, sound well on the plucked instrument. The fugue, however, offers sizable difficulties and seems better suited to the clavier. The authenticity of this movement has been quite rightly questioned.[1]

A separate *Fugue in G minor* (BWV 1000) is an arrangement of the fugue in the first of the sonatas for unaccompanied violin (BWV 1001). The medium of the lute is apt to provide a more precise expression for the implied polyphony of the original, but some of the violin composition's lustre is lost in the transcription. Later Bach even went further in his adaptation of the model by arranging the fugue for the organ (BWV 539, cf. p. 237).

His lute compositions offered Bach an opportunity to satisfy his urge for reshaping his ideas. Although they are not numerous and hardly significant, as compared to his great contributions, they help us to understand the restless mind of a man who never tired of exploring new avenues of artistic pursuit.

Bach's attitude toward the Baroque trio sonata for two melody instruments and figured bass is significant because of the changes it shows in his artistic thinking. During the Cöthen years the venerable combination served him mainly as a point of departure for new musical exploits which were to prove highly important for the future. By the end of his career, however, he deliberately returned to the form, in-

---

1. Cf. J. Schreyer, *Beiträge zur Bach-Kritik*, II, Leipzig, 1913, p. 35 ff. Of doubtful authenticity are also the Suite in E minor (BWV 996) and the Partita in C minor (BWV 997) which fit into the output of neither the Leipzig nor the Cöthen years. An arrangement of the Partita in E major for unaccompanied violin, preserved in Bach's own hand (BWV 1006a), is occasionally enumerated among Bach's lute compositions. The composer did not indicate the instrument on which the work should be played. It seems well suited for a plucked instrument, but from the nature of the arrangement it appears doubtful that Bach had the lute in mind. Neemann (*BJ* 1931, p. 86) suggests the use of a harp.

serting a trio sonata in the traditional style as the heart-piece into his 'Musical Offering.'[1]

Before 1723 Bach wrote a Sonata in G major for two flutes supported by figured bass (BWV 1039). This work also exists in two other versions: as a Sonata for viola da gamba with cembalo obbligato (BWV 1027); and three of its movements (Nos. 1, 2, 4) in arrangements for organ or pedal clavier.[2]

It seems probable that the composition for two flutes and bass served as the basis for the viola da gamba Sonata. Bach might have entrusted the part of the first flute to the right hand of the harpsichord player, while the bass part was assigned to the clavierist's left hand. The part of the second flute was transposed an octave down and given to the viola da gamba. Thus, without any radical change, a transformation of great significance was achieved. A trio which normally needed a minimum of three performers for its realization could, in its altered guise, be played by only two.[3]

Bach did not initiate the 'trio' for clavier and a melody instrument. This form was conceived at least a century earlier.[4] But no other composer used this combination as systematically and as successfully. It includes some of his outstanding chamber music compositions.

Apart from the G major *Sonata for harpsichord and viola da gamba* (BWV 1027), there are two more sonatas for the same instrumental combination (BWV 1028, 1029), two *Sonatas for harpsichord and flute* (BWV 1030, 1032), and six *Sonatas for harpsichord and violin* (BWV 1014-19).

Bach's zest for experimenting induced him to employ in these compositions a wealth of different forms and devices. He fused his sonatas with elements of the concerto, using da capo and rondo forms and inserting long solo sections. At times he employed the harpsichord as a mere accompanying instrument, or its upper part as a unison reinforce-

---

1. Cf. the analysis of this work on p. 332.

2. See BWV 1027a, KB to NBA, VI/3, p. 51 f.; and H. Eppstein, 'J. S. B.s Triosonate G-dur (BWV 1039) und ihre Beziehung zur Sonate für Gambe und Cembalo G-dur (BWV 1027),' *Musikforschung*, vol. 18, 1965, pp. 126-37.

3. The three voices of the flute trio were even assigned to a single performer, who could play them on the manuals and pedal of an organ (BWV 1027a).

4. Cf. A. Schering, 'Zur Geschichte der Solosonate in der 1. Hälfte des 17. Jahrhunderts,' in *Riemann Festschrift*, 1909.

ment of the melody. At other times the clavier was given the leading voice while the melody instrument accompanied; Bach even wrote a movement for cembalo solo without violin (BWV 1019/3).[1] Bach did not confine himself to the conventional three parts; occasionally he used four, five, or even six voices, double stops in either instrument, arpeggios, and full chords. There are movements in canonic (BWV 1015/3) or ostinato (BWV 1016/3) forms, and pieces of a prelude-like character (BWV 1018/3). The number of movements in individual sonatas also varies. Four movements (slow-fast-slow-fast) predominate; but compositions in three (BWV 1029, 1032) and five movements (BWV 1019) also occur.

The variety of technical devices is matched by an abundance of different moods. There are pieces that are happy and gay, energetic, stubborn, tender, melancholy, or tragic in character. To emphasize the wide range of feeling, individual movements are given such unorthodox headings as 'Cantabile, ma un poco Adagio' (BWV 1019a), 'Largo e dolce' (BWV 1030).

It seems that these eleven sonatas originated in the Cöthen years, but some of them were later revised in Leipzig, where Bach may have performed them in his 'Collegium' concerts. The composer apparently wrote the viola da gamba sonatas for Prince Leopold of Anhalt-Cöthen, who liked to play the instrument, or for Christian Ferdinand Abel, the eminent virtuoso. The delicate, silvery tone of the cello-like instrument was particularly well suited to blend with the sound of the harpsichord. In the G major Sonata (BWV 1027) the character of the original flute composition seems still to linger. The Andante, with its slowly shifting arpeggios, is gentle and poetical, while the fast movements surrounding it provide a cheerful and energetic contrast. Performance of the G minor Sonata (BWV 1029) requires outstanding technique and we can well imagine Abel and the composer enrapturing an audience with their rendition. For all its brilliance the sonata has a striking intellectual character; in particular the last movement displays intricate elaborations of the thematic material.

The only sonata for cembalo and flute that has been preserved in its entirety (BWV 1030) was also originally conceived in G minor. Later, possibly in the middle 1730's, Bach revised and transposed it to the key

1. See also NBA, VI, vol. 1, p. 204 ff.

of B minor, thus putting the wind instrument part in a more suitable range. An extended Andante in three-part form leads to a brief middle movement related to a noble siciliano. The finale starts with a humorous and brisk three-part fugue. Before reaching its full development, it surprisingly stops on a dominant chord, and a bustling gigue ensues, which is based on a variation of the fugue theme. Thus a light-hearted mood is recaptured at the end of this beautiful work, which Spitta quite rightly called 'the finest flute sonata in existence.'

The Flute Sonata in A major (BWV 1032) has had a rather peculiar fate. When Bach wrote his Concerto for two claviers and strings in C minor (BWV 1062), he found that the score did not quite fill the sheets of his manuscript paper. At the bottom of each page three lines remained empty, and the thrifty composer felt that a sonata for harpsichord and flute was tailor-made to fill the unused space. Unfortunately the bottom of sheets 9-14 was later cut off, resulting in a gap of close to fifty measures in the first movement.[1] As no other source for the work could be found, the loss seems irretrievable. The gently singing second movement and the spirited, dance-like finale in broadly contoured three-part form make it appear particularly regrettable that we know the sonata only as a torso.

Within the works of this group the violin compositions are once more the leading ones. Forkel praised them enthusiastically: 'They may be reckoned among Bach's supreme achievements in this field. . . . The violin part requires a master. Bach knew the possibilities of that instrument and spared it as little as he did his clavier.' On the other hand it testifies to the great interest Bach felt for these compositions that one sonata has been preserved in two and another even in three versions.[2] In the Adagio of the fifth Sonata (BWV 1018) the motion of the accompanying harpsichord was increased from sixteenth to thirty-second notes. The result was a composition of an almost impressionistic char-

1. Cf. BG, vol. 9, p. xix. The autograph in question disappeared during World War II. The flute sonata in E flat major (BWV 1031), whose authenticity was already questioned by Wilhelm Rust (BG vol. 9, p. xxv), was excluded from the publication of B.'s flute compositions in the NBA.

2. Cf. K. H. Köhler, 'Zur Problematik der Violinsonaten mit obligatem Cembalo,' BJ 1958, p. 114 ff., and H. Eppstein, 'Zur Problematik von J. S. B.s Sonate für Violine und Cembalo G dur (BWV 1019),' Archiv für Musikwissenschaft, XXI, 1964. pp. 217-42.

acter. The first version of the sixth Sonata (BWB 1019) started with a fast movement in G major; three slow pieces followed, and a literal repetition of the first movement concluded the work. Bach may have found this arrangement too monotonous. In a new version one of the slow movements was eliminated, while two new pieces, one a solo for the cembalo, the other a solo for the violin, were inserted. This revision consisted of six movements, the restatement of the initial piece at the end of the composition being maintained. Bach was still not satisfied and undertook a third, particularly radical remodeling of the work. He retained only the first two movements[1] and added three new ones, thus creating an unorthodox but well-proportioned form: fast-slow-fast-slow-fast. A piece for harpsichord solo, different from that in the second version, served as the third movement and thus became the contrasting centerpiece of the composition.

These different sonatas show Bach's eagerness to explore all the possibilities to be derived from the transformation of an antiquated combination into a workable new one. He planted precious seeds for the growth of chamber music, establishing, for the benefit of later generations, one of the most significant and cherished forms of joint music-making.

Bach was greatly concerned with the structure and technique of the *Concerto.* His interest in the *stile concertato,* inspired by Baroque concepts, and, specifically, in the concerto form, had already manifested itself in his early works. At Weimar he was able to study Italian concertos thoroughly while arranging them for the keyboard, but before he came to Cöthen he had no proper incentive to write concertos of his own. When composing such works, he did not simply follow the methods adopted in his models; he imbued the structure developed by the Venetian Antonio Vivaldi with significant new ideas. Bach both clarified and simplified the Italian composer's rondo form of the first movement. He often reinforced its architectural solidity by using the da capo form of the Italian aria or a symmetrical construction in which not

1. Of two of the movements discarded from the second version, the cembalo solo became the Courante, the violin solo the Gavotte in the Clavier Partita No. VI (BWV 830).

only the first and last sections correspond, but a certain connection is established between the second part and the one next to the last. The slow middle movements are less intricate. They usually employ a lighter and thinner orchestration; often they are built on a widely spun-out cantilena or on a few motives. Ostinato figures occur frequently in the bass. In the finales Bach favors a combination of concerto and fugue forms. Here the tutti often correspond to the entrances of the subject, the solos to the episodes. All concerto movements by Bach are distinguished by most careful elaboration. Even in homophonic movements Bach tends to have the figurations of the solo instrument accompanied by thematic ideas (*Ex. 63*) rather than by the simple chords customary in Vivaldi's works.

Ex. 63. *Brandenburg Concerto* No. IV, First movement

In order to understand the nature of Bach's concertos, we should remember that the Baroque concerto, unlike the concerto of a later period, is not necessarily meant as a vehicle to display the soloist's virtuosity. The composer explores the interplay between various sound elements, the tutti and one or more solo instruments. Although technical brilliance is not lacking in Bach's concertos, it is often avoided, as it might disturb the subtle balance in the game of contrasting effects. Actually some of Bach's chamber music pieces offer greater technical difficulties than the solo parts in certain concertos.

It seems strange that only two *concertos for violin solo and string orchestra* and one *concerto for two violins and string orchestra,* all three probably written in Cöthen, should be preserved, while there exist considerably more transcriptions of such works for solo harpsichord and strings (cf. p. 322 ff). Did Bach discard some of the original compositions as soon as the arrangements were completed? Did these models only exist in his imagination and were never put to paper; or were some violin concertos lost after his death, possibly through the negligence of his eldest son, Wilhelm Friedemann? These questions probably will never be answered. Anyway, judging from the transcriptions extant, we may safely say that the three works preserved must have been among the very best Bach wrote in this field.

The first movement of the Violin Concerto in E major (BWV 1042), written in da capo form, displays Bach's mastery in handling the concertato style. The solo instrument and the accompanying orchestra confront each other or join forces in a most effective manner. At the very beginning of the solo section Bach introduces, in a kind of stretto, the first and second tutti measures simultaneously, and moreover implies in the bass an imitation of the triadic theme (*Ex. 64*). In

Ex. 64. Violin Concerto in E major

Violino solo

Violino I, Ripieno

Basso

this movement the three notes of the major chord assume almost the character of a germ motive. They serve as a firm basis for the rich ornamentation of the solo instrument. Similarly the initial movement of the solo Concerto in A minor (BWV 1041) grows with inexorable logic

out of ideas presented in the monumental first ritornel. In the Double
Concerto in D minor (BWV 1043) the first movement starts with a
tutti section in the form of a fugal exposition, which is a feature
unusual at the beginning of a Bach concerto. Apparently this piece is
influenced by Torelli's Violin Concerto No. 8, known to Bach from
an arrangement for organ made by his friend, J. G. Walther.[1]

The slow movements of the solo concertos exhibit recurring bass figures, the serious character of which contrasts more effectively with the
poignant sweetness of the solo violin's utterances. Of equal beauty is
the 'Largo, ma non tanto' in the Double Concerto, one of the most intimate and heart-stirring cantilenas Bach ever wrote. While the orchestra
is used here merely to support the soloists, the finale of the concerto
presents a remarkable instance of the inversion of the traditional relationship between principal instrument and orchestra. The solo violins
are entrusted with broad organistic chords and the melody is supplied
in vigorous unison by the orchestra (Ex. 65). In the last movements of

Ex. 65

the solo concertos the composer progresses along more accepted lines.
The finale of the E major work is gay, almost jubilant, with a decisive
leaning toward a dance character. In the A minor Concerto a quieter,
more sedate spirit prevails, additional solidity being achieved through
the introduction of fugal elements.[2]

1. Cf. A. Schering, *Geschichte des Instrumentalkonzerts*, Leipzig, 1905.
2. The fragment of a movement from a Violin Concerto in D major preserved in
Bach's own hand (BWV 1045) may have been intended as the instrumental introduction to a church cantata, apparently lost today. The rich orchestration with two
oboes, three trumpets, and timpani startlingly contrasts with the extremely modest
musical invention. It seems unlikely that this pretentious, yet uninspired, piece was
composed by Bach himself.

The six so-called *Brandenburg Concertos*[1] (BWV 1046–51), which Bach dedicated in the spring of 1721 to Christian Ludwig Margrave of Brandenburg (cf. p. 49), are not concertos for a single solo instrument but examples of older forms of concerted music, showing, in the German fashion, a preference for wind instruments. In three of them (Nos. 1, 3, 6) the orchestra is composed of evenly balanced instrumental choirs which toss the themes to and fro among themselves in charming conversation, only occasionally surrendering the lead to a single instrument out of their midst. Such compositions, based upon the old Venetian *canzona,* with its contrasting instrumental choirs, are known as 'orchestra concertos' or 'concerto-symphonies.' There are also three 'concerti grossi' in the set (Nos. 2, 4, 5), in which accompanying string players, the *ripieni,* are confronted by the *concertino,* consisting of three or four solo instruments. Bach likes to single out one of the concertino's members as its protagonist and leader; the part of this solo instrument is usually more brilliant and technically exacting than that of the other soloists. Thus these concerti grossi seem to operate with three groups of instruments. The largest is formed by the ripienists; a smaller second one by the common members of the concertino; and the third one by a single instrument, which makes up by its display of virtuosity for its numerical inferiority.

Even the Bach student who expects the utmost variety in every work of the master, must be amazed at the abundance of changing scenes in these musical gems.

No. 2, which in its perfect proportions seems to be the very prototype of the concerto grosso, employs a concertino of trumpet, recorder,

1. Bach's predilection for the Brandenburg Concertos is demonstrated by the various arrangements he made of specific movements. Especially Concerto I seemed suitable to him for such purposes. Its first movement was adapted as introductory sinfonia to Cantata 52, *Falsche Welt, dir trau ich nicht.* The third movement and the second trio to the minuet were used in Cantata 207, *Vereinigte Zwietracht,* the former appearing as chorus No. 1, the latter as a ritornello after the duet No. 5. In the chorus the orchestration is changed, but the vocal lines follow the instrumental parts almost without deviation. Moreover, the parody of BWV 207, the 'dramma per musica,' *Auf schmetternde Töne* (BWV 207a) employs the concerto's third movement as introductory chorus. Of Concerto III the first movement appears as sinfonia in Cantata 174, *Ich liebe den Höchsten,* with two obbligato horns and three oboes added. — Concerto IV was adapted in its entirety as a Harpsichord Concerto in F major (BWV 1057; cf. p. 325).

oboe, and violin. A particular coloristic appeal is gained by using the brass instrument in the high clarino register; indeed the trumpet is treated in so brilliant a manner that the work at times assumes the character of a solo concerto. Almost excessive demands are made on the player's skill. Without the benefit of valves, not invented until the 19th century, he has to produce fast passages leading up to an incredibly high g''' (two and half octaves above middle c). In the tender, melancholy middle movement, though, he is kept silent, and most of the accompanying strings are omitted as well. The finale again puts the brass instrument in the forefront of musical activity. It sounds the jolly main subject and also concludes the dashing piece. This movement deviates from accepted norms, as the fugue-like passages are entrusted to the four soloists and the continuo, while the ripieni provide the filling parts.

No. 4 is written for a concertino of two recorders and a violin. Here the string instrument assumes a dominant position, greater demands being made on its nimbleness than in any of Bach's concertos for violin solo. A cheerful pastoral character is created in the broadly contoured first movement, which uses the da capo form. The following andante is the only slow movement of the set in which Bach does not reduce the size of his orchestra. A stirring dialogue between concertino and orchestra conjures up the idiom of Bach's great contemporary Handel. After a 'Phrygian cadence'[1] it leads into the finale, a fugue displaying good-natured jocularity. Near the end, at the peak of the contrapuntal motion, Bach three times inserts powerful chords which harmonize the thinly disguised main theme. A last entrance of the subject in the recorders brings the piece to its joyous conclusion.

In No. 5, written for a concertino of flute, violin, and harpsichord, the keyboard instrument dominates; it is even entrusted with an unaccompanied solo cadenza of 65 measures in the initial movement. Here the humble harpsichord, whose role in ensembles had mostly been that of supporting other instruments, assumes the proud part of the leader. Obviously this work was from the outset intended for the harpsichord and must be considered as the first original clavier concerto ever written. Maybe Bach, who played the part himself, was inspired

1. The first inversion of a subdominant chord in the minor mode, followed by a dominant chord in root position.

to compose it by the exquisite harpsichord he had purchased in 1719 for his Prince in Berlin.[1] The buoyant and dramatic first movement is followed by a melancholic 'Affettuoso,' played by the three soloists and continuo. A different mood prevails in the finale which is free of any attempt at introspection. A strong sense of humor prevails in this lightweight piece, which cleverly combines elements of fugue and concerto with the form of the da capo aria, the first 78 measures being literally repeated at the end.[2]

The concerto-symphony No. 1 employs the tiny *violino piccolo* (tuned a minor third above the ordinary violin), together with three oboes, bassoon, two horns, strings, and cembalo. The traditional three movements are followed by a gay Menuet. This is uttered four times, alternating with a Trio, a Polonaise and a second Trio. Each of these dances is steeped in a different coloristic garb. While the Menuet is scored for the full orchestra, the first insertion is entrusted to two oboes and bassoon, the second to the strings, and the third again to wind instruments, which achieve, through the combination of horns and oboes, some droll sound effects. This little group of dances seems meant to provoke applause, like the *licenza* at the end of a comic opera.[3]

The third Concerto introduces three powerful choirs of strings, each subdivided into three parts. A sense of drama pervades the majestic first movement, with its clashing melodic forces and the occasional appearance of somber minor keys. Bach omits a slow movement and inserts in its place two chords of a 'Phrygian cadence,' which allow for a cadenza the performers might improvise. The necessary contrast between the

1. In this score Bach prescribes the transverse flute and not the recorder as he felt the need for a more powerful woodwind instrument to balance the clavier's strong sounds. It is noteworthy that among the ripieni only a single violin is prescribed instead of the customary two. Obviously Bach who usually played one of the string instruments, was not available as he performed on the clavier (Cf. F. Smend, *B. in Köthen*, p. 24).

2. A second Concerto for harpsichord, flute and violin in A minor (BWV 1044) is discussed on p. 266.

3. An earlier version of this Concerto has been preserved, designated as 'Sinfonia' (BWV 1046A = 1071). The *violino piccolo* is not used there, and the third movement and the polonaise of the fourth movement are missing. The Sinfonia assumes the more regular pattern: fast movement—Adagio—Menuet with 2 Trios. (Cf. NBA, vol. VII/2, p. 225 ff., and H. Besseler in KB to NBA, vol. VII/2, p. 37 ff.)

two fast movements is achieved through structural changes. The first movement uses the customary concerto form, the finale the two-part form of contemporary dances.

The most unusual scoring is to be found in No. 6, written for two violas, two viole da gamba, cello, and continuo.[1] One of the gamba parts may have been intended for Prince Leopold, as it offers virtually no technical difficulties. Bach himself most likely played the first viola, since he entrusted it with interesting tasks.[2] The composition's most striking feature is the two-part canon in the tutti-ritornel of the first movement. Here the imitating voice enters after an eighth note rest. Bach's pupil, J. P. Kirnberger, used this in his *Kunst des reinen Satzes* as illustration for counterpoint in its strictest form. It is characteristic of the vitality of Bach's music that the hearer, unaware of the polyphonic intricacies, will yet derive full enjoyment from the piece's brilliance. The Adagio omits the viole da gamba. The violas utter the main melody, and their expressive cantilena evokes a mood of deep nostalgia. The energetic finale, however, restores the initial spirit. It is imbued with an optimistic mood and driven by irresistible rhythmic forces.

The Brandenburg Concertos seem to embody the splendor and effervescence of court life at Cöthen, and, moreover, they reveal the composer's delight in writing for a group of highly trained instrumentalists. There is an exuberance and abundance of inspiration in this music which only a genius, aware of his newly achieved full mastery, could call forth. Craftsmanship and richly flowing melodic invention, logic and zest for experimenting, counterpoise each other here to an extent rarely equaled again even by Bach himself.

Several *Concertos for harpsichord and string orchestra* (BWV 1052-58) originated during the Leipzig years. At that time Bach felt a pressing need for clavieristic material, as he and his sons required effective compositions for their appearances in the Collegium Musicum. To produce such works the composer resorted to a method he had used while writing his sonatas for a melody instrument and clavier obbligato. He gave the solo part of a previously composed violin con-

---

1. Stress on the numbers 3 and 6 respectively in the instrumentation of the third and sixth concertos may be due to Bach's predilection for number symbolism.
2. Cf. KB to NBA VII/2, p. 21.

certo to the right hand of the keyboard player, whose left hand reinforced or paraphrased the bass of the composition. In this manner a violin concerto was transformed into a clavier concerto, while the harpsichordist, who had previously served as a continuo player, was promoted to the rank of principal performer. This role he often combined with part of his former duties, by solidifying the composition's texture, particularly in the tutti sections. Occasionally the responsibilities were divided; one harpsichordist appeared as soloist, while a second one elaborated the continuo part.

Although more than half of the models Bach used for these arrangements can no longer be traced, it is possible to reconstruct the method he employed in these transcriptions. In many instances the pitch of the original composition was transposed one tone down, since the claviers in Bach's time as a rule went up to d''' and did not have e''', the traditional top note of the violin concertos.[1] The composer wrote and rewrote the same arrangement several times, and in the course of this process his language became increasingly idiomatic. A good example is offered by the Clavier Concerto in D minor (BWV 1052), which the edition of the BG presents in different stages of its development.[2] An early version of the clavier part[3] displays obvious violinistic features. But it may well be that there was even an earlier setting than the one for violin. Some of the arpeggios in the first movement, as well as double stops in fourths, seem to indicate that the Concerto was conceived for a bowed instrument with seven strings, tuned partly in fourths, like the viola d'amore. Later it may have been changed to a violin concerto, and this, in turn, to a harpsichord concerto. Even then the transformation went on, and certain sections of the keyboard part were rewritten three times.[4] How significant these changes were can

1. Cf. Howard Shanet, 'Why Did J. S. B. Transpose His Arrangements?', *MQ*, 1950.

2. BG, vol. 17, pp. 3-42 and 275-313. Cf. also U. Siegele, *Kompositionsweise*.

3. The first two movements of this version were also used in Cantata 146, whereby the harpsichord part was entrusted to the organ. In the cantata's introduction two oboes and English horn were added, and so was a vocal quartet in the first chorus. Apparently Bach also intended to use the concerto as introduction to Cantata 188.

4. Cf. BG, vol. 17, p. xvi ff. and xxii; A. Aber in *BJ* 1913, p. 5 ff.; P. Hirsch in *BJ* 1929, p. 153 ff., and in *BJ* 1930, p. 143 ff. It has been questioned whether the Thomas Cantor was the author of this fascinating composition. Quite rightly H.

be seen in some measures from the finale presented in two versions. (*Ex. 66*)

Ex. 66. *BWV* 1052

The larger notes are found in an early version; in a later arrangement Bach added the notes reproduced in smaller type.

The composition is well worth the extreme effort Bach expended on it. A demonic first movement driven by irresistible forces is followed by a poignant Adagio, in which the tender cantilena of the keyboard instrument is supported by a majestic ostinato. The lively and high-spirited dance of the finale, played in the brisk tempo Bach is reported to have used for such movements, must have excited the sedate burghers.

Apparently the Concertos in E major (BWV 1053) and in F minor (BWV 1056)[1] are likewise transcriptions of violin concertos. Accordingly successful reconstructions were carried out of the Violin Concerto in G minor which may have served as a model for BWV 1056.[2] The performance of the two clavier works is highly gratifying both to players and listeners. In particular the melodious Siciliano of the E major Concerto and the serenade-like Largo of the F minor Concerto have

---

Keller exclaims, however: 'Who, but Bach, could have composed such a concerto!' (Cf. *Die Klavierwerke B.s*, p. 257).

1. Material from these concertos was also used in Bach's church cantatas. The first movement of BWV 1053 appears as introduction to Cantata 169. Here the solo is given to the organ, and three oboes are added to the score. The second movement was employed with an added vocal part for an aria in the same cantata, while the last movement, with added oboe d'amore, made up the introductory sinfonia in Cantata 49. The second movement of BWV 1056 appears in the introduction to Cantata 156. Obviously the lost violin concerto served here as Bach's model. No organ solo is to be found in this score and the cantilena is entrusted to a melody instrument, the oboe.

2. G. Schreck arranged it for C. F. Peters, Leipzig; Jackson and Whittaker for Oxford University Press, London.

great warmth and beauty. The finale of the latter work assumes a mischievous character through its numerous echo effects.

Only the first nine measures of Bach's score have been preserved of a second Harpsichord Concerto in D minor (BWV 1059), which seems also to have grown out of a violin concerto. Nevertheless this work need not be considered as lost. The composer used all three movements in his Cantata 35 so that the substance of the highly attractive composition is known to us.[1]

The Concerto in A major (BWV 1055) is the only work of this group whose harpsichord part is comparatively free of violinistic features. Moreover a separate part for the thorough bass has been preserved in the original orchestral material. It indicates that Bach wanted to free the solo harpsichord from its secondary function as filling continuo instrument and to entrust a second clavier with this task. It may well be that Bach conceived this work originally for the harpsichord, as he had done in the fifth Brandenburg Concerto.[2] The gay and playful character of the initial allegro is emphasized by the indication 'spiccato' (with a bouncing bow) at the beginning of the string parts. The following Larghetto in F sharp minor, with its noble dialogue between the strings and harpsichord, seems to conjure up the atmosphere of a Greek drama. The humorous finale restores the mood of the beginning. So infectious is its gaiety that the composer even feels the need to restrain the performers somewhat by the indication 'allegro ma non tanto' (joyful, but within reason).

The Concertos in D major, in G minor, and in F major (BWV 1054, 1058, 1057) are derived from the violin concertos in E major and A minor and from the fourth Brandenburg Concerto. Those based on the violin works do not quite reach the high level of the models and accordingly are but rarely performed. More successful is the adaptation of the fourth Brandenburg Concerto (BWV 1057), incidentally, Bach's only clavier concerto to use two recorders in the accompaniment.

1. The concerto formed the basis of Nos. 1, 2, and 5 in Cantata No. 35. In the usual manner the harpsichord solo was entrusted to the organ. To the instrumental composition's orchestra of strings and oboe, the cantata added a second oboe, an English horn and, in No. 2, a contralto voice. (Cf. p. 171, fn. 4.)

2. On the other hand an attempt was also made to reconstruct an 'original version' of the concerto. In 1958 it was performed at Warburg, Germany, in a version for oboe d'amore and orchestra. (Cf. *Freie Presse*, Bielefeld, December 15, 1958.)

Bach did not confine himself to writing concertos for a single solo harpsichord but also composed concertos for two, three, and four solo claviers accompanied by string orchestra. Maybe he did so partly in order to have pieces he could perform together with his brilliant sons.

These works seem once again to be derived from earlier versions. Among the *Concertos for two harpsichords and string orchestra* one, in C minor, (BWV 1062), is based on Sebastian's own Concerto for two violins in D minor. A second C minor Concerto (BWV 1060) is probably the transcription of a concerto for oboe and violin, no longer in existence. In these two concertos the orchestra fully shares in the musical elaboration, and attractive dialogues unfold between keyboard instruments and strings. The soloists are not always given leading parts; frequently one or both of them fulfill the cembalo's original task of serving as filling and reinforcing continuo instrument. Often the left hand of one of the two clavierists is entrusted with a middle part, and so the musical texture is enriched.

The Concerto in C major (BWV 1061) is somewhat different, for it appears to be an original clavier composition. Its two keyboard parts exist in autograph, while the string parts, which mainly provide reinforcement, are not preserved in Bach's own writing. Thus it seems quite likely that the orchestration was a later addition, and that the work was originally written for two harpsichords only. In the middle movement, an 'Adagio ovvero Largo' in the character of a siciliano, the accompanying strings keep altogether silent. In the finale too they participate only briefly. This is a fugue which is clearly divided into four sections. Each of them starts with an extensive solo of the claviers and reaches a climax near its end through the entrance of the reinforcing orchestral instruments. It might be mentioned that there also exist in Sebastian's hand the parts to a *Concerto a duoi cembali concertati* without any accompaniment, which his son Friedemann composed at an early age, possibly under the influence of BWV 1061.[1]

All the concertos for three and four claviers and string orchestra[2]

1. Cf. BWV Anh. 188. Friedemann's composition was erroneously printed as a work of his father in BG, 43/1, p. 47.

2. Cf. H. Boas in BJ 1913, p. 31 ff., and M. Krause in *Die Musik-Woche*, Leipzig, 1902, No. 20.

seem to be arrangements, and it is doubtful whether Bach wrote the original compositions.[1] The C major Concerto for three claviers (BWV 1064) is probably based on a Concerto for three violins, while the D minor Concerto for three claviers (BWV 1063) might be derived from a Concerto for flute, violin, and oboe. The Concerto for four harpsichords in A minor (BWV 1065) is the only work whose antecedence is clear. Bach arranged it from Vivaldi's Concerto in B minor for four violins and strings. The work appears as No. 10 in Vivaldi's op. 3, a set of twelve concertos, among which Bach had previously arranged three works for harpsichord alone and two for organ alone.

In the D minor Concerto the claviers prevail, and the first harpsichord, which was probably played by Sebastian, is given preferential treatment. The strings are relegated to a role of lesser significance. The mood of the concerto is weirdly serious and imbued with tremendous energy. Even the 'Alla Siciliana' of the middle movement fails to convey the traditional tenderness and breathes a stern spirit. Greater independence is granted to the orchestra in the C major Concerto,[2] which accords no special favor to the first harpsichordist. This is a majestic and forceful work of great dignity. If Bach was not its author, he must at least have contributed a great deal to the definite shaping of the brilliant composition. The Vivaldi Concerto, on the other hand, did not offer a particularly inspired model. Bach may have chosen it because he was tempted by the technical problem of operating with four keyboard instruments. The opportunity it presented to collaborate with three of his pupils may also have offered a strong inducement. The arrangement is colorful and done with the thoroughness and skill of the master. But unfortunately Bach remained too faithful to Vivaldi's work, and failed to impart the significant improvements we admire in his other arrangements. His most extensive clavier concerto is by no means the best.

By and large Bach's harpsichord concertos are more significant from

1. The authenticity of the arrangements for three claviers has likewise been questioned (cf. J. Schreyer, II, p. 39 ff.), but the arguments proffered do not seem fully convincing.

2. Several, apparently later, sources present the work in the key of D major also. Cf. BG, vol. 31, p. vi.

a historical than from an aesthetic point of view. The composer did pioneer work in this field. He created the form, thus blazing a trail for the pianoforte concerto of later generations.

Bach's *four Overtures or Suites for Orchestra* (BWV 1066-69) have features which link them to his concertos. No. 1 repeatedly assumes the character of a concerto grosso, No. 2 that of a solo concerto, while No. 3 and No. 4 reveal certain features of orchestral concertos. They were designated as overtures on account of their initial movement. Each work starts with a stately introduction employing dotted rhythms. There follows a section using fugal elements, while the conclusion again displays a solemn mood. This extended movement forms the first half of the composition. The second half, the suite proper, consists of a free sequence of dances and character-pieces with French titles. Despite the foreign elements introduced here, these four works are true products of the German soil, inspired by the folklore of the country. The decisive contrast between the more elaborate and extensive introduction and the concise dances enhances their appeal.

So far it has not been possible to ascertain with any degree of certitude when these works were written. No. 1, which seems less advanced than the rest, might be an earlier composition. Autograph parts of No. 2 written after 1735 have been preserved. They may have been intended for the excellent Dresden flutist Buffardin; but there is no proof that Bach composed the work at this late date; he may well have copied a Cöthen manuscript. The three trumpets prescribed in the scores of No. 3 and No. 4 exceeded the orchestral resources at the Cöthen court. On the other hand the overture of No. 4 was also used for the initial chorus of Cantata 110, first performed in 1725. This might indicate that this work, and possibly also the closely related No. 3, belong to the early Leipzig years.[1] We can well imagine that Bach played these four cheerful works with his Collegium Musicum.

No. 1 in C major is scored for a trio of two oboes and bassoon, in addition to strings and continuo. Passages in concertato style, played by

1. Cf. A. Dürr in *BJ* 1957, p. 83 ff., G. v. Dadelsen, p. 113, and M. Bernstein in Report of the 8th Congress of the IMS, New York, 1961, vol. II, p. 127 ff. Bernstein suggests also that No. 1 might not be a work of Bach, but rather a suite by J. F. Fasch, who is represented with several works in the Leipzig Thomas School.

the three wind instruments, may be found throughout the composition, in particular in the middle section of the Overture and in the second Bourrée which is exclusively entrusted to them. The chain of dances is longer here than in the other suites. It includes the lively Forlane, a dance of northern Italy, popular with opera composers of the Baroque period. Two high-spirited Passepieds make for an unconventional ending.

No. 2 in B minor is the most intimate of the suites. It is scored for flute, strings, and continuo only. Dispersed throughout the suite are tutti numbers in which the flute doubles the part of violin I. These important sections, which provide solidity to the work's structure, include the piquant Rondeau, displaying the character of a gavotte, and the following Sarabande, introducing a canon of the twelfth between melody and bass line, a tour de force Bach but rarely attempted. The gems of the score are, however, the effervescent solos in Bach's favorite flute key of B minor. Dashing, truly idiomatic flute passages can be found in the fugal episodes of the overture. There is, moreover, the Double, where scintillating arabesques are woven around the Polonaise's melody, and, most of all, the impudent 'Badinerie' (banter), which provides the flutist with supreme opportunities for displaying virtuosity. No doubt this movement ranks among the most captivating showpieces written for the woodwind instrument.

Suites No. 3 and 4 are in the same key of D major, and scored for nearly the same group of instruments. They both use two oboes, three trumpets, timpani, strings, and continuo; No. 4 adds to this orchestration a third oboe and a bassoon. When young Mendelssohn played the magnificent initial number of No. 3 on the piano to Goethe in May 1830, the aged poet remarked: 'There is such pomp and ceremony here that one can actually see a procession of elegantly dressed people descending a vast flight of stairs.'[1] For the introductory movement to No. 4, Bach himself seems to have provided a program. He used this Overture for the initial chorus of his Christmas Cantata 110, based on Psalm 126, v.2: 'Then was our mouth filled with laughter and our tongue with singing.' It does not require too much imagination to detect ripples of laughter in the fugal middle section of this joyous piece.

1. See F. Mendelssohn, *Reisebriefe aus den Jahren 1830-32*, 8th ed., Leipzig, 1869, p. 17.

The best-known movement in the two compositions is the lofty Air from No. 3; but it is regrettable that this poignant cantilena owes its reputation to an arrangement of questionable value.[1] An earthy sense of humor prevails in the two Gavottes following the Air, and a turbulent Gigue serves as the finale. In No. 4 a character piece, with the French heading 'Réjouissance' (rejoicing), appears as the last number. The same title might well be used for this whole group of suites, in which Bach never overwhelms us with his stupendous mastery, but captivates us with wit, grace, and charm.

In his last period of composition Bach created only two ensemble works, but they are among the greatest he ever wrote.

The *Musicalisches Opfer* (Musical Offering; BWV 1079) belongs to the series of contrapuntal variations the composer concentrated on during the later part of his life. This time the basis of the variations is the theme which Frederick the Great offered Bach for elaboration on the latter's visit to the palace at Potsdam.[2] Bach felt that he had by no means exhausted all the possibilities of the royal theme (hereafter abbreviated r.t.) in his improvisations before the king. He therefore worked on it after his return to Leipzig, and the result seemed so satisfying to him that he had the whole cycle engraved. Composition and production must have proceeded very rapidly, since the dedication to the king is dated July 7, 1747, just two months following the actual visit. Apparently the composer wanted to send his 'Offering' while his host's memory of the visit was still fresh.

The great speed of the production may have been partly responsible for the disconnected form of the original publication. It consists of four separate sections, two of which are engraved in oblong size and two in upright form. Bach may have neglected to give precise instructions to J. G. Schübler, who engraved the work for him. Thus Schübler followed the practice of the time, using the oblong size for pieces he considered keyboard music and the upright one for the chamber music, including the bulk of the canons. Three canons that could not

1. A. Wilhelmj rewrote the Air in 1871 for the violin G string, and it has been a favorite encore with violin virtuosos.

2. It seems unlikely that Bach changed the idea given to him by the king, as H. Keller suggests (*Musica*, 1950). Such an action would have annoyed the king, who was a good enough musician to remember what theme he had given Bach.

be fitted in were squeezed into the oblong sheets.[1] The confusing arrangement made it difficult to comprehend the architecture of the work —particularly since the autograph of the 'Musical Offering' is lost.[2] Indeed, so outstanding an expert as Philipp Spitta described this composition as a 'strange conglomerate of pieces, wanting not only internal connection but external uniformity.'[3] It seems hardly possible to recognize the structure of the work from the order in which the numbers appear in the first publication.[4] Clarification can be achieved only by a thorough investigation of the music.[5]

The ten canons of the 'Musical Offering' clearly fall into two groups. Five of them (Nos. 2, 3b-e) are two-part canons, to which, in a third voice, a variation of the r.t. is added as a cantus firmus. Five others (Nos. 3a, 4, 6, 7, 9) use variations of the r.t. in canonic elaboration. There are also two Ricercars (fugues) based on the r.t., one in three parts and one in six parts, and, as the most extensive piece, a Trio Sonata for flute, violin and figured bass. Written in the traditional four movements, this 'church sonata' introduces a fugue into its first fast movement in which the r.t. appears as a kind of cantus firmus, while a fugue in the second fast movement employs the r.t. as its subject. This suggests a symmetrical arrangement of the thirteen pieces, with the three-part Ricercar at the beginning, the six-part Ricercar at the end. The Sonata would be located in the center, while the five canons with

1. One oblong section contains the three-part Ricercar and the three-part canon at the double octave (Nos. 1, 2); the other the six-part Ricercar, the two-part canon by inversion and the four-part canon (Nos. 5-7). One of the upright sections presents six canons (Nos. 3a-e, and 4); the other the Trio Sonata and the 'Mirror' Canon (Nos. 8, 9). The numbers used here in parentheses are those of the BWV list.

2. Only one of the thirteen pieces is preserved. C. P. E. Bach retained a holograph of the six-part Ricercar, but this version is not identical with that of the print.

3. II, p. 676.

4. Attempts to offer internal reasons for the arrangement in the original print made by A. Orel (*Die Musik*, 1937-38, p. 82 ff; 165 ff), H. Husmann (*BJ* 1938, p. 56 ff.) and E. Schenk (*Anzeiger der philosophisch-historischen Klasse der österreichischen Akademie der Wissenschaften*, Jg. 1953, No. 3, p. 51 ff.) are not fully convincing.

5. H. T. David (new edition of the work and booklet accompanying it, published by G. Schirmer, New York, 1945), R. Gerber (*Das Musikleben*, I, 1948, p. 65 ff.), and W. Pfannkuch (*Die Musikforschung*, VII, 1954, p. 440 ff.) have tried to reconstruct the form Bach wanted to give to the 'Musical Offering.' Among these David's theory seems most convincing.

the r.t. as cantus firmus precede it and the five canons elaborating the r.t. follow it. The resulting structure corresponds to the form of countless other Bach works:

RICERCAR	5 CANONS	TRIO SONATA	TRIO SONATA	5 CANONS	RICERCAR
three-part fugue based on r.t.	in three voices, using the r.t. as cantus firmus	Fugue No. 1, introducing r.t. as cantus firmus	Fugue No. 2, using r.t. as fugue subject	subjecting r.t. to canonic elaboration	six-part fugue based on r.t.

Example 67 illustrates the manner of variation Bach employed in different numbers.

Ex. 67. *Musical Offering,* Theme and two variations

The first and the last Ricercars lend themselves to performance on keyboard instruments.[1] They are directly connected with the visit to

1. The original edition has the three-part Ricercar on two staves, the six-part Ricercar in open score. The latter can also be performed without difficulty by a single clavierist, and the autograph which belonged to C. P. E. Bach presents it on two

Potsdam, when Bach improvised on one of the king's claviers a three-part fugue based on the r.t., but evaded the suggestion of employing the same subject in a six-part fugue. The six-part composition which the master played in Potsdam was on a theme of his own choice, and the respective elaboration of the r.t. was carried out after his return. Accordingly the two Ricercars are quite different in character. The first lacks the supreme logic and perfect balance of the last; it obviously represents Bach's improvisation and may be taken as an example of his extemporizing in strict forms. The six-part Ricercar, on the other hand, ranks as one of the most magnificent fugues Bach ever wrote. This is a large-sized work whose profundity of thought, magnificent poise, and loftiness of sound make it one of the sublime monuments of polyphonic music.

While in these two pieces preference is shown for the clavier, the remaining eleven compositions are obviously intended for chamber music combinations. The Trio Sonata and one of the canons (No. 9) expressly prescribe flute, violin, and figured bass; a canon with imitation in unison (No. 3b) calls for two violins and bass. For the remainder of the pieces no instrumentation is indicated, but string instruments and flute are logical choices for their execution.

The ten canons are predominantly retrospective in character. In his untiring quest for new solutions of formal problems, the composer investigated here some types of canon he had bypassed in the 'Goldberg' and in the 'Canonic' Variations. Their presentation in the printed edition tests the ingenuity of the performers. As a rule the canons are not printed in full score, and Bach uses special hints to indicate his intentions. Two clefs are often used in immediate succession to indicate the interval of imitation. One of them may stand on its head to signify melodic inversion. If the clef is placed at the end of the composition, this means retrograde motion. Usually the place is indicated where the imitating voice is to come in. If such an instruction is missing the performer has a substantial problem to solve. At No. 6 the original edition remarks rather provocatively 'quaerendo invenietis' (if you seek, you will find).

In each of these ten canons Bach sets himself a different task. The

___

staves. However, other media of performance should not be excluded. H. Keller transcribed the six-part Ricercar for organ, E. Fischer for string orchestra, A. Webern for full orchestra.

canons with the r.t. in a separate cantus firmus are all in three parts. In one of them (No. 2) the r.t. is surrounded by imitative voices, in another (No. 3b) the melody lies in the bass, while two soprano voices pursue each other. A canon 'per motum contrarium' (No. 3c) introduces the inversion of the imitating voice, each step upward being answered by a simple step downward and vice versa. Even more complicated is the canon 'per augmentationem, contrario motu' (No. 3d), in which the imitative voice appears in inversion and in notes of doubled value as well. A spiral canon (No. 3e), designated shortly after Bach's death as 'canon per tonos' (canon through the keys), modulates in its eight measures one whole tone up. This peculiar piece, which belongs to a very rarely used type of composition, has to be performed six times before all the parts return to the original key of C minor.

The canons transforming the r.t. into imitative voices show even greater variety. One of the pieces in two voices (No. 3a) is a 'crab canon,' in which the imitating voice proceeds backward, starting with the last note and ending with the first. In another two-part composition, a canon by inversion (No. 6), Bach leaves it to the ingenuity of the performer to ascertain where the second voice is to come in. Actually more than one solution of the problem is possible.[1] In the original print the only four-part canon of the set (No. 7) follows this two-part composition.[2] Here too Bach neglected to indicate where the imitative voices are to set in, and it requires some effort to realize that the successive entrances appear at intervals of seven measures each. On the other hand, one canon was completely resolved in the first edition. The so-called 'mirror canon' (No. 9) uses a freely invented figured bass to accompany two canonic voices proceeding in inversion. As Bach twice changed the interval at which the imitative voice sets in, an abbreviated notation was inappropriate for this piece. Particularly ingenious is the 'Fuga canonica in epidiapente' (No. 4). Two voices imitating each other at the interval of a fifth are accompanied by an initially

1. BG, vol. 31/2, p. 49 ff., presents the piece in four different versions.

2. This is also the only piece in the set which does not appear in the key of C used for all the other pieces. However, David (p. 176 ff.) convincingly stated that the four-part canon was likewise meant to be performed in the basic key. The abbreviated notation of the original, presenting four voices in a single line, suggested the transposition to avoid the additional use of awkward leger lines.

independent bass. Fugal and canonic elements are here significantly combined, and a climax is reached when the bass triumphantly intones the r.t., thus enriching the contrapuntal web with the entrance of a third thematic voice.

The learned character of the 'Musical Offering' also shows itself in some additional Latin entries made into the copy Bach sent to Potsdam. On the first page was an acrostic, the initial letters of each word forming the word 'ricercar': *Regis Iussu Cantio Et Reliqua Canonica Arte Resoluta* (according to the order of the King the tune and the remainder are resolved with canonic art). To the canon in augmentation was written: *Notulis crescentibus crescat Fortuna Regis* (may the fortune of the King grow with the length of the notes), and likewise the spiral canon bears the annotation: *Ascendenteque Modulatione ascendat Gloria Regis* (and may the Glory of the King rise with the rising modulation).

In the 'Musical Offering' the contrapuntal complications and the puzzle canons of earlier centuries are resurrected. Likewise the frequent omission of any indication regarding the instruments to be used reminds us of much older music. It would be wrong, however, to consider the work as merely an attempt to revive ancient tenets of musical learning. The solid harmonic foundation of these contrapuntal gems, the peculiar character of the modulating spiral canon, and, most of all, the content of the Sonata prove that the work's foundation is in 18th-century music. This beautiful Trio for flute, violin and continuo, which forms the centerpiece of the set, is a composition of great dignity and beauty, one of the outstanding works of its kind written by Bach.

By and large the 'Musical Offering' appears as a creation in which the composer attempts to fuse past and present. It succeeds in drawing in compact and monumental form a synthesis of musical thought from the Middle Ages to Bach's own time.

At this point it seems appropriate to discuss individual *Canons*[1] that were not included in larger sets. Only a handful of such pieces is

---

1. Among the various analyses of B.'s canons the following might be singled out: A. Dörffel in BG, vol. 45, p. xliiff.; Spitta, I, p. 386, II, pp. 478, 506, 708, 717; F. Smend, *J. S. B. Kirchenkantaten*, III, p. 9 ff., F. Smend, *J. S. B. bei seinem Namen gerufen*, Kassel, 1950, p. 11ff.

known, all written for special occasions, and usually quite intimate in character. Some of them offer puzzles that are extremely difficult to solve, and, at times, the composer resorts to non-musical devices, such as the use of an acrostichon, or of number symbolism, to convey a secret message. While most of the classical canons are vocal compositions whose texts clearly express the composer's intentions, Bach amused himself in producing instrumental pieces which forced the interpreter to expend considerable skill and energy to discover their hidden meaning. They illuminate the composer's peculiar brand of highly sophisticated humor.

A four-part canon (BWV 1073) written 1713 in Weimar was probably intended for Bach's friend and kinsman, J. G. Walther. Although the piece is written in a single line, Bach gives the necessary instructions, and offers a canon whose realization seems hardly difficult. There is, however, a hidden meaning to the composition, as Smend pointed out. The entrances of the canon's four successive voices are on c, g, d', a'; written out in full score it has a length of 14 measures, while each of the voices comprises 82 notes. According to the number alphabet 14 represents Bach; 41, the retrograde version of 14, J. S. Bach, and 82 Walther ($\underset{\text{W}}{21}+\underset{\text{A}}{1}+\underset{\text{L}}{11}+\underset{\text{T}}{19}+\underset{\text{H}}{8}+\underset{\text{E}}{5}+\underset{\text{R}}{17} = 82$); c, g, d', a' are the open strings of the viola, the instrument which Bach usually played in the orchestra. Thus the composer referred to himself both in notes and with the help of the number alphabet. Walther is also introduced through a number, and the composer makes an elegant tribute to him by implying that Walther (82) is twice as much as J. S. Bach (41).

The difficulties in a four-part puzzle canon (BWV 1074) which Bach wrote in 1727 for his Hamburg friend, L. F. Hudemann, are of a purely musical nature. The composer indicated in his notation the intervals of imitation; he failed, however, to state where the individual voices had to come in, thus leaving a tidy problem to the ingenuity of the performer. The little piece intrigued Bach's contemporaries, and no lesser artists than Telemann, Mattheson, and Marpurg worked on it, proudly presenting the solution in their own publications.[1]

---

1. Telemann, *Der getreue Musik-Meister*, 1728; Mattheson, *Der vollkommene Capellmeister*, 1739; Marpurg, *Abhandlung von der Fuge*, 1753. The solution was also offered by L. Mizler in *Neu eröffnete musikalische Bibliothek*, part 3, 1747.

The best-known piece of the group is the six-part puzzle canon (BWV 1076) Bach wrote in 1747 when he considered joining the Mizler *Societät*. In the portrait by E. G. Haussmann, painted in the same year, he is seen with the manuscript of the little composition in his hand. The sheet is held in such a way that the notes can be easily read, as if Bach wanted to challenge the spectator to solve the riddle.

This, however, is by no means easy. Bach presents three voices, each of which is to be imitated canonically by another voice. But the composer neglects to indicate the interval or the nature of the imitation (augmented, diminished, inverted); nor does he reveal the places where the new voices are to come in. Thus it took more than a century before the enigma was solved.[1] The composer wanted the imitating voices to enter with unchanged note values, but in inverted form, after one measure.

Bach was willing to join the *Societät* after he learned that Handel had done so. He liked the idea of this connection with his great contemporary, and thus he included subtle references to the highly esteemed artist in his work. The bass of the canon is borrowed from a chaconne by Handel.[2] The composition's first measure contains eight notes, and the whole piece, including the imitations, sixty notes. A person conversant with the number-alphabet would not find it difficult to discover the hidden meaning. Apparently 8 stands for the first letter of Handel (8 = H) and 60 for his full name[3]

$$\begin{matrix} G & F & H & A & E & N & D & E & L \\ (7 & +6 & +8 & +1 & +5 & +13 & +4 & +5 & +11 = 60).^4 \end{matrix}$$

Bach's last canon (BWV 1078) was written in 1749. It is a composition in seven parts in which six imitative voices proceed over a constantly repeated ground bass. No problems face the performer here, but the names of both the composer and the person to whom it is dedicated are missing from the manuscript. They have to be guessed from indirect hints.

1. In C. L. Hilgenfeldt, *J. S. B.s Leben, Wirken und Werke.* Leipzig, 1850.
2. Bach used it also in a second canon (BWV 1077) written in 1747.
3. For an additional example of Bach's use of number symbolism in connection with his membership in Mizler's *Societät*, see p. 94.
4. In German, Handel's name is spelled as Händel, with an umlaut on the letter 'a'. When using capitals, it is customary to transcribe an umlaut as ae.

The ground bass is committed to paper in musical notation as well as in letters (*Ex.* 68). This seems to refer to the name 'Faber' and the

assumption is confirmed by a Latin acrostic which Bach wrote at the end of the composition. It reads:

> Domine Possessor
> Fidelis Amici Beatum Esse Recordari
> tibi haud ignotum: itaque
> Bonae Artis Cultorem Habeas
> Lipsiae d. 1 Martii 1749   verum amIcum Tuum[1]

The second line of the acrostic also emphasizes the name 'Faber,' the fourth, 'Bach.' The letters I and T singled out in the last line are, as Spitta has already pointed out,[2] to be interpreted as abbreviations of 'Isenaco Thuringum,' a reference to Bach's native city Eisenach in Thuringia.

We know of no friend of Bach's by the name of Faber. However, Faber is also the Latinized form of the very common German name Schmidt. The composer was in contact with several men of this name, and the canon might, for instance, have been dedicated to Balthasar Schmidt, publisher of the 'Goldberg' Variations. Smend[3] thinks he can offer final proof that the little composition was written for a person called Schmidt. According to the number alphabet 'Faber,' 'Bach I.T.' can be substituted for 'Schmidt':

$$F \ A \ B \ E \ R \ \ B \ A \ C \ H \ I \ \ T$$
$$6+1+2+5+17+2+1+3+8+9+19 = 73$$

$$S \ \ C \ H \ M \ \ I \ \ D \ \ T$$
$$18+3+8+12+9+4+19 = 73$$

1. This reads, in a free English translation: 'Honored owner, it is not unknown to you that it is fortunate to have a faithful friend. Accept therefore a man, active in the fine arts, as your true friend. Leipzig, 1 March 1749.'

2. II, p. 718.

3. *Kirchenkantaten*, III/11.

It should also be considered that Bach neither before nor afterwards used the letters I T after his name. He may well have done it here to make the amusing equation come out right.

Thus it seems that even near the end of his life Bach did not tire of such *lusus ingenii* which offered him welcome respite from the great tasks he set himself.

Die Kunst der Fuge (The Art of the Fugue; BWV 1080) is Bach's last great composition. The master seems to have been engaged in this tremendous task after the completion of the 'Musical Offering,' and in this case, too, he planned to have the work printed. Part of the engraving seems to have taken place in his lifetime, but before this assignment was carried out, and before Bach even had a chance of completing his manuscript, he died. The 'Art of the Fugue' remained a torso, and neither the autograph nor the original print issued shortly after Bach's death,[1] can give an exact idea of his intentions. There are doubts regarding the precise order in which the different numbers were meant to appear, and the choice of individual sections has been questioned. We do not know what end the composer had planned for his work, and it is possible that even the title, *Die Kunst der Fuge*, was not conceived by Bach himself.[2]

Yet, the sections which were preserved are of such awe-inspiring majesty that even in its fragmentary form the 'Art of the Fugue' appears as one of the truly great creations of the human mind. The composition seems to be a sequel to the 'Musical Offering.' It, too, is a set

1. The work was printed end of 1750 or beginning of 1751. A second edition, with a preface by F. W. Marpurg, came out in 1752. As the sales were disappointingly low, C. P. E. Bach tried in 1756 to dispose of the engraved copper plates. Since no publisher seemed willing to acquire them he sold them as old metal.

2. Among the various editions of the work attempting to deal with these problems the following might be singled out: W. Rust (BG, v. XXV), W. Gräser (Neue Bach Gesellschaft, XXVIII/1), H. Husmann (Steingräber No. 2695), H. T. David (Peters No. 3940a), D. F. Tovey (Oxford University Press). The very extensive literature concerned with this work includes studies by H. Riemann (in *Handbuch der Fugenkomposition*, III, Berlin, 1916[3]), W. Gräser (*BJ* 1924, p. 1), H. T. David (*Jahrbuch Peters* 1927), J. Müller-Blattau (*Grundzüge einer Geschichte der Fuge*, Kassel, 1931, p. 122 ff.), D. F. Tovey (*A Companion to the Art of Fugue*, London, 1931), H. Husmann (*BJ* 1938, p. 1 ff.), E. Schwebsch (*J. S. B. und die Kunst der Fuge*, Kassel, 1955[2]).

of contrapuntal variations, all based on the same idea and all in the
same key; there is even a certain melodic resemblance between the
subjects of the two works. Again, in most of the variations, Bach omits
any indication as to which instruments should be used. It seems likely
that the composer meant his final work to be primarily keyboard
music,[1] but the 'Art of the Fugue' sounds even more impressive when
played by a string quartet or varying ensembles.[2] While in the former
work the emphasis was on canonic elaboration, all the possibilities of
fugal writing are explored here. Even the four canons which are included in the 'Art of the Fugue' illustrate certain aspects of fugal composition.

Despite, or perhaps because of, its deceptively plain and unobtrusive
character, the short theme of the 'Art of the Fugue' is well suited to
serve as a foundation for the monumental edifice. It is completely regular and symmetrical in its construction; it forms a fine basis for variations and readily lends itself to treatment in inversion and strettos.

While Bach presents his theme in ever-changing rhythmic and
melodic alterations (Ex. 69), he gradually unfolds a comprehensive

Ex. 69. The theme of the *Art of the Fugue* with two variations

manual of fugal composition. Each *Contrapunctus* (as he calls the individual variations, to emphasize their learned character) gives a definite solution to basic problems of fugal writing.

1. Cf. the studies by Tovey and Husmann mentioned above as well as the essay
by G. M. Leonhardt (The Hague, 1952). Numerous editions of the work for piano
are available.

2. String quartet versions were prepared by Klemm and Weymar (Ries & Erler),
and Harris and Norton (G. Schirmer); an orchestral arrangement by Gräser (Breitkopf & Härtel).

The composition begins with a group of four fugues, two of which
(Nos. 1 and 2)[1] present the theme in its original shape, two others
(Nos. 3, 4) in contrary motion. These are finely wrought masterpieces
of great structural beauty. They are still comparatively simple and
avoid great contrapuntal complications. The striking No. 3 introduces
mysterious chromatic counterpoints. The graceful, yet highly expressive No. 4 appears to have been added later to the set; in the autograph,
which seems to present an earlier phase of the work, this piece is still
missing. Next the composer introduces three 'counterfugues' (Nos.
5-7) employing as an answer the inversion of the subject. At the same
time these pieces are also 'stretto fugues' presenting the theme in different voices in such close succession that a new statement begins before the previous one is completed. No. 5 fills in the thirds of the theme
with stepwise progressions. There is a magnificent climax near the
end when the subject is introduced simultaneously in direct and in
contrary motion (*Ex.* 70) while, at the same time, the number of

Ex. 70. *Art of the Fugue*, end of Contrapunctus V

voices is increased from four to six. A solemn and noble fugue in 'stile
francese' (No. 6) presents the dotted rhythms of the slow section of a
French overture. Here Bach makes use of the device of thematic diminution. In the following fugue ('per Augmentationem et Diminu-
tionem') he employs both the extension and the reduction of the note
values in the statements of his theme.

After the basic idea has been thoroughly developed, Bach follows
with a group of fugues (Nos. 8-11) in which this theme is combined
with other subjects. Nos. 9 and 10 are double fugues, with one theme
added to the main tune, Nos. 8 and 11 triple fugues, with two additional subjects. No. 9 'alla Duodecima' is invented in double counterpoint of the twelfth. This means that the new idea can be placed either

1. The following analysis uses the numbering in BWV. A table given on p. 607
of this work compares the list with the order of Bach's autograph, and the editions
by Rust, Gräser, Husmann, and David. The edition of D. F. Tovey employs approximately the same order as BWV.

below or above the main theme; in the latter case it is transposed a twelfth (octave plus fifth) up (cf. b. 35 and 89). Similarly No. 10, 'alla Decima,' offers a double counterpoint of the tenth, the required transposition being an octave plus third (cf. b. 75 and 115).[1] The two triple fugues, No. 8 in three parts and No. 11 in four parts, are thematically interrelated. Bach uses the inversion of the three themes from the earlier fugue in the latter piece. A chromatic progression[2] might even be considered a fourth subject; thus this triple fugue seems to approach the character of a quadruple fugue.

Up to this point the arrangement of the fugues is logical, and Bach himself appears to have been able to witness the production of his work. It is also significant that a page of the autograph contains a list of mistakes found in the fugues 7-11 of the original edition. No such evidence exists, however, for the remainder of the set. From No. 12 on, the arrangement of the material seems arbitrary, and we may well assume that at this point of the production the guiding hand was removed because of Bach's death.

Rather surprisingly a group of four two-part canons appear; their melodic lines grow out of variations of the main theme. In the sprightly No. 15 the imitation is at the interval of an octave, the tune being presented in its original form and inverted (b. 41). In his canon 'per augmentationem in contrario motu' (No. 14) Bach introduces the melody first in the treble, with the augmented and inverted imitation in the bass. In the middle the relationship is reversed, with the bass assuming the lead. This problem must have been of particular interest to the composer. The piece has been preserved in two versions, both in Bach's own hand. The remaining two canons, on the other hand, seem to be of later origin, as they are missing in the autograph. One of them is 'alla Decima' (No. 16), the other 'alla Duodecima' (No. 17). They show the traditional subdivision into two sections, with a change of

1. Actually Bach complicated the task by occasionally doubling the themes in thirds or sixths. No. 10 appears in the autograph in a condensed and more primitive form (No. 10a) while the manuscript of the final version is lost. Owing to an oversight, the earlier setting slipped into the original edition which presents this single number in two stages of development. Most 20th-century editions, however, omit 10a.

2. It is introduced in b.28 and combined with the three other ideas near the fugue's end.

roles in the middle. Once more they are invented in double counter-point of the tenth and twelfth respectively, which brings them into a direct relationship with the double fugues 9 and 10.

The most stunning, though not necessarily the most complicated, pieces of the whole set are three pairs of 'mirror' fugues, which in the original edition both precede and follow the canons. In a pair of four-part fugues (No. 12:1 and 2) Bach presents all the voices first in their original form, and then, like a reflected image, in complete inversion. To make the mirror reflection doubly realistic, the soprano of the first fugue becomes the bass of the second fugue, the alto changes into a tenor, the tenor into an alto, and the bass into a treble, with the result that No. 12:2 appears like 12:1 standing on its head. There is a some-what different approach in a pair of three-part 'mirror' fugues (No. 13:1 and 2). Here the middle part of the first fugue is transformed into the treble of the second fugue, the bass changes into the middle part, and the treble into the bass.[1]

Bach must have been both amused and delighted by these tours de force, because he created a third pair of 'mirror' fugues (No. 18:1 and 2) which is nothing but an enlarged keyboard version of the fugues of No. 13. On a clavier the original pieces could only be performed by two players, as the voices were too widely spaced to be executed by two hands. Since these are three-part compositions, one of the four hands of the performers would remain idle, which seemed a waste to the practical-minded musician. He therefore added filling parts both to the *rectus* and the *inversus*, thus transforming the original three-part compositions into four-part pieces for two claviers. It is characteristic, however, that these added voices are freely invented and do not form part of the highly artistic contrapuntal web of the 'mirror' fugues. Theoretically this foreign body, added merely for practical reasons, destroys the pure construction of the polyphonic masterpieces, but it produces easily playable and attractive music which seemed important to Bach.

A great deal of controversy has been sparked by the mighty unfin-ished fugue (No. 19), which in the original edition concludes the 'Art of the Fugue.' According to a brief note at the back of the title page,

---

1. In these 'mirror fugues' the original form is usually referred to as *rectus* and the inversion of all the voices as *inversus*.

Bach was prevented from finishing the composition through his failing health and subsequent death. The monumental fragment has the
appearance of a triple fugue which is clearly divided into three sections,
the first developing a majestic theme in long notes, the second a
busily running subject in eighth notes (b. 114), the third a powerful
idea growing out of the notes B-A-C-H (b. 193). Like an artist of the
Renaissance portraying himself in his picture, Bach inserted his own
name into the work. At the place where the three themes are combined (b. 235-9), the autograph abruptly stops,[1] and later generations
were faced with the fascinating, albeit dangerous, task of guessing the
master's intentions. Earlier historians like M. Hauptmann, W. Rust,
and P. Spitta assumed that the incomplete *contrapunctus*, which did
not contain the main subject of the whole cycle, did not really belong
to the work. G. Nottebohm, the famous interpreter of Beethoven's
sketches, discovered,[2] however, that the three subjects of the fugue
could be combined with the main theme of the 'Art of the Fugue' (*Ex.
71*), and he concluded that Bach meant to write a quadruple fugue for
his work. This shrewd theory inspired Riemann,[3] Busoni,[4] and Tovey[5]

Ex. 71. *Art of the Fugue*; the four themes of No. 19

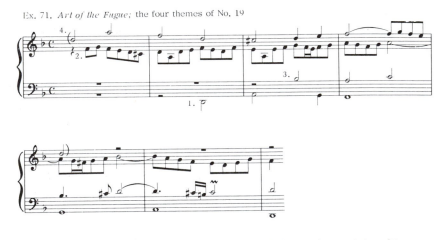

    1. Curiously enough, the original edition ends with b.232, thus omitting this com-
bination of themes.
    2. *Musikwelt*, 1880, Nos. 21, 22.
    3. In his edition of the 'Art of the Fugue' published by Schott, Mainz.
    4. Fantasia Contrappuntistica, op. 10.
    5. Page 104 of his edition.

to attempt completions of the piece, by enlarging Bach's fragment of a triple fugue into the quadruple fugue he seems to have envisioned.[1]

To the question whether Bach intended to end his work with the quadruple fugue, an affirmative answer can be given. The torso of the piece that has been preserved is considerably longer than any other *contrapunctus* of the set, and in its completed form the fugue would certainly have reached the impressive dimensions that might be expected in the finale of so awe-inspiring a set. A true quadruple fugue would, moreover, form an admirable conclusion of the work, and the fact that Bach's own name is conspicuously introduced in the third section, also appears to indicate that the composer intended to use this as an endpiece. It seems hard to imagine that this monumental piece could have been followed by an even greater number.[2]

Altogether there are not many works of Bach in which his intellectual processes are as evident as in the 'Art of the Fugue.' This was a didactic composition, and as such it offers the quintessence of contrapuntal mastery. But even if he had wanted to do so, Bach would have been unable to write only dry instructive precepts. Under his hands the textbook changed into a poem imbued with the mystery of pure beauty. The solemn pathos which permeates each of the contrapuntal variations gives this farewell of a genius the transcendental character of art conceived on the threshold of eternity.

1. Having heard performances of the complete work in which, without ritard, the great fugue suddenly breaks off, this writer would not exchange the deeply moving experience for an effective new ending, however scholarly the execution.

2. The remark in Mizler's *Musikalische Bibliothek* of 1754 (IV, p. 168) is often quoted that Bach left the last fugue but one unfinished and was unable to write the ultimate fugue which was to contain four themes, subsequently inverted throughout. Tovey (p. 41 ff.) interpreted this to mean that not only the ending of the quadruple fugue, but also a complete mirror fugue with four themes was missing. Müller-Blattau (p. 138) suggests, on the other hand, that the paragraph in question refers to the incomplete third section and the ultimate section of the quadruple fugue (No. 19). Owing to the generous proportions of this torso each of its *sections* might well have been designated as a fugue. Even in the torso two of the themes are inverted and the missing part of the fugue might have made further use of this device.

EPILOGUE

EPILOGUE

THE first part of Bach's artistic career appeared bright and promising. As soon as he had finished his apprenticeship, he was highly successful; especially so in Weimar, where his fame as a brilliant organ virtuoso and expert spread rapidly. In Cöthen he occupied a greatly respected position and enjoyed the friendship of a prince. Some of the most admired clavier music the 18th century produced was conceived at this little court.

A drastic change took place when Bach, at the age of thirty-eight, moved to Leipzig. From the outset people showed little enthusiasm for the work of the new Cantor, and in the following quarter of a century his compositions found less and less acclaim. His gigantic output in the field of church cantata, passion and oratorio was almost ignored. The overcomplicated works, wrought with the deepest symbolic meaning, yet presented in student performances of mediocre quality, were tolerated, but hardly enjoyed by the congregations. The half-hearted bids Bach later made for public acclaim were not much more successful. His association with the Telemann Collegium Musicum, the compositions written in honor of generally respected personalities, and the publication of various keyboard compositions of his did not turn the tide. Bach was unwilling to offer the uncomplicated, 'natural' kind of music expected in this era of rationalistic thinking; on the other hand his contemporaries paid little heed to the involved and seemingly outdated compositions he did present. It was Bach's tragic fate that he was unable to envision the reaction of people outside his own circle. The composer sent to the Margrave of Brandenburg concertos which were hardly suitable for the Prince's small band of musicians, and to the King of Prussia the intricate 'Musical Offering,' which the monarch may have found too difficult to understand. Likewise he had no compunction in presenting the simple burghers in Leipzig with highly sophisticated artistic compositions, instead of the plain, entertaining

349

music they wanted to hear. Bach provided the crowning glory to the art of a vanishing era, but he refused to be drawn into the orbit of light and sentimental Rococo music, fashionable at the time. When he died, hardly a voice of regret was raised. He had few personal friends, and only a small number of pupils and direct followers realized the overwhelming grandeur of his work.

It is due to this tiny group of admirers that Bach's compositions were not altogether forgotten and that his fame gradually grew to a size nobody in his lifetime could have forseen.[1] Dedicated men like Agricola, Kirnberger, Marpurg, and Bach's son Philipp Emanuel transmitted his work to later generations. At first only few of the seeds they scattered fell onto fertile soil, but the small number of plants that grew were of utmost significance. The Baron Gottfried van Swieten, who was initiated through Emanuel Bach and Kirnberger into Bach's art, passed the message on to the Viennese classical composers. Joseph Haydn acquired Sebastian's 'Well-tempered Clavier,' the Motets, and the B minor Mass. Their influence can be detected in the choral polyphony of Haydn's last masses and oratorios. Mozart was thrilled by Bach's clavier works and fugues, which he avidly studied, copied and arranged. In the finale of the 'Jupiter' Symphony, in the C minor Mass, the Requiem, and The Magic Flute, ample documentation may be found for the strong impression the Thomas Cantor's work made on Mozart's artistic thinking. Beethoven studied as a child the 'Well-tempered Clavier' with C. G. Neefe (who had been trained in Leipzig). Later he was also indoctrinated by van Swieten. The last string quartets and piano sonatas, the Ninth Symphony and the Missa Solemnis clearly proclaim how much Bach's work meant to the composer who had reached the summit of his life's work.

It is interesting to note that at the beginning of the 19th century the attitude toward Bach revealed by the greatest composers was gradually being shared by wider circles of music lovers. The trend toward more profound expression manifest in the romantic period, the reawakened interest in the art of the past, and the stronger emphasis on religious experience, all produced a new awareness of the significance of Bach's music. In 1801 the 'Well-tempered Clavier' was printed simultaneously

1. Cf. F. Blume, *J.S.B. im Wandel der Geschichte*, Kassel, 1947 (English ed., London, 1950), and *Bach Reader*, p. 358 ff.

by two German publishers and a Swiss firm. In the following two years the motets were issued. The beginning of the new century witnessed also another effort in favor of Bach's art. In 1802 J. N. Forkel's biography of the master was published, a work largely based on information the author had received from Emanuel Bach. This book, which was quickly translated into English, has remained a solid foundation for all research on Bach's life and work ever since.

The next decisive steps were taken by leading musicians of the time. C. F. Zelter, director of the Berlin Singakademie, owned a large collection of Bach works which had formerly been the property of Kirnberger and Agricola. His young pupil Felix Mendelssohn-Bartholdy was given an opportunity to study these scores. It was due to Mendelssohn's unwavering enthusiasm that in 1829, a century after the Leipzig performance, the St. Matthew Passion was produced under his leadership in Berlin. This was a dazzling revelation to the musical world since—apart from infrequent performances of the motets—hardly any of Bach's great vocal works had been heard before. In the following years, as a direct result of the performance, the two Passions and, in 1845, the Mass in B minor were published.

With the active support of Robert Schumann, the *Bach Gesellschaft* was founded in 1850, one hundred years after the master's death; it set itself the highly ambitious task of printing Bach's complete works in a reliable critical edition. Wilhelm Rust, grandson of a pupil of Friedemann Bach, served for many years as the publication's main editor. It took half a century to produce the forty-six volumes of this monumental edition.[1]

The *Neue Bach Gesellschaft* founded in 1900 on completion of the critical edition of Bach's works, presented the composer's music in practical editions, inaugurated Bach festivals, and, most of all, published the *Bach Jahrbuch*. This highly important periodical, which reached fifty volumes by the end of 1964, is a treasure chest of shorter studies on individual aspects of Bach research. From 1907 to 1939 it was edited by Arnold Schering, a leading Bach scholar of the 20th century who also made significant contributions to the Yearbook.

Likewise a number of basic biographical studies on Bach were writ-

---

1. A supplement appeared in 1932. The forty-six volumes of the original edition were reprinted by Edwards, Ann Arbor, Michigan, 1948.

ten during the 19th and 20th centuries. C. H. Bitter's pioneering effort
of 1865 was superseded by the contribution of Philipp Spitta. In the
years 1873 to 1880 the scholar offered the great biography of the composer, an epoch-making work which analyzes Bach's life and music
against the general trends of the era. This magnificent opus, written
with deep understanding and unerring sensitivity, has been rightly
considered the cornerstone of Bach research. Contrary to Spitta's philo-
logical and historical approach, Albert Schweitzer's biography of 1905
investigated problems connected with the aesthetic evaluation and the
performance of Bach's works. He threw light on the pictorial elements
prevailing in the composer's music, thus opening up new paths to a
better understanding of the Baroque idiom. Charles Sanford Terry, the
English historian, reviewed all biographical evidence and in 1928 offered a vivid account of Bach's life.

The bicentenary of Bach's death in 1950 stimulated Bach research
to new efforts. Among the numerous publications of this year Wolfgang Schmieder's *Bach Werke Verzeichnis* might be singled out. It offers the first scientifically reliable thematic catalogue of all the works of
Bach, together with valuable bibliographical information on each composition. Of paramount importance is a project jointly inaugurated by
the Bach Institute in Göttingen and the Bach Archives in Leipzig. It
was felt that the old collected edition of Bach's works no longer met
the scientific requirements of present-day research. For this reason the
Neue Ausgabe sämtlicher Werke was started and set itself the goal of
presenting each work of Bach in all its authentic versions and revisions.
The new edition faithfully follows the original sources, but it also offers a suitable basis for practical performances. In order to provide the
best possible text for each volume the editors undertake painstaking
re-evaluations of all the material accessible. Bach's own writing, that of
his helpers and copyists, the watermarks of the papers they used and
many other important criteria are being carefully re-examined. The
critical reports accompanying each volume of the new edition are
mines of fruitful information. Even in this third century after Bach's
death discoveries are being made and new vistas are being opened up
into the creative mind of one of the giants in the realm of music.

Friedrich Blume seems to go too far when attempting to use the recent
discoveries as basis for a "new Bach picture" relegating the composer's

sacred music to a comparatively modest position. The abiding faith radiating from Bach's church music cannot be denied; for centuries it has afforded inspiration and strength to countless music lovers. That Bach was able to exhibit equal creative power when dealing with works destined for secular purposes, supplies once more proof for his greatness and universality.

The intense preoccupation of the scholars with Bach's work reflects a trend prevailing all over the musical world. Bach's music plays a basic role in concert programs and its impact on 19th- and 20th-century composers can hardly be overestimated. Brahms, Reger, and Busoni; Schönberg, Berg, and Hindemith; Casella, Malipiero, and Respighi; Franck, Widor, and Honegger; Elgar, Walton, and Britten; Copland, Harris, and Piston belong to the very large group of creative artists vitally stimulated by the Thomas Cantor's works.

It often happens in the history of the arts that a genius far in advance of his time is accorded recognition only after his death. In Bach's case the picture is somewhat different. In his own time his music was frequently considered antiquated. Yet to later generations it has proved to be an inexhaustible source of inspiration, a vital force within Western man's musical heritage.

A SELECTED BACH-BIBLIOGRAPHY

(Additional studies dealing with individual compositions or specific problems are cited in the footnotes.)

ADLER, G., *Handbuch der Musikgeschichte*, 2nd ed., Berlin, 1930.

ADLUNG, J., *Musica Mechanica Organoedi* (1768), reprinted by C. Mahrenholz, Kassel, 1931.

ALDRICH, P., *Ornamentation in J. S. Bach's Organ Works*, New York, 1951.

Bach Gedenkschrift, compiled by the International Bach Society, ed. by K. Matthaei, Zürich, 1950.

BESCH, H., *J. S. Bach. Frömmigkeit und Glaube*, vol. I, *Deutung und Wirklichkeit*, 2nd ed., Kassel, 1950.

BESSELER, H., *Fünf echte Bildnisse J. S. Bachs*, Kassel, 1956.

BITTER, C. H., *Johann Sebastian Bach*, 2nd ed., Berlin, 1881.

BLANKENBURG, W., 'Zwölf Jahre Bachforschung,' *Acta Musicologica*, vol. XXXVII, 1965, p. 95 ff.

BLUME, F., 'J. S. Bach' in *Die Musik in Geschichte und Gegenwart*, Kassel, 1949, vol. I, 962 ff.

————, *Two Centuries of Bach. An Account of Changing Taste*, transl. by S. Godman, New York, 1950.

————, 'Outlines of a New Picture of Bach,' transl. by S. Godman, *Music and Letters*, July 1963.

————, *Geschichte der evangelischen Kirchenmusik*, Kassel, 1965.

BODKY, E., *The Interpretation of Bach's Keyboard Works*, Cambridge, Mass., 1960.

BOUGHTON, R., *Bach, the Master*, New York, 1930.

BOYDEN, D. D., 'The Violin and Its Technique in the 18th Century,' *MQ*, 1950.

BUCHER, E., *J. S. Bach. L'oeuvre et la vie*, Paris, 1963.

BUKOFZER, M., *Music in the Baroque Era*, New York, 1947.

CHAILLEY, J., *Les Passions de J. S. Bach*, Paris, 1963.

CHERBULIEZ, A. E., *J. S. Bach, sein Leben und sein Werk*, Olten, 1946.

DADELSEN, G. VON, *Bemerkungen zur Handschrift J. S. Bachs*, Tübinger Bach-Studien 1, Trossingen, 1957.

————, *Beiträge zur Chronologie der Werke J. S. Bachs*, Tübinger Bach-Studien 4/5, Trossingen, 1958.

DANCKERT, W., *Beiträge zur Bachkritik*, Kassel, 1934.

DAVID, H. T. AND MENDEL, A., *The Bach Reader*, New York, 1945.

DAVISON, A. T., *Bach and Handel*, Cambridge, 1951.

DAY, J., *The Literary Background to Bach's Cantatas*, London, 1961.

DEHNERT, M., *Das Weltbild J. S. Bachs*, Leipzig, 1948.

DICKINSON, A. E. F., *The Art of Bach*, London, 1936.

———, *Bach's Fugal Works*, London, 1956.

DIETRICH, F., 'J. S. Bachs Orgelchoral und seine geschichtlichen Wurzeln,' *BJ* 1929.

———, 'Analogieformen in Bachs Tokkaten und Präludien für die Orgel,' *BJ* 1931.

DONINGTON, R., *Tempo and Rhythm in Bach's Organ Music*, London, 1960.

DRINKER, H. S., *Texts of the Choral Works of J. S. Bach*, New York, 1942-43.

DUFOURCQ, N., *J. S. Bach, le maître de l'orgue*, Paris, 1948.

———, *Le Clavecin*, Paris, 1949.

DÜRR, A., *Studien über die frühen Kantaten J. S. Bachs*, Leipzig, 1951.

———, 'Zur Chronologie der Leipziger Vokalmusik J. S. Bachs,' *BJ* 1957.

EMERY, W., *Notes on Bach's Organ Works*, London, 1953 ff.

———, *Bach's Ornaments*, London, 1953.

ENGEL, H., *J. S. Bach*, Berlin, 1950.

FIELD, L. N., *J. S. Bach*, Minneapolis, 1943.

FINLAY, J., *J. S. Bachs weltliche Kantaten*, Göttingen, 1950.

FISCHER, E., *J. S. Bach*, Bern, 1948.

FLORAND, F., *Jean-Sebastien Bach; l'oeuvre d'orgue*, Paris, 1947.

FOCK, G., *Der junge Bach in Lüneburg*, Hamburg, 1950.

FORKEL, J. N., *Über J. S. Bachs Leben, Kunst und Kunstwerke*, reprint of the edition of 1802: Kassel, 1950. English translation London, 1820, reprinted in David and Mendel, *The Bach Reader*. New York, 1945. New translation by C. S. Terry, London, 1920.

FREYSE, C., *Eisenacher Dokumente um Sebastian Bach*, Leipzig, 1933.

———, 'Das Bach-Haus zu Eisenach,' *BJ* 1939, 1940-48.

FROTSCHER, G., *Geschichte des Orgelspiels und der Orgelkomposition*, Berlin, 1935.

———, *J. S. Bach und die Musik des 17. Jhdts.*, Wädenswil, 1939.

GEIRINGER, K., *Musical Instruments*, London, 1943.

———, 'Artistic Interrelations of the Bachs,' *MQ*, 1950.

———, *The Lost Portrait of J. S. Bach*, New York, 1950.

———, *The Bach Family*, New York, 1954.

———, *Symbolism in the Music of Bach*, Washington, D.C., 1956.

———, 'Es ist genug' in G. Reese and R. Brandel, *The Commonwealth of Music*. New York, 1965.

GRACE, H., *The Organ Works of Bach*, London, 1922.

GURLITT, W., *J. S. Bach. Der Meister und sein Werk*, 3rd ed., Kassel, 1949. Engl. translation, St. Louis, 1957.

HAAS, R., *Musik des Barocks*, Potsdam, 1929.

HAMEL, F., *J. S. Bach. Geistige Welt*, Göttingen, 1951.

HASSE, K., *J. S. Bach*, Leipzig, 1946.

HERZ, G., *J. S. Bach im Zeitalter des Rationalismus und der Frühromantik*, Bern, 1936.

———, 'Bach's Religion,' *Journal of Renaissance and Baroque Music*, 1946.

HINDEMITH, P., *J. S. Bach. Heritage and Obligation*, New Haven, 1952.

HULL, A. E., *Bach's Organ Works*, London, 1929.

JANSEN, M., 'Bachs Zahlensymbolik an seinen Passionen untersucht.' *BJ* 1937.

KAEGI, W., *Die simultane Denkweise in J. S. Bachs Inventionen, Sinfonien und Fugen*, Basel, 1951.

KELLER, H., *J. S. Bach. Der Künstler und sein Werk*, Lorch, 1947.

———, *Die Orgelwerke Bachs*, Leipzig, 1948. (Engl. transl. by Helen Hewitt in prep.)

———, *Die Klavierwerke Bachs*, Leipzig, 1950.

KINSKY, G., *Die Originalausgaben der Werke J. S. Bachs*, Wien, 1937.

KLOTZ, H., *Über die Orgelkunst der Gotik, der Renaissance und des Barock*, Kassel, 1934.

———, 'Bachs Orgeln und seine Orgelmusik,' *Die Musikforschung*, 1950.

KURTH, E., *Grundlagen des linearen Kontrapunkts*, Bern, 4th ed., 1946.

MENDEL, A., 'Accompaniments to Bach's Leipzig Church Music.' *MQ*, 1950.

———, 'On the Pitches in Use in Bach's Time.' *MQ*, 1955.

———, *see also* David, H. T.

MENKE, W., *History of the Trumpet of Bach and Handel*, London, 1934.

MILES, R. H., *J. S. Bach*, Englewood Cliffs, N. J., 1962.

MIZLER, L. C., *Neu eröffnete Musikalische Bibliothek*, Leipzig, 1736-54.

MOSER, H. J., *J. S. Bach*, 2nd ed., Berlin, 1943.

MÜLLER, v.Asow, E. AND H., *J. S. Bach, Briefe. Gesamtausgabe*, 2nd ed., Regensburg, 1950.

NEUMANN, W., *J. S. Bach's Chorfuge*, Leipzig, 1938.

———, *Handbuch der Kantaten J. S. Bachs*, Leipzig, 1947; 2nd ed., 1953.

———, 'Das Bachische Collegium Musicum,' *BJ* 1960.

———, *Auf den Lebenswegen J. S. Bachs*, Berlin, 1957; Engl. ed., New York, 1961.

———, *Bach, eine Bildbiographie*, München, 1960.

———, *J. S. Bach. Sämtliche Kantatentexte*, Leipzig, 1956.

——— AND SCHULZE, H. J., *Bach Dokumente*, Kassel, 1963.

NEWMAN, W. S., *The Sonata in the Baroque Era*, Chapel Hill, N. C., 1959.

PARRY, C. H. H., *J. S. Bach*, London, 1909.

PAUMGARTNER, B., *J. S. Bach. Leben und Werk*, I, Zürich, 1950.

PETZOLDT, R. AND WEINHOLD, L., *Johann Sebastian Bach. Das Schaffen des Meisters in Spiegel einer Stadt*, Leipzig, 1950.

PIRRO, A., *L'Orgue de Jean-Sébastien Bach*, Paris, 1895.

————, *J. S. Bach,* Paris, 1906; Engl. ed., New York, 1957.

————, *L'Esthétique de Jean-Sébastien Bach,* Paris, 1907.

PITROU, R., *Jean-Sébastien Bach,* Paris, 1941.

POTTGIESSER, K., 'Die Briefentwürfe des J. Elias Bach,' *Die Musik,* 1912-13.

RAUPACH, H., *Das wahre Bildnis J. S. Bachs,* Wolfenbüttel, 1950.

RIEMENSCHNEIDER, A., *The Use of the Flutes in the Works of J. S. Bach,* Washington, D.C., 1950.

SCHEIBE, J. A., *Critischer Musicus,* Leipzig, 1745.

SCHEIDE, W. H., *J. S. Bach as a Biblical Interpreter,* Princeton, 1952.

————, 'J. S. Bach's Sammlung von Kantaten seines Vetters Johann Ludwig Bach,' *BJ* 1959, 1961, 1962.

SCHERING, A., *Geschichte des Instrumentalkonzerts,* Leipzig, 1905.

————, 'Kleine Bachstudien,' *BJ* 1933.

————, *J. S. Bach's Leipziger Kirchenmusik,* Leipzig, 1936.

————, *Bach und das Musikleben Leipzigs im 18. Jhdt,* Leipzig, 1941.

————, *Das Symbol in der Musik,* Leipzig, 1941.

————, *Über Kantaten J. S. Bachs,* with preface by F. Blume, Leipzig, 1942.

SCHMIEDER, W., *Thematisch-systematisches Verzeichnis der musikalischen Werke von J. S. Bach,* Leipzig, 1950.

SCHMITZ, A., *Die Bildlichkeit der wortgebundenen Musik J. S. Bachs,* Mainz, 1950.

SCHNEIDER, M., *Bach Urkunden* in Veröffentlichungen der Neuen Bach Gesellschaft, XVII/3, 1916.

SCHRADE, L., 'Bach: the Conflict between the Sacred and the Secular,' *Journal of the History of Ideas,* 1946.

SCHREYER, J., *Beiträge zur Bachkritik,* Leipzig, 1911-13.

SCHULZE, H. J., *see* Neumann.

SCHWEITZER, A., *J. S. Bach,* Paris, 1905; Leipzig, 1908; Engl. transl. by E. Newman, London, 1911; rev. ed., 1952.

SEIFFERT, M., *Geschichte der Klaviermusik,* Leipzig, 1899.

SMEND, F., 'Neue Bach-Funde,' *Archiv f. Musikforschung,* 1942.

————, *J. S. Bach: Kirchenkantaten,* 6 vols., Berlin, 1948-49.

————, *J. S. Bach bei seinem Namen gerufen,* Kassel, 1950.

————, *Bach in Köthen,* Berlin, 1951.

SPITTA, P., *J. S. Bach,* Leipzig, 1873-80; 4th ed., Leipzig, 1930; Engl. ed. transl. by Clara Bell and J. A. Fuller-Maitland, London, 1884-85; reprint, New York, 1951.

————, 'Über die Beziehungen J. S. Bachs zu C. F. Hunold and M. v. Ziegler,' *Historische und philologische Aufsätze,* Berlin, 1884.

STEGLICH, R., *J. S. Bach,* Potsdam, 1935.

————, *Wege zu Bach,* Regensburg, 1949.

TAGLIAVINI, L. F., *Studi sui testi delle cantate sacre di J. S. Bach,* Padua, 1956.

TERRY, C. S., *Bach's Chorals,* Cambridge, 1915-1921.

————, *J. S. Bach, Cantata Texts*, London, 1926.

————, *Bach: A Biography*, London, 1928.

————, *Bach: The Historical Approach*, New York, 1930.

————, *Bach's Orchestra*, London, 1932.

————, *The Music of Bach, An Introduction*, New York, 1933.

THIELE, E., *Die Chorfugen J. S. Bachs*, Bern, 1936.

TIERSOT, J., *J. S. Bach*, Paris, 1934.

VAN TUYLL VAN SEROOSKERKEN, H. O. R., *Probleme des Bachporträts*, Biltho-ven, 1956.

VETTER, W., *Der Kapellmeister Bach. Versuch einer Deutung*, Potsdam, 1950.

———— AND MEYER, E. H., *Bericht über die wissenschaftliche Bachtagung*, Leipzig, 1951.

WERKER, W., *Studien über die Symmetrie im Bau der Fugen und die moti-vische Zusammengehörigkeit der Präludien und Fugen des Wohltem-perierten Klaviers von J. S. Bach*, Leipzig, 1922.

WHITTAKER, W. G., *The Cantatas of J. S. Bach*, London, 1959.

WIEGAND, F., *J. S. Bach und seine Verwandten in Arnstadt*, Arnstadt, 1950.

WINTERFELD, C. VON, *Der evangelische Kirchengesang und sein Verhältnis zur Kunst des Tonsatzes*, Leipzig, 1843-47.

WUSTMANN, R., *J. S. Bachs Kantatentexte*, Leipzig, 1913.

INDEX OF COMPOSITIONS

INDEX OF PERSONS AND PLACES